D1599579

readings in current
personality theories

readings in current personality theories

raymond j corsini

F. E. PEACOCK PUBLISHERS, INC. ITASCA, ILLINOIS 60143

To Heinz L. and Rowena R. Ansbacher

CONTENTS

Preface ix

Chapter 1: Psychoanalysis 1
    The Origin and Development of Psychoanalysis,
    Sigmund Freud 2

Chapter 2: Individual Psychology 31
    Compulsion Neurosis, Alfred Adler 32

Chapter 3: Analytical Psychology 50
    Phenomena Resulting From the Assimilation of the
    Unconscious, Carl G. Jung 51

Chapter 4: Person-Centered Theory 63
    Persons or Science? A Philosophical Question,
    Carl R. Rogers 64

Chapter 5: Personalism 80
    Traits Revisited, Gordon W. Allport 81

Chapter 6: Operant Reinforcement 94
    Freedom and the Control of Men, B. F. Skinner 95

Chapter 7: Personal Constructs 106
    Man's Construction of His Alternatives, George A. Kelly ... 107

Chapter 8: Existential Theory 128
    The Differentiation Between Human Existence and
    Animal Being, Ludwig Binswanger 129

Chapter 9: Sociological Theory 138
    Language and the Development of the Self,
    George H. Mead 139

Chapter 10: Constitutional Theory 151
    Social Traits and Morphologic Types, William H. Sheldon .. 152

Chapter 11: Constitutional Theory 159
    Sex Designations of Right and Left Body Sides and Assumptions about Male-Female Superiority, Seymour Fisher 160

Chapter 12: Constitutional Theory 166
    On Emotions: Considerations from the Organismic Point
    of View, Kurt Goldstein 167

Chapter 13: Soviet Personality Theory 177
    The Parent as Upbringer, A. 'S. Makarenko 178
Chapter 14: Soviet Personality Theory 188
    Personality and Neuroses, V. M. Myasishchev 189
Chapter 15: Asian Personality Theory 202
    The Mystique of "Western" Psychotherapy: An Eastern
    Interpretation, Shashi K. Pande 203
Chapter 16: Asian Personality Theory 212
    Amae: A Key Concept for Understanding Japanese
    Personality Structure, L. Takeo Doi 213
Chapter 17: Psychosocial Theory 220
    The Poignancy of Neurotic Conflicts, Karen Horney 221
Chapter 18: Sociometric Theory 226
    Spontaneity-Creativity and Energy Systems, J. L. Moreno . . 227
Chapter 19: Self-Actualization Theory 238
    The Instinctoid Nature of Basic Needs, A. H. Maslow 239
Chapter 20: Needs-Press Theory 254
    Thematic Apperception Test, Henry A. Murray 255
Chapter 21: Transactional Analysis 266
    The Formal Aspects of Transactional Analysis, Eric Berne . . 267
Chapter 22: Developmental Theory 276
    Memorandum on Youth, Erik H. Erikson 277
Chapter 23: Gestalt Theory 285
    Time: Past and Future, Past and Present, Frederick S. Perls 286
Chapter 24: Rational-Emotive Theory 297
    Toward a Theory of Personality, Albert Ellis . . . . : 298
Chapter 25: Reality Therapy Theory 312
    Basic Concepts in Reality Therapy,
    William Glaser and Leonard Zunin 313
Chapter 26: Social Learning Theory 321
    Behavior Theory and Identificatory Learning,
    Albert Bandura 322
Chapter 27: Typology Theory 331
    The Structure of Personality, H. J. Eysenck 332
Chapter 28: Direct Decision Theory 345
    Treatment of the Psychopath, Harold Greenwald 346

PREFACE

This book consists of 28 selections concerning 24 theories of personality, most of which were written by the originators of a number of "schools" of personality theory. These selections are coordinated with materials in a textbook I edited, *Current Personality Theories* (Itasca, Ill.: F. E. Peacock Publishers, Inc., 1977), which includes chapters by 15 other contributors and myself. *Readings in Current Personality Theories*, however, can be read independently of or in conjunction with this or any similar text; indeed, it can serve as the primary source book for courses in this field.

While the organization of the text, *Current Personality Theories,* is highly structured and disciplined, *Readings* is based on two simple principles. First, each of the 24 theories discussed in the text must be given space proportionate to its importance; and second, each selection had to be meaningful and interesting.

The contents of this book represent my own view of what is important in this field, but no person, no matter how well read, can make optimal selections from the enormous literature in this field. What saves this book from being purely an idiosyncratic gleaning is that I had the assistance of 15 experts in various aspects of personality theory, the authors of chapters in *Current Personality Theories*. From their nominations of articles or chapters in books, I made final the selections for inclusion in *Readings*. Therefore I am indebted to the following individuals who made the initial suggestions: Heinz L. Ansbacher, Peter L. Giovacchini, T. L. Holdstock, Suzanne Kobasa, Robert W. Lundin, Salvatore Maddi, Renaldo Maduro, Paul B. Pedersen, Carl R. Rogers, William Sahakian, Lee Sechrest, Franklin Shontz, Anselm Strauss, Joseph Wheelwright and Isidore Ziferstein. Generally, they agreed that the final choices were appropriate for a book of this kind.

Considerable help was obtained from a variety of sources. I learned that a book of readings is not easy to complete. The first people to be thanked are a dozen or so librarians at the University of Hawaii who, in person and via telephone, were always helpful in finding or obtaining difficult-to-locate material. Mrs. Janet Terner of the Library of Congress was especially helpful in locating some materials not locally available. Dr. Anthony Marsella of the Psychology Department of the University of Hawaii lent me books from his extensive library and offered advice. Dr. Heinz Ansbacher served as a long-distance counselor and helped make some fine judgments. William and Maureen Dinker were helpful in a variety of technical tasks, such as translating the highly idiosyncratic citations into American Psychological Association style. My wife, Dr. Kleona Rigney, as usual, helped by permitting me to play with my papers while she did some of my chores, but she also was a source of encouragement and helped me make some judgments. Tom LaMarre, editor at F. E. Peacock Publishers, Inc., was, as usual, most helpful in a variety of situations, including dealings with copyright holders.

The reader now is in for an exciting and fascinating adventure. You are about to read the concentrated thoughts of some of the best and most original minds of the century about what is and what will always be the last frontier of science—the mysteries of the human mind.

Raymond J. Corsini

CHAPTER 1

Psychoanalysis

Introduction

On September 6, 1909, one of the most important events in the history of American psychology occurred when Sigmund Freud (1856-1939) delivered the first of five scheduled addresses at Clark University in Worcester, Massachusetts. This was probably also the most important event in his professional life to that date; he said, on receiving an honorary doctorate at the conclusion of his lectures: "This is the first official recognition of our endeavors."

Freud had decided to engage in research after being graduated from medical school, but for economic reasons he switched to medical practice, specializing in neurology. He studied in Paris with Jean-Martin Charcot, a man who made respectable the up-to-then disreputable practice of hypnosis.

With Josef Breuer, Freud published a paper in 1893 entitled "On the Psychical Mechanism of Hysterical Phenomena," and in 1895 they co-authored *Studies on Hysteria*. These early publications were more or less ignored, but with further publications on his own, such as *Interpretation of Dreams* (1900) and *Psychopathology of Everyday Life* (1901), Freud's reputation began to grow, despite Victorian attitudes towards sexuality.

This set of lectures shows Freud at the height of his powers, with an unparalleled ability to persuade. Even today they can be read with profit for their content; they provide a compact summary of psychoanalysis, delivered by a master propagandist.

SIGMUND FREUD
The origin and development of psychoanalysis

FIRST LECTURE

Ladies and Gentlemen: It is a new and somewhat embarrassing experience for me to appear as lecturer before students of the New World. I assume that I owe this honor to the association of my name with the theme of psychoanalysis, and consequently it is of psychoanalysis that I shall aim to speak. I shall attempt to give you in very brief form an historical survey of the origin and further development of this new method of research and cure.

Granted that it is a merit to have created psychoanalysis, it is not my merit. I was a student, busy with the passing of my last examinations, when another physician of Vienna, Dr. Joseph Breuer, made the first application of this method to the case of an hysterical girl (1880–82). We must now examine the history of this case and its treatment, which can be found in detail in *Studies on Hysteria* (Breuer & Freud, 1895), later published by Dr. Breuer and myself.

But first one word. I have noticed, with considerable satisfaction, that the majority of my hearers do not belong to the medical profession. Now do not fear that a medical education is necessary to follow what I shall have to say. We shall now accompany the doctors a little way, but soon we shall take leave of them and follow Dr. Breuer on a way which is quite his own.

Sigmund Freud, "The Origin and Development of Psychoanalysis." Reprinted from *The American Journal of Psychology*, 1910, *12*, 181–218, with permission of the University of Illinois Press.

Dr. Breuer's patient was a girl of twenty-one, of a high degree of intelligence. She had developed in the course of her two years' illness a series of physical and mental disturbances which well deserved to be taken seriously. She had a severe paralysis of both right extremities, with anasthesia, and at times the same affection of the members of the left side of the body; disturbance of eye-movements, and much impairment of vision; difficulty in maintaining the position of the head, an intense nervous cough, nausea when she attempted to take nourishment, and at one time for several weeks of loss of the power to drink, in spite of tormenting thirst. Her power of speech was also diminished, and this progressed so far that she could neither speak nor understand her mother tongue; and, finally, she was subject to states of "absence," of confusion, delirium, alteration of her whole personality. These states will later claim our attention.

When one hears of such a case, one does not need to be a physician to incline to the opinion that we are concerned here with a serious injury, probably of the brain, for which there is little hope of cure and which will probably lead to the early death of the patient. The doctors will tell us, however, that in one type of cases with just as unfavorable symptoms, another, far more favorable, opinion is justified. When one finds such a series of symptoms in the case of a young girl, whose vital organs (heart, kidneys), are shown by objective tests to be normal, but who has suffered from strong emotional disturbances, and when the symptoms differ in certain finer characteristics from what one might logically expect, in a case like this the doctors are not too much disturbed. They consider that there is present no organic lesion of the brain, but that enigmatical state, known since the time of the Greek physicians as hysteria, which can simulate a whole series of symptoms of various diseases. They consider in such a case that the life of the patient is not in danger and that a restoration to health will probably come about of itself. The differentiation of such an hysteria from a severe organic lesion is not always very easy. But we do not need to know how a differential diagnosis of this kind is made; you may be sure that the case of Breuer's patient was such that no skillful physician could fail to diagnose an hysteria. We may also add a word here from the history of the case. The illness first appeared while the patient was caring for her father, whom she tenderly loved, during the severe illness which led to his death, a task which she was compelled to abandon because she herself fell ill.

So far it has seemed best to go with the doctors, but we shall soon part company with them. You must not think that the outlook of a patient with regard to medical aid is essentially bettered when the diagnosis points to hysteria rather than to organic disease of the brain. Against the serious brain diseases medical skill is in most cases powerless, but also in the case of hysterical affections the doctor can do nothing. He must leave it to benign nature, when and how his hopeful prognosis will be realized.[1] Accordingly,

with the recognition of the disease as hysteria, little is changed in the situation of the patient, but there is a great change in the attitude of the doctor. We can observe that he acts quite differently toward hystericals than toward patients suffering from organic diseases. He will not bring the same interest to the former as to the latter, since their suffering is much less serious and yet seems to set up the claim to be valued just as seriously.

But there is another motive in this action. The physician, who through his studies has learned so much that is hidden from the laity, can realize in his thought the causes and alterations of the brain disorders in patients suffering from apoplexy or dementia, a representation which must be right up to a certain point, for by it he is enabled to understand the nature of each symptom. But before the details of hysterical symptoms, all his knowledge, his anatomical-physiological and pathological education, desert him. He cannot understand hysteria. He is in the same position before it as the layman. And that is not agreeable to any one, who is in the habit of setting such a high valuation upon his knowledge. Hystericals, accordingly, tend to lose his sympathy; he considers them persons who overstep the laws of his science, as the orthodox regard heretics; he ascribes to them all possible evils, blames them for exaggeration and intentional deceit, "simulation," and he punishes them by withdrawing his interest.

Now Dr. Breuer did not deserve this reproach in this case; he gave his patient sympathy and interest, although at first he did not understand how to help her. Probably this was easier for him on account of those superior qualities of the patient's mind and character, to which he bears witness in his account of the case.

His sympathetic observation soon

---

[1] I know that this view no longer holds today, but in the lecture I take myself and my hearers back to the time before 1880. If things have become different since that time it has been largely due to the work the history of which I am sketching.

found the means which made the first help possible. It had been noticed that the patient, in her states of "absence," of psychic alteration, usually mumbled over several words to herself. These seemed to spring from associations with which her thoughts were busy. The doctor, who was able to get these words, put her in a sort of hypnosis and repeated them to her over and over, in order to bring up any associations that they might have. The patient yielded to his suggestion and reproduced for him those psychic creations which controlled her thoughts during her "absences," and which betrayed themselves in these single spoken words. These were fancies, deeply sad, often poetically beautiful, day dreams, we might call them, which commonly took as their starting point the situation of a girl beside the sick-bed of her father. Whenever she had related a number of such fancies, she was, as it were, freed and restored to her normal mental life. This state of health would last for several hours, and then give place on the next day to a new "absence," which was removed in the same way by relating the newly-created fancies. It was impossible not to get the impression that the psychic alteration which was expressed in the "absence" was a consequence of the excitations originating from these intensely emotional fancy-images. The patient herself, who at this time of her illness strangely enough understood and spoke only English, gave this new kind of treatment the name "talking cure," or jokingly designated it as "chimney sweeping."

The doctor soon hit upon the fact that through such cleansing of the soul more could be accomplished than a temporary removal of the constantly recurring mental "clouds." Symptoms of the disease would disappear when in hypnosis

the patient could be made to remember the situation and the associative connections under which they first appeared, provided free vent was given to the emotions which they aroused. "There was in the summer a time of intense heat, and the patient had suffered very much from thirst; for, without any apparent reason, she had suddenly become unable to drink. She would take a glass of water in her hand, but as soon as it touched her lips she would push it away as though suffering from hydrophobia. Obviously for these few seconds she was in her absent state. She ate only fruit, melons and the like, in order to relieve this tormenting thirst. When this had been going on about six weeks, she was talking one day in hypnosis about her English governess, whom she disliked, and finally told, with every sign of disgust, how she had come into the room of the governess, and how that lady's little dog, that she abhorred, had drunk out of a glass. Out of respect for the conventions the patient had remained silent. Now, after she had given energetic expression to her restrained anger, she asked for a drink, drank a large quantity of water without trouble, and woke from hypnosis with the glass at her lips. The symptom thereupon vanished permanently."

Permit me to dwell for a moment on this experience. No one had ever cured an hysterical symptom by such means before, or had come so near understanding its cause. This would be a pregnant discovery if the expectation could be confirmed that still other, perhaps the majority of symptoms, originated in this way and could be removed by the same method. Breuer spared no pains to convince himself of this and investigated the pathogenesis of the other more serious symptoms in a more orderly way. Such was indeed the case; almost all the symptoms originated in exactly this way, as remnants, as precipitates, if you like, of affectively-toned experiences, which for that reason we later called "psychic traumata." The nature of the symptoms became clear through their relation to the scene which caused them. They were, to use the technical term, "determined" by the scene whose memory traces they embodied, and so could no longer be described as arbitrary or enigmatical functions of the neurosis.

Only one variation from what might be expected must be mentioned. It was not always a single experience which occasioned the symptom, but usually several, perhaps many similar, repeated traumata co-operated in this effect. It was necessary to repeat the whole series of pathogenic memories in chronological sequence, and of course in reverse order, the last first and the first last. It was quite impossible to reach the first and often most essential trauma directly, without first clearing away those coming later.

You will of course want to hear me speak of other examples of the causation of hysterical symptoms beside this of inability to drink on account of the disgust caused by the dog drinking from the glass. I must, however, if I hold to my programme, limit myself to very few examples. Breuer relates, for instance, that his patient's visual disturbances could be traced back to external causes, in the following way. "The patient, with tears in her eyes, was sitting by the sick-bed when her father suddenly asked her what time it was. She could not see distinctly, strained her eyes to see, brought the watch near her eyes so that the dial seemed very large, or else she tried hard to suppress her tears, so that the sick man might not see them."

All the pathogenic impressions sprang from the time when she shared in the care of her sick father. "Once she was watching at night in the greatest anxiety for the patient, who was in a high fever, and in suspense, for a surgeon was expected from Vienna, to operate on the patient. Her mother had gone out for a little while, and Anna sat by the sick-bed, her right arm hanging over the back of her chair. She fell into a revery and saw a black snake emerge, as it were, from the wall and approach the sick man as though to bite him. (It is very probable that several snakes had actually been seen in the meadow behind the house, that she had already been frightened by them, and that these former experiences furnished the material for the hallucination.) She tried to drive off the creature, but was as though paralyzed. Her right arm, which was hanging over the back of the chair, had 'gone to sleep,' become anasthetic and paretic, and as she was looking at it, the fingers changed into little snakes with death-heads. (The nails.) Probably she attempted to drive away the snake with her paralyzed right hand, and so the anasthesia and paralysis of this member formed associations with the snake hallucination. When this had vanished, she tried in her anguish to speak, but could not. She could not express herself in any language, until finally she thought of the words of an English nursery song, and thereafter she could think and speak only in this language." When the memory of this scene was revived in hypnosis the paralysis of the right arm, which had existed since the beginning of the illness, was cured and the treatment ended.

When, a number of years later, I began to use Breuer's researches and treatment on my own patients, my experiences completely coincided with his. In the case of a woman of about forty, there was a tic, a peculiar smacking noise which manifested itself whenever she was laboring under any excitement, without any obvious cause. It had its origin in two experiences which had this common element, that she attempted to make no noise, but that by a sort of counter-will this noise broke the stillness. On the first occasion, she had finally after much trouble put her sick child to sleep, and she tried to be very quiet so as not to awaken it. On the second occasion, during a ride with both her children in a thunderstorm the horses took fright, and she carefully avoided any noise for fear of frightening them still more. I give this example instead of many others which are cited in the *Studies on Hysteria.*

Ladies and gentlemen, if you will permit me to generalize, as is indispensable in so brief a presentation, we may express our results up to this point in the formula: *Our hysterical patients suffer from reminiscences.* Their symptoms are the remnants and the memory symbols of certain (traumatic) experiences.

A comparison with other memory symbols from other sources will perhaps enable us better to understand this symbolism. The memorials and monuments with which we adorn our great cities, are also such memory symbols. If you walk through London you will find before one of the greatest railway stations of the city a richly decorated Gothic pillar—"Charing Cross." One of the old Plantagenet kings, in the thirteenth century, caused the body of his beloved queen Eleanor to be borne to Westminster, and had Gothic crosses erected at each of the stations where the coffin was set down. Charing Cross is the last of these monuments, which preserve the memory of this sad journey. In another part of the city, you will see a high pillar of more modern construction, which is merely called "the monument." This is in memory of the great fire which broke out in the neighborhood in the year 1666, and destroyed a great part of the city. These monuments are memory symbols like the hysterical symptoms; so far the comparison seems justified. But what would you say to a Londoner who to-day stood sadly before the monument to the funeral of Queen Eleanor, instead of going about his business with the haste engendered by modern industrial conditions, or rejoicing with the young queen of his own heart? Or to another, who before the "Monument" bemoaned the burning of his loved native city, which long since has arisen again so much more splendid than before?

Now hystericals and all neurotics behave like these two unpractical Londoners, not only in that they remember the painful experiences of the distant past, but because they are still strongly affected by them. They cannot escape from the past and neglect present reality in its favor. This fixation of the mental life on the pathogenic traumata is an essential, and practically a most significant characteristic of the neurosis. I will willingly concede the objection which you are probably formulating, as you think over the history of Breuer's patient. All her traumata originated at the time when she was caring for her sick father, and her symptoms could only be regarded as memory symbols of his sickness and death. They corresponded to mourning, and a fixation on thoughts of the dead so short a time after death is certainly not pathological, but rather corresponds to normal emotional behavior. I concede this: there is nothing abnormal in the fixation of feeling on the trauma shown by Breuer's patient. But in other cases, like that of the tic that I have mentioned, the occasions for which lay ten and fifteen years back, the characteristic of this abnormal clinging to the past is very clear, and Breuer's patient would probably have developed it, if she had not come under the "cathartic treatment" such a short time after the traumatic experiences and the beginning of the disease.

We have so far only explained the relation of the hysterical symptoms to the life history of the patient; now by considering two further moments which Breuer observed, we may get a hint as to the processes of the beginning of the illness and those of the cure. With regard to the first, it is especially to be noted that Breuer's patient in almost all pathogenic situations had to suppress a strong excitement, instead of giving vent to it by appropriate words and deeds. In the little experience with her governess' dog, she suppressed, through regard for the conventions, all manifestations of her very intense disgust. While she was seated by her father's sick-bed, she was careful to betray nothing of her anxiety and her painful depression to the patient. When, later, she reproduced the same scene before the physician, the emotion which she had suppressed on the occurrence of the scene burst out with especial strength, as though it had been pent up all along. The symptom which had been caused by that scene reached its greatest intensity while the doctor was striving to revive the memory of the scene, and vanished after it had been fully laid bare. On the other hand, experience shows that if the patient is reproducing the traumatic scene to the physician, the process has no curative effect if, by some peculiar chance, there is no development of emotion. It is apparently these emotional processes upon which the illness of the patient and the restoration to health are dependent. We feel justified in regarding "emotion" as a quantity which may become increased,

derived and displaced. So we are forced to the conclusion that the patient fell ill because the emotion developed in the pathogenic situation was prevented from escaping normally, and that the essence of the sickness lies in the fact that these "imprisoned" emotions undergo a series of abnormal changes. In part they are preserved as a lasting charge and as a source of constant disturbance in psychical life; in part they undergo a change into unusual bodily innervations and inhibitions, which present themselves as the physical symptoms of the case. We have coined the name "hysterical conversion" for the latter process. Part of our mental energy is, under normal conditions, conducted off by way of physical innervation and gives what we call "the expression of emotions." Hysterical conversion exaggerates this part of the course of a mental process which is emotionally colored; it corresponds to a far more intense emotional expression, which finds outlet by new paths. If a stream flows in two channels, an overflow of one will take place as soon as the current in the other meets with an obstacle.

You see that we are in a fair way to arrive at a purely psychological theory of hysteria, in which we assign the first rank to the affective processes. A second observation of Breuer compels us to ascribe to the altered condition of consciousness a great part in determining the characteristics of the disease. His patient showed many sorts of mental states, conditions of "absence," confusion and alteration of character, besides her normal state. In her normal state she was entirely ignorant of the pathogenic scenes and of their connection with her symptoms. She had forgotten those scenes, or at any rate had dissociated them from their pathogenic connection. When the patient was hypnotized, it was possible, after considerable difficulty, to recall those scenes to her memory, and by this means of recall the symptoms were removed. It would have been extremely perplexing to know how to interpret this fact, if hypnotic practice and experiments had not pointed out the way. Through the study of hypnotic phenomena, the conception, strange though it was at first, has become familiar, that in one and the same individual several mental groupings are possible, which may remain relatively independent of each other, "know nothing" of each other, and which may cause a splitting of consciousness along lines which they lay down. Cases of such a sort, known as "double personality," occasionally appear spontaneously. If in such a division of personality consciousness remains constantly bound up with one of the two states, this is called the *conscious* mental state, and the other the *unconscious*. In the well-known phenomena of so-called post hypnotic suggestion, in which a command given in hypnosis is later executed in the normal state as though by an imperative suggestion, we have an excellent basis for understanding how the unconscious state can influence the conscious, although the latter is ignorant of the existence of the former. In the same way it is quite possible to explain the facts in hysterical cases. Breuer came to the conclusion that the hysterical symptoms originated in such peculiar mental states, which he called "hypnoidal states." Experiences of an emotional nature, which occur during such hypnoidal states easily become pathogenic, since such states do not present the conditions for a normal draining off of the emotion of the exciting processes. And as a result there arises a peculiar product of this exciting process, that is, the symptom, and this is projected like a foreign body into the normal state. The latter has, then, no conception of the significance of the hypnoidal pathogenic situation. Where a symptom arises, we also find an amnesia, a memory gap, and the filling of this gap includes the removal of the conditions under which the symptom originated.

I am afraid that this portion of my treatment will not seem very clear, but you must remember that we are dealing here with new and difficult views, which perhaps could not be made much clearer. This all goes to show that our knowledge in this field is not very far advanced. Breuer's idea of the hypnoidal states has, moreover, been shown to be superfluous and a hindrance to further investigation, and has been dropped from present conceptions of psychoanalysis. Later I shall at least suggest what other influences and processes have been disclosed besides that of the hypnoidal states, to which Breuer limited the causal moment.

You have probably also felt, and rightly, that Breuer's investigations gave you only a very incomplete theory and insufficient explanation of the phenomena which we have observed. But complete theories do not fall from Heaven, and you would have had still greater reason to be distrustful, had any one offered you at the beginning of his observations a well-rounded theory, without any gaps; such a theory could only be the child of his speculations and not the fruit of an unprejudiced investigation of the facts.

SECOND LECTURE

Ladies and Gentlemen: At about the same time that Breuer was using the "talking-cure" with his patient, M. Charcot began in Paris, with the hystericals of the Salpetrière, those researches which were to lead to a new understanding of the disease. These results were, however, not yet known in Vienna. But when about ten years later Breuer and I published our preliminary communication on the psychic mechanism of hysterical phenomena, which grew out of the cathartic treatment of Breuer's first patient, we were both of us under the spell of Charcot's investigations. We made the pathogenic experiences of our patients, which acted as psychic traumata, equivalent to those physical traumata whose influence on hysterical paralyses Charcot had determined; and Breuer's hypothesis of hypnoidal states is itself only an echo of the fact that Charcot had artificially reproduced those traumatic paralyses in hypnosis.

The great French observer, whose student I was during the years 1885–86, had no natural bent for creating psychological theories. His student, P. Janet, was the first to attempt to penetrate more deeply into the psychic processes of hysteria, and we followed his example, when we made the mental splitting and the dissociation of personality the central points of our theory. Janet propounds a theory of hysteria which draws upon the principal theories of heredity and degeneration which are current in France. According to his view hysteria is a form of degenerative alteration of the nervous system, manifesting itself in a congenital "weakness" of the function of psychic synthesis. The hysterical patient is from the start incapable of correlating and unifying the manifold of his mental processes, and so there arises the tendency to mental dissociation. If you will permit me to use a banal but clear illustration, Janet's hysterical reminds one of a weak woman who has been shopping, and is now on her way home, laden with packages and bundles of every description. She cannot manage the whole lot with her two arms and her ten fingers, and soon she drops one. When she stoops to pick this up, another breaks loose, and so it goes on.

Now it does not agree very well with this assumed mental weakness of hystericals, that there can be observed in hysterical cases, besides the phenomena of lessened functioning, examples of a partial increase of functional capacity, as a sort of compensation. At the time when Breuer's patient had forgotten her mother-tongue and all other languages save English, her control of English attained such a level that if a German book was put before her she could give a fluent, perfect translation of its contents at sight. When later I undertook to continue on my own account the investigations begun by Breuer, I soon came to another view of the origin of hysterical dissociation (or splitting of consciousness). It was inevitable that my views should diverge widely and radically, for my point of departure was not, like that of Janet, laboratory researches, but attempts at therapy. Above everything else, it was practical needs that urged me on. The cathartic treatment, as Breuer had made use of it, presupposed that the patient should be put in deep hypnosis, for only in hypnosis was available the knowledge of his pathogenic associations, which were unknown to him in his normal state. Now hypnosis, as a fanciful, and so to speak, mystical, aid, I soon came to dislike; and when I discovered that, in spite of all my efforts, I could not hypnotize by any means all of my patients, I resolved to give up hypnotism and to make the cathartic method independent of it.

Since I could not alter the psychic state

of most of my patients at my wish, I directed my efforts to working with them in their normal state. This seems at first sight to be a particularly senseless and aimless undertaking. The problem was this: to find out something from the patient that the doctor did not know and the patient himself did not know. How could one hope to make such a method succeed? The memory of a very noteworthy and instructive proceeding came to my aid, which I had seen in Bernheim's clinic at Nancy. Bernheim showed us that persons put in a condition of hypnotic somnambulism, and subjected to all sorts of experiences, had only apparently lost the memory of those somnambulic experiences, and that their memory of them could be awakened even in the normal state. If he asked them about their experiences during somnambulism, they said at first that they did not remember, but if he persisted, urged, assured them that they did know, then every time the forgotten memory came back.

Accordingly I did this with my patients. When I had reached in my procedure with them a point at which they declared that they knew nothing more, I would assure them that they did know, that they must just tell it out, and I would venture the assertion that the memory which would emerge at the moment that I laid my hand on the patient's forehead would be the right one. In this way I succeeded, without hypnosis, in learning from the patient all that was necessary for a construction of the connection between the forgotten pathogenic scenes and the symptoms which they had left behind. This was a troublesome and in its length an exhausting proceeding, and did not lend itself to a finished technique. But I did not give it up without drawing definite conclusions from the data which I had gained. I had substantiated the fact that

the forgotten memories were not lost. They were in the possession of the patient, ready to emerge and form associations with his other mental content, but hindered from becoming conscious, and forced to remain in the unconscious by some sort of a force. The existence of this force could be assumed with certainty, for in attempting to drag up the unconscious memories into the consciousness of the patient, in opposition to this force, one got the sensation of his own personal effort striving to overcome it. One could get an idea of this force, which maintained the pathological situation, from the resistance of the patient.

It is on this idea of *resistance* that I based my theory of the psychic processes of hystericals. It had been found that in order to cure the patient it was necessary that this force should be overcome. Now with the mechanism of the cure as a starting point, quite a definite theory could be constructed. These same forces, which in the present situation as resistances opposed the emergence of the forgotten ideas into consciousness, must themselves have caused the forgetting, and repressed from consciousness the pathogenic experiences. I called this hypothetical process "repression" and considered that it was proved by the undeniable existence of resistance.

But now the question arose: what were those forces, and what were the conditions of this repression, in which we were now able to recognize the pathogenic mechanism of hysteria? A comparative study of the pathogenic situations, which the cathartic treatment has made possible, allows us to answer this question. In all those experiences, it had happened that a wish had been aroused, which was in sharp opposition to the other desires of the individual, and was not capable of being reconciled with the ethical, aesthetic and personal pretensions of the patient's personality. There had been a short conflict, and the end of this inner struggle was the repression of the idea which presented itself to consciousness as the bearer of this irreconcilable wish. This was, then, repressed from consciousness and forgotten. The incompatibility of the idea in question with the "ego" of the patient was the motive of the repression, the ethical and other pretensions of the individual were the repressing forces. The presence of the incompatible wish, or the duration of the conflict, had given rise to a high degree of mental pain; this pain was avoided by the repression. This latter process is evidently in such a case a device for the protection of the personality.

I will not multiply examples, but will give you the history of a single one of my cases, in which the conditions and the utility of the repression process stand out clearly enough. Of course for my purpose I must abridge the history of the case and omit many valuable theoretical considerations. It is that of a young girl, who was deeply attached to her father, who had died a short time before, and in whose care she had shared—a situation analogous to that of Breuer's patient. When her older sister married, the girl grew to feel a peculiar sympathy for her new brother-in-law, which easily passed with her for family tenderness. This sister soon fell ill and died, while the patient and her mother were away. The absent ones were hastily recalled, without being told fully of the painful situation. As the girl stood by the bedside of her dead sister, for one short moment there surged up in her mind an idea, which might be framed in these words: "Now he is free and can marry me." We may be sure that this idea, which betrayed to her consciousness her intense love for her brother-in-law, of which she had not been

conscious, was the next moment consigned to repression by her revolted feelings. The girl fell ill with severe hysterical symptoms, and, when I came to treat the case, it appeared that she had entirely forgotten that scene at her sister's bedside and the unnatural, egoistic desire which had arisen in her. She remembered it during the treatment, reproduced the pathogenic moment with every sign of intense emotional excitement, and was cured by this treatment.

Perhaps I can make the process of repression and its necessary relation to the resistance of the patient, more concrete by a rough illustration, which I will derive from our present situation.

Suppose that here in this hall and in this audience, whose exemplary stillness and attention I cannot sufficiently commend, there is an individual who is creating a disturbance, and, by his ill-bred laughing, talking, by scraping his feet, distracts my attention from my task. I explain that I cannot go on with my lecture under these conditions, and thereupon several strong men among you get up, and, after a short struggle, eject the disturber of the peace from the hall. He is now "repressed," and I can continue my lecture. But in order that the disturbance may not be repeated, in case the man who has just been thrown out attempts to force his way back into the room, the gentlemen who have executed my suggestion take their chairs to the door and establish themselves there as a "resistance," to keep up the repression. Now, if you transfer both locations to the psyche, calling this "consciousness," and the outside the "unconscious," you have a tolerably good illustration of the process of repression.

We can see now the difference between our theory and that of Janet. We do not derive the psychic fission from a congenital lack of capacity on the part of the mental apparatus to synthesize its experiences, but we explain it dynamically by the conflict of opposing mental forces, we recognize in it the result of an active striving of each mental complex against the other.

New questions at once arise in great number from our theory. The situation of psychic conflict is a very frequent one; an attempt of the ego to defend itself from painful memories can be observed everywhere, and yet the result is not a mental fission. We cannot avoid the assumption that still other conditions are necessary, if the conflict is to result in dissociation. I willingly concede that with the assumption of "repression" we stand, not at the end, but at the very beginning of a psychological theory. But we can advance only one step at a time, and the completion of our knowledge must await further and more thorough work.

Now do not attempt to bring the case of Breuer's patient under the point of view of repression. This history cannot be subjected to such an attempt, for it was gained with the help of hypnotic influence. Only when hypnosis is excluded can you see the resistances and repressions and get a correct idea of the pathogenic process. Hypnosis conceals the resistances and so makes a certain part of the mental field freely accessible. By this same process the resistances on the borders of this field are heaped up into a rampart, which makes all beyond inaccessible.

The most valuable things that we have learned from Breuer's observations were his conclusions as to the connection of the symptoms with the pathogenic experiences or psychic traumata, and we must not neglect to evaluate this result properly from the standpoint of the repression-theory. It is not at first evident how we can get from the repression to the creation of the symptoms. Instead of giving a complicated theoretical derivation, I will return at this point to the illustration which I used to typify repression.

Remember that with the ejection of the rowdy and the establishment of the watchers before the door, the affair is not necessarily ended. It may very well happen that the ejected man, now embittered and quite careless of consequences, gives us more to do. He is no longer among us, we are free from his presence, his scornful laugh, his half-audible remarks, but in a certain sense the repression has miscarried, for he makes a terrible uproar outside, and by his outcries and by hammering on the door with his fists interferes with my lecture more than before. Under these circumstances it would be hailed with delight if possibly our honored president, Dr. Stanley Hall, should take upon himself the role of peacemaker and mediator. He would speak with the rowdy on the outside, and then turn to us with the recommendation that we let him in again, provided he would guarantee to behave himself better. On Dr. Hall's authority we decide to stop the repression, and now quiet and peace reign again. This is in fact a fairly good presentation of the task devolving upon the physician in the psychoanalytic therapy of neuroses. To say the same thing more directly: we come to the conclusion, from working with hysterical patients and other neurotics, that they have not fully succeeded in repressing the idea to which the incompatible wish is attached. They have, indeed, driven it out of consciousness and out of memory, and apparently saved themselves a great amount of psychic pain, *but in the unconscious the suppressed wish still exists,* only waiting for its chance to become active, and finally succeeds in sending into consciousness, instead of the repressed idea, a disguised and unrecognizable surrogate-creation, to which the same painful sensations associate themselves that the patient thought he was rid of through his repression. This surrogate of the suppressed idea—the symptom—is secure against further attacks from the defences of the ego, and instead of a short conflict there originates now a permanent suffering. We can observe in the symptom, besides the tokens of its disguise, a remnant of traceable similarity with the originally repressed idea; the way in which the surrogate is built up can be discovered during the psychoanalytic treatment of the patient, and for his cure the symptom must be traced back over the same route to the repressed idea. If this repressed material is once more made part of the conscious mental functions—a process which supposes the overcoming of considerable resistance—the psychic conflict which then arises, the same which the patient wished to avoid, is made capable of a happier termination, under the guidance of the physician, than is offered by repression. There are several possible suitable decisions which can bring conflict and neurosis to a happy end; in particular cases the attempt may be made to combine several of these. Either the personality of the patient may be convinced that he has been wrong in rejecting the pathogenic wish, and he may be made to accept it either wholly or in part; or this wish may itself be directed to a higher goal which is free from objection, by what is called sublimation; or the rejection may be recognized as rightly motivated, and the automatic and therefore insufficient mechanism of repression be reinforced by the higher, more characteristically human mental faculties: one succeeds in mastering his wishes by conscious thought.

Forgive me if I have not been able to present more clearly these main points of the treatment which is to-day known as "psychoanalysis." The difficulties do not lie merely in the newness of the subject.

Regarding the nature of the unacceptable wishes, which succeed in making their influence felt out of the unconscious, in spite of repression; and regarding the question of what subjective and constitutional factors must be present for such a failure of repression and such a surrogate or symptom creation to take place, we will speak in later remarks.

THIRD LECTURE

Ladies and Gentlemen: It is not always easy to tell the truth, especially when one must be brief, and so to-day I must correct an incorrect statement that I made in my last lecture.

I told you how when I gave up using hypnosis I pressed my patients to tell me what came into their minds that had to do with the problem we were working on, I told them that they would remember what they had apparently forgotten, and that the thought which irrupted into consciousness would surely embody the memory for which we were seeking. I claimed that I substantiated the fact that the first idea of my patients brought the right clue and could be shown to be the forgotten continuation of the memory. Now this is not always so; I represented it as being so simple only for purposes of abbreviation. In fact, it would only happen the first times that the right forgotten material would emerge through simple pressure on my part. If the experience was continued, ideas emerged in every case which could not be the right ones, for they were not to the purpose, and the patients themselves rejected them as incorrect. Pressure was of no further service here, and one could only regret again having given up hypnosis. In this state of perplexity I clung to a prejudice which years later was proved by my friend C. G. Jung of the University of Zürich, and his pupils, to have a scientific justification. I must confess that it is often of great advantage to have prejudices. I put a high value on the strength of the determination of mental processes, and I could not believe that any idea which occurred to the patient, which originated in a state of concentrated attention, could be quite arbitrary and out of all relation to the forgotten idea that we were seeking. That it was not identical with the latter, could be satisfactorily explained by the hypothetical psychological situation. In the patients whom I treated there were two opposing forces: on the one hand the conscious striving to drag up into consciousness the forgotten experience which was present in the unconscious; and on the other hand the resistance which we have seen, which set itself against the emergence of the suppressed idea or its associates into consciousness. In case this resistance was nonexistent or very slight, the forgotten material could become conscious without disguise. It was then a natural supposition that the disguise would be the more complete, the greater the resistance to the emergence of the idea. Thoughts which broke into the patient's consciousness instead of the ideas sought for, were accordingly made up just like symptoms; they were new, artificial, ephemeral surrogates for the repressed ideas, and differed from these just in proportion as they had been more completely disguised under the influence of the resistances. These surrogates must, however, show a certain similarity with the ideas which are the object of our search, by virtue of their nature as symptoms; and when the

resistance is not too intensive it is possible from the nature of these irruptions to discover the hidden object of our search. This must be related to the repressed thought as a sort of allusion, as a statement of the same thing in *indirect* terms.

We know cases in normal psychology in which analogous situations to the one which we have assumed give rise to similar experiences. Such a case is that of wit. By my study of psychoanalytic technique I was necessarily led to a consideration of the problem of the nature of wit. I will give one example of this sort, which, too, is a story that originally appeared in English.

The anecdote runs: Two unscrupulous business men had succeeded by fortunate speculations in accumulating a large fortune, and then directed their efforts to breaking into good society. Among other means they thought it would be of advantage to be painted by the most famous and expensive artist of the city, a man whose paintings were considered as events. The costly paintings were first shown at a great soirée and both hosts led the most influential connoisseur and art critic to the wall of the salon on which the portraits were hung, to elicit his admiring judgment. The artist looked for a long time, looked about as though in search of something, and then merely asked, pointing out the vacant space between the two pictures; "And where is the Saviour?"

I see that you are all laughing over this good example of wit, which we will now attempt to analyse. We understand that the critic means to say; "You are a couple of malefactors, like those between whom the Saviour was crucified." But he does not say this, he expresses himself instead in a way that at first seems not to the purpose and not related to the matter in hand, but which at the next moment we recognize as an *allusion* to the insult at which he aims, and as a perfect surrogate for it. We cannot expect to find in the case of wit all those relations that our theory supposes for the origin of the irruptive ideas of our patients, but it is my desire to lay stress on the similar motivation of wit and irruptive idea. Why does not the critic say directly what he has to say to the two rogues? Because, in addition to his desire to say it straight out, he is actuated by strong opposite motives. It is a proceeding which is liable to be dangerous to offend people who are one's hosts, and who can call to their aid the strong arms of numerous servants. One might easily suffer the same fate that I used in the previous lecture to illustrate repression. On this ground, the critic does not express the particular insult directly, but in a disguised form, as an allusion with omission. The same constellation comes into play, according to our hypothesis, when our patient produces the irruptive idea as a surrogate for the forgotten idea which is the object of the quest.

Ladies and gentlemen, it is very useful to designate a group of ideas which belong together and have a common emotive tone, according to the custom of the Zürich school (Bleuler, Jung and others), as a "complex." So we can say that if we set out from the last memories of the patient to look for a repressed complex, that we have every prospect of discovering it, if only the patient will communicate to us a sufficient number of the ideas which come into his head. So we let the patient speak along any line that he desires, and cling to the hypothesis that nothing can occur to him except what has some indirect bearing on the complex that we are seeking. If this method of discovering the repressed complexes seems too circumstantial, I can at least assure you that it is the only available one.

In practicing this technique, one is further bothered by the fact that the patient often stops, is at a stand-still, and considers that he has nothing to say; nothing occurs to him. If this were really the case and the patient were right, our procedure would again be proven inapplicable. Closer observation shows that such an absence of ideas never really occurs, and that it only appears to when the patient holds back or rejects the idea which he perceives, under the influence of the resistance, which disguises itself as critical judgment of the value of the idea. The patient can be protected from this if he is warned in advance of this circumstance, and told to take no account of the critical attitude. He must say anything that comes into his mind, fully laying aside such critical choice, even though he may think it unessential, irrelevant, nonsensical, especially when the idea is one which is unpleasant to dwell on. By following this prescription we secure the material which sets us on the track of the repressed complex.

These irruptive ideas, which the patient himself values little, if he is under the influence of the resistance and not that of the physician, are for the psychologist like the ore, which by simple methods of interpretation he reduces from its crude state to valuable metal. If one desires to gain in a short time a preliminary knowledge of the patient's repressed complexes, without going into the question of their arrangement and associations, this examination may be conducted with the help of the association experiments, as Jung and his pupils have perfected them. This procedure is to the psychologist what qualitative analysis is to the chemist; it may be dispensed with in the therapy of neurotic patients, but is indispensable in the investigations of the psychoses, which have been begun by the Zürich school with such valuable results.

This method of work with whatever comes into the patient's head when he submits to psychoanalytic treatment, is not the only technical means at our disposal for the widening of consciousness. Two other methods of procedure serve the same purpose, the interpretation of his dreams and the evaluation of acts which he bungles or does without intending to.

I might say, esteemed hearers, that for a long time I hesitated whether instead of this hurried survey of the whole field of psychoanalysis, I should not rather offer you a thorough consideration of the analysis of dreams; a purely subjective and apparently secondary motive decided me against this. It seemed rather an impropriety that in this country, so devoted to practical pursuits, I should pose as "interpreter of dreams," before you had a chance to discover what significance the old and despised art can claim.

Interpretation of dreams is in fact the *via regia* to the interpretation of the unconscious, the surest ground of psychoanalysis and a field in which every worker must win his convictions and gain his education. If I were asked how one could become a psychoanalyst, I should answer, through the study of his own dreams. With great tact all opponents of the psychoanalytic theory have so far either evaded any criticism of *The Interpretation of Dreams* (Freud, 1900) or have attempted to pass over it with the most superficial objections. If, on the contrary, you will undertake the solution of the problems of dream life, the novelties which psychoanalysis present to

your thoughts will no longer be difficulties.

You must remember that our nightly dream productions show the greatest outer similarity and inner relationship to the creations of the insane, but on the other hand are compatible with full health during waking life. It does not sound at all absurd to say that whoever regards these normal sense illusions, these delusions and alterations of character as matter for amazement instead of understanding, has not the least prospect of understanding the abnormal creations of diseased mental states in any other than the lay sense. You may with confidence place in this lay group all the psychiatrists of today. Follow me now on a brief excursion through the field of dream problems.

In our waking state we usually treat dreams with as little consideration as the patient treats the irruptive ideas which the psychoanalyst demands from him. It is evident that we reject them, for we forget them quickly and completely. The slight valuation which we place on them is based, with those dreams that are not confused and nonsensical, on the feeling that they are foreign to our personality, and, with other dreams, on their evident absurdity and senselessness. Our rejection derives support from the unrestrained shamelessness and the immoral longings which are obvious in many dreams. Antiquity, as we know, did not share this light valuation of dreams. The lower classes of our people today stick close to the value which they set on dreams; they, however, expect from them, as did the ancients, the revelation of the future. I confess that I see no need to adopt mystical hypotheses to fill out the gaps in our present knowedge, and so I have never been able to find anything that supported the hypothesis of the prophetic nature of dreams. Many other things, which are wonderful enough, can be said about them.

And first, not all dreams are so foreign to the character of the dreamer, are incomprehensible and confused. If you will undertake to consider the dreams of young children from the age of a year and a half on, you will find them quite simple and easy to interpret. The young child always dreams of the fulfillment of wishes which were aroused in him the day before and were not satisfied. You need no art of interpretation to discover this simple solution, you only need to inquire into the experiences of the child on the day before (the "dream day"). Now it would certainly be a most satisfactory solution of the dream-riddle, if the dreams of adults, too, were the same as those of children, fulfillments of wishes which had been aroused in them during the dream day. This is actually the fact; the difficulties which stand in the way of this solution can be removed step by step by a thorough analysis of the dream.

There is, first of all, the most weighty objection, that the dreams of adults generally have an incomprehensible content, which shows wish-fulfillment least of anything. The answer is this: these dreams have undergone a process of disguise, the psychic content which underlies them was originally meant for quite different verbal expression. You must differentiate between the *manifest dream-content,* which we remember in the morning only confusedly, and with difficulty clothe in words which seem arbitrary, and the *latent dream-thoughts,* whose presence in the unconscious we must assume. This distortion of the dream is the same process which has been revealed to you in the investigations of the creations (*symptoms*) of hysterical subjects; it points to the fact that the same

opposition of psychic forces has its share in the creation of dreams as in the creation of symptoms.

The manifest dream-content is the disguised surrogate for the unconscious dream-thoughts, and this disguising is the work of the defensive forces of the ego, of the resistances. These prevent the repressed wishes from entering consciousness during the waking life, and even in the relaxation of sleep they are still strong enough to force them to hide themselves by a sort of masquerading. The dreamer, then, knows just as little the sense of his dream as the hysterical knows the relation and significance of his symptoms. That there are latent dream-thoughts and that between them and the manifest dream-content there exists the relations just described—of this you may convince yourselves by the analysis of dreams, a procedure the technique of which is exactly that of psychoanalysis. You must abstract entirely from the apparent connection of the elements in the manifest dream and seek for the irruptive ideas which arise through free association, according to the psychoanalytic laws, from each separate dream element. From this material the latent dream thoughts may be discovered, exactly as one divines the concealed complexes of the patient from the fancies connected with his symptoms and memories. From the latent dream thoughts which you will find in this way, you will see at once how thoroughly justified one is in interpreting the dreams of adults by the same rubrics as those of children. What is now substituted for the manifest dream-content is the real sense of the dream, is always clearly comprehensible, associated with the impressions of the day before, and appears as the fulfilling of an unsatisfied wish. The manifest dream, which we remember after waking, may then be described as a *disguised* fulfillment of *repressed* wishes.

It is also possible by a sort of synthesis to get some insight into the process which has brought about the disguise of the unconscious dream-thoughts as the manifest dream-content. We call this process "dream-work." This deserves our fullest theoretical interest, since here as nowhere else we can study the unsuspected psychic processes which are existent in the unconscious, or, to express it more exactly, *between* two such separate systems as the conscious and the unconscious. Among these newly discovered psychic processes, two, condensation and displacement or transvaluation, change of psychic accent, stand out most prominently. Dream work is a special case of the reaction of different mental groupings on each other, and as such is the consequence of psychic fission. In all essential points it seems identical with the work of disguise, which changes the repressed complex in the case of failing repression into symptoms.

You will furthermore discover by the analysis of dreams, most convincingly your own, the unsuspected importance of the role which impressions and experiences from early childhood exert on the development of men. In the dream life the child, as it were, continues his existence in the man, with a retention of all his traits and wishes, including those which he was obliged to allow to fall into disuse in his later years. With irresistible might it will be impressed on you by what processes of development, of repression, sublimation and reaction there arises out of the child, with its peculiar gifts and tendencies, the so-called normal man, the bearer and partly the victim of our painfully acquired civilization. I will also direct your attention to the fact that we

have discovered from the analysis of dreams that the unconscious makes use of a sort of symbolism, especially in the presentation of sexual complexes. This symbolism in part varies with the individual, but in part is of a typical nature, and seems to be identical with the symbolism which we suppose to lie behind our myths and legends. It is not impossible that these latter creations of the people may find their explanation from the study of dreams.

Finally, I must remind you that you must not be led astray by the objection that the occurrence of anxiety-dreams contradicts our idea of the dream as a wish-fulfillment. Apart from the consideration that anxiety-dreams also require interpretation before judgment can be passed on them, one can say quite generally that the anxiety does not depend in such a simple way on the dream content as one might suppose without more knowledge of the facts, and more attention to the conditions of neurotic anxiety. Anxiety is one of the ways in which the ego relieves itself of repressed wishes which have become too strong, and so is easy to explain in the dream, if the dream has gone too far towards the fulfilling of the objectionable wish.

You see that the investigation of dreams was justified by the conclusions which it has given us concerning things otherwise hard to understand. But we came to it in connection with the psychoanalytic treatment of neurotics. From what has been said you can easily understand how the interpretation of dreams, if it is not made too difficult by the resistance of the patient, can lead to a knowledge of the patient's concealed and repressed wishes and the complexes which he is nourishing. I may now pass to that group of everyday mental phenomena whose study has become a technical help for psychoanalysis.

These are the bungling of acts among normal men as well as among neurotics, to which no significance is ordinarily attached; the forgetting of things which one is supposed to know and at other times really does know (for example the temporary forgetting of proper names); mistakes in speaking, which occur so frequently; analogous mistakes in writing and in reading, the automatic execution of purposive acts in wrong situations and the loss or breaking of objects, etc. These are trifles, for which no one has ever sought a psychological determination, which have passed unchallenged as chance experiences, as consequences of absent-mindedness, inattention and similar conditions. Here, too, are included the acts and gestures executed without being noticed by the subject, to say nothing of the fact that he attaches no psychic importance to them; as playing and trifling with objects, humming melodies, handling one's person and clothing and the like.

These little things, the bungling of acts, like the symptomatic and chance acts are not so entirely without meaning as is generally supposed by a sort of tacit agreement. They have a meaning, generally easy and sure to interpret from the situation in which they occur, and it can be demonstrated that they either express impulses and purposes which are repressed, hidden if possible from the consciousness of the individual, or that they spring from exactly the same sort of repressed wishes and complexes which we have learned to know already as the creators of symptoms and dreams.

It follows that they deserve the rank of symptoms, and their observation, like that of dreams, can lead to the discovery of the hidden complexes of the psychic life. With their help one will usually betray the most intimate of his secrets. If these occur so easily and commonly among people in health, with whom repression has on the whole succeeded fairly well, this is due to their insignificance and their inconspicuous nature. But they can lay claim to high theoretic value, for they prove the existence of repression and surrogate creations even under the conditions of health. You have already noticed that the psychoanalyst is distinguished by an especially strong belief in the determination of the psychic life. For him there is in the expressions of the psyche nothing trifling, nothing arbitrary and lawless, he expects everywhere a widespread motivation, where customarily such claims are not made; more than that, he is even prepared to find a manifold motivation of these psychic expressions, while our supposedly inborn causal need is satisfied with a single psychic cause.

Now keeping in mind the means which we possess for the discovery of the hidden, forgotten, repressed things in the soul life: the study of the irruptive ideas called up by free association, the patient's dreams, and his bungled and symptomatic acts; and adding to these the evaluation of other phenomena which emerge during the psychoanalytic treatment, on which I shall later make a few remarks under the heading of "transfer," you will come with me to the conclusion that our technique is already sufficiently efficacious for the solution of the problem of how to introduce the pathogenic psychic material into consciousness, and so to do away with the suffering brought on by the creation of surrogate symptoms.

The fact that by such therapeutic endeavors our knowledge of the mental life of the normal and the abnormal is widened and deepened, can of course only be regarded as an especial attraction and superiority of this method.

I do not know whether you have gained the impression that the technique through whose arsenal I have led you is a peculiarly difficult one. I consider that on the contrary, for one who has mastered it, it is quite adapted for use. But so much is sure, that it is not obvious, that it must be learned no less than the histological or the surgical technique.

You may be surprised to learn that in Europe we have heard very frequently judgments passed on psychoanalysis by persons who knew nothing of its technique and had never practised it, but who demanded scornfully that we show the correctness of our results. There are among these people some who are not in other things unacquainted with scientific methods of thought, who for example would not reject the result of a microscopical research because it cannot be confirmed with the naked eye in anatomical preparations, and who would not pass judgment until they had used the microscope. But in matters of psychoanalysis circumstances are really more unfavorable for gaining recognition. Psychoanalysis will bring the repressed in mental life to conscious acknowledgment, and every one who judges it is himself a man who has such repressions, perhaps only maintained with difficulty. It will consequently call forth the same resistances from him as from the patient, and this resistance can easily succeed in disguising itself as intellectual rejection, and bring forward arguments similar to those from which we protect our patients by the basic principles of psychoanalysis. It is not difficult to substantiate in our opponents the same impairment of intelligence produced by emotivity which we may observe every day with our patients. The arrogance of consciousness which for example rejects dreams so lightly, belongs—quite generally—to the strongest protective apparatus which guards us against the breaking through of the unconscious complexes, and as a result it is hard to convince people of the reality of the unconscious, and to teach them anew, what their conscious knowledge contradicts.

FOURTH LECTURE

Ladies and Gentlemen: At this point you will be asking what the technique which I have described has taught us of the nature of the pathogenic complexes and repressed wishes of neurotics.

One thing in particular: psychoanalytic investigations trace back the symptoms of disease with really surprising regularity to impressions from the sexual life, show us that the pathogenic wishes are of the nature of erotic impulse-components, and necessitate the assumption that to disturbances of the erotic sphere must be ascribed the greatest significance among the etiological factors of the disease. This holds of both sexes.

I know that this assertion will not willingly be credited. Even those investigators who gladly follow my psychological labors, are inclined to think that I overestimate the etiological share of the sexual moments. They ask me why other mental excitations should not lead to the phenomena of repression and surrogate-creation which I have described. I can give them this answer; that I do not know why they should not do this, I have no objection to their doing it, but experience shows that they do not possess such a significance, and that they merely support the effect of the sexual moments, without being able to supplant them. This conclusion was not a theoretical postulate; in *Studies on Hysteria,* published in 1895 with Dr. Breuer, I did not stand on this ground. I was converted to it when my experience was richer and had led me deeper into the nature of the case. Gentlemen, there are among you some of my closest friends and adherents, who have travelled to Worcester with me. Ask them, and they will tell you that they all were at first completely sceptical of the assertion of the determinative significance of the sexual etiology, until they were compelled by their own analytic labors to come to the same conclusion.

The conduct of the patients does not make it any easier to convince one's self of the correctness of the view which I have expressed. Instead of willingly giving us information concerning their sexual life, they try to conceal it by every means in their power. Men generally are not candid in sexual matters. They do not show their sexuality freely, but they wear a thick overcoat—a fabric of lies—to conceal it, as though it were bad weather in the world of sex. And they are not wrong; sun and wind are not favorable in our civilized society to any demonstration of sex life. In truth no one can freely disclose his erotic life to his neighbor. But when your patients see that in your treatment they may disregard the conventional restraints, they lay aside this veil of lies, and then only are you in a position to formulate a judgment on the question in dispute. Unfortunately physicians are not favored above the rest of the children of men in their personal relationship to the questions of the sex life. Many of them

are under the ban of that mixture of prudery and lasciviousness which determines the behaviour of most polite people in affairs of sex.

Now to proceed with the communication of our results. It is true that in another series of cases psychoanalysis at first traces the symptoms back not to the sexual, but to banal traumatic experiences. But the distinction loses its significance through other circumstances. The work of analysis which is necessary for the thorough explanation and complete cure of a case of sickness does not stop in any case with the experience of the time of onset of the disease, but in every case it goes back to the adolescence and the early childhood of the patient. Here only do we hit upon the impressions and circumstances which determine the later sickness. Only the childhood experiences can give the explanation for the sensitivity to later traumata and only when these memory traces, which almost always are forgotten, are discovered and made conscious, is the power developed to banish the symptoms. We arrive here at the same conclusion as in the investigation of dreams—that it is the incompatible, repressed wishes of childhood which lend their power to the creation of symptoms. Without these the reactions upon later traumata discharge normally. But we must consider these mighty wishes of childhood very generally as sexual in nature.

Now I can at any rate be sure of your astonishment. Is there an infantile sexuality? you will ask. Is childhood not rather that period of life which is distinguished by the lack of the sexual impulse? No, gentlemen, it is not at all true that the sexual impulse enters into the child at puberty, as the devils in the gospel entered into the swine. The child has his sexual impulses and activities from the beginning, he brings them with him into the world, and from these the so-called normal sexuality of adults emerges by a significant development through manifold stages. It is not very difficult to observe the expressions of this childish sexual activity; it needs rather a certain art to overlook them or to fail to interpret them.

As fate would have it, I am in a position to call a witness for my assertions from your own midst. I show you here the work of one Dr. Sanford Bell, published in 1902 in the *American Journal of Psychology*. The author was a fellow of Clark University, the same institution within whose walls we now stand. In this thesis, entitled "A Preliminary Study of the Emotion of Love between the Sexes," which appeared three years before my *Three Contributions to the Theory of Sex* (Freud, 1905), the author says just what I have been saying to you: "The emotion of sex . . . does not make its appearance for the first time at the period of adolescence as has been thought." He has, as we should say in Europe, worked by the American method, and has gathered not less than 2,500 positive observations in the course of fifteen years, among them 800 of his own. He says of the signs by which this amorous condition manifests itself: "The unprejudiced mind, in observing these manifestations in hundreds of couples of children, cannot escape referring them to sex origin. The most exacting mind is satisfied when to these observations are added the confessions of those who have as children experienced the emotion to a marked degree of intensity, and whose memories of childhood are relatively distinct." Those of you who are unwilling to believe in infantile sexuality will be most astonished to hear that among those children who fell in love

so early not a few are of the tender ages of three, four, and five years.

It would not be surprising if you should believe the observations of a fellow-countryman rather than my own. Fortunately a short time ago from the analysis of a five-year-old boy who was suffering from anxiety, an analysis undertaken with correct technique by his own father, I succeeded in getting a fairly complete picture of the bodily expressions of the impulse and the mental productions of an early stage of childish sexual life. And I must remind you that my friend, Dr. C. G. Jung, read you a few hours ago in this room an observation on a still younger girl who from the same cause as my patient—the birth of a little child in the family—betrayed certainly almost the same secret excitement, wish and complex-creation. Accordingly I am not without hope that you may feel friendly toward this idea of infantile sexuality that was so strange at first. I might also quote the remarkable example of the Zürich psychiatrist, E. Bleuler, who said a few years ago openly that he faced my sexual theories incredulous and bewildered, and since that time by his own observations had substantiated them in their whole scope. If it is true that most men, medical observers and others, do not want to know anything about the sexual life of the child, the fact is capable of explanation only too easily. They have forgotten their own infantile sexual activity under the pressure of education for civilization and do not care to be reminded now of the repressed material. You will be convinced otherwise if you begin the investigation by a self-analysis, by an interpretation of your own childhood memories.

Lay aside your doubts and let us evaluate the infantile sexuality of the earliest years. The sexual impulse of the child manifests itself as a very complex one, it permits of an analysis into many components, which spring from different sources. It is entirely disconnected from the function of reproduction which it is later to serve. It permits the child to gain different sorts of pleasure sensations, which we include, by the analogues and connections which they show, under the term sexual pleasures. The great source of infantile sexual pleasure is the auto-excitation of certain particularly sensitive parts of the body; besides the genitals are included the rectum and the opening of the urinary canal, and also the skin and other sensory surfaces. Since in this first phase of child sexual life the satisfaction is found on the child's own body and has nothing to do with any other object, we call this phase after a word coined by Havelock Ellis, that of "auto-erotism." The parts of the body significant in giving sexual pleasure we call "erogenous zones." The thumb-sucking or passionate sucking of very young children is a good example of such an auto-erotic satisfaction of an erogenous zone. The first scientific observer of this phenomenon, a specialist in children's diseases in Budapest by the name of Lindner, interpreted these rightly as sexual satisfaction and described exhaustively their transformation into other and higher forms of sexual gratification. Another sexual satisfaction of this time of life is the excitation of the genitals by masturbation, which has such a great significance for later life and, in the case of many individuals, is never fully overcome. Besides this and other auto-erotic manifestations we see very early in the child the impulse-components of *sexual pleasure,* or, as we may say, of the *libido,* which presupposes a second person as its object. These impulses appear in opposed pairs, as active and passive. The most important represen-

tatives of this group are the pleasure in inflicting pain (sadism) with its passive opposite (masochism) and active and passive exhibition-pleasure. From the first of these later pairs splits off the curiosity for knowledge, as from the latter the impulse toward artistic and theatrical representation. Other sexual manifestations of the child can already be regarded from the view-point of object-choice, in which the second person plays the prominent part. The significance of this was primarily based upon motives of the impulse of self-preservation. The difference between the sexes plays, however, in the child no very great role. One may attribute to every child, without wronging him, a bit of the homosexual disposition.

The sexual life of the child, rich, but dissociated, in which each single impulse goes about the business of arousing pleasure independently of every other, is later correlated and organized in two general directions, so that by the close of puberty the definite sexual character of the individual is practically finally determined. The single impulses subordinate themselves to the overlordship of the genital zone, so that the whole sexual life is taken over into the service of procreation, and their gratification is now significant only so far as they help to prepare and promote the true sexual act. On the other hand, object-choice prevails over auto-erotism, so that now in the sexual life all components of the sexual impulse are satisfied in the loved person. But not all the original impulse-components are given a share in the final shaping of the sexual life. Even before the advent of puberty certain impulses have undergone the most energetic repression under the impulse of education, and mental forces like shame, disgust and morality are developed, which, like sentinels, keep the repressed wishes in subjection. When there comes, in puberty, the high tide of sexual desire it finds dams in this creation of reactions and resistances. These guide the outflow into the so-called normal channels, and make it impossible to revivify the impulses which have undergone repression.

The most important of these repressed impulses are coprophilism, that is, the pleasure in children connected with the excrements; and, further, the tendencies attaching themselves to the persons of the primitive object-choice.

Gentlemen, a sentence of general pathology says that every process of development brings with it the germ of pathological dispositions in so far as it may be inhibited, delayed, or incompletely carried out. This holds for the development of the sexual function, with its many complications. It is not smoothly completed in all individuals, and may leave behind either abnormalities or disposition to later diseases by the way of later falling back or *regression*. It may happen that not all the partial impulses subordinate themselves to the rule of the genital zone. Such an impulse which has remained disconnected brings about what we call a perversion, which may replace the normal sexual goal by one of its own. It may happen, as has been said before, that the auto-erotism is not fully overcome, as many sorts of disturbances testify. The originally equal value of both sexes as sexual objects may be maintained and an inclination to homosexual activities in adult life result from this, which, under suitable conditions, rises to the level of exclusive homosexuality. This series of disturbances corresponds to the direct inhibition of development of the sexual function, it includes the perversions and the general *infantilism* of the sex life that are not seldom met with.

The disposition to neuroses is to be derived in another way from an injury to the development of the sex life. The neuroses are related to the perversions as the negative to the positive; in them we find the same impulse-components as in perversions, as bearers of the complexes and as creators of the symptoms; but here they work from out the unconscious. They have undergone a repression, but in spite of this they maintain themselves in the unconscious. Psychoanalysis teaches us that overstrong expression of the impulse in very early life leads to a sort of fixation, which then offers a weak point in the articulation of the sexual function. If the exercise of the normal sexual function meets with hindrances in later life, this repression, dating from the time of development, is broken through at just that point at which the infantile fixation took place.

You will now perhaps make the objection: "But all that is not sexuality." I have used the word in a very much wider sense than you are accustomed to understand it. This I willingly concede. But it is a question whether you do not rather use the word in much too narrow a sense when you restrict it to the realm of procreation. You sacrifice by that the understanding of perversions; of the connection between perversion, neurosis and normal sexual life; and have no means of recognizing, in its true significance, the easily observable beginning of the somatic and mental sexual life of the child. But however you decide about the use of the word, remember that the psychoanalyst understands sexuality in that full sense to which he is led by the evaluation of infantile sexuality.

Now we turn again to the sexual development of the child. We still have much to say here, since we have given more attention to the somatic than to the mental expressions of the sexual life. The primitive object-choice of the child, which is derived from his need of help, demands our further interest. It first attaches to all persons to whom he is accustomed, but soon these give way in favor of his parents. The relation of the child to his parents is, as both direct observation of the child and later analytic investigation of adults agree, not at all free from elements of sexual accessory-excitation. The child takes both parents, and especially one, as an object of his erotic wishes. Usually he follows in this the stimulus given by his parents, whose tenderness has very clearly the character of a sex manifestation, though inhibited so far as its goal is concerned. As a rule, the father prefers the daughter, the mother the son; the child reacts to this situation, since, as son, he wishes himself in the place of his father, as daughter, in the place of the mother. The feelings awakened in these relations between parents and children, and, as a resultant of them, those among the children in relation to each other, are not only positively of a tender, but negatively of an inimical sort. The complex built up in this way is destined to quick repression, but it still exerts a great and lasting effect from the unconscious. We must express the opinion that this with its ramifications presents the *nuclear complex* of every neurosis, and so we are prepared to meet with it in a not less effectual way in the other fields of mental life. The myth of King Oedipus, who kills his father and wins his mother as a wife is only the slightly altered presentation of the infantile wish, rejected later by the opposing barriers of incest. Shakespeare's tale of Hamlet rests on the same basis of an incest complex, though better concealed. At the time when the child is still ruled by the still unrepressed nuclear complex, there begins a very significant part of his mental activity which serves sexual interest. He begins to investigate the question of where children come from and guesses more than adults imagine of the true relations by deduction from the signs which he sees. Usually his interest in this investigation is awakened by the threat to his welfare through the birth of another child in the family, in whom at first he sees only a rival. Under the influence of the partial impulses which are active in him he arrives at a number of "infantile sexual theories," as that the same male genitals belong to both sexes, that children are conceived by eating and born through the opening of the intestine, and that sexual intercourse is to be regarded as an inimical act, a sort of overpowering.

But just the unfinished nature of his sexual constitution and the gaps in his knowledge brought about by the hidden condition of the feminine sexual canal, cause the infant investigator to discontinue his work as a failure. The facts of this childish investigation itself as well as the infant sex theories created by it are of determinative significance in the building of the child's character, and in the content of his later neuroses.

It is unavoidable and quite normal that the child should make his parents the objects of his first object-choice. But his *libido* must not remain fixed on these first chosen objects, but must take them merely as a prototype and transfer from these to other persons in the time of definite object-choice. The breaking loose of the child from his parents is thus a problem impossible to escape if the social virtue of the young individual is not to be impaired. During the time that the repressive activity is making its choice among the partial sexual impulses and later, when the influence of the parents, which in the most essential way has furnished the material for these repressions, is lessened, great problems fall to the work of education, which at present certainly does not always solve them in the most intelligent and economic way.

Gentlemen, do not think that with these explanations of the sexual life and the sexual development of the child we have too far departed from psychoanalysis and the cure of neurotic disturbances. If you like, you may regard the psychoanalytic treatment only as a continued education for the overcoming of childhood-remnants.

FIFTH LECTURE

Ladies and Gentlemen: With the discovery of infantile sexuality and the tracing back of the neurotic symptoms to erotic impulse-components we have arrived at several unexpected formulae for expressing the nature and tendencies of neurotic diseases. We see that the individual falls ill when in consequence of outer hindrances or inner lack of adaptability the satisfaction of the erotic needs in the sphere of reality is denied. We see that he then flees to sickness, in order to find with its help a surrogate satisfaction for that denied him. We recognize that the symptoms of illness contain fractions of the sexual activity of the individual, or his whole sexual life, and we find in the turning away from reality the chief tendency and also the chief injury of the sickness. We may guess that the resistance of our patients against the cure is not a simple one, but is composed of many motives. Not only does the ego of the patient strive against the giving up of the repressions by which it has changed itself from its original

constitution into its present form, but also the sexual impulses may not renounce their surrogate satisfaction so long as it is not certain that they can be offered anything better in the sphere of reality.

The flight from the unsatisfying reality into what we call, on account of its biologically injurious nature, disease, but which is never without an individual gain in pleasure for the patient, takes place over the path of regression, the return to earlier phases of the sexual life, when satisfaction was not lacking. This regression is seemingly a twofold one, a *temporal,* in so far as the *libido* or erotic need falls back to a temporally earlier stage of development, and a *formal,* since the original and primitive psychic means of expression are applied to the expression of this need. Both sorts of regression focus in childhood and have their common point in the production of an infantile condition of sexual life.

The deeper you penetrate into the pathogenesis of neurotic diseases, the more the connection of neuroses with other products of human mentality, even the most valuable, will be revealed to you. You will be reminded that we men, with the high claims of our civilization and under the pressure of our repressions, find reality generally quite unsatisfactory and so keep up a life of fancy in which we love to compensate for what is lacking in the sphere of reality by the production of wish-fulfillments. In these phantasies is often contained very much of the particular constitutional essence of personality and of its tendencies, repressed in real life. The energetic and successful man is he who succeeds by dint of labor in transforming his wish fancies into reality. Where this is not successful in consequence of the resistance of the outer world and the weakness of the individual, there begins the turning away from reality. The individual takes refuge in his satisfying world of fancy. Under certain favorable conditions it still remains possible for him to find another connecting link between these fancies and reality, instead of permanently becoming a stranger to it through the regression into the infantile. If the individual who is displeased with reality is in possession of that *artistic talent* which is still a psychological riddle, he can transform his fancies into artistic creations. So he escapes the fate of a neurosis and wins back his connection with reality by this round-about way. Where this opposition to the real world exists, but this valuable talent fails or proves insufficient, it is unavoidable that the *libido*, following the origin of the fancies, succeeds by means of regression in revivifying the infantile wishes and so producing a neurosis. The neurosis takes, in our time, the place of the cloister, in which were accustomed to take refuge all those whom life had undeceived or who felt themselves too weak for life. Let me give at this point the main result at which we have arrived by the psychoanalytic investigation of neurotics, namely, that neuroses have no peculiar psychic content of their own, which is not also to be found in healthy states; or, as C. G. Jung has expressed it, neurotics fall ill of the same complexes with which we sound people struggle. It depends on quantitative relationships, on the relations of the forces wrestling with each other, whether the struggle leads to health, to a neurosis, or to compensatory over-functioning.

Ladies and gentlemen, I have still withheld from you the most remarkable experience which corroborates our assumptions of the sexual impulse-forces of neurotics. Every time that we treat a neurotic psychoanalytically, there occurs in him the so-called phenomenon of *transfer*, that is, he applies to the person of the physician a great amount of tender emotion, often mixed with enmity, which has no foundation in any real relation, and must be derived in every respect from the old wish-fancies of the patient which have become unconscious. Every fragment of his emotive life, which can no longer be called back into memory, is accordingly lived over by the patient in his relations to the physician, and only by such a living of them over in the "transfer" is he convinced of the existence and the power of these unconscious sexual excitations. The symptoms, which, to use a simile from chemistry, are the precipitates of earlier love experiences (in the widest sense), can only be dissolved in the higher temperature of the experience of transfer and transformed into other psychic products. The physician plays in this reaction, to use an excellent expression of Sandor Ferenczi, the role of a *catalytic ferment*, which temporarily attracts to itself the affect which has become free in the course of the process.

The study of transfer can also give you the key to the understanding of hypnotic suggestion, which we at first used with our patients as a technical means of investigation of the unconscious. Hypnosis showed itself at that time to be a therapeutic help, but a hindrance to the scientific knowledge of the real nature of the case, since it cleared away the psychic resistances from a certain field, only to pile them up in an unscalable wall at the boundaries of this field. You must not think that the phenomenon of transfer, about which I can unfortunately say only too little here, is created by the influence of the psychoanalytic treatment. The transfer arises spontaneously in all human relations and in the relations of the patient to the physician; it is everywhere the especial bearer of therapeutic influences, and it works the stronger the less one knows of its presence. Accordingly psychoanalysis does not create it, it merely discloses it to consciousness, and avails itself of it, in order to direct the psychic processes to the wished for goal. But I cannot leave the theme of transfer without stressing the fact that this phenomenon is of decisive importance to convince not only the patient, but also the physician. I know that all my adherents were first convinced of the correctness of my views through their experience with transfer, and I can very well conceive that one may not win such a surety of judgment so long as he makes no psychoanalysis, and so has not himself observed the effects of transfer.

Ladies and gentlemen, I am of the opinion that there are, on the intellectual side, two hindrances to acknowledging the values of the psychoanalytic viewpoint: first, the fact that we are not accustomed to reckon with a strict determination of mental life, which holds without exception, and second, the lack of knowledge of the peculiarities through which unconscious mental processes differ from those conscious ones with which we are familiar. One of the most widespread resistances against the work of psychoanalysis with patients as with persons in health reduces to the latter of the two moments. One is afraid of doing harm by psychoanalysis, one is anxious about calling up into consciousness the repressed sexual impulses of the patient, as though there were danger that they could overpower the higher ethical strivings and rob him of his cultural acquisitions. One can see that the patient has sore places in his soul life, but one is afraid to touch them, lest his suffering be increased. We may use this analogy. It is, of course, better not to touch diseased places when one can only cause pain. But

we know that the surgeon does not refrain from the investigation and reinvestigation of the seat of illness, if his invasion has as its aim the restoration of lasting health. Nobody thinks of blaming him for the unavoidable difficulties of the investigation or the phenomena of reaction from the operation, if these only accomplish their purpose, and gain for the patient a final cure by temporarily making his condition worse. The case is similar in psychoanalysis; it can lay claim to the same things as surgery; the increase of pain which takes place in the patient during the treatment is very much less than that which the surgeon imposes upon him, and especially negligible in comparison with the pains of serious illness. But the consequence which is feared, that of a disturbance of the cultural character by the impulse which has been freed from repression, is wholly impossible. In relation to this anxiety we must consider what our experiences have taught us with certainty, that the somatic and mental power of a wish, if once its repression has not succeeded, is incomparably stronger when it is unconscious than when it is conscious, so that by being made conscious it can only be weakened. The unconscious wish cannot be influenced, is free from all strivings in the contrary direction, while the conscious is inhibited by those wishes which are also conscious and which strive against it. The work of psychoanalysis accordingly presents a better substitute, in the service of the highest and most valuable cultural strivings, for the repression which has failed.

Now what is the fate of the wishes which have become free by psychoanalysis, by what means shall they be made harmless for the life of the individual? There are several ways. The general consequence is, that the wish is consumed during the work by the correct mental activity of those better tendencies which are opposed to it. The repression is supplanted by a condemnation carried through with the best means at one's disposal. This is possible, since for the most part we have to abolish only the effects of earlier developmental stages of the ego. The individual for his part only repressed the useless impulse, because at that time he was himself still incompletely organized and weak; in his present maturity and strength he can, perhaps, conquer without injury to himself that which is inimical to him. A second issue of the work of psychoanalysis may be that the revealed unconscious impulses can now arrive at those usefu applications which, in the case of undisturbed development, they would have found earlier. The extirpation of the infantile wishes is not at all the ideal aim of development. The neurotic has lost, by his repressions, many sources of mental energy whose contingents would have been very valuable for his character building and his life activities. We know a far more purposive process of development, the so-called *sublimation,* by which the energy of infantile wish-excitations is not secluded, but remains capable of application, while for the particular excitations, instead of becoming useless, a higher, eventually no longer sexual, goal is set up. The components of the sexual instinct are especially distinguished by such a capacity for the sublimation and exchange of their sexual goal for one more remote and socially more valuable. To the contributions of the energy won in such a way for the functions of our mental life we probably owe the highest cultural consequences. A repression taking place at an early period excludes the sublimation of the repressed impulse; after the removal of the repression the way to sublimation is again free.

We must not neglect, also, to glance at the third of the possible issues. A certain part of the suppressed libidinous excitation has a right to direct satisfaction and ought to find it in life. The claims of our civilization make life too hard for the greater part of humanity, and so further the aversion to reality and the origin of neuroses, without producing an excess of cultural gain by this excess of sexual repression. We ought not to go so far as to fully neglect the original animal part of our nature, we ought not to forget that the happiness of individuals cannot be dispensed with as one of the aims of our culture. The plasticity of the sexual-components, manifest in their capacity for sublimation, may cause a great temptation to accomplish greater culture-effects by a more and more far reaching sublimation. But just as little as with our machines we expect to change more than a certain fraction of the applied heat into useful mechanical work, just as little ought we to strive to separate the sexual impulse in its whole extent of energy from its peculiar goal. This cannot succeed, and if the narrowing of sexuality is pushed too far it will have all the evil effects of a robbery.

I do not know whether you will regard the exhortation with which I close as a presumptuous one. I only venture the indirect presentation of my conviction, if I relate an old tale, whose application you may make yourselves. German literature knows a town called Schilda, to whose inhabitants were attributed all sorts of clever pranks. The wiseacres, so the story goes, had a horse, with whose powers of work they were well satisfied, and against whom they had only one grudge, that he consumed so much expensive oats. They concluded that by good management they would break him of this bad habit, by cutting down his rations by several stalks each day, until he had learned to do without them altogether. Things went finely for a while, the horse was weaned to one stalk a day, and on the next day he would at last work without fodder. On the morning of this day the malicious horse was found dead; the citizens of Schilda could not understand why he had died. We should be inclined to believe that the horse had starved, and that without a certain ration of oats no work could be expected from an animal.

I thank you for calling me here to speak, and for the attention which you have given me.

REFERENCES

Breuer, J. & Freud, S. *Studies on hysteria.* New York: Basic Books, 1957. (Originally published, 1895.)

Freud, S. *The interpretation of dreams.* New York: Random House, 1938. (Originally published, 1900.)

Freud, S. *Three contributions to the theory of sex.* London: Hogarth Press, 1953. (Originally published, 1905.)

CHAPTER 2

Individual Psychology

Introduction

The relationship between Sigmund Freud and Alfred Adler (1870–1937) would make a fascinating study of two contrasting personalities; they might be compared, for example, to Don Quixote and Sancho Panza. Freud, like Don Quixote, used grandiloquent and fanciful language and had extremely unusual ideas; Adler, like Sancho Panza, spoke simply and with great common sense.

Freud invited Adler to join the select circle of people interested in the developing topic of psychoanalysis who met in his apartment to present and discuss papers and ideas. As time went on it became apparent that the views of these two individuals were too different to be reconciled. In 1911 Adler left Freud's group and went on his own. Eventually he established his own school of thought, which he labeled Individual Psychology.

Freud became a bitter enemy of Adler and never forgave his defection. While a great many other people who joined with Freud later separated from him, including Carl Jung and Otto Rank, apparently Adler's departure from the group caused Freud the greatest degree of hurt and anger.

Adler represented a humanistic, commonsense point of view, while Freud's was essentially mechanistic and biological. As can be seen in this selection, Adler wrote in terse, no-nonsense terms and aimed constantly for simplicity. The difference is seen, for example, in their contrasting views of the personality. Freud separated the self into the contending forces of the ego, the id, and the superego, while Adler saw the personality as a unified entity.

ALFRED ADLER
Compulsion neurosis

In the last several decades the medical profession has shown an especial interest in psychological studies. This is largely owing to the fact that the physician has found that psychology provides him with a means for observing and understanding certain developments that occur commonly in life, but which generally pass undetected. Early preparatory descriptive steps were taken in France, and in Vienna by Krafft-Ebing. It represented a great advance toward clarification when later Westphal decided to include under the term "compulsion neurosis" a certain group of neurotic disturbances. Since then the literature on the subject has grown to vast proportions. In this article I shall indicate the contribution that Individual Psychology has made to the understanding of compulsion neurosis; but to do this I must begin far back.

The efforts of Individual Psychology have always been mainly directed toward grasping the "Why?" of phenomena— why (toward what end) a human being behaves in a manner which seems to us extraordinary and pathological. Other psychologists have been more inclined to study the "How?"—how certain particular symptoms come into being. Each group, it must be understood, takes both questions—both the Why? (the Whither) and the How? (the Whence)—into consideration, but each always lays the chief stress upon one or the other approach.

In view of our comprehensive general outlook, it is understandable that we should throw into relief the question of why a human being behaves in such a way as not to solve his life problems in the manner *generally expected* in his culture. Accordingly, in 1907, shortly after the completion of my *Study of Organ Inferiority and Its Psychical Compensation* (Adler, 1907, 1917), I began to round out the definitive viewpoint of Individual Psychology, and came to the conclusion that we must look upon the psychic life as a movement, directed toward the solution of certain almost immutable problems of existence. And this activity, it should be added, coexists with a tendency on the part of each individual to arrange factors of the external world in a fashion that, from his standpoint, he feels will best enable him to attain his ideal, his goal. It is evident that the question of the best way of dealing with these inescapable life problems is, to a degree, a matter of arbitrary judgment; it can be considered from different points of view, and solutions can be attempted in various ways. This explains the countless variants in cultural forms.

Alfred Adler, "Compulsion Neurosis." Reprinted from H. L. Ansbacher and R. R. Ansbacher (eds.), *Superiority and Social Interest* (Evanston, Ill.: Northwestern University Press, 1970), pp. 112-138.

For Adler mental disorder was the expression of a faulty, immature style of life, . . . The important matter was to comprehend the individual life style. Not much attention was paid to diagnostic categories; there were no pure cases. Yet one specific type of neurosis was to Adler apparently the prototype of all—compulsion neurosis. He wrote more on this form than on any other.—From Heinz L. Ansbacher and Rowena R. Ansbacher (eds.). *Superiority and Social Interest.*

In 1908 I hit upon the idea that every individual really exists in a state of permanent aggression, and I was imprudent enough to call this attitude the "aggression drive." But I soon realized that I was not dealing with drive, but with a partly conscious, partly irrational attitude toward the tasks which life imposes; and I gradually arrived at an understanding of the social element in personality, the extent of which is always determined by the individual's opinion of the facts and the difficulties of life. The individual's attitude reflects not the actual facts, not the thing-in-itself as a permanent "reality principle," but what he thinks of the demands which the external world makes on him, and what he thinks of his ability to fulfill them. Individual Psychology conceives of the individual as living within a closed circle of social relations, but does so with the understanding that each person always follows his own particular route toward what he regards as a successful adaptation to the social scheme. Individual Psychology arrived at the point where it was concerned with determining the social import of life styles and of actually measuring, in every psychic movement, the capacity for social cooperation and its ratio to a striving for security and superiority.

By way of transition to my special topic, let me mention that in 1918 I delivered an address on compulsion neurosis before the Medical Association in Zurich (Adler, 1927). In this paper I expressed a view which I believe is discernible today, albeit in modified form, in the theory of every school of psychiatry. I asserted that, under all circumstances, a neurotic symptom is produced whenever a person attempts to evade the problems of life because he feels fundamentally unable to solve them in a manner compatible with his striving for superiority.

HESITATING ATTITUDE

The compulsion neurotic regularly displays signs of anxiety if he fails to develop other symptoms in a given difficult situation. He feels compelled to do something, to perform a compulsive action which he himself feels is absurd—and which he recognizes as being out of joint with social living. Yet he must yield to the compulsion, or else fall victim to anxiety. The compulsion neurotic has a feeling of insecurity and inadequacy, a feeling of not being able. (The feeling of insecurity and inadequacy is traceable to a deeply rooted biological basis and is not to be thought of as something having purely a psychological significance.)

Anxiety is one of the most distinct manifestations of the sense of inferiority. It serves a definite purpose, the purpose of protection. For example, a woman patient under treatment for anxiety neurosis had progressed so well that she could go out by herself. One night when she came home she found a stranger standing by the door. She screamed out, "Why don't you go away? Can't you see I'm afraid?" The use of anxiety as a means to power is very important from the social viewpoint.

In the paper published in 1918 I also pointed out that the compulsion neurotic apparently retires to a secondary field of action on which he expends all his energies instead of devoting them, as we should expect, to solving his primary problem. He impresses us as a veritable Don Quixote, fighting windmills—concerning himself with matters that have no proper place in our social world but which serve only to waste time. For time seems to him his most dangerous foe, always making some demand on him and always importuning him to solve problems which he feels to be beyond his powers.

We can always corroborate the fact that the patient is inadequately prepared to meet the problems of life (which are always social in nature); and this inadequacy in preparation—whether real or only imaginary—prevents him from moving forward. He lapses into a hesitating attitude; and in this state of vacillation the compulsion neurotic turns to his secondary field of action. We must not fail to note that such an evasion does not occur unless he is afraid of a failure. So long as the compulsion neurotic is sure of himself, he gets on well enough, is impeded by no compulsions, and surmounts his difficulties. Only in certain phases of his existence—either in his business and professional affairs, or frequently in his love life—do we find an extreme development of his tendency to ward off failures by retreating to a secondary field of action and eliminating the compelling duties of life by means of a counter-compulsion. The counter-compulsion gives him a feeling of success—according to his style.

I must also touch upon one other point, which has already been made clear in Individual Psychology, but which often gives rise to mistaken notions. This is the phenomenon of indecision or doubt. Doubt seems often to constitute a special entity in psychology and is frequently so considered. But if we observe this state of mind in its general context and ask ourselves the question, "What part does doubt play in relation to specific achievement in social life?" we will discover that its purpose is to maintain the *status quo,* to prevent change. This is the hesitating attitude of which I have often spoken. Excessive doubt and long-continued indecision represent nothing more than attempts to waste time—to waste time in order to gain time.

I have found that the sense of degradation and humility so common among the mentally sick is simply another device for wasting time.

STRIVING FOR GODLIKENESS AND DEPRECIATION OF OTHERS

I further mentioned that rarely is the striving for superiority so clearly defined as it is in a compulsion neurosis. Many writers on the subject had already noted the patients' belief in the magical efficacy and omnipotence of words and ideas, but, lacking the criteria of Individual Psychology, apparently did not fully understand. Recourse to "primitive, archaic thought," is not an atavism and does not stem from the "collective unconscious," but represents an ever feasible, childish device for achieving a sense of power. It arises from the striving for a unique sort of superiority which I have described as godlikeness. The compulsion neurotic strives after the clearest expression of his godlike quality; but naturally he cannot achieve this end in the realm of social life since he lacks even the first requisite to success in social life—an interest in others.

We may ignore the opinions to the effect that the compulsion neurotic is distinguished from other individuals by a morbid objectivity. On the contrary, he stands in great need of others; he clearly reveals his feelings of inferiority in the manifestations of his uncertainty and anxiety, and draws another person into his sphere as he advances to an overt inferiority complex. The compulsion neurotic endeavors to overcome this anxiety, and tries to represent himself in the form to which he originally aspired—

as a demigod, who exalts himself above humankind and who depreciates everyone else and puts them in the shade. He covers over his inferiority complex with a superiority complex and thus appears magnificent enough in his own eyes—for *only* his compulsive idea, so he feels, prevents him from fulfilling his triumphant mission. His fantastic notion of superiority is fully and wholly revealed in his compulsion.

And I found, too, that the so-called sadistic bent in compulsion neurosis is only one of the thousand subtle variations on the theme of seeking ascendancy over others; it is only a manifestation of the desire to dominate, to exalt oneself, by depreciating others. In compulsion neurosis, if it is manifest, it is expressed in a way so that the clear, direct, sadistic intent is covered by the patient's horror of it and his consequent feeling of guilt. But perhaps the absurd struggle of the compulsion neurotic—his effort to raise himself above everyone else in so abrupt and startling a manner—is not without an element of cruelty, since he (like the user of violent profanity) approaches the realm of practical activity with the purpose of depreciating other individuals.

CRITIQUE OF AMBIVALENCE, CONFLICT, AND GUILT

I mentioned further that what some writers on the subject have described as ambivalence, ambiguity, contradictoriness in mental dispositions and feelings, and split personality is simply a matter of contrasting means to the same end, and not a change in the end itself.

This brings us to a question which is of the greatest importance to the whole theory of neurosis. Individual Psychology, since it so strongly emphasizes the unity of the individual's life and

endeavors, had to take cognizance of the idea of ambivalence. It explains that the movement of a person who wishes to evade reality—in order to raise himself to godlikeness in his imagination and emotions—must naturally show a point of beginning and an end point. Individual Psychology has always stressed the fact that it regards psychic life as movement, and considers form, expression, function as a kind of frozen movement. Hence, if an individual purposes to raise himself from a lower level to a higher, we should expect to find two seemingly contrasting points in the movement, namely, the point away from which the movement goes and the point toward which it is directed. It is from these points that we are able to learn something of the direction of the movement.

Furthermore, we can realize that the multiplicity and variety of life styles show that there is no one ideal movement upward. Many paths to significance and superiority may be followed.

Inaccurately considered, the disparities between reality and the ideals of courage, truthfulness, activity, etc., can always be presented as contrasts, when, indeed, we are dealing here with varieties and degrees. It is a pity that we do not have uniform terms and concepts for the variants of a psychic movement. If we did, this error would certainly not have insinuated itself into our thought. Of course, we will also observe the so-called pleasure in suffering which finally gives the neurotic the feeling that he is unique and godlike, and which really is nothing more than the pleasure which a person feels when he has paid the forfeit that exempts him from a greater evil. Such a life style constitutes a palpable failure in life.

We cannot properly speak of a "conflict" in compulsion neurosis, since the patient never deviates from the road of evasion, which he paves with good intentions or feelings of guilt. Conflict means only a standstill. These good intentions, which may appear as feelings of guilt, are absolutely dead; they signify nothing as to any real change in the life of the patient. It means nothing, so far as altered behavior in the patient is concerned, that he makes a great display of his feelings of guilt; he has the assurance that, by acknowledging his guilt and raising trivialities to a rank of importance and dignity, he can appear to be more genteel and more honest than any of his fellows. That these much bewailed trivialities have no "deeper" significance is evident from the fact that, in compulsion neurosis as in melancholia, the patient contents himself with merely expressing a sense of guilt, and would never think of exercising active contrition, shown in the form of improved behavior.

COMPULSION AS SAFEGUARD

The compulsion neurotic early employs and trains an absurd process of reasoning in order to allow himself a sense of great personal importance and worth without achieving anything objectively tangible. A properly conducted inquiry into his past history will reveal certain characteristic traits: a pedantic striving for faultlessness and perfect accuracy; a tendency to side-step difficult tasks by confusing them with unrelated, simple ones; the practice of formalized religious exercises and rituals, with the idea of "tempting God"; the habit of stressing the difficulty of situations in order to make a greater triumph of their solution; a desire to elude rivalries; a pride in a grotesquely exaggerated family tradition. The compulsion neurotic is always a person who reveals the neurotic disposition which I attempted to describe in my book, *The Neurotic Constitution* (Adler, 1912, 1926). He is a person who feels that he is set apart from other individuals; who thinks only of himself; who is imbued with self-love, and has no interest in the general welfare. He believes that he is incapable of realizing his great potentialities in the social stream of the world, and for this reason he sets himself a high personal goal, above the aspirations of other mortals.

Further, I noted a trait which I called the neurotic tendency to create safeguards, and which is especially prominent in compulsion neurosis. This tendency is not merely a protective device, and certainly cannot be considered a defense against suppressed sexual desires. It is a system of psychic forms of expression, resulting from careful training, and is skillfully contrived to permit the individual actually to attain, in the neurotic 'manner, his goal of personal superiority. The patient who feels a compulsion to jump out of windows builds up this compulsion into a safeguard; he acquires a sense of superiority by successfully overcoming the urge, and employs the whole situation as an excuse for his failure in life.

I come now to an important fact that seems to have escaped the writers on this topic. They always seem to consider the compulsion as if it resided in the obsessions or compulsive ideas. They regard obsession or obsessional action as if it were wholly divorced from the normal processes of thought; as if thinking were charged with compulsion and rises up from time to time, like a demon from a pit, to overpower and take possession of its victim; as if the compulsion had an individuality of its own. Freud, with incomparable grace and ease, invests each of his postulated "instincts" with human attributes. The compulsion does not reside in the compulsive idea or action; it originates outside—in the sphere of our normal social life. This is the source of the patient's neurotic compulsion or urge. He *must* evade the realities of life, since he feels incompetent to face them and since his high-flown ambition must elude any sort of palpable failure. He retreats farther and farther before the bayonets of life from outside, which he feels are closing in on him—until he finds a secluded cranny of life where he is put to no real test and can make use of the notions that give him a feeling of complete superiority. By exerting all his force he acquires a sense of omnipotence in overcoming some variety of self-created, imaginary fears. Herein lies the significance of the safeguarding tendency that I have described. The compulsion, therefore, does not reside in the obsessive symptom, but in the actualities of life which seem terrifying to the individual concerned. Furthermore, I was able to determine with great certainty that the compulsion neurotic is characterized from childhood on (as we can see from his earliest experiences) by sudden successful efforts to pull himself together.

A short case history will clarify this point. The patient is a man of forty-five, in good circumstances. You will readily understand that individuals who strive for [personal] superiority may occasionally achieve quite estimable results in life. In fact, it is surprisingly common for the compulsion neurotic to occupy a prominent social position. He accomplishes something, but he is never satisfied with what he accomplishes. Such is the case with our 45-year-old patient, who complains of a continual obsession that he must jump out of a window. The obsession is most pronounced when he is in an upper story of a high building. For twenty-five years he has felt this compulsion. Yet now he stands before me in the flesh. He has never jumped out; he has always conquered his obsession. He has triumphed over himself. He feels heroic.

To the untrained mind this explanation may at first seem farfetched or artificial. But we know as a familiar fact that we ourselves often take a particular pride in mastering our inclinations and overcoming one or another of our desires. This same sort of pride gives our patient a sense of omnipotence. He feels heroic when he can say to himself: "I have been able to bear up under a whole mountain of woe—wretched Atlas that I am!" Like every neurotic, he does not fix his attention on the really important point, but on a secondary issue. He has an eye to his anxiety, since he needs it as something to overcome; but he does not understand his fantastic struggle for omnipotence or his sense of inferiority which, he feels, compels him to travel on easy byways. He is a fighter of windmills: a hero in his own mind if not to the outside world.

Now let us glance back at the patient's childhood. Individual Psychology has succeeded in making a new science of interpreting childhood recollections; these old memories have begun to talk and tell their tale. Our patient was the youngest child, and his mother's favorite. Like many pampered children he was timid, and his anxiety increased when he entered school. This was revealed on one occasion when a bullying schoolmate singled him out for abuse. But, in the emergency, he mustered up all his energies, attacked the other boy, and knocked him down. Anyone capable of finding the dynamics in childhood recollections cannot help seeing that the patient has followed the same tactics throughout his life. First he is afraid; then he overcomes his fear. This is his method of acquiring a sense of superiority.

SELF-CREATED CAUSALITY

Furthermore, I have found that a personality like that of the compulsion neurotic never comes about as a result of a mechanistic process. According to Freud, the instincts have the power of choice. They can think; they have a consciousness, and know their direction; they have a purposive, creative energy, etc. In short, everything that he finds in the psychic life of the individual is attributed to the instincts. We cannot, however, find the explanation of the origin of compulsion neurosis in instincts or drives, for a drive, as we understand it, is without direction. We are equally unable to lay the blame on heredity, since all the factors entering into the neurosis—character, passions, emotions—are shaped within the framework of human society.

We must consider the great potentialities for mistaken interpretation residing in the human mind if we hope to understand neurotic symptoms. These errors are wholly devoid of causality. No one is forced into neurosis, either by heredity or by instincts, but only enticed, within certain latitudes of probability. The pampered child—and almost all neurotics are pampered children—does not act according to the law of cause and effect when he picks one experience out of thousands and makes it the basis of his subsequent life. We cure the neurotic by freeing him from a false, self-created causality and adapting him to real life.

In trying to understand some given behavior one must turn back to the past life of the patient. For a person's behavior is always based upon the materials of his life experience, and these naturally lie in

the past. After his fourth or fifth year every individual possesses an established life style, and, according to his life style, the individual assimilates, applies, and digests the data of all later experiences. He draws from them only such conclusions as fit into his already established apperception schema, attaching importance only to those aspects of any experience which correspond with the picture of the world which he has already formed and with the particular life style which he has developed for coping with that world.

It should be pointed out further that the life style of the compulsion neurotic—this most patent and futile form of striving for godlikeness—naturally accepts everything that suits its purposes, and rejects everything that runs counter to them. I shall illustrate this fact with an example—which probably needs further inquiry and a better foundation, but will serve to clarify a great deal which, even today, is uncritically referred to the province of the unconscious.

The example I shall use is a medical student who, from childhood on, has despaired of his ability to catch up with his brother. This brother has taken life at a canter. The oldest child in the family, and a stepson, he was less pampered and had the courage to make good headway. As a result, the patient continually lived in the obscuring shadow of his overpowering older brother. At present the patient is studying medicine and finds it easy to master the theoretical branches. But now, faced with the necessity of deciding whether to continue his studies, and still looking up to his brother, he suddenly discovers that he is unable to enter the dissecting room, that it is impossible for him to attend an operation, etc.

If we bear in mind the connection between these symptoms and the patient's overestimation of his brother, we can understand his fear, his unwillingness to make a final decision. The patient's dread of attending an operation fits in with his diffident attitude toward his medical studies. He looks into the future, senses a possible defeat, and prepares a means of rescuing his self-esteem. At some later date he will be able to say: If I hadn't felt this mysterious dread, I would have surpassed my brother. He postpones the test which will decide his defeat or victory, and arms himself against an encroachment on his personal ambition. But it seems that his is only the humanly intelligible aim of emulating his brother and not one that expressly strives for godlikeness. His goal is merely a superiority over his brother, and not the absolute superiority to which the compulsion neurotic aspires.

Perhaps Individual Psychology alone is fully cognizant that compulsion neurosis can develop only in cases of considerable estrangement from social interest. At all events, however, we can clearly observe in this patient an automatism which seems peculiar to the human psyche, one which we find in individuals who approximate the normal as well as in those who are designated abnormal. This is the instinctive tendency to single out and stress those experiences which fit into one's life style, and to exclude all those which do not fit in, or to transform them until they do. Each human being evaluates all experiences according to his life style.

EMPHASIS ON RATIONAL PROCESSES

At this point I should like to take up a fundamental issue. Although the problem of compulsion neurosis may be considered as if the chief concern were of an intellectual nature and had to do only with ideas, yet we know that the element of thought cannot be detached from the structure of the whole psychic make-up, which includes feelings as well. Whenever one conceives an idea, one arouses in himself also a series of corresponding feelings and emotions, not only because he realizes that the idea should connote these emotions, but because he actually transports himself into a sphere of thought which is affected and altered by the idea. The various psychic functions, thought and feeling, cannot be divorced from one another. If, for instance, I think of being in a beautiful city, my mental picture gives rise to feelings and emotions such as I might have if I were actually approaching the city, or were already there. This process is especially important as an essential factor in our dream dynamics. When we dream, we awaken feelings and emotions. We do this by conjuring up images with which certain feelings are associated which strongly affect us and move us in a certain definite direction. The same process is at work in a compulsion neurosis. In the thought of absolute superiority we can plainly detect the feeling or emotion of absolute superiority.

The chief disturbance in the psychic life of the compulsion neurotic takes place in the rational processes, in the realm of thought rather than emotion. The unity and indivisibility of the psychic life was earlier and more forcibly stressed by Individual Psychology than by any other psychological school. But I have also stressed the complexity and uniqueness of every individual and the great diversity of life styles. Certain elements, certain aspects of the whole, certain particular psychic movements, are found to be especially emphasized in various individual cases. These particular aspects we may artificially isolate for the purpose of discussion. They may be either chiefly rational or chiefly emotional in character, and may take the form of either active or passive attitudes. Of all the phases of psychic life, the rational is most strongly stressed in individuals who suffer from compulsion neurosis, but it is an ideational life directed in such a way that it runs counter to social interest, and hence to common sense.

This tendency to rationalize and formulate, to pay regard to formal routine and orderly arrangement, is not restricted to the obsessional ideas but reveals itself also in other phases of the patient's life. Often he has a marked feeling for words; he is fond of brooding over ideas; he loves to pick about at maxims and precepts; he acts as if he firmly believed that "in the beginning was the Word." We must grant that persons with these inclinations may achieve fine things, provided that they follow the path of the social good. But, unless turned to the advantage of society, the tendency is futile and results in empty form. This is the case with the phrase-mongering of the compulsion neurotic, and is manifest in his addiction to compulsive prayers, to repetition of ritual-like performances, and to love of formulas; in his overt curses and libels; in his earnest faith in the potency of his anathemas. Certain repetitive actions can easily be understood as expressing an obsessional idea—for instance, the washing compulsion which shouts more loudly than words that everyone but the patient is a dirty swine.

From practice, one gets the impression often that words and thoughts have been set at so high a premium in these compulsion cases because the patient began in childhood to consider the power of linguistic expression as a vital problem in his life. He may have grown up as a self-pampered child in an environment which

he felt to be hostile, and in which he was continually put to a disadvantage by others who were more adept than he at turning thoughts, words, and curses to advantageous ends. Words and ideas played an important role in his life. Occasionally the child's own timidity and reticence gives him the impression that:

> With words 'tis excellent disputing;
> Systems to words 'tis easy suiting.[1]

Here we have another evident point of comparison with schizophrenia which also manifests itself chiefly in a disturbance of the thought processes, and very frequently involves the coining of words, phrases, and maxims, either voiced or silent.

Of course the other elements of the psychic life—other than the one artificially isolated for the purpose of discussion—are not absent, but they seem to follow in the wake of the more dominant element. The dominant element may be, for instance, high-strung emotionalism, anxiety, hypersensitivity. Whatever it is, it corresponds to the individual's lifelong training and shows especially at the time of the shock which the patient suffers when he is confronted by the forthcoming tasks of life for which he is not prepared. Such a shock must inevitably be produced in him as soon as his childish philosophy of life collides with a reality quite different from the one he has trained for, and he feels forced into a retreat. This retreat the patient accomplishes by strengthening his dominant characteristic, which reflects what he has considered as a vital problem ever since his childhood, but which he begins

---

[1]Goethe, J. W. v. *Faust*. Part 1. Bayard Taylor's translation, lines 1997-1998.—Translator's note.

automatically to regard as the very keynote of his existence.

To the best of our knowledge (and the best is none too adequate), we can safely assume that individuals differ considerably in their natural capacities for intellectual and linguistic development. Exactly how much they differ no one can say at the present time, since most of the students of heredity make the mistake of working backwards and trying to deduce the amount of innate capacity from the finished products, or degree of development. We can, however, assume that any superior capacity for language, like any other superior natural endowment, is a definite advantage when properly used; that is, when it is developed, in the stream of evolution and human progress, as a useful contribution to the welfare of humanity as a whole. But if it is imprisoned in a false conception of life, it may be useless or even injurious. This is the case in compulsion neurosis and paranoia.

It is, however, probable (though not inevitable) that the processes of thought and speech will be brought into the foreground through the creative power of the child, and will be more highly developed, if the child experiences his own speech development as a source of inferiority, either in his struggle with his environment or because the environment intentionally or unintentionally impresses this problem on his mind. In such an event, the feeling of inferiority may set in so strongly that the child takes one of two courses. He can go through intensive training to better his results in this respect (either on the useful or the useless side of life), or else give up the battle. Granted possibilities of development in his natural endowment, he may choose either alternative.

In many cases of compulsion neurosis, I have found that continual nagging, scolding, derision, and faultfinding can exert so profound an influence on the child that, whatever his natural capacities, he will make a frantic effort to improve his faculty of self-expression, adopting the same tone that is used toward him, acquiring a nimble tongue or continually searching for words, ignoring affronts or lapsing into the limping sort of wit that stumbles on the proper retort only when it is too late. Or he may invent a standard rejoinder—usually derogatory—which occurs to him on every occasion when his pride and vanity are injured. The compulsion neurotic is generally of the latter type.

One of my patients, who suffered from a washing and tidying mania, had grown up as the youngest, rather helpless, child in a family where shouting and cursing were everyday practices, and she was continually scolded and ridiculed for her faulty pronunciation. Shortly after her marriage, when her husband fell into the same habit of reproving and criticizing her, she began to draw the long bow herself, and freed herself from him and all her other responsibilities by an incessant urge to clean and arrange the house. This was tantamount to her saying, "You fool, now you see what happens when I give in to your critical wishes for order and cleanliness!" If anything was not exactly in keeping with her mania for cleanliness, she immediately gave expression to a formula which was puzzling to those around her who did not understand its purpose. She cried: "Help! Help!"

I once presented these views before a group of physicians that included a good many psychiatrists. In the general discussion which followed my talk, one of the psychiatrists began to attack my statements by picking out individual words and misinterpreting them to suit his purposes. In reply, I innocently tried to make myself clearer with an illustration. "Take yourself, for example," I said, "with your tendency to pick apart words and ideas and attach your own meanings to them. If you were ever so unfortunate as to acquire a neurosis, it would probably be a compulsion neurosis." I was not a little surprised to discover that my words had produced an unforeseen effect. My colleague was speechless; he turned pale, and seemed greatly disturbed. I apologized as best I could, but later on I learned that this psychiatrist had for two years been under unsuccessful treatment for compulsion neurosis.

TWELVE CASES

I have spoken plainly enough on the subject of causality and its slight importance in relation to the understanding of the psychic life, since it governs at best only the physiological processes, not the psychological. And I have described the structure of compulsion neurosis. With all this in mind, we should be able to discover why one particular compulsive symptom and not another appears under a given set of circumstances. A brief account of a few cases will illustrate practically the nature of compulsion neurosis, and show that the application of our principles advances the understanding of it.

1. A common form of compulsion is the impulse to *jump out of windows*. A young singer, who seemed confident that he had a fine voice but felt thrust into the background by his father and his older brother, engaged in an incessant struggle against such an obsession. He believed that it was only his puzzling obsession which prevented him from becoming "the greatest tenor." He was free of it only so

long as someone was at his side, and this, of course, was impossible in a theatre or on the concert platform where he would have had to appear if he were to go on with his profession of concert singer. So we can see that his compulsive idea served as a means of putting at a distance the test of his greatness. He was really not sure that the test would result in his favor. He felt that he must surpass his father and brother in some way. Now if he prevents himself from ever coming to the test he can always save his vanity from being hurt. And he can maintain his personal prestige in his own eyes by having arranged a situation in which he can say and believe, "I could have been greater than they if I had not been burdened with this fear. But I was."

By the arrangement of the compulsive idea his real capacity for achievement is prevented from being put to the test. Thus he is safeguarded from any possibility of failure. At the same time, he successfully fought the compulsion; he had never jumped. So he assured himself time and again of the feeling of victory, the sense of heroic triumph.

2. A rarer type of compulsion is to be seen in the case of a girl who could not go out into society because of her impulse to *imitate a cock's crow*. Here we have the masculine protest—an important concept in Individual Psychology—expressed in such a way that the young woman is spared the necessity of proving her superiority in a more difficult way—by useful achievement. She felt that, as a girl, she played a subordinate, inferior part in society. This feeling of hers certainly has no causal foundation. A great many girls, as well as men, are still possessed of the old superstition that women are inferior beings; and so it is not surprising that an ambitious girl who wants to occupy a leading place should

feel that the social system itself compels her to eschew her role as woman in a society where she believes women are valued less than men. Being a woman, she feels, means falling into a low position of no value. She wants a high position of value, and sees it only in the masculine role.

It seems unlikely that this case involves sadistic tendencies. A much more probable explanation is this: The girl sees a kind of godlike superiority in the role of man as compared to the role of woman, in the "masculine principle," and goes a-tilting against windmills. She usurps the role of the male in an easy but useless way, and so spares herself the pains of proving by means of achievements valuable from an objective standpoint her capacity to fill it. This is a common characteristic of the compulsion neurotic; he has a sense of absolute superiority, and at the same time excludes all social ties from his life.

3. Another case concerns a girl whose symptoms set in at a time when she had suffered a defeat in her struggle for superiority. (The neurosis and all the special disturbances always put in their appearance whenever the patient feels that he is challenged to prove his superiority.) She was the younger of two sisters, and felt overshadowed by the older; but she was keenly intelligent and brilliantly endowed for her studies and her chosen work. For a long time she showed no signs of obsessions; but, like all compulsion neurotics, she was engaged in a frantic struggle for absolute superiority. The obsessive symptoms did not appear until she had lost her position through an unfortunate speculation, and a man in whom she was interested gave her clearly to understand that he preferred her sister. Now the patient developed an obsession. Whenever she met a woman

carrying a market basket, she was tormented by the thought that *a rusty coin might jump out of her purse* into the basket and poison the woman's family.

She, too, was a fighter against windmills; she strove, futilely, to become a god and save mankind. Her obsession also took other forms. She declared that all books, especially Bibles, were sacrosanct; and if a book or a Bible chanced to fall on the floor, she discarded it and bought a new one. In this harmless way she plainly showed that she was superior to her sister in her esteem for religion and erudition. She was more pious and more ethical, more considerate of others' welfare, and also more respectful toward learning and religion. Thus she found a cheap means of triumphing over her sister, not by way of useful achievement in real life. Her philosophy of life remained the same. She asked herself only the one question: How can I exalt myself above my sister and everyone else?

4. And now another case, from an insane asylum: a man who had suffered since childhood from an inclination to represent himself in quite petty matters as ethical, noble-minded, and superior to all others. His earliest recollections extend back to his first days in kindergarten. He recalls that at some time or other he had made a mistake that escaped the notice of his teacher. For two years he suffered from pangs of conscience, and then, at his father's advice, he went to the teacher and confessed his secret shortcoming. Brought up in a family with a cultural tradition, he felt that his best chances for success lay in the direction of proving himself more noble than others. His life was not without achievement. But every time that he was faced by a real test of his powers, compulsive symptoms set in, and he was unable to meet the test. For this reason he frequently changed his occupation. One

day, when he was confronted by such an emergency, he went to church and threw himself on the floor before the altar in the crowded church, and loudly proclaimed that he was "the *greatest sinner* on earth." After this he was committed to an institution, and thus succeeded in evading the test of his worth that goes with living productively.

The desire for a godlike superiority, so plainly revealed in this episode, evinced itself on other occasions as well. One day he appeared stark naked in the dining hall. By this expedient he postponed his dismissal from the institution and put off another imminent test of his powers in a field outside, where he felt uncertain and sensed a possible defeat. He was really a very handsome man, with a fine physique; in that regard he felt superior to others. And so his compulsion—the product of the emergency—revealed itself again as an effort, on the useless side of life, to maintain his exaggerated sense of personal importance by flaunting his superiority over other people.

5. Another patient, who had suffered for many years from a variety of compulsive symptoms, improved notably under treatment. He was the oldest child of a family in which the father occupied a dominant position. The father had hopes that his son would turn out to be a genius, and the boy, extremely devoted to his father, took these high expectations as a matter of course until, when he was five years old, a sister was born. Then the father's affections were diverted to the sister and the boy suddenly began to feel an overpowering urge to *climb up on his father's shoulders,* stand over his head, *and break open his skull.* Later on, he also developed very pedantic traits, and was troubled by gruesome, and sometimes filthy, thoughts whenever he felt slighted.

Under such circumstances someone else might have expressed his resentment in a stream of threats and curses.

Compulsive thoughts mean a kind of attack, more than an outburst of profanity and less than a physical assault. Up to the time of his treatment and improvement, the patient was firmly convinced that, even though he failed to meet his father's great expectations, he would certainly have outstripped his father if it had not been for his terrible obsessions. Here we can see how a kind of superiority grows out of the obsession, or out of the aggressive tendency that manifests itself in the obsession. Behind his symptoms the patient sees a star of hope—the hope of quieting his fear of defeat. He looks into a Promised Land, where he sees the possibility of consoling himself with the thought that he could have been superior to his father if only he had not been so unfortunately handicapped by a mysterious ailment which no doctor ever succeeded in controlling. In this manner he saves his self-esteem and guards his vanity from injury. The difficulties in the treatment of a compulsion neurotic are indicated. The therapeutic method of Individual Psychology is not only a science, but an art—the art of invalidating the patient's hollow alibi and teaching him to develop and rely on his actual capacities.

6. Very often the obsession takes the form of an impulse to inflict an injury on someone whenever the patient sees a knife. For example, a woman, who had grown up as an only child and had always been the center of attention, discovered that she was being deceived and slighted by her husband, and she then developed *the urge to take up a knife* and attack either him or her child. This urge reveals about the same frame of mind that moves

certain people to blurt out threats such as, "I'd like to kill that man!" In the present case the mood is expressed in a kind of pantomime, but the feeling is not translated into overt action. Each time it arises the impulse is overcome; and thus the patient experiences a sense of triumph. At the same time she depreciates her husband by showing her lack of regard for him. She takes a cheap and easy short cut to establish a kind of superiority whenever she feels her value threatened.

7. In another case, a much-pampered young woman began to feel this impulse to *"do something" with a knife* because her husband—a very kindly, well-intentioned man—had the inclination to pick up a book and read instead of amusing himself with her. This was sufficient cause for her to feel the urge to attack him whenever she happened to see a knife. Here again a sense of superiority is plainly revealed—but in such a form that she was content to make a harmless show of her resentment and anger. Her husband was forced by her obsession to concern himself with her.

8. It is only natural that the "runaway" tendency, always evident in neurosis, should clearly reveal itself in individuals who feel too weak to meet the problems of life. In many cases of neurosis, when the problem of sex seems overly difficult, it takes the form of homosexuality. That we often find evidence of compulsion in such cases is easily understandable. As an example, let us take the case of a man who deliberately trained himself, from childhood on, to enchant everyone with his physical attractiveness. Of course, in our culture a girl can do this more easily than a boy; and so the patient early began to practice playing the part of a girl. Once, in a school entertainment, he filled the role of a girl so convincingly that a man in the audience fell in love with him on the spot. The desire to achieve further successes of this kind brought him within the province of homosexuality.

And now the time came for this man to prepare for a profession and to pass the necessary examinations; that is, he was expected to take the normal means—by useful achievement—of acquiring prestige and securing the place of glory that he had always anticipated. But he felt it was much more likely that he would meet with failure in trying to acomplish an objectively useful task than in merely enchanting someone and trying to be charming. It turned out now that whenever he attended a lecture, he suffered from a *sleep compulsion*. This served, of course, as a perfect precaution. It protected him against having to take the coming examination. And in case he did take it, it supplied a perfect alibi for failure. "If I can't help falling asleep," he could say, "no one can expect me to pass the examination." And he really did fail, but with an easier conscience than if he had paid attention in class and failed anyway.

9. Another patient is a married woman who incessantly busied herself with *putting her linen in order,* and in so doing aroused herself to a high pitch of excitement. This ordeal took up the greater part of the day, and clearly indicated a compulsion incident to her striving for a godlike superiority. A servant girl always did the actual work, but under the patient's constant supervision. This woman grew up in a family where there was continual bickering and she had had her full share of slaps and aspersions. She recollected that at one time she said to herself: "Just wait till I grow up and I'll

boss other people the way they boss me now." Here we have a clear illustration of what I mean by life style. This motive force, this desire to rule, so common in neurotically disposed children, we see operating time and again in both the greatest and the least of our fellow men. It reduces itself to the thought, "Someday *I'll* be the boss."

It proved that this patient's compulsive symptom served the end of keeping her out of society, where she never felt sure of maintaining a dominant position. She never failed to produce friction and ill-feeling wherever she went, and so consistently offended people that they frankly avoided her. She found herself left alone. By way of compensation, she played God Almighty in her own household, praising or punishing her children as the spirit moved her, and keeping her husband completely under her thumb. Her parents and sisters might take a special pride in their linen, but she outdid them. No one could set a linen closet to rights as well as she. And to have a slave at one's beck and call, to give orders and to see them carried out in an artistic fashion—this she felt to be the very apogee of power. She made herself the reigning queen of the little spot that she had set off for herself, and within her narrow realm no one could make any demands upon her.

10. An especially common form of compulsion is the *washing mania*—the urge to be continually cleaning and scouring. Here we see an inclination to depreciate others by implying that everyone but the patient is dirty. No one but the patient is allowed to touch anything, and he alone is crowned with a gloriole of purity and superiority. This, too, is only another means of wasting time, thus deferring the solution of some vital problem and evading the necessity of proving one's importance through actual achievements and contributions.

One case of this type concerned a girl who was the younger of two daughters. The older sister had felt neglected after the birth of her younger sister and revolted against the situation which she felt intolerable. All the parents' affections were concentrated on the younger daughter. She was a model child, lauded, loved, and showered with presents. And she came to expect a great deal of life. But her first experiment in living away from the pampering home life, at school, resulted in failure; after that she never completed anything she undertook. She was punished for her laziness, but no one questioned her potential ability; and she accepted the punishment and reproofs rather than risk displaying her inferiority. As a married woman she felt that her position was extremely degrading. Her husband was much older than herself, remarkably dried-up, and in her eyes totally unfit for love and marriage. Her washing compulsion set in when she finally married—after much hesitation. She pronounced her husband unclean, and banished him from bed and board. It is interesting and rather surprising to note that the house of a person obsessed with the idea of cleanliness is often unclean. The reason is that the whole social harmony of the home is destroyed, and the prevailing desire is to find dirt everywhere.

11. The compulsion may also take the form of continual *blushing*. A woman, for example, had suffered since childhood from a lability of the surface blood vessels which manifested itself in frequent blushing. She was downright proud when someone noticed this and remarked about it. Here again we can see the unim-

portance of causality. At first, her blushing actually gave her pleasure. But when she had her first baby, in a loveless marriage, and an aunt began to irritate her with advice on the proper way to bring up children, this extremely ambitious woman suddenly acquired the notion that her blushing was quite a terrible thing, and that because of it she would have to shun society—as a vanquished hero, but a hero none the less. She made full use of her blushing mania as a source of special privileges within her home, however. Here she was the mistress; and by reducing her sphere of action to the narrowest possible dimensions, she was able to satisfy her thirst for power.

12. And now one other case, which may not seem to fall within the category of compulsion neurosis. I once knew a housemaid who had an odd habit: whenever she was told to do something, she always repeated the order in the first person. If her mistress asked her to arrange a cupboard, she would say, "*I'll* arrange the cupboard this afternoon." Here we see the rejection of authority. She could act only if she had the sense of acting on her own volition.

This peculiarity of the human mind—the desire to be the leader, to do things on one's own initiative—is recognized in some armies, where the soldier must repeat every command in the first person and actually make himself feel that he is the commander. This tradition is certainly based on a profound knowledge of human nature.

A related case is that of a strikingly beautiful woman who developed the following compulsion: whenever she was faced with a piece of housework that seemed degrading in view of her prestige as a beauty, she always had to give herself the order to do it. This symptom, together with compulsive blushing, appeared when she was reminded by quite insignificant experiences that she was growing older and would eventually lose her beauty.

RECAPITULATION AND CONCLUDING REMARKS

The study of compulsion neurosis reveals the following factors and tendencies:

1. A striving for personal superiority which, from fear of betraying an actual inferiority, is diverted into easy and generally useless channels.

2. This striving for an exclusive superiority is encouraged in childhood by excessive pampering or self-indulgence, and develops into a desire for godlike supremacy which is less mitigated and qualified by a concrete social goal (objective success in the world of reality), by actual useful achievement, than is the case in other forms of neurosis.

3. Compulsion neurosis occurs in the face of actual situations (problems of social living, occupation, or love), where the dread of failure or a blow to vanity leads to a hesitating attitude. This hesitating attitude finds expression in killing time, in seeking out and repeating a single routine or expressive movement or idea which will preclude further contact with the terrifying problems of life. (It is a hesitation that represents a "no" in disguise in response to some difficulty or problem of life.)

4. These means of relief from a difficult situation, once fixed upon, provide the patient with an excuse for failing to reach the pinnacle of existence. Successes in life loom much larger if achieved despite the handicap of a compulsion neurosis; and the kind of superiority obtained by means of obsessions and

compulsions also serves to alleviate the patient's strong sense of inferiority, even though it fails to satisfy completely his great vanity. Hence, the form of compulsion—generally plural—is so chosen that the patient can express his striving for tremendous personal superiority (godlikeness) in a fictive guise.

5. The construction of the compulsion neurosis is identical with the structure of the entire life style and personality. The abnormal conduct appears first when the patient faces a problem which demands greater social interest than was developed in his childhood.

6. By reason of his prestige policy, the patient employs a counter-compulsion to meet and evade the compulsion exerted by the social requirements.

During more recent years I have been able to add the following points:

1. The compulsion does not reside in the compulsive actions themselves, but originates in the demands of social living, which the patient feels as a menace and threat to his prestige. He feels compelled to create a safeguard in order to heighten his sense of superiority and to serve as a means of evading failures and preventing a revelation of his inferiority.

2. This energetic quest for personal superiority characterizes the patient from early childhood on, and leads him, in accordance with his training, to a compulsion neurosis, not to other aberrations.

3. An early-developed, unified personality like that of the compulsion neurotic cannot be produced by causal, mechanical means—such as the operation of instincts, heredity, brain injuries, environment, or the endocrine glands. It is the final product of a particular choice and way of training. The patient is only misdirected and led into a mistaken attitude toward life by such factors as physical inferiority, the influences of

environment, or the imitation of examples. Although the error may to a degree be intelligible, we cannot grant the existence of any causal relationship. The development of the child's psyche can never be understood from the point of view of cause and effect; it begins as a groping process of trial and error, plausible perhaps, but never scientifically calculable and predictable. After about his fifth year, the child experiences, apperceives, and assimilates according to a life pattern which by this time he has definitely established and unified.

4. The life style of the compulsion neurotic adopts all the forms of expression that suit its purpose, and rejects the rest.

5. The feelings of guilt or humility, almost always present in compulsion neurosis, are elaborations of the effort to kill time. They show kinship with melancholia, and are so contrived that the patient's environment can easily detect in them the unstable, distorted, pathological element. Like extravagant exercises of penance, they very often serve the purpose of demonstrating the patient's unexampled virtue and magnanimity. But they never lead to any change of conduct or active contrition in the form of improved behavior.

The prognosis of compulsion neurosis is fundamentally the same as that of any other neurosis. There is no doubt that some forms of neurosis or psychosis begin with an apparent compulsive symptom, and there is no doubt that these compulsive symptoms may border on either cyclothymia or schizophrenia and resolve themselves into one or the other. In some rare cases it is difficult to determine whether we are still dealing with a compulsion neurosis or with melancholia or an early stage of schizophrenia. But certain factors, of course, are bound to mark the difference. Several psychiatrists have keenly noted the similarities to cyclothymia; and others, the resemblances to schizophrenia. All three groups of symptoms are variants of a single condition—characterized by an extreme superiority complex and differing degrees of capacity for cooperation. The compulsion symptoms appear as soon as the patient comes into conflict with social responsibilities and tasks which call for more social interest than he has. Then he can only maintain the position of superiority which he claims by falling back into his imaginary and emotional life.

The cure, therefore, must consist of reconciling the patient with the problems of life. He must be made to see the defects in his life style, and he must develop his social interest, important elements of which are active social contribution and a generally courageous attitude toward life. Only self-knowledge can achieve these results. And Individual Psychology—with its subtle technique, neither easily learned nor easily understood—is a good guide to this end.

REFERENCES

Adler, A. *Study of organ inferiority and its psychical compensations.* New York: Nervous and Mental Disease Publishing Co., 1917. (Originally published, 1907.)

Adler, A. *The neurotic constitution.* New York: Dodd Mead, 1926. (Originally published, 1912.)

Adler, A. Compulsion neurosis. In A. Adler, *The practice and theory of Individual Psychology.* New York: Harcourt Brace, 1927.

CHAPTER **3**

Analytical Psychology

Introduction

The youngest of the big three of the early days of psychoanalysis was Carl Jung (1875–1961), who was 5 years younger than Alfred Adler and 19 years Sigmund Freud's junior. Jung's strong philosophical and religious orientation made him quite different in personality from both the austere Freud and the sociable Adler; Jung was warm but nevertheless introverted. He had a tremendous intellectual capacity, as did the other two, but he perhaps exceeded both of them in terms of depth and breadth of intellectual interest. Jung was an interior person, and his psychology is truly one of the person inside.

Jung was attracted to Freud in 1906, and the two had a warm personal relationship until their breakup in 1912, a year after Adler had separated from Freud. The issue had to do with Jung's belief that people have many elements in their libido that could have been major contributors to neuroses, in defiance of Freud's insistence that sex alone is the major drive that leads to personality problems.

The passage reprinted here gives a clear indication of Jung's thinking. In contrast to most of his writings, which are highly convoluted and difficult to follow, this selection has literary qualities. Jung shows his considerable erudition, breadth of thinking, and amazing capacity to jump from topic to topic with ease. His scholarship, wisdom, and common sense are demonstrated, as well as his revolutionary conceptualizations of the human mind.

CARL G. JUNG
Phenomena resulting from the assimilation
of the unconscious

The process of assimilating the unconscious yields some very remarkable phenomena. In some patients it leads to an unmistakable, and often unpleasant, accentuation of ego-consciousness, a heightened self-confidence; they know everything, they are completely *au fait* with their unconscious, and they believe themselves to be fully acquainted with everything that comes out of it. At any rate with every interview the doctor sees them getting more and more above themselves. Others, on the contrary, are depressed, even crushed by the contents of the unconscious. Their self-confidence dwindles, and they look on with resignation at all the extraordinary things the unconscious produces. Patients of the former sort, in the exuberance of their self-confidence, assume a responsibility for the unconscious that goes much too far, beyond all reasonable bounds: whereas the latter sort finally give up all sense of responsibility in an overwhelming realization of the powerlessness of the ego against the fate that rules it from the unconscious.

If we submit these two extreme modes of reaction to closer analytical scrutiny, we discover that behind the optimistic self-confidence of the first there lurks an equally deep, or rather far deeper, helplessness, for which the conscious optimism acts as an unsuccessful compensation. And behind the pessimistic resignation of the second there is a defiant will to power, far surpassing in cocksureness the conscious optimism of the first.

With these two modes of reaction I have sketched only the two rough extremes. A finer shading would have been truer to reality. As I have said elsewhere, every analysand starts by unconsciously misusing his newly won knowledge in the interests of his abnormal, neurotic attitude, unless he is sufficiently freed from his symptoms in the early stages to be able to dispense with further treatment altogether. A very important contributory factor is that in the early stages everything is still understood on the objective level, i.e., without distinction between imago and object, so that everything is directly related to the object. Hence the man for whom "other people" are the objects of prime importance will conclude from any self-knowledge he may have imbibed at this stage of the analysis: "Aha! so that is what other people are like!" He will therefore feel it his duty, according to his nature, tolerant or otherwise, to enlighten the world. But the other man, who feels himself to be more the object of his fellows than their subject, will be weighed down by this self-knowledge and become correspondingly depressed. (I am

Source: *The Collected Works of C. G. Jung,* ed. Herbert Read, Michael Fordham, Gerhard Adler, William McGuire; trans. R. F. C. Hull. Bollingen Series XX. Vol. 7, *Two Essays on Analytical Psychology* © 1953 and 1966 by Bollingen Foundation. "Phenomena Resulting from the Assimilation of the Unconscious," pp. 139–155, paragraphs 221–242, reprinted by permission of Princeton University Press, Princeton, N.J.

naturally leaving out of account those numerous and more superficial natures who experience these problems only by the way.) In both cases the relation to the object is strengthened—in the first case in an active, in the second case in a reactive sense. The collective element is markedly accentuated. The one extends the sphere of his action, the other the sphere of his suffering.

Adler has employed the term "godlikeness"—or "god-almightiness"— to characterize certain basic features of neurotic power psychology. If I likewise borrow the same idea from *Faust,* I use it here more in the sense of that well-known passage where Mephisto writes in the student's album and makes the following aside:

> Just follow the old advice
> And my cousin the snake,
> And one day your likeness to God
> Will make you quiver and quake.[1]

Godlikeness evidently refers to knowledge, the knowledge of good and evil. The analysis and conscious realization of unconscious contents engender a certain superior tolerance, thanks to which even relatively indigestible portions of one's unconscious characterology can be accepted. This tolerance may look very wise and superior, but often it is no more than a grand gesture that brings all sorts of consequences in its train. Two spheres have been brought together which before were kept anxiously apart. After considerable resistances have been overcome, the union of opposites is successfully achieved, at least to all appearances. The deeper understanding thus gained, the juxtaposition of what was before separated, and hence the apparent overcoming of the moral conflict, give rise to a feeling of superiority that may

well express itself in the form of "godlikeness." But this same juxtaposition of good and evil can have a very different effect on a different kind of temperament. Not everyone will feel himself a superman, holding in his hands the scales of good and evil. It may also seem as though he were a helpless object caught between hammer and anvil; not in the least a Hercules at the parting of the ways, but rather a rudderless ship buffeted between Scylla and Charybdis. For without knowing it, he is caught up in perhaps the greatest and most ancient of human conflicts, experiencing the throes of eternal principles in collision. Well might he feel himself like a Prometheus chained to the Caucasus, or as one crucified. This would be a "godlikeness" in suffering. Godlikeness is certainly not a scientific concept, although the term expresses the psychological facts very graphically. Nor do I imagine that every reader will immediately grasp the peculiar state of mind implied by "godlikeness." The term belongs too exclusively to the sphere of *belles-lettres.* So I should probably be better advised to give a more circumspect description of this state. The insight and understanding, then, gained by the analysand usually reveal much to him that was before unconscious. He naturally applies this knowledge to his environment; in consequence he sees, or thinks he sees, many things that were before invisible. Since his knowledge was helpful to him, he readily assumes that it would be useful also to others. In this way he is liable to become arrogant; it may be well meant, but it is nonetheless annoying to other people. He feels as though he possesses a key that opens many, perhaps even all, doors. Psychoanalysis itself has this same bland unconsciousness of its limitations, as can clearly be seen from the way it meddles with works of art.

Since human nature is not compounded

---

[1] *Faust,* Part I, 3rd scene in Faust's study.

wholly of light, but also abounds in shadows, the insight gained in practical analysis is often somewhat painful, the more so if, as is generally the case, one has previously neglected the other side. Hence there are people who take their newly won insight very much to heart, far too much in fact, quite forgetting that they are not unique in having a shadow-side. They allow themselves to get unduly depressed and are then inclined to doubt everything, finding nothing right anywhere. That is why many excellent analysts with very good ideas can never bring themselves to publish them, because the psychic problem, as they see it, is so overwhelmingly vast that it seems to them almost impossible to tackle it scientifically. One man's optimism makes him overweening, while another's pessimism makes him over-anxious and despondent. Such are the forms which the great conflict takes when reduced to a smaller scale. But even in these lesser proportions the essence of the conflict is easily recognized: the arrogance of the one and the despondency of the other share a common uncertainty as to their boundaries. The one is excessively expanded, the other excessively contracted. Their individual boundaries are in some way obliterated. If we now consider the fact that, as a result of psychic compensation, great humility stands very close to pride, and that "pride goeth before a fall," we can easily discover behind the haughtiness certain traits of an anxious sense of inferiority. In fact we shall see clearly how his uncertainty forces the enthusiast to puff up his truths, of which he feels none too sure, and to win proselytes to his side in order that his followers may prove to himself the value and trustworthiness of his own convictions. Nor is he altogether so happy in his fund of knowledge as to be able to hold out alone; at bottom he feels isolated by it, and the secret fear of

being left alone with it induces him to trot out his opinions and interpretations in and out of season, because only when convincing some one else does he feel safe from gnawing doubts.

It is just the reverse with our despondent friend. The more he withdraws and hides himself, the greater becomes his secret need to be understood and recognized. Although he speaks of his inferiority he does not really believe it. There arises within him a defiant conviction of his unrecognized merits, and in consequence he is sensitive to the slightest disapprobation, always wearing the stricken air of one who is misunderstood and deprived of his rightful due. In this way he nurses a morbid pride and an insolent discontent—which is the very last thing he wants and for which his environment has to pay all the more dearly.

Both are at once too small and too big; their individual mean, never very secure, now becomes shakier than ever. It sounds almost grotesque to describe such a state as "godlike." But since each in his way steps beyond his human proportions, both of them are a little "superhuman" and therefore, figuratively speaking, godlike. If we wish to avoid the use of this metaphor, I would suggest that we speak instead of "psychic inflation." The term seems to me appropriate in so far as the state we are discussing involves an extension of the personality beyond individual limits, in other words, a state of being puffed up. In such a state a man fills a space which normally he cannot fill. He can only fill it by appropriating to himself contents and qualities which properly exist for themselves alone and should therefore remain outside our bounds. What lies outside ourselves belongs either to someone else, or to everyone, or to no one. Since psychic inflation is by no means a phenomenon induced exclusively by analysis, but occurs just as often in ordinary life, we can investigate it equally well in other cases. A very common instance is the humourless way in which many men identify themselves with their business or their titles. The office I hold is certainly my special activity; but it is also a collective factor that has come into existence historically through the co-operation of many people and whose dignity rests solely on collective approval. When, therefore, I identify myself with my office or title, I behave as though I myself were the whole complex of social factors of which that office consists, or as though I were not only the bearer of the office, but also and at the same time the approval of society. I have made an extraordinary extension of myself and have usurped qualities which are not in me but outside me. *L'état c'est moi* is the motto for such people.

In the case of inflation through knowledge we are dealing with something similar in principle, though psychologically more subtle. Here it is not the dignity of an office that causes the inflation, but very significant fantasies. I will explain what I mean by a practical example, choosing a mental case whom I happened to know personally and who is also mentioned in a publication by Maeder. The case is characterized by a high degree of inflation. (In mental cases we can observe all the phenomena that are present only fleetingly in normal people, in a cruder and enlarged form.)[2] The

patient suffered from paranoid dementia with megalomania. He was in telephonic communication with the Mother of God and other great ones. In human reality he was a wretched locksmith's apprentice who at the age of nineteen had become incurably insane. He had never been blessed with intelligence, but he had, among other things, hit upon the magnificent idea that the world was his picture-book, the pages of which he could turn at will. The proof was quite simple: he had only to turn round, and there was a new page for him to see.

This is Schopenhauer's "world as will and idea" in unadorned, primitive concreteness of vision. A shattering idea indeed, born of extreme alienation and seclusion from the world, but so naïvely and simply expressed that at first one can only smile at the grotesqueness of it. And yet this primitive way of looking lies at the very heart of Schopenhauer's brilliant vision of the world. Only a genius or a madman could so disentangle himself from the bonds of reality as to see the world as his picture-book. Did the patient actually work out or build up such a vision, or did it just befall him? Or did he perhaps fall into it? His pathological disintegration and inflation point rather to the latter. It is no longer *he* that thinks and speaks, but *it* thinks and speaks within him: he hears voices. So the difference between him and Schopenhauer is that, in him, the vision remained at the stage of a mere spontaneous growth, while Schopenhauer abstracted it and expressed it in language of universal validity. In so doing he raised it out of its subterranean beginnings into the clear light of collective consciousness. But it would be quite wrong to assume that the patient's vision had a purely personal character or value, as though it were something that belonged to him. If that were so, he would be a philosopher. A

___

[2] When I was still a doctor at the psychiatric clinic in Zurich, I once took an intelligent layman through the sick-wards. He had never seen a lunatic asylum from the inside before. When we had finished our round, he exclaimed, "I tell you, it's just like Zurich in miniature! A quintessence of the population. It is as though all the types one meets every day on the streets had been assembled here in their classical purity. Nothing but oddities and picked specimens from top to bottom of society!" I had never looked at it from this angle, but my friend was not far wrong.

man is a philosopher of genius only when he succeeds in transmuting the primitive and wholly natural vision into an abstract idea belonging to the common stock of consciousness. This achievement, and this alone, constitutes his personal value, for which he may take credit without necessarily succumbing to inflation. But the sick man's vision is an impersonal value, a natural growth against which he is powerless to defend himself, by which he is actually swallowed up and "wafted" clean out of the world. Far from *his* mastering the idea and expanding *it* into a philosophical view of the world, it is truer to say that the undoubted grandeur of his vision blew *him* up to pathological proportions. The personal value lies entirely in the philosophical achievement, not in the primary vision. To the philosopher as well this vision comes as so much increment, accruing to him from the common human store in which, theoretically, every one of us shares. The golden apples drop from the same tree, whether they be gathered by an imbecile locksmith's apprentice or a Schopenhauer.

There is, however, yet another thing to be learnt from this example, namely that these transpersonal contents are not just inert or dead matter that can be annexed at will. Rather they are living entities which exert an attractive force upon the conscious mind. Identification with one's office or one's title is very attractive indeed, which is precisely why so many men are nothing more than the decorum accorded to them by society. In vain would one look for a personality behind this husk. Underneath all the padding one would find a very pitiable little creature. That is why the office—or whatever this outer husk may be—is so attractive: it offers easy compensation for personal deficiencies.

Outer attractions, such as offices, titles, and other social regalia are not the only things that cause inflation. These are simply impersonal quantities that lie outside in society, in the collective consciousness. But just as there is a society outside the individual, so there is a collective psyche outside the personal psyche, namely the collective unconscious, concealing, as the above example shows, elements that are no whit less attractive. And just as a man may suddenly step into the world on his professional dignity ("Messieurs, à présent je suis Roy"), so another may disappear out of it equally suddenly when it is his lot to behold one of those mighty images that put a new face upon the world. These are the magical *représentations collectives* which underlie the slogan, the catchword, and, on a higher level, the language of the poet and mystic. I am reminded of another mental case who was neither a poet nor anything very outstanding, just a naturally quiet and rather sentimental youth. He had fallen in love with a girl and, as so often happens, had failed to ascertain whether his love was requited. His primitive *participation mystique* took it for granted that his agitations were plainly the agitations of the other, which on the lower levels of human psychology is naturally very often the case. Thus he built up a sentimental love-fantasy which precipitately collapsed when he discovered that the girl would have none of him. He was so desperate that he went straight to the river to drown himself. It was late at night, and the stars gleamed up at him from the dark water. It seemed to him that the stars were swimming two by two down the river, and a wonderful feeling came over him. He forgot his suicidal intentions and gazed fascinated at the strange, sweet drama. And gradually he became aware that every star was a face, and that all these pairs were lovers, who were carried along locked in a dreaming embrace. An entirely new understanding came to him: all had changed—his fate, his disappointment, even his love, receded and fell away. The memory of the girl grew distant, blurred; but instead, he felt with complete certainty that untold riches were promised him. He knew that an immense treasure lay hidden for him in the neighbouring observatory. The result was that he was arrested by the police at four o'clock in the morning, attempting to break into the observatory.

What had happened? His poor head had glimpsed a Dantesque picture, whose loveliness he could never have grasped had he read it in a poem. But he saw it, and it transformed him. What had hurt him most was now far away; a new and undreamed-of world of stars, tracing their silent courses far beyond this grievous earth, had opened out to him the moment he crossed "Proserpine's threshold." The intuition of untold wealth—and could any fail to be touched by this thought?—came to him like a revelation. For his poor turnip-head it was too much. He did not drown in the river, but in an eternal image, and its beauty perished with him.

Just as one man may disappear in his social role, so another may be engulfed in an inner vision and be lost to his surroundings. Many fathomless transformations of personality, like sudden conversions and other far-reaching changes of mind, originate in the attractive power of a collective image,[3] which, as the present example shows, can cause such a high degree of inflation that the entire personality is disintegrated. This disintegration is a mental disease, of a transitory or a permanent nature, a "splitting of the mind" or "schizophrenia," in Bleuler's term. The pathological inflation naturally depends on some innate weakness of the personality against the autonomy of collective unconscious contents.

We shall probably get nearest to the truth if we think of the conscious and personal psyche as resting upon the broad basis of an inherited and universal psychic disposition which is as such unconscious, and that our personal psyche bears the same relation to the collective psyche as the individual to society.

But equally, just as the individual is not unique and separate, but is also a social being, so the human psyche is not a self-contained and wholly individual phenomenon, but also a collective one. And just as certain social functions or instincts are opposed to the interests of single individuals, so the human psyche exhibits certain functions or tendencies which, on account of their collective nature, are opposed to individual needs. The reason for this is that every man is born with a highly differentiated brain and is thus assured of a wide range of possible mental functioning which he has neither acquired ontogenetically nor developed himself. To the degree that human brains are uniformly differentiated, the mental functioning thereby made possible is also collective and universal. This explains the interesting fact that the unconscious processes of the most remotely separated peoples and races show a quite remarkable correspondence, which displays itself, among other things, in the well-authenticated similarity between the themes and forms of autochthonous myths. The universal similarity of the brain yields the universal possibility of a similar mental functioning. This func-

---

[3] Cf. the definition "Image" in my *Psychological Types* (Jung, 1920), Part II, Def. 26. Léon Daudet, in *L'Hérédo* (Paris, 1916), calls this process "autofécondation interieure," by which he means the reawakening of an ancestral soul.

tioning is the collective psyche. In so far as differentiations exist that correspond to race, tribe, or even family, there exists also a collective psyche limited to race, tribe, or family over and above the "universal" collective psyche. To borrow an expression from Janet the collective psyche comprises *les parties inférieures* of the psychic functions, that is to say, the deep-rooted, well-nigh automatic, hereditary elements that are ubiquitously present, hence the impersonal or transpersonal portions of the individual psyche. Consciousness plus the personal unconscious constitutes *les parties supérieures* of the psychic functions, those portions, therefore, that are ontogenetically acquired and developed. Consequently, the individual who assimilates the pre-existing and unconscious heritage of the collective psyche into his own ontogenetic equipment, as though it were a part of the latter, extends the bounds of his personality in an illegitimate way, with corresponding results. Because the collective psyche comprises *les parties inférieures* of the psychic functions and is therefore the basis underlying every personality, it has the effect of crushing and humiliating the personality. This shows itself in inflation, taking the form either of a smothering of self-confidence or else of an unconscious intensification of the ego's importance to the point of a pathological will to power.

By raising the personal unconscious to consciousness, the analysis makes the subject aware of things which he is generally aware of in others, but never in himself. This discovery makes him therefore less individually unique, and more collective. His collectivization is not always a step to the bad; it may sometimes be a step to the good. There are people who repress their good qualities and consciously give free reign to their infantile desires. The lifting of personal repression at first brings purely personal contents into consciousness; but attached to them are the collective elements of the unconscious, the ever-present instincts, qualities, and ideas (images) as well as all those "statistical" fractions of average virtue and average vice which we recognize when we say, "Everyone has in him something of the criminal, the genius, and the saint." Thus a living picture emerges, containing pretty well everything that moves upon the checkerboard of the world, the good and the bad, the fair and the foul. A sense of solidarity with the world is gradually built up, which is felt by many natures as something very positive and in certain cases actually is the deciding factor in the treatment of neurosis. I have myself seen cases who, in this condition, managed for the first time in their lives to arouse love, and even to experience it themselves; or, by daring to leap into the unknown, they get involved in the very fate for which they were suited. I have seen not a few who, taking this condition as final, remained for years in a state of enterprising euphoria. I have often heard such cases referred to as shining examples of analytical therapy. But I must point out that cases of this euphoric and enterprising type are so utterly lacking in differentiation from the world that nobody could pass them as fundamentally cured. To my way of thinking they are as much cured as not cured. I have had occasion to follow up the lives of such patients, and it must be owned that many of them showed symptoms of maladjustment, which, if persisted in, gradually leads to the sterility and monotony so characteristic of those who have divested themselves of their egos. Here too I am speaking of the border-line cases, and not of the less valuable, normal, average folk for whom the question of adaptation is more technical than problematical. If I were more of a therapist than an investigator, I would naturally be unable to check a certain optimism of judgment, because my eyes would then be glued to the number of cures. But my conscience as an investigator is concerned not with quantity but with quality. Nature is aristocratic, and one person of value outweighs ten lesser ones. My eye followed the valuable people, and from them I learned the dubiousness of the results of a purely personal analysis, and also to understand the reasons for this dubiousness.

If, through assimilation of the unconscious, we make the mistake of including the collective psyche in the inventory of personal psychic functions, a dissolution of the personality into its paired opposites inevitably follows. Besides the pair of opposites already discussed, megalomania and the sense of inferiority, which are so painfully evident in neurosis, there are many others, from which I will single out only the specifically moral pair of opposites, namely good and evil. The specific virtues and vices of humanity are contained in the collective psyche like everything else. One man arrogates collective virtue to himself as his personal merit, another takes collective vice as his personal guilt. Both are as illusory as the megalomania and the inferiority, because the imagined virtues and the imagined wickednesses are simply the moral pair of opposites contained in the collective psyche, which have become perceptible or have been rendered conscious artificially. How much these paired opposites are contained in the collective psyche is exemplified by primitives: one observer will extol the greatest virtues in them, while another will record the very worst impressions of the selfsame tribe.

For the primitive, whose personal differentiation is, as we know, still in its infancy, both propositions are true, because his psyche is essentially collective and therefore for the most part unconscious. He is still more or less identical with the collective psyche, and accordingly has all the collective virtues and vices without any personal attribution and without inner contradiction. The contradiction arises only when the personal development of the psyche begins, and when reason discovers the irreconcilable nature of the opposites. The consequence of this discovery is the conflict of repression. We want to be good, and therefore must repress evil; and with that the paradise of the collective psyche comes to an end. Repression of the collective psyche was absolutely necessary for the development of personality. In primitives, development of personality, or more accurately, development of the person, is a question of magical prestige. The figure of the medicine-man or chief leads the way: both make themselves conspicuous by the singularity of their ornaments and their mode of life, expressive of their social roles. The singularity of his outward tokens marks the individual off from the rest, and the segregation is still further enhanced by the possession of special ritual secrets. By these and similar means the primitive creates around him a shell, which might be called a persona (mask). Masks, as we know, are actually used among primitives in totem ceremonies—for instance, as a means of enhancing or changing the personality. In this way the outstanding individual is apparently removed from the sphere of the collective psyche, and to the degree that he succeeds in identifying himself with his persona, he actually is removed. This removal means magical prestige. One could easily assert that the impelling motive in this development is the will to power. But that would be to forget that the building up of prestige is always a product of collective compromise: not only must there be one who wants prestige, there must also be a public seeking somebody on whom to confer prestige. That being so, it would be incorrect to say that a man creates prestige for himself out of his individual will to power; it is on the contrary an entirely collective affair. Since society as a whole needs the magically effective figure, it uses the needful will to power in the individual, and the will to submit in the mass, as a vehicle, and thus brings about the creation of personal prestige. The latter is a phenomenon which, as the history of political beginnings shows, is of the utmost importance for the comity of nations.

The importance of personal prestige can hardly be overestimated, because the possibility of regressive dissolution in the collective psyche is a very real danger, not only for the outstanding individual but also for his followers. This possibility is most likely to occur when the goal of prestige—universal recognition—has been reached. The person then becomes a collective truth, and that is always the beginning of the end. To gain prestige is a positive achievement not only for the outstanding individual but also for the clan. The individual distinguishes himself by his deeds, the many by their abdication from power. So long as this attitude needs to be fought for and defended against hostile influences, the achievement remains positive; but as soon as there are no more obstacles and universal recognition has been attained, prestige loses its positive value and usually becomes a dead letter. A schismatic movement then sets in, and the whole process begins again from the beginning.

Because personality is of such paramount importance for the life of the community, everything likely to disturb its development is sensed as a danger. But the greatest danger of all is the premature dissolution of prestige by an invasion of the collective psyche. Absolute secrecy is one of the best known primitive means of exorcising this danger. Collective thinking and feeling and collective effort are far less of a strain than individual functioning and effort; hence there is always a great temptation to allow collective functioning to take the place of individual differentiation of the personality. Once the personality has been differentiated and safeguarded by magical prestige, its levelling down and eventual dissolution in the collective psyche (e.g., Peter's denial) occasions a "loss of soul" in the individual, because an important personal achievement has been either neglected or allowed to slip into regression. For this reason taboo infringements are followed by Draconian punishments altogether in keeping with the seriousness of the situation. So long as we regard these things from the causal point of view, as mere historical survivals and metastases of the incest taboo,[4] it is impossible to understand what all these measures are for. If, however, we approach the problem from the teleological point of view, much that was quite inexplicable becomes clear.

For the development of personality, then, strict differentiation from the collective psyche is absolutely necessary, since partial or blurred differentiation leads to an immediate melting away of the individual in the collective. There is now a danger that in the analysis of the unconscious the collective and the personal psyche may be fused together, with, as I

---

[4] Freud, *Totem and Taboo* (1913).

have intimated, highly unfortunate results. These results are injurious both to the patient's life-feeling and to his fellow men, if he has any influence at all on his environment. Through his identification with the collective psyche he will infallibly try to force the demands of his unconscious upon others, for identity with the collective psyche always brings with it a feeling of universal validity—"godlikeness"—which completely ignores all differences in the personal psyche of his fellows. (The feeling of universal validity comes, of course, from the universality of the collective psyche.) A collective attitude naturally presupposes this same collective psyche in others. But that means a ruthless disregard not only of individual differences but also of differences of a more general kind within the collective psyche itself, as for example differences of race. This disregard for individuality obviously means the suffocation of the single individual, as a consequence of which the element of differentiation is obliterated from the community. The element of differentiation is the individual. All the highest achievements of virtue, as well as the blackest villainies, are individual. The larger a community is, and the more the sum total of collective factors peculiar to every large community rests on conservative prejudices detrimental to individuality, the more will the individual be morally and spiritually crushed, and, as a result, the one source of moral and spiritual progress for society is choked up. Naturally the only thing that can thrive in such an atmosphere is sociality and whatever is collective in the individual. Everything individual in him goes under, i.e., is doomed to repression. The individual elements lapse into the unconscious, where, by the law of necessity, they are transformed into something

essentially baleful, destructive, and anarchical. Socially, this evil principle shows itself in the spectacular crimes—regicide and the like—perpetrated by certain prophetically-inclined individuals; but in the great mass of the community it remains in the background, and only manifests itself indirectly in the inexorable moral degeneration of society. It is a notorious fact that the morality of society as a whole is in inverse ratio to its size; for the greater the aggregation of individuals, the more the individual factors are blotted out, and with them morality, which rests entirely on the moral sense of the individual and the freedom necessary for this. Hence every man is, in a certain sense, unconsciously a worse man when he is in society than when acting alone; for he is carried by society and to that extent relieved of his individual responsibility. Any large company composed of wholly admirable persons has the morality and intelligence of an unwieldy, stupid, and violent animal. The bigger the organization, the more unavoidable is its immorality and blind stupidity *(Senatus bestia, senatores boni viri)*. Society, by automatically stressing all the collective qualities in its individual representatives, puts a premium on mediocrity, on everything that settles down to vegetate in an easy, irresponsible way. Individuality will inevitably be driven to the wall. This process begins in school, continues at the university, and rules all departments in which the State has a hand. In a small social body, the individuality of its members is better safeguarded; and the greater is their relative freedom and the possibility of conscious responsibility. Without freedom there can be no morality. Our admiration for great organizations dwindles when once we become aware of the other side of the wonder: the tremendous piling up and accentuation of all that is primitive in man, and the unavoidable destruction of his individuality in the interests of the monstrosity that every great organization in fact is. The man of today, who resembles more or less the collective ideal, has made his heart into a den of murderers, as can easily be proved by the analysis of his unconscious, even though he himself is not in the least disturbed by it. And in so far as he is normally "adapted" to his environment, it is true that the greatest infamy on the part of his group will not disturb him, so long as the majority of his fellows steadfastly believe in the exalted morality of their social organization. Now, all that I have said here about the influence of society upon the individual is identically true of the influence of the collective unconscious upon the individual psyche. But, as is apparent from my examples, the latter influence is as invisible as the former is visible. Hence it is not surprising that its inner effects are not understood, and that those to whom such things happen are called pathological freaks and treated as crazy. If one of them happened to be a real genius, the fact would not be noted until the next generation or the one after. So obvious does it seem to us that a man should drown in his own dignity, so utterly incomprehensible that he should seek anything other than what the mob wants, and that he should vanish permanently from view in this other. One could wish both of them a sense of humour, that—according to Schopenhauer —truly "divine" attribute of man which alone befits him to maintain his soul in freedom.

The collective instincts and fundamental forms of human thought and feeling whose activity is revealed by the analysis of the unconscious are, for the conscious personality, an acquisition which it cannot assimilate without considerable disturbance. It is therefore of the utmost importance in practical treatment to keep the integrity of the personality constantly in mind. For, if the collective psyche is taken to be the personal possession of the individual, it will result in a distortion or an overloading of the personality which is very difficult to deal with. Hence it is imperative to make a clear distinction between personal contents and those of the collective psyche. This distinction is far from easy, because the personal grows out of the collective psyche and is intimately bound up with it. So it is difficult to say exactly what contents are to be called personal and what collective. There is no doubt, for instance, that archaic symbolisms such as we frequently find in fantasies and dreams are collective factors. All basic instincts and basic forms of thought and feeling are collective. Everything that all men agree in regarding as universal is collective, likewise everything that is universally understood, universally found, universally said and done. On closer examination one is always astonished to see how much of our so-called individual psychology is really collective. So much, indeed, that the individual traits are completely overshadowed by it. Since, however, individuation[5] is an ineluctable psychological requirement, we can see from the superior force of the collective what very special attention must be paid to this delicate

---

[5] Cf. *Psychological Types* (Jung, 1920), Def. 29: "Individuation is a process of differentiation, having for its goal the development of the individual personality."—"Since the individual is not only a single entity, but also, by his very existence, presupposes a collective relationship, the process of individuation does not lead to isolation, but to an intenser and more universal collective solidarity."

plant "individuality" if it is not to be completely smothered.

Man has one capacity which is of the greatest possible value for collective purposes, but most pernicious for individuation, and that is the faculty of imitation. Social psychology can never dispense with imitation, for without it mass organizations, the State, and the ordering of society are simply impossible. It is not the law that makes for social order, but imitation, which concept also includes suggestibility, suggestion, and mental contagion. But daily we see how the mechanism of imitation is used, or rather misused, for the purpose of personal differentiation: people are content to ape some outstanding personality, some striking characteristic or activity, thus achieving an outward distinction from their immediate environment. We could almost say that as a punishment for this the essential uniformity of their minds with the environment is intensified to the point of unconscious, compulsive fixation. Usually these specious attempts at individual differentiation stiffen into a pose, and the imitator remains at the same level as he always was, only several degrees more sterile than before. In order to discover what is authentically individual in ourselves, profound reflection is needed; and suddenly we realize how uncommonly difficult the discovery of individuality in fact is.

REFERENCES

Freud, S. *Totem and taboo.* New York: Random House, 1946. (Originally published, 1913.)

Jung, C. G. *Psychological types.* In *Collected Works* (Vol. 6). New York: Pantheon, 1953. (Originally published, 1920.)

CHAPTER 4

Person-Centered Theory

Introduction

This selection by Carl Rogers (1902–   ) was written during the time I was in training with him at the University of Chicago in 1954. One of my own concerns at that time about psychotherapy—*Was it science or was it not?*—can be seen in this classic statement.

Rogers's style is immensely personal. He talks about himself freely and he communicates so lucidly and persuasively that the reader feels an empathy with him, as though they were reasoning together. Perhaps Rogers puts the reader in the position of a therapist, listening to the exposition of a person concerned with an important problem. Indeed, the topic of this selection is one that troubles or at least concerns all those who would dare to be therapists.

Students of psychotherapy would do well to follow Rogers's career through his writings. As in the case of Karen Horney, the various stages of his growth and development are dramatic and exciting.

CARL R. ROGERS
Persons or science? A philosophical question

This is a highly personal document, written primarily for myself, to clarify an issue which has become increasingly puzzling. It will be of interest to others only to the extent that the issue exists for them. I shall therefore describe first something of the way in which the paper grew.

As I have acquired experience as a therapist, carrying on the exciting, rewarding experience of psychotherapy, and as I have worked as a scientific investigator to ferret out some of the truth about therapy, I have become increasingly conscious of the gap between these two roles. The better therapist I have become (as I believe I have), the more I have been vaguely aware of my complete subjectivity when I am at my best in this function. And as I have become a better investigator, more "hardheaded" and more scientific (as I believe I have) I have felt an increasing discomfort at the distance between the rigorous objectivity of myself as scientist and the almost mystical subjectivity of myself as therapist. This paper is the result.

What I did first was to let myself go as therapist, and describe, as well as I could do in a brief space, what is the essential nature of psychotherapy as I have lived it with many clients. I would stress the fact that this is a very fluid and personal formulation, and that if it were written by another person, or if it were written by me

two years ago, or two years hence, it would be different in some respects. Then I let myself go as scientist—as tough-minded fact-finder in this psychological realm—and endeavored to picture the meaning which science can give to therapy. Following this I carried on the debate which existed in me, raising the questions which each point of view legitimately asks the other.

When I had carried my efforts this far I found that I had only sharpened the conflict. The two points of view seemed more than ever irreconcilable. I discussed the material with a seminar of faculty and students, and found their comments very helpful. During the following year I continued to mull over the problem until I began to feel an integration of the two views arising in me. More than a year after the first sections were written I tried to express this tentative and perhaps temporary integration in words.

Thus the reader who cares to follow my struggles in this matter will find that it has quite unconsciously assumed a dramatic form—all of the dramatis personae being contained within myself; First Protagonist, Second Protagonist, The Conflict, and finally, The Resolution. Without more ado let me introduce the first protagonist, myself as therapist, portraying as well as I can, what the *experience* of therapy seems to be.

Carl R. Rogers, "Persons or Science? A Philosophical Question." From *The American Psychologist*, 1955, 10, 267–278. Copyright © 1955 by the American Psychological Association. Reprinted by permission.

THE ESSENCE OF THERAPY IN TERMS OF ITS EXPERIENCE

I launch myself into the therapeutic relationship having a hypothesis, or a faith, that my liking, my confidence, and my understanding of the other person's inner world, will lead to a significant process of becoming. I enter the relationship not as a scientist, not as a physician who can accurately diagnose and cure, but as a person, entering into a personal relationship. Insofar as I see him only as an object, the client will tend to become only an object.

I risk myself, because if, as the relationship deepens, what develops is a failure, a regression, a repudiation of me and the relationship by the client, then I sense that I will lose myself, or a part of myself. At times this risk is very real, and is very keenly experienced.

I let myself go into the immediacy of the relationship where it is my total organism which takes over and is sensitive to the relationship, not simply my consciousness. I am not consciously responding in a planful or analytic way, but simply in an unreflective way to the other individual, my reaction being based (but not consciously) on my total organismic sensitivity to this other person. I live the relationship on this basis.

The essence of some of the deepest parts of therapy seems to be a unity of experiencing. The client is freely able to experience his feeling in its complete intensity, as a "pure culture," without intellectual inhibitions or cautions, without having it bounded by knowledge of contradictory feelings; and I am able with equal freedom to experience my understanding of this feeling, without any conscious thought about it, without any apprehension or concern as to where this will lead, without any type of diagnostic or analytic thinking, without any cognitive or emotional barriers to a complete "letting go" in understanding. When there is this complete unity, singleness, fullness of experiencing in the relationship, then it acquires the "out-of-this-world" quality which many therapists have remarked upon, a sort of trance-like feeling in the relationship from which both the client and I emerge at the end of the hour, as if from a deep well or tunnel. In these moments there is, to borrow Buber's phrase, a real "I-Thou" relationship, a timeless living in the experience which is *between* the client and me. It is at the opposite pole from seeing the client, or myself, as an object. It is the height of personal subjectivity.

I am often aware of the fact that I do not *know,* cognitively, where this immediate relationship is leading. It is as though both I and the client, often fearfully, let ourselves slip into the stream of becoming, a stream or process which carries us along. It is the fact that the therapist has let himself float in this stream of experience or life previously, and found it rewarding, that makes him each time less fearful of taking the plunge. It is my confidence that makes it easier for the client to embark also, a little bit at a time. It often seems as though this stream of experience leads to some goal. Probably the truer statement, however, is that its rewarding character lies within the process itself, and that its major reward is that it enables both the client and me, later, independently, to let ourselves go in the process of becoming.

As to the client, as therapy proceeds he finds that he is daring to become himself, in spite of all the dread consequences which he is sure will befall him if he permits himself to become himself. What does this becoming one's self mean? It appears to mean less fear of the organismic, nonreflective reactions which one has, a gradual growth of trust in and even affection for the complex, varied, rich assortment of feelings and tendencies which exist in one at the organic or organismic level. Consciousness, instead of being the watchman over a dangerous and unpredictable lot of impulses, of which few can be permitted to see the light of day, becomes the comfortable inhabitant of a richly varied society of impulses and feelings and thoughts, which prove to be very satisfactorily self-governing when not fearfully or authoritatively guarded.

Involved in this process of becoming himself is a profound experience of personal choice. He realizes that he can choose to continue to hide behind a facade, or that he can take the risks involved in being himself; that he is a free agent who has it within his power to destroy another, or himself, and also the power to enhance himself and others. Faced with this naked reality of decision, he chooses to move in the direction of being himself.

But being himself doesn't "solve problems." It simply opens up a new way of living in which there is more depth and more height in the experience of his feelings, more breadth and more range. He feels more unique and hence more alone, but he is so much more real that his relationships with others lose their artificial quality, become deeper, more satisfying, and draw more of the realness of the other person into the relationship.

Another way of looking at this process, this relationship, is that it is a learning by the client (and by the therapist, to a lesser extent). But it is a strange type of learning. Almost never is the learning notable by its complexity, and at its deepest the learnings never seem to fit well into verbal symbols. Often the learnings take such simple forms as "I *am* different from others"; "I do feel hatred for him"; "I *am* fearful of feeling dependent"; "I do feel sorry for myself"; "I am self-centered"; "I do have tender and loving feelings"; "I could be what I want to be"; etc. But in spite of their seeming sim-plicity these learnings are vastly significant in some new way which is very difficult to define. We can think of it in various ways. They are self-appropriated learnings, for one thing, based somehow in experience, not in symbols. They are analogous to the learning of the child who knows that "two and two make four" and who one day playing with two objects and two objects, suddenly realizes in *experience* a totally new learning, that "two and two *do* make four."

Another manner of understanding these learnings is that they are a belated attempt to match symbols with meanings in the world of feelings, an undertaking long since achieved in the cognitive realm. Intellectually, we match carefully the symbol we select with the meaning which an experience has for us. Thus I say something happened "gradually," having quickly (and largely unconsciously) reviewed such terms as "slowly," "imperceptibly," "step-by-step," etc., and rejected them as not carrying the precise shade of meaning of the experience. But in the realm of feelings, we heave never learned to attach symbols to experience with any accuracy of meaning. This something which I feel welling up in myself, in the safety of an acceptant relationship—what is it? Is it sadness, is it anger, is it regret, is it sorrow for myself, is it anger at lost opportunities—I stumble around trying out a wide range of symbols, until one "fits," "feels right," seems really to match the organismic experience. In doing this type of thing the client discovers that he has to learn the language of feeling and emotion as if he were an infant learning to speak; often, even worse, he finds he must unlearn a false language before learning the true one.

Let us try still one more way of defining this type of learning, this time by describing what it is not. It is a type of learning which cannot be taught. The essence of it is the aspect of self-discovery. With "knowledge" as we are accustomed to think of it, one person can teach it to another, providing each has adequate motivation and ability. But in the significant learning which takes place in therapy, one person *cannot* teach another. The teaching would destroy the learning. Thus I might teach a client that it is safe for him to be himself, that freely to realize his feelings is not dangerous, etc. The more he learned this, the less he would have learned it in the significant, experiential, self-appropriating way. Kierkegaard regards this latter type of learning as true subjectivity, and makes the valid point that there can be no direct communication of it, or even about it. The most that one person can do to further it in another is to create certain conditions which make this type of learning *possible*. It cannot be compelled.

A final way of trying to describe this learning is that the client gradually learns to symbolize a total and unified state, in which the state of the organism, in experience, feeling, and cognition may all be described in one unified way. To make the matter even more vague and unsatisfactory, it seems quite unnecessary that this symbolization should be expressed. It usually does occur, because the client wishes to communicate at least a portion of himself to the therapist, but it is probably not essential. The only necessary aspect is the inward realization of the total, unified, immediate, "at-the-instant," state of the organism which is me. For example, to realize fully that at this moment the oneness in me is simply that "I am deeply frightened at the possibility of becoming something different" is of the essence of therapy. The client who realizes this will be quite

certain to recognize and realize this state of his being when it recurs in somewhat similar form. He will also, in all probability, recognize and realize more fully some of the other existential feelings which occur in him. Thus he will be moving toward a state in which he is more truly himself. He will *be*, in more unified fashion, what he organismically *is*, and this seems to be the essence of therapy.

THE ESSENCE OF THERAPY IN TERMS OF SCIENCE

I shall now let the second protagonist, myself as scientist, take over and give his view of this same field.

In approaching the complex phenomena of therapy with the logic and methods of science, the aim is to work toward an *understanding* of the phenomena. In science this means an objective knowledge of events and of functional relationships between events. Science may also give the possibility of increased prediction of and control over these events, but this is not a necessary outcome of scientific endeavor. If the scientific aim were fully achieved in this realm, we would presumably know that, in therapy, certain elements were associated with certain types of outcomes. Knowing this it is likely that we would be able to predict that a particular instance of a therapeutic relationship would have a certain outcome (within certain probability limits) because it involved certain elements. We could then very likely control outcomes of therapy by our manipulation of the elements contained in the therapeutic relationship.

It should be clear that no matter how profound our scientific investigation, we could never by means of it discover any absolute truth, but could only describe relationships which had an increasingly high probability of occurrence. Nor could we discover any underlying reality in regard to persons, interpersonal relationships, or the universe. We could only describe relationships between observable events. If science in this field followed the course of science in other fields, the working models of reality which would emerge (in the course of theory building) would be increasingly removed from the reality perceived by the senses. The scientific description of therapy and therapeutic relationships would become increasingly *unlike* these phenomena as they are experienced.

It is evident at the outset that since therapy is a complex phenomenon, measurement will be difficult. Nevertheless "anything that exists can be measured," and since therapy is judged to be a significant relationship, with implications extending far beyond itself, the difficulties may prove to be worth surmounting in order to discover laws of personality and interpersonal relationships.

Since, in client-centered therapy, there already exists a crude theory (though not a theory in the strictly scientific sense), we have a starting point for the selection of hypotheses. For purposes of this discussion, let us take some of the crude hypotheses which can be drawn from this theory, and see what a scientific approach will do with them. We will, for the time being, omit the translation of the total theory into a formal logic which would be acceptable, and consider only a few of the hypotheses.

Let us first state three of these in their crude form.

1. Acceptance of the client by the therapist leads to an increased acceptance of self by the client.

2. The more the therapist perceives the client as a person rather than as an object,

the more the client will come to perceive himself as a person rather than an object.

3. In the course of therapy an experiential and effective type of learning about self takes place in the client.

How would we go about translating each of these[1] into operational terms and how would we test the hypotheses? What would be the general outcomes of such testing?

This paper is not the place for a detailed answer to these questions, but research already carried on supplies the answers in a general way. In the case of the first hypothesis, certain devices for measuring acceptance would be selected or devised. These might be attitude tests, objective or projective, Q technique or the like. Presumably the same instruments, with slightly different instructions or mind set, could be used to measure the therapist's acceptance of the client, and the client's acceptance of self. Operationally then, the degree of therapist acceptance would be equated to a certain score on this instrument. Whether client self-acceptance changed during therapy would be indicated by pre- and post-measurements. The relationship of any change to therapy would be determined by comparison of changes in therapy to changes during a control period or in a control group. We would finally be able to say whether a relationship existed between therapist acceptance and client self-acceptance, as operationally defined, and the correlation between the two.

---

[1] I believe it is now commonly accepted that the most subjective feelings, apprehensions, tensions, satisfactions, or reactions, may be dealt with scientifically, providing only that they may be given clear-cut operational definition. William Stephenson, among others, presents this point of view forcefully (in his "Postulates of Behaviorism," 1953), and, through his Q technique, has contributed importantly to the objectification of such subjective materials for scientific study.

The second and third hypotheses involve real difficulty in measurement, but there is no reason to suppose that they could not be objectively studied, as our sophistication in psychological measurement increases. Some type of attitude test or Q sort might be the instrument for the second hypothesis, measuring the attitude of therapist toward client, and of client toward self. In this case the continuum would be from objective regard of an external object to a personal and subjective experiencing. The instrumentation for hypothesis there might be physiological, since it seems likely that experiential learning has physiologically measurable concomitants. Another possibility would be to infer experiential learning from its effectiveness, and thus measure the effectiveness of learning in different areas. At the present stage of our methodology hypothesis three might be beyond us, but certainly within the foreseeable future, it too could be given operational definition and tested.

The findings from these studies would be of this order. Let us become suppositious, in order to illustrate more concretely. Suppose we find that therapist acceptance leads to client self-acceptance, and that the correlation is in the neighborhood of .70 between the two variables. In hypothesis two we might find the hypothesis unsupported, but find that the more the therapist regarded the client as a person, the more the client's self-acceptance increased. Thus we would have learned that person-centeredness is an element of acceptance, but that it has little to do with the client becoming more of a person to himself. Let us also suppose hypothesis three upheld with experiential learning of certain describable sorts taking place much more in therapy than in the control subjects.

Glossing over all the qualifications and ramifications which would be present in the findings, and omitting reference to the unexpected leads into personality dynamics which would crop up (since these are hard to imagine in advance), the preceding paragraph gives us some notion of what science can offer in this field. It can give us a more exact description of the events of therapy and the changes which take place. It can begin to formulate some tentative laws of the dynamics of human relationships. It can offer public and replicable statements, that if certain operationally definable conditions exist in the therapist or in the relationship, then certain client behaviors may be expected with a known degree of probability. It can presumably do this for the field of therapy and personality change as it is in the process of doing for such fields as perception and learning. Eventually theoretical formulations should draw together these different areas, enunciating the laws which appear to govern alteration in human behavior, whether in the situations we classify as perception, those we classify as learning, or the more global and molar changes which occur in therapy, involving both perception and learning.

SOME ISSUES

Here are two different methods of perceiving the essential aspects of psychotherapy, two different approaches to forging ahead into new territory in this field. As presented here, and as they frequently exist, there seems almost no common meeting ground between the two descriptions. Each represents a vigorous way of seeing therapy. Each seems to be an avenue to the significant truths of therapy. When each of these is held by a different individual or group, it constitutes a basis of sharp disagreement. When each of these approaches seems true to one individual, like myself, then he feels himself conflicted by these two views. Though they may superficially be reconciled, or regarded as complementary to each other, they seem to me to be basically antagonistic in many ways. I should like to raise certain issues which these two viewpoints pose for me.

The scientist's questions

First let me pose some of the questions which the scientific viewpoint asks of the experiential (using scientific and experiential simply as loose labels to indicate the two views). The hardheaded scientist listens to the experiential account, and raises several searching questions.

1. First of all he wants to know, "How can you know that this account, or any account given at a previous or later time, is true? How do you know that it has any relationship to reality? If we are to rely on this inner and subjective experience as being the truth about human relationships or about ways of altering personality, then Yogi, Christian Science, dianetics, and the delusions of a psychotic individual who believes himself to be Jesus Christ, are all true, just as true as this account. Each of them represents the truth as perceived inwardly by some individual or group of individuals. If we are to avoid this morass of multiple and contradictory truths, we must fall back on the only method we know for achieving an ever-closer approximation to reality, the scientific method."

2. "In the second place, this experiential approach shuts one off from improving his therapeutic skill, or discovering the less than satisfactory

elements in the relationship. Unless one regards the present description as a perfect one, which is unlikely, or the present level of experience in the therapeutic relationship as being the most effective possible, which is equally unlikely, then there are unknown flaws, imperfections, blind spots, in the account as given. How are these to be discovered and corrected? The experiential approach can offer nothing but a trial-and-error process for achieving this, a process which is slow and which offers no real guarantee of achieving this goal. Even the criticisms or suggestions of others are of little help, since they do not arise from within the experience and hence do not have the vital authority of the relationship itself. But the scientific method, and the procedures of a modern logical positivism, have much to offer here. Any experience which can be described at all can be described in operational terms. Hypotheses can be formulated and put to test, and the sheep of truth can thus be separated from the goats of error. This seems the only sure road to improvement, self-correction, growth in knowledge."

3. The scientist has another comment to make. "Implicit in your description of the therapeutic experience seems to be the notion that there are elements in it which *cannot* be predicted—that there is some type of spontaneity or (excuse the term) free will operative here. You speak as though some of the client's behavior—and perhaps some of the therapist's—is not caused, is not a link in a sequence of cause and effect. Without desiring to become metaphysical, may I raise the question as to whether this is defeatism? Since surely we can discover what causes *much* of behavior—you yourself speak of creating the conditions where certain behavioral results follow—then why give

up at any point? Why not at least *aim* toward uncovering the causes of *all* behavior? This does not mean that the individual must regard himself as an automaton, but in our search for the facts we shall not be hampered by a belief that some doors are closed to us."

4. Finally, the scientist cannot understand why the therapist, the experientialist, should challenge the one tool and method which is responsible for almost all the advances which we value. "In the curing of disease, in the prevention of infant mortality, in the growing of larger crops, in the preservation of food, in the manufacture of all the things that make life comfortable, from books to nylon, in the understanding of the universe, what is the foundation stone? It is the method of science, applied to each of these, and to many other problems. It is true that it has improved methods of warfare, too, serving man's destructive as well as his constructive purposes, but even here the potentiality for social usefulness is very great. So why should we doubt this same approach in the social science field? To be sure advances here have been slow, and no law as fundamental as the law of gravity has as yet been demonstrated, but are we to give up this approach out of impatience? What possible alternative offers equal hope? If we are agreed that the social problems of the world are very pressing indeed, if psychotherapy offers a window onto the most crucial and significant dynamics of change in human behavior, then surely the course of action is to apply to psychotherapy the most rigorous canons of scientific method, on as broad a scale as possible, in order that we may most rapidly approach a tentative knowledge of the laws of individual behavior and of attitudinal change."

The questions of the experientialist

While the scientist's questions may seem to some to settle the matter, his comments are far from being entirely satisfying to the therapist who has lived the experience of therapy. Such an individual has several points to make in regard to the scientific view.

1. "In the first place," this "experientialist" points out, "science always has to do with the other, the object. Various logicians of science, including Stevens, show that it is a basic element of science that it always has to do with the observable object, the observable other. This is true, even if the scientist is experimenting on himself, for to that degree he treats himself as the observable other. It never has anything to do with the experiencing me. Now does not this quality of science mean that it must forever be irrelevant to an experience such as therapy, which is intensely personal, highly subjective in its inwardness, and dependent entirely on the relationship of two individuals each of whom is an experiencing me? Science can of course study the events which occur, but always in a way which is irrelevant to what is occurring. An analogy would be to say that science can conduct an autopsy of the dead events of therapy, but by its very nature it can never enter into the living physiology of therapy. It is for this reason that therapists recognize—usually intuitively—that any advance in therapy, any fresh knowledge of it, any significant new hypotheses in regard to it must come from the experience of the therapists and clients, and can never come from science. Again, to use an analogy, certain heavenly bodies were discovered solely from examination of the scientific measurements of the courses of the stars.

Then the astronomers searched for these hypothesized bodies and found them. It seems decidedly unlikely that there will ever be a similar outcome in therapy, since science has nothing to say about the internal personal experience which 'I' have in therapy. It can only speak of the events which occur in 'him.' "

2. "Because science has as its field the 'other,' the 'object,' it means that everything it touches is transformed into an object. This has never presented a problem in the physical sciences. In the biological sciences it has caused certain difficulties. A number of medical men feel some concern as to whether the increasing tendency to view the human organism as an object, in spite of its scientific efficacy, may not be unfortunate for the patient. They would prefer to see him again regarded as a person. It is in the social sciences, however, that this becomes a genuinely serious issue. It means that the people studied by the social scientist are always objects. In therapy, both client and therapist become objects for dissection, but not persons with whom one enters a living relationship. At first glance, this may not seem important. We may say that only in his role as scientist does the individual regard others as objects. He can also step out of this role and become a person. But if we look a little further we will see that this is a superficial answer. If we project ourselves into the future, and suppose that we had the answers to most of the questions which psychology investigates today, what then? Then we would find ourselves increasingly impelled to treat all others, and even ourselves, as objects. The knowledge of all human relationships would be so great that we would know it rather than live the relationships unreflectively. We see some

foretaste of this in the attitude of sophisticated parents who know that affection 'is good for the child.' This knowledge frequently stands in the way of their being themselves, freely, unreflectively, affectionate or not. Thus the development of science in a field like therapy is either irrelevant to the experience, or may actually make it more difficult to live the relationship as a personal, experiential event."

3. The experientialist has a further concern. "When science transforms people into objects, as mentioned above, it has another effect. The end result of science is to lead toward manipulation. This is less true in fields like astronomy, but in the physical and social sciences, the knowledge of the events and their relationships leads to manipulation of some of the elements of the equation. This is unquestionably true in psychology, and would be true in therapy. If we know all about how learning takes place, we use that knowledge to manipulate persons as objects. This statement places no value judgment on manipulation. It may be done in highly ethical fashion. We may even manipulate ourselves as objects, using such knowledge. Thus, knowing that learning takes place more rapidly with repeated review rather than long periods of concentration of one lesson, I may use this knowledge to manipulate my learning of Spanish. But knowledge is power. As I learn the laws of learning I use them to manipulate others through advertisements, through propaganda, through prediction of their responses, and the control of those responses. It is not too strong a statement to say that the growth of knowledge in the social sciences contains within itself a powerful tendency toward social control, toward control of the many by the few. An equally strong

tendency is toward the weakening or destruction of the existential person. When all are regarded as objects, the subjective individual, the inner self, the person in the process of becoming, the unreflective consciousness of being, the whole inward side of living life, is weakened, devalued, or destroyed. Perhaps this is best exemplified by two books. Skinner's *Walden Two* is a psychologist's picture of paradise. To Skinner it must have seemed desirable, unless he wrote it as a tremendous satire. At any rate it is a paradise of manipulation, in which the extent to which one can be a person is greatly reduced, unless one can be a member of the ruling council. Huxley's *Brave New World* is frankly satire, but portrays vividly the loss of personhood which he sees as associated with increasing psychological and biological knowledge. Thus, to put it bluntly, it seems that a developing social science (as now conceived and pursued) leads to social dictatorship and individual loss of personhood. The dangers perceived by Kierkegaard a century ago in this respect seem much more real now, with the increase in knowledge, than they could have then.''

4. "Finally," says the experientialist, "doesn't all this point to the fact that ethics is a more basic consideration than science? I am not blind to the value of science as a tool, and am aware that it can be a very valuable tool. But unless it is the tool of ethical *persons,* with all that the term persons implies, may it not become a Juggernaut? We have been a long time recognizing this issue, because in physical science it took centuries for the ethical issue to become crucial, but it has at last become so. In the social sciences the ethical issues arise much more quickly,

because persons are involved. But in psychotherapy the issue arises most quickly and most deeply. Here is the maximizing of all that is subjective, inward, personal; here a relationship is lived, not examined, and a person, not an object, emerges; a person who feels, chooses, believes, acts, not as an automaton, but as a person. And here too is the ultimate in science—the objective exploration of the most subjective aspects of life; the reduction to hypotheses, and eventually to theorems, of all that has been regarded as most personal, most completely inward, most thoroughly a private world. And because these two views come so sharply into focus here, we must make a choice—an ethical personal choice of values. We may do it by default, by not raising the question. We may be able to make a choice which will somehow conserve both values—but choose we must. And I am asking that we think long and hard before we give up the values that pertain to being a person, to experiencing, to living a relationship, to becoming, that pertain to one's self as a process, to one's self in the existential moment, to the inward subjective self that lives.''

The dilemma

There you have the contrary views as they occur sometimes explicitly, more often implicitly, in current psychological thinking. There you have the debate as it exists in me. Where do we go? What direction do we take? Has the problem been correctly described or is it fallacious? What are the errors of perception? Or if it is essentially as described, must we choose one or the other? And if so, which one? Or is there some broader, more inclusive formulation which can happily encompass both of these views without damage to either?

A CHANGED VIEW OF SCIENCE

In the year which has elapsed since the foregoing material was written, I have from time to time discussed the issues with students, colleagues, and friends. To some of them I am particularly indebted for ideas which have taken root in me.[2] Gradually I have come to believe that the most basic error in the original formulation was in the description of science. I should like, in this section, to attempt to correct that error, and in the following section to reconcile the revised points of view.

The major shortcoming was, I believe, in viewing science as something "out there," something spelled with a capital S, a "body of knowledge," existing somewhere in space and time. In common with many psychologists I thought of science as a systematized and organized collection of tentatively verified fact, and saw the methodology of science as the socially approved means of accumulating this body of knowledge, and continuing its verification. It has seemed somewhat like a reservoir into which all and sundry may dip their buckets to obtain water— with a guarantee of 99% purity. When viewed in this external and impersonal fashion, it seems not unreasonable to see Science not only as discovering knowledge in lofty fashion, but as involving depersonalization, a tendency to manipulate, a denial of the basic freedom of choice which I have met experientially in therapy. I should like now to view the scientific approach from a different, and I hope, a more accurate perspective.

Science in persons

Science exists only in people. Each scientific project has its creative inception, its process, and its tentative conclusion, in a person or persons. Knowledge—even scientific knowledge— is that which is subjectively acceptable. Scientific knowledge can be communicated only to those who are subjectively ready to receive its communication. The utilization of science also occurs only through people who are in pursuit of values which have meaning for them. These statements summarize very briefly something of the change in emphasis which I would like to make in my description of science. Let me follow through the various phases of science from this point of view.

The creative phases

Science has its inception in a particular person who is pursuing aims, values, purposes, which have personal and subjective meaning for him. As a part of this pursuit, he, in some area, "wants to find out." Consequently, if he is to be a good scientist, he immerses himself in the relevant experience, whether that be the physics laboratory, the world of plant or animal life, the hospital, the psychological laboratory or clinic, or whatever. This immersion is complete and subjective, similar to the immersion of the therapist in therapy, described previously. He senses the field in which he is interested. He lives it. He does more than "think" about it—he lets his organism take over and react to it, both on a

---

[2] I would like to mention my special debt to discussions with, and published and unpublished papers by Robert M. Lipgar, Ross L. Mooney, David A. Rodgers, and Eugene Streich. My own thinking has fed so deeply on theirs, and become so intertwined with theirs, that I would be at a loss to acknowledge specific obligations. I only know that in what follows there is much which springs from them, through me. I have also profited from correspondence regarding the paper with Anne Roe and Walter Smet.

knowing and on an unknowing level. He comes to sense more than he could possibly verbalize about his field, and reacts organismically in terms of relationships which are not present in his awareness.

Out of this complete subjective immersion comes a creative forming, a sense of direction, a vague formulation of relationships hitherto unrecognized. Whittled down, sharpened, formulated in clearer terms, this creative forming becomes a hypothesis—a statement of a tentative, personal, subjective faith. The scientist is saying, drawing upon all his known and unknown experience, that "I have a hunch that such and such a relationship exists, and the existence of this phenomenon has relevance to my personal values."

What I am describing is the initial phase of science, probably its most important phase, but one which American scientists, particularly psychologists, have been prone to minimize or ignore. It is not so much that it has been denied as that it has been quickly brushed off. Kenneth Spence has said that this aspect of science is "simply taken for granted."[3] Like many experiences taken for granted, it also tends to be forgotten. It is indeed in the matrix of immediate personal, subjective experience that all science, and each individual scientific research, has its origin.

---

[3] It may be pertinent to quote the sentences from which this phrase is taken. ". . . the data of all sciences have the same origin—namely, the immediate experience of an observing person, the scientist himself. That is to say, immediate experience, the initial matrix out of which all sciences develop, is no longer considered a matter of concern for the scientist. He simply takes it for granted and then proceeds to the task of describing the events occurring in it and discovering and formulating the nature of the relationships holding among them." Kenneth W. Spence, in *Psychological Theory,* M. H. Marx (Ed.), Macmillan, 1951, p. 173.

Checking with reality

The scientist has then creatively achieved his hypothesis, his tentative faith. But does it check with reality? Experience has shown each one of us that it is very easy to deceive himself, to believe something which later experience shows is not so. How can I tell whether this tentative belief has some real relationship to observed facts? I can use, not one line of evidence only, but several. I can surround my observation of the facts with various precautions to make sure I am not deceiving myself. I can consult with others who have also been concerned with avoiding self-deception, and learn useful ways of catching myself in unwarranted beliefs, based on misinterpretation of observations. I can, in short, begin to use all the elaborate methodology which science has accumulated. I discover that stating my hypothesis in operational terms will avoid many blind alleys and false conclusions. I learn that control groups can help me to avoid drawing false inferences. I learn that correlations, and *t* tests and critical ratios and a whole array of statistical procedures can likewise aid me in drawing only reasonable inferences.

Thus scientific methodology is seen for what it truly is—a way of preventing me from deceiving myself in regard to my creatively formed subjective hunches which have developed out of the relationship between me and my material. It is in this context, and perhaps only in this context, that the vast structure of operationism, logical positivism, research design, tests of significance, etc., have their place. They exist, not for themselves, but as servants in the attempt to check the subjective feeling or hunch or hypothesis of a person with the objective fact.

And even throughout the use of such rigorous and impersonal methods, the important choices are all made subjectively by the scientist. To which of a number of hypotheses shall I devote time? What kind of control group is most suitable for avoiding self-deception in this particular research? How far shall I carry the statistical analysis? How much credence may I place in the findings? Each of these is necessarily a subjective personal judgment, emphasizing that the splendid structure of science rests basically upon its subjective use by persons. It is the best instrument we have yet been able to devise to check upon our organismic sensing of the universe.

The findings

If, as scientist, I like the way I have gone about my investigation, if I have been open to all the evidence, if I have selected and used intelligently all the precautions against self-deception which I have been able to assimilate from others or to devise myself, then I will give my tentative belief to the findings which have emerged. I will regard them as a springboard for further investigation and further seeking.

It seems to me that in the best of science, the primary purpose is to provide a more satisfactory and dependable hypothesis, belief, faith, for the investigator himself. To the extent that the scientist is endeavoring to prove something to someone else—an error into which I have fallen more than once—then I believe he is using science to bolster a personal insecurity, and is keeping it from its truly creative role in the service of the person.

In regard to the findings of science, the subjective foundation is well shown in the fact that at times the scientist may refuse to believe his own findings. "The experiment showed thus and so but I believe it is wrong," is a theme which every scientist has experienced at some time or other. Some very fruitful scientific discoveries have grown out of the persistent *disbelief,* by a scientist, in his own findings and those of others. In the last analysis he may place more trust in his total organismic reactions than in the methods of science. There is no doubt that this can result in serious error as well as in scientific discoveries, but it indicates again the leading place of the subjective in the use of science.

Communication of scientific findings

Wading along a coral reef in the Caribbean this morning, I saw a blue fish—I think. If you, quite independently, saw it too, then I feel more confidence in my own observation. This is what is known as intersubjective verification, and it plays an important part in our understanding of science. If I take you (whether in conversation or in print or behaviorally) through the steps I have taken in an investigation, and it seems to you too that I have not deceived myself, and that I have indeed come across a new relationship which is relevant to my values, and that I am justified in having a tentative faith in this relationship, then we have the beginnings of Science with a capital S. It is at this point that we are likely to think we have created a body of scientific knowledge. Actually there is no such body of knowledge. There are only tentative beliefs, existing subjectively, in a number of different persons. If these beliefs are not tentative, then what exists is dogma, not science. If on the other hand, no one but the investigator believes the finding, then this finding is either a personal and deviant matter, an instance of psychopathology, or else it is an unusual truth discovered by a genius, which as yet no one is subjectively ready to believe. This leads me to comment on the group which can put tentative faith in any given scientific finding.

Communication to whom?

It is clear that scientific findings can be communicated only to those who have agreed to the same ground rules of investigation. The Australian bushman will be quite unimpressed with the findings of science regarding bacterial infection. He knows that illness truly is caused by evil spirits. It is only when he too agrees to scientific method as a good means of preventing self-deception, that he will be likely to accept its findings.

But even among those who have adopted the ground rules of science, tentative belief in the findings of a scientific research can only occur where there is a subjective readiness to believe. One could find many examples. Most psychologists are quite ready to believe evidence showing that the lecture system produces significant increments of learning, and quite unready to believe that the turn of an unseen card may be called through an ability labeled extrasensory perception. Yet the scientific evidence for the latter is considerably more impeccable than for the former. Likewise when the so-called "Iowa studies" first came out, indicating that intelligence might be considerably altered by environmental conditions, there was great disbelief among psychologists, and many attacks on the imperfect scientific methods used. The scientific evidence for this finding is not much better today than it was when the Iowa studies first appeared, but the subjective readiness of psychologists to believe such a finding has altered greatly.

A historian of science has noted that empiricists, had they existed at the time, would have been the first to disbelieve the findings of Copernicus.

It appears then that whether I believe the scientific findings of others, or those of my own studies, depends in part on my readiness to put a tentative belief in such findings.[4] One reason we are not particularly aware of this subjective fact is that in the physical sciences particularly, we have gradually agreed that in a very large area of experience we are ready to believe any finding which can be shown to rest upon the rules of the scientific game, properly played.

The use of science

But not only is the origin, process, and conclusion of science something which exists only in the subjective experience of persons—so also is its utilization. "Science" will never depersonalize, or manipulate, or control individuals. It is only persons who can and will do that. This is surely a most obvious and trite ob-

---

[4] One example from my own experience may suffice. In 1941 a research study done under my supervision showed that the future adjustment of delinquent adolescents was best predicted by a measure of their realistic self-understanding and self-acceptance. The instrument was a crude one, but it was a better predictor than measures of family environment, hereditary capacities, social milieu, and the like. At that time I was simply not ready to believe such a finding, because my own belief, like that of most psychologists, was that such factors as the emotional climate in the family and the influence of the peer group were the real determinants of future delinquency and nondelinquency. Only gradually, as my experience with psychotherapy continued and deepened, was it possible for me to give my tentative belief to the findings of this study and of a later one (1944) which confirmed it. (For a report of these two studies see "The role of self understanding in the prediction of behavior" by C. R. Rogers, B. L. Kell, and H. McNeil, *Journal of Consulting Psychology*, 1948, *12*, 174–186.)

servation, yet a deep realization of it has had much meaning for me. It means that the use which will be made of scientific findings in the field of personality is and will be a matter of subjective personal choice—the same type of choice as a person makes in therapy. To the extent that he has defensively closed off areas of his experience from awareness, the person is more likely to make choices which are socially destructive. To the extent that he is open to all phases of his experience we may be sure that this person will be more likely to use the findings and methods of science (or any other tool or capacity) in a manner which is personally and socially constructive.[5] There is, in actuality then, no threatening entity of "Science" which can in any way affect our destiny. There are only people. While many of them are indeed threatening and dangerous in their defensiveness, and modern scientific knowledge multiplies the social threat and danger, this is not the whole picture. There are two other significant facets. (1) There are many other persons who are relatively open to their experience and hence likely to be socially constructive. (2) Both the subjective experience of psychotherapy and the scientific findings regarding it indicate that individuals are motivated to change, and may be helped to change, in the direction of greater openness to experience, and hence in the direction of behavior which is enhancing of self and society, rather than destructive.

To put it briefly, Science can never threaten us. Only persons can do that. And while individuals can be vastly destructive with the tools placed in their

hands by scientific knowledge, this is only one side of the picture. We already have subjective and objective knowledge of the basic principles by which individuals may achieve the more constructive social behavior which is natural to their organismic process of becoming.

A NEW INTEGRATION

What this line of thought has achieved for me is a fresh integration in which the conflict between the "experientialist" and the "scientific" tends to disappear. This particular integration may not be acceptable to others, but it does have meaning to me. Its major tenets have been largely implicit in the preceding section, but I will try to state them here in a way which takes cognizance of the arguments between the opposing points of view.

Science, as well as therapy, as well as all other aspects of living, is rooted in and based upon the immediate, subjective experience of a person. It springs from the inner, total, organismic experiencing which is only partially and imperfectly communicable. It is one phase of subjective living.

It is because I find value and reward in human relationships that I enter into a relationship known as therapeutic, where feelings and cognition merge into one unitary experience which is lived rather than examined, in which awareness is nonreflective, and where I am participant rather than observer. But because I am curious about the exquisite orderliness which appears to exist in the universe and in this relationship I can abstract myself from the experience and look upon it as an observer, making myself and/or others the objects of that observation. As observer I use all of the hunches which grow out of the living experience. To avoid deceiving myself as observer, to gain a

---

[5] I have spelled out much more fully the rationale for this view in two recent papers: "The Concept of the Fully Functioning Person" (unpublished manuscript), and "Toward a Theory of Creativity" *ETC,* 1954, *11,* 249–260.

more accurate picture of the order which exists, I make use of all the canons of science. Science is not an impersonal something, but simply a person living subjectively another phase of himself. A deeper understanding of therapy (or of any other problem) may come from living it, or from observing it in accordance with the rules of science, or from the communication within the self between the two types of experience. As to the subjective experience of choice, it is not only primary in therapy, but it is also primary in the use of scientific method by a person. I have even come to see that freedom of choice is not necessarily antithetical to the determinism which is a part of our framework for thinking scientifically. Since I have recently tried to spell out this relationship elsewhere,[6] I will not take the space to do so here.

What I will do with the knowledge gained through scientific method— whether I will use it to understand, enhance, enrich, or use it to control, manipulate, and destroy—is a matter of subjective choice dependent upon the values which have personal meaning for me. If, out of fright and defensiveness, I block out from my awareness large areas of experience—if I can see only those facts which support my present beliefs, and am blind to all others—if I can see only the objective aspects of life, and cannot perceive the subjective—if in any way I cut off my perception from the full range of its actual sensitivity—then I am likely to be socially destructive, whether I use as tool the knowledge and instruments of science, or the power and emotional

strength of a subjective relationship. And on the other hand if I am open to my experience, and can permit all of the sensings of my intricate organism to be available to my awareness, then I am likely to use myself, my subjective experience, *and* my scientific knowledge, in ways which are realistically constructive.

This, then, is the degree of integration I have currently been able to achieve between two approaches first experienced as conflicting. It does not completely resolve all the issues posed in the earlier section, but it seems to point toward a resolution. It rewrites the problem or reperceives the issue, by putting the subjective, existential person, with the values which he holds, at the foundation and the root of the therapeutic relationship and of the scientific relationship. For science too, at its inception, is an "I-Thou" relationship with the world of perceived objects, just as therapy at its deepest is an "I-Thou" relationship with a person or persons. And only as a subjective person can I enter either of these relationships.

REFERENCES

Rogers, C. R. The concept of the fully functioning person. *Unpublished manuscript,* n.d.

Rogers, C. R. Toward a theory of creativity. *ETC: A Review of General Semantics,* 1954, *11,* 249–260.

Rogers, C. R., Kell, B., & McNeil, H. The role of self-understanding in the prediction of behavior. *Journal of Consulting Psychology,* 1948, *12,* 174–186.

Spence, K. W. Types of constructs in psychology. In M. H. Marx (Ed.), *Psychological Theory.* New York: Macmillan, 1951.

Stephenson, W. Postulates of behaviorism. *Philosophy of Science,* 1953, *20,* 110–120.

---

[6] In my paper on "The Concept of the Fully Functioning Person."

CHAPTER 5

Personalism

Introduction

If there is anyone who deserves the title of "Mr. Personality Theorist" it is Gordon W. Allport (1897–1967), who was the first person in the United States to teach a course in personality. His classic book, *Personality: A Psychological Interpretation* (1937), was the definitive text for some 20 years. In a variety of ways—editing the *Journal of Abnormal and Social Psychology,* doing basic research, writing newspaper articles on rumors and morale during World War II—he contributed more than anyone else to the growth and development of personality as a science.

Allport was not the founder of a school of thought but rather a hard and careful worker in the field of personality. One of his views, reflected in this selection from a speech he gave on being awarded an honor from a learned society, is the basic concept of the importance of traits. You will have the opportunity to read the reasoned conceptualization of a great personality researcher and theorist in the following pages.

GORDON W. ALLPORT
Traits revisited

Years ago I ventured to present a paper before the Ninth International Congress at New Haven (G. W. Allport, 1931). It was entitled "What Is a Trait of Personality?" For me to return to the same topic on this honorific occasion is partly a sentimental indulgence, but partly too it is a self-imposed task to discover whether during the past 36 years I have learned anything new about this central problem in personality theory.

In my earlier paper I made eight bold assertions. A trait, I said,

1. Has more than nominal existence.
2. Is more generalized than a habit.
3. Is dynamic, or at least determinative, in behavior.
4. May be established empirically.
5. Is only relatively independent of other traits.
6. Is not synonymous with moral or social judgment.
7. May be viewed either in the light of the personality which contains it, or in the light of its distribution in the population at large.

To these criteria I added one more:

8. Acts, and even habits, that are inconsistent with a trait are not proof of the nonexistence of the trait.

While these propositions still seem to me defensible they were originally framed

Gordon W. Allport, "Traits Revisited." From *The American Psychologist*, 1966, *21*, 1–10. Copyright © 1966 by the American Psychological Association. Reprinted by permission.

in an age of psychological innocence. They now need reexamination in the light of subsequent criticism and research.

CRITICISM OF THE CONCEPT OF TRAIT

Some critics have challenged the whole concept of trait. Carr and Kingsbury (1938) point out the danger of reification. Our initial observation of behavior is only in terms of adverbs of action: John behaves aggressively. Then an adjective creeps in: John has an aggressive disposition. Soon a heavy substantive arrives, like William James' cow on the doormat: John has a trait of aggression. The result is the fallacy of misplaced concreteness.

The general positivist cleanup starting in the 1930s went even further. It swept out (or tried to sweep out) all entities, regarding them as question-begging redundancies. Thus Skinner (1953) writes:

When we say that a man eats *because* he is hungry, smokes a great deal *because* he has the tobacco habit, fights *because* of the instinct of pugnacity, behaves brilliantly *because* of his intelligence, or plays the piano well *because* of his musical ability, we seem to be referring to causes. But on analysis these phrases prove to be merely redundant descriptions. (p. 31)

It is clear that this line of attack is an assault not only upon the concept of trait, but upon all intervening variables whether they be conceived in terms of expectancies, attitudes, motives, capacities, sentiments, or traits. The resulting postulate of the "empty organism" is by now familiar to us all, and is the scientific credo of some. Carried to its logical extreme this reasoning would scrap the concept of personality itself—an eventuality that seems merely absurd to me.

More serious, to my mind, is the argument against what Block and Bennett (1955) called "traitology" arising from many studies of the variability of a person's behavior as it changes from situation to situation. Every parent knows that an offspring may be a hellion at home and an angel when he goes visiting. A businessman may be hardheaded in the office and a mere marshmallow in the hands of his pretty daughter.

Years ago the famous experiment by La Piere (1934) demonstrated that an innkeeper's prejudice seems to come and go according to the situation confronting him.

In recent months Hunt (1965) has listed various theories of personality that to his mind require revision in the light of recent evidence. Among them he questions the belief that personality traits are the major sources of behavior variance. He, like Miller (1963), advocates that we shift attention from traits to interactions among people, and look for consistency in behavior chiefly in situationally defined roles. Helson (1964) regards trait as the residual effect of previous stimulation, and thus subordinates it to the organism's present adaptation level.

Scepticism is likewise reflected in many investigations of "person perception." To try to discover the traits residing within a personality is regarded as either naive or impossible. Studies, therefore, concentrate only on the *process* of perceiving or judging, and reject the problem of validating the perception and judgment. (Cf. Tagiuri & Petrullo, 1958.)

Studies too numerous to list have ascribed chief variance in behavior to situational factors, leaving only a mild residue to be accounted for in terms of idiosyncratic attitudes and traits. A prime example is Stouffer's study of *The American Soldier* (Stouffer et al., 1949). Differing opinions and preferences are ascribed so far as possible to the GI's age, martial status, educational level, location of residence, length of service, and the like. What remains is ascribed to "attitude." By this procedure personality becomes an appendage to demography (see G. W. Allport, 1950). It is not the integrated structure within the skin that determines behavior, but membership in a group, the person's assigned roles—in short, the prevailing situation. It is especially the sociologists and anthropologists who have this preference for explanations in terms of the "outside structure" rather than the "inside structure" (cf. F. H. Allport, 1955, Ch. 21).

I have mentioned only a few of the many varieties of situationism that flourish today. While not denying any of the evidence adduced I would point to their common error of interpretation. If a child is a hellion at home, an angel outside, he obviously has two contradictory tendencies in his nature, or perhaps a deeper genotype that would explain the opposing phenotypes. If in studies of person perception the process turns out to be complex and subtle, still there would be no perception at all unless there were something out there to perceive and to judge. If, as in Stouffer's studies, soldiers' opinions vary with their martial status or length of service, these opinions are still their own. The fact that my age, sex, social status help form my outlook on life does not change the fact that the outlook is a functioning part of me. Demography deals with distal forces—personality study with proximal forces.

The fact that the innkeeper's behavior varies according to whether he is, or is not, physically confronted with Chinese applicants for hospitality tells nothing about his attitude structure, except that it is complex, and that several attitudes may converge into a given act of behavior.

Nor does it solve the problem to explain the variance in terms of statistical interaction effects. Whatever tendencies exist reside in a person, for a person is the sole possessor of the energy that leads to action. Admittedly different situations elicit differing tendencies from my repertoire. I do not perspire except in the heat, nor shiver except in the cold; but the outside temperature is not the mechanism of perspiring or shivering. My capacities and my tendencies lie within.

To the situationist I concede that our theory of traits cannot be so simple-minded as it once was. We are now challenged to untangle the complex web of tendencies that constitute a person, however contradictory they may seem to be when activated differentially in various situations.

ON THE OTHER HAND

In spite of gunfire from positivism and situationism, traits are still very much alive. Gibson (1941) has pointed out that the "concept of set or attitude is nearly universal in psychological thinking." And in an important but neglected paper—perhaps the last he ever wrote—McDougall (1938) argued that *tendencies* are the "indispensable postulates of all psychology." The concept of *trait* falls into this genre. As Walker (1964) says, trait, however else defined, always connotes an enduring tendency of some sort. It is the structural counterpart of such functional concepts as "expectancy," and "goal-directedness."

After facing all the difficulties of situational and mood variations, also many of the methodological hazards such as response set, halo, and social desirability, Vernon (1964) concludes, "We could go a long way towards predicting behavior if we could assess these stable features in which people differ from one another" (p. 181). The powerful contributions of Thurstone, Guilford, Cattell, and Eysenck, based on factor analysis, agree that the search for traits should provide eventually a satisfactory taxonomy of personality and of its hierarchical structure. The witness of these and other thoughtful writers helps us withstand the pessimistic attacks of positivism and situationism.

It is clear that I am using "trait" as a generic term, to cover all the "permanent possibilities for action" of a generalized order. Traits are cortical, subcortical, or postural dispositions having the capacity to gate or guide specific phasic reactions. It is only the phasic aspect that is visible; the tonic is carried somehow in the still mysterious realm of neurodynamic structure. Traits, as I am here using the term, include long-range sets and attitudes, as well as such variables as "perceptual response dispositions," "personal constructs," and "cognitive styles."

Unlike McClelland (1951) I myself would regard traits (i.e., some traits) as motivational (others being merely stylistic). I would also insist that traits may be studied at two levels: (1) dimensionally, that is as an aspect of the psychology of individual differences, and (2) individually, in terms of *personal dispositions*. (Cf. G. W. Allport, 1961, Ch. 15.) It is the latter approach that brings us closest to the person we are studying.

As for factors, I regard them as a mixed

blessing. In the investigations I shall soon report, factorial analysis, I find, has proved both helpful and unhelpful. My principal question is whether the factorial unit is idiomatic enough to reflect the structure of personality as the clinician, the counselor, or the man in the street apprehends it. Or are factorial dimensions screened so extensively and so widely attenuated—through item selection, correlation, axis manipulation, homogenization, and alphabetical labeling—that they impose an artifact of method upon the personal neural network as it exists in nature?

A HEURISTIC REALISM

This question leads me to propose an epistemological position for research in personality. Most of us, I suspect, hold this position although we seldom formulate it even to ourselves. It can be called a *heuristic realism*.

Heuristic realism, as applied to our problem, holds that the person who confronts us possesses inside his skin generalized action tendencies (or traits) and that it is our job scientifically to discover what they are. Any form of realism assumes the existence of an external structure ("out there") regardless of our shortcomings in comprehending it. Since traits, like all intervening variables, are never directly observed but only inferred, we must expect difficulties and errors in the process of discovering their nature.

The incredible complexity of the structure we seek to understand is enough to discourage the realist, and to tempt him to play some form of positivistic gamesmanship. He is tempted to settle for such elusive formulations as: "If we knew enough about the situation we wouldn't need the concept of personality"; or

"One's personality is merely the way other people see one"; or "There is no structure in personality but only varying degrees of consistency in the environment."

Yet the truly persistent realist prefers not to abandon his commitment to find out what the other fellow is really like. He knows that his attempt will not wholly succeed, owing partly to the complexity of the object studied, and partly to the inadequacy of present methods. But unlike Kant, who held that the *Ding an Sich* is doomed to remain unknowable, he prefers to believe that it is at least partly or approximately knowable.

I have chosen to speak of *heuristic* realism, because to me special emphasis should be placed on empirical methods of discovery. In this respect heuristic realism goes beyond naive realism.

Taking this epistemological point of view, the psychologist first focuses his attention on some limited slice of personality that he wishes to study. He then selects or creates methods appropriate to the empirical testing of his hypothesis that the cleavage he has in mind is a trait (either a dimensional trait or a personal disposition). He knows that his present purposes and the methods chosen will set limitations upon his discovery. If, however, the investigation achieves acceptable standards of validation he will have progressed far toward his identification of traits. Please note, as with any heuristic procedure the process of discovery may lead to important corrections of the hypothesis as originally stated.

Empirical testing is thus an important aspect of heuristic realism, but it is an empiricism restrained throughout by rational considerations. Galloping empiricism, which is our present occupational disease, dashes forth like a headless horseman. It has no rational objective; uses no rational method other than mathematical; reaches no rational conclusion. It lets the discordant data sing for themselves. By contrast heuristic realism says, "While we are willing to rest our case for traits on empirical evidence, the area we carve out for study should be rationally conceived, tested by rational methods; and the findings should be rationally interpreted."

THREE ILLUSTRATIVE STUDIES

It is now time for me to illustrate my argument with sample studies. I have chosen three in which I myself have been involved. They differ in the areas of personality carved out for study, in the methods employed, and in the type of traits established. They are alike, however, in proceeding from the standpoint of heuristic realism. The presentation of each study must of necessity be woefully brief. The first illustrates what might be called *meaningful dimensionalism;* the second *meaningful covariation;* the third *meaningful morphogenesis.*

Dimensions of values

The first illustration is drawn from a familiar instrument, dating almost from the stone age, *The Study of Values* (Allport & Vernon, 1931). While some of you have approved it over the years, and some disapproved, I use it to illustrate two important points of my argument.

First, the instrument rests on an a priori analysis of one large region of human personality, namely, the region of generic evaluative tendencies. It seemed to me 40 years ago, and seems to me now, that Eduard Spranger (1922) made a persuasive case for the existence of six

fundamental types of subjective evaluation or *Lebensformen.* Adopting this rational starting point we ourselves took the second step, to put the hypothesis to empirical test. We asked: Are the six dimensions proposed—the *theoretic,* the *economic,* the *esthetic, social, political,* and *religious*— measurable on a multidimensional scale? Are they reliable and valid? Spranger defined the six ways of looking at life in terms of separate and distinct ideal types, although he did not imply that a given person belongs exclusively to one and only one type.

It did not take long to discover that when confronted with a forced-choice technique people do in fact subscribe to all six values, but in widely varying degrees. Within any pair of values, or any quartet of values, their forced choices indicate a reliable pattern. Viewed then as empirical continua, rather than as types, the six value directions prove to be measurable, reproducible, and consistent. But are they valid? Can we obtain external validation for this particular a priori conception of traits? The test's *Manual* (Allport & Vernon, 1931) contains much such evidence. Here I would add a bit more, drawn from occupational studies with women subjects. (The evidence for men is equally good.) The data in Table 5.1 are derived partly from

TABLE 5.1. Mean scores for occupational groups of women: Study of values

	Female collegiate norms (N = 2,475)	Graduate nurses training for teaching (N = 328)	Graduate students of business administration (N = 77)	Peace Corps teachers (N = 131)
Theoretical. .	36.5	40.2	37.3	40.6
Economic. . .	36.8	32.9	40.4	29.9
Esthetic	43.7	43.1	46.8	49.3
Social.	41.6	40.9	35.0	41.2
Political	38.0	37.2	41.8	39.7
Religious . . .	43.1	45.7	38.7	39.2

the *Manual,* partly from Guthrie and McKendry (1963) and partly from an unpublished study by Elizabeth Moses.

For present purposes it is sufficient to glance at the last three columns. For the *theoretic* value we note that the two groups of teachers or teachers in preparation select this value significantly more often than do graduate students of business administration. Conversely the young ladies of business are relatively more *economic* in their choices. The results for the *esthetic* value probably reflect the higher level of liberal arts background for the last two groups. The *social* (philanthropic) value is relatively low for the business group, whereas the *political* (power) value is relatively high. Just why nurses should more often endorse the *religious* value is not immediately clear.

Another study of external validation, showing the long-range predictive power of the test is an unpublished investigation by Betty Mawardi. It is based on a follow-up of Wellesley graduates 15 years after taking the Study of Values.

Table 5.2 reports the significant deviations (at the 5% level or better) of various occupational groups from the mean scores of Wellesley students. In virtually every case we find the deviation meaningful (even necessary) for the occupation in question. Thus women in business are significantly high in

economic interests; medical, government, and scientific workers in *theoretical;* literary and artistic workers in *esthetic;* social workers in *social;* and religious workers in *religious* values.

One must remember that to achieve a relatively high score on one value, one must deliberately slight others. For this reason it is interesting to note in the table the values that are systematically slighted in order to achieve a higher score on the occupationally relevant value. (In the case of social workers it appears that they "take away" more or less uniformly from other values in order to achieve a high social value.)

Thus, even at the college age it is possible to forecast in a general way modal vocational activity 15 years hence. As Newcomb, Turner, and Converse (1965) say, this test clearly deals with "inclusive values" or with "basic value postures" whose generality is strikingly broad. An evaluative posture toward life saturates, or guides, or gates (choose your own metaphor) specific daily choices over a long expanse of years.

One reason I have used this illustration of trait research is to raise an important methodological issue. The six values are not wholly independent. There is a slight tendency for theoretic and esthetic values to covary; likewise for economic and political values; and so too with social and religious. Immediately the thought arises,

TABLE 5.2. Significant deviations of scores on the study of values for occupational groups of Wellesley alumni from Wellesley mean scores

Occupational groups	N	Theoretical	Economic	Esthetic	Social	Political	Religious
Business workers	64	Lower	Higher				
Medical workers	42	Higher	Lower			Lower	
Literary workers	40	Higher	Lower	Higher			
Artistic workers	37			Higher	Lower		
Scientific workers	28	Higher		Lower			
Government workers	24	Higher			Lower		Lower
Social workers	26				Higher		
Religious workers	11					Lower	Higher

"Let's factor the whole matrix and see what orthogonal dimensions emerge." This step has been taken several times (see *Manual*), but always with confusing results. Some investigators discover that fewer than six factors are needed—some that we need more. And in all cases the clusters that emerge seem strange and unnamable. Here is a case, I believe, where our empiricism should submit to rational restraint. The traits as defined are meaningful, reliably measured, and validated. Why sacrifice them to galloping gamesmanship?

Covariation: Religion and prejudice

Speaking of covariation I do not mean to imply that in restraining our empirical excesses we should fail to explore the patterns that underlie covariation when it seems reasonable to do so.

Take, for example, the following problem. Many investigations show conclusively that on the broad average church attenders harbor more ethnic prejudice than nonattenders. (Some of the relevant studies are listed by Argyle, 1959, and by Wilson, 1960.) At the same time many ardent workers for civil rights are religiously motivated. From Christ to Gandhi and to Martin Luther King we note that equimindedness has been associated with religious devoutness. Here then is a paradox: Religion makes prejudice; it also unmakes prejudice.

First we tackle the problem rationally and form a hypothesis to account for what seems to be a curvilinear relation. A hint for the needed hypothesis comes from *The Authoritarian Personality* (Adorno, Frenkel-Brunswik, Levinson, & Sanford, 1950) which suggests that acceptance of institutional religion is not as important as the *way* in which it is accepted. Argyle (1959) sharpens the

hypothesis. He says, "It is not the genuinely devout who are prejudiced but the conventionally religious" (p. 84).

In our own studies we have tentatively assumed that two contrasting but measurable forms of religious orientation exist. The first form we call the *extrinsic* orientation, meaning that for the church-goer religious devotion is not a value in its own right, but is an instrumental value serving the motives of personal comfort, security, or social status. (One man said he went to church because it was the best place to sell insurance.) Elsewhere I have defined this utilitarian orientation toward religion more fully (G. W. Allport, 1960, 1963). Here I shall simply mention two items from our scale, agreement with which we assume indicates the extrinsic attitude:

What religion offers me most is comfort when sorrows and misfortune strike.

One reason for my being a church member is that such membership helps to establish a person in the community.

By contrast the *intrinsic* orientation regards faith as a supreme value in its own right. Such faith strives to transcend self-centered needs, takes seriously the commandment of brotherhood that is found in all religions, and seeks a unification of being. Agreement with the following items indicated an intrinsic orientation:

My religious beliefs are what really lie behind my whole approach to life.

If not prevented by unavoidable circumstances, I attend church, on the average (more than once a week) (once a week) (two or three times a month) (less than once a month).

This second item is of considerable interest, for many studies have found that it is the irregular attenders who are by far the most prejudiced (e.g., Holtzmann, 1956; Williams, 1964). They take their

TABLE 5.3. Correlations between measures of religious orientation among churchgoers and various prejudice scales

Denominational sample	N	r
Unitarian	50	
Extrinsic—anti-Catholicism . . .		.56
Intrinsic—anti-Catholicism. . . .		—.36
Extrinsic—anti-Mexican		.54
Intrinsic—anti-Mexican		—.42
Catholic	66	
Extrinsic—anti-Negro.		.36
Intrinsic—anti-Negro		—.49
Nazarene	39	
Extrinsic—anti-Negro.		.41
Intrinsic—anti-Negro		—.44
Mixed*	207	
Extrinsic—anti-Semitic.		.65

* From Wilson (1960).

religion in convenient doses and do not let it regulate their lives.

Now for a few illustrative results in Table 5.3. If we correlate the extrinsicness of orientation with various prejudice scales we find the hypothesis confirmed. Likewise, as predicted, intrinsicness of orientation is negatively correlated with prejudice.

In view of the difficulty of tapping the two complex traits in question, it is clear from these studies that our rationally derived hypothesis gains strong support. We note that the trend is the same when different denominations are studied in relation to differing targets for prejudice.

Previously I have said that empirical testing has the ability to correct or extend our rational analysis of patterns. In this particular research the following unexpected fact emerges. While those who approach the intrinsic pole of our continuum are on the average less prejudiced than those who approach the extrinsic pole, a number of subjects show themselves to be disconcertingly illogical. They accept both intrinsically worded items and extrinsically worded items, even when these are contradictory, such as:

My religious beliefs are what really lie behind my whole approach to life.

Though I believe in my religion, I feel there are many more important things in my life.

It is necessary, therefore, to inspect this sizable group of muddleheads who refuse to conform to our neat religious logic. We call them "inconsistently proreligious." They simply like religion; for them it has "social desirability" (cf. Edwards, 1957).

TABLE 5.4. Types of religious orientation and mean prejudice scores

	Mean prejudice scores			
	Consistently intrinsic	Consistently extrinsic	Moderately inconsistent (proreligion)	Extremely inconsistent (proreligion)
Anti-Negro .	28.7	33.0	35.4	37.9
Anti-Semitic.	22.6	24.6	28.0	30.1

Note: $N = 309$, mixed denominations. All differences significant at .01 level.

The importance of recognizing this third mode of religious orientation is seen by comparing the prejudice scores for the groups presented in Table 5.4. In the instruments employed the lowest possible prejudice score is 12, the highest possible, 48. We note that the mean prejudice score rises steadily and significantly from the intrinsically consistent to the inconsistently proreligious. Thus subjects with an undiscriminated proreligious response set are on the average most prejudiced of all.

Having discovered the covariation of prejudice with both the extrinsic orientation and the "pro" response set, we are faced with the task of rational explanation. One may, I think, properly argue that these particular religious attitudes are instrumental in nature; they provide safety, security, and status—all within a self-serving frame. Prejudice, we know, performs much the same function within some personalities. The needs for status, security, comfort, and a feeling of self-rightness are served by both ethnic hostility and by tailoring one's religious orientation to one's convenience. The economy of other lives is precisely the reverse: It is their religion that centers their existence, and the only ethnic attitude compatible with this intrinsic orientation is one of brotherhood, not of bigotry.

This work, along with the related investigations of Lenski (1961), Williams (1964), and others, signifies that we gain important insights when we refine our conception of the nature of the religious sentiment and its functions. Its patterning properties in the economy of a life are diverse. It can fuse with bigotry or with brotherhood according to its nature.

As unfinished business I must leave the problem of nonattenders. From data available it seems that the unchurched are less prejudiced on the average than either the extrinsic or the inconsistent churchgoers, although apparently more prejudiced on the average than those whose religious orientation is intrinsic. Why this should be so must form the topic of future research.

Personal dispositions: An idiomorphic approach

The final illustration of heuristic realism has to do with the search for the natural cleavages that mark an individual life. In this procedure there is no reference to common dimensions, no comparison with other people, except as is implied by the use of the English language. If, as Allport and Odbert (1936) have found, there are over 17,000 available trait names, and if these may be used in combinations, there is no real point in arguing that the use of the available lexicon of a language necessarily makes

all trait studies purely nomothetic (dimensional).

A series of 172 published *Letters from Jenny* (G. W. Allport, 1965) contains enough material for a rather close clinical characterization of Jenny's personality, as well as for careful quantitative and computational analysis. While there is no possibility in this case of obtaining external validation for the diagnosis reached by either method, still by employing both procedures an internal agreement is found which constitutes a type of empirical validation for the traits that emerge.

The *clinical* method in this case is close to common sense. Thirty-nine judges listed the essential characteristics of Jenny as they saw them. The result was a series of descriptive adjectives, 198 in number. Many of the selected trait names were obviously synonymous; and nearly all fell readily into eight clusters.

The *quantitative* analysis consisted of coding the letters in terms of 99 tag words provided by the lexicon of the General Inquirer (Stone, Bales, Namenwirth, & Ogilvie, 1962). The frequency with which these basic tag words are associated with one another in each letter forms the basis for a factor analysis (see G. W. Allport, 1965, p. 200).

Table 5.5 lists in parallel fashion the clusters obtained by clinical judgment based on a careful reading of the series,

TABLE 5.5. Central traits in Jenny's personality as determined by two methods

Common-Sense Traits	Factorial Traits
Quarrelsome-suspicious } Aggressive }	Aggression
Self-centered (possessive)	Possessiveness
Sentimental	{ Need for affiliation { Need for family acceptance
Independent-autonomous	Need for autonomy
Esthetic-artistic	Sentience
Self-centered (self-pitying)	Martyrdom
(No parallel)	Sexuality
Cynical-morbid	(No parallel)
Dramatic-intense	("Overstate")

along with the factors obtained by Jeffrey Paige in his unpublished factorial study.

In spite of the differences in terminology the general paralleling of the two lists establishes some degree of empirical check on both of them. We can say that the direct common-sense perception of Jenny's nature is validated by quantification, coding, and factoring. (Please note that in this case factor analysis does not stand alone, but is tied to a parallel rational analysis.)

While this meaningful validation is clearly present, we gain (as almost always) additional insights from our attempts at empirical validation of the traits we initially hypothesize. I shall point to one instance of such serendipity. The tag words (i.e., the particular coding system employed) are chiefly substantives. For this reason, I suspect, *sexuality* can be identified by coding as a minor factor; but it is not perceived as an independent quality by the clinical judges. On the other hand, the judges, it seems, gain much from the running style of the letters. Since the style is constant it would not appear in a factorial analysis which deals only with variance within the whole. Thus the common-sense traits *cynical-morbid* and *dramatic-intense* are judgments of a pervading expressive style in Jenny's personality and seem to be missed by factoring procedure.

Here, however, the computer partially redeems itself. Its program assigns the tag "overstate" to strong words such as *always, never, impossible,* etc., while words tagged by "understate" indicate reserve, caution, qualification. Jenny's letters score exceedingly high on overstate and exceedingly low on understate, and so in a skeletonized way the method does in part detect the trait of dramatic intensity.

One final observation concerning this essentially idiomorphic trait study.

Elsewhere I have reported a small investigation (G. W. Allport, 1958) showing that when asked to list the "essential characteristics" of some friend, 90% of the judges employ between 3 and 10 trait names, the average number being 7.2. An "essential characteristic" is defined as "any trait, quality, tendency, interest, that you regard as of major importance to a description of the person you select." There is, I submit, food for thought in the fact that in these two separate studies of Jenny, the common-sense and the factorial, only 8 or 9 central traits appear. May it not be that the essential traits of a person are few in number if only we can identify them?

The case of Jenny has another important bearing on theory. In general our besetting sin in personality study is irrelevance, by which I mean that we frequently impose dimensions upon persons when the dimensions fail to apply. (I am reminded of the student who was told to interview women patients concerning their mothers. One patient said that her mother had no part in her problem and no influence on her life; but that her aunt was very important. The student answered, "I'm sorry, but our method requires that you tell about your mother." The *method* required it, but the *life* did not.)

In ascribing a list of traits to Jenny we may seem to have used a dimensional method, but such is not the case. Jenny's traits emerge from her own personal structure. They are not imposed by predetermined but largely irrelevant schedules.

CONCLUSION

What then have I learned about traits in the last four decades? Well, I have learned that the problem cannot be avoided—

neither by escape through positivism or situationism, nor through statistical interaction effects. Tendencies, as McDougall (1937) insisted, remain the "indispensable postulates of all psychology."

Further, I have learned that much of our research on traits is overweighted with methodological preoccupation; and that we have too few restraints holding us to the structure of a life as it is lived. We find ourselves confused by our intemperate empiricism which often yields unnamable factors, arbitrary codes, unintelligible interaction effects, and sheer flatulence from our computers.

As a safeguard I propose the restraints of "heuristic realism" which accepts the common-sense assumption that persons are real beings, that each has a real neuropsychic organization, and that our job is to comprehend this organization as well as we can. At the same time our profession uniquely demands that we go beyond common-sense data and either establish their validity or else—more frequently—correct their errors. To do so requires that we be guided by theory in selecting our trait slices for study, that we employ rationally relevant methods, and be strictly bound by empirical verification. In the end we return to fit our findings to an improved view of the person. Along the way we regard him as an objectively real being whose tendencies we can succeed in knowing—at least in part—beyond the level of unaided common sense. In some respects this recommended procedure resembles what Cronbach and Meehl (1955) call "construct validation," with perhaps a dash more stress on external validation.

I have also learned that while the major foci of organization in a life may be few in number, the network of organization, which includes both minor and con-

tradictory tendencies, is still elusively complex.

One reason for the complexity, of course, is the need for the "inside" system to mesh with the "outside" system—in other words, with the situation. While I do not believe that traits can be defined in terms of interaction effects (since all tendencies draw their energy from within the person), still the vast variability of behavior cannot be overlooked. In this respect I have learned that my earlier views seemed to neglect the variability induced by ecological, social, and situational factors. This oversight needs to be repaired through an adequate theory that will relate the inside and outside systems more accurately.

The fact that my three illustrative studies are so diverse in type leads me to a second concession: that trait studies depend in part upon the investigator's own purposes. He himself constitutes a situation for his respondents, and what he obtains from them will be limited by his purpose and his method. But this fact need not destroy our belief that, so far as our method and purpose allow, we can elicit real tendencies.

Finally, there are several problems connected with traits that I have not here attempted to revisit. There are, for example, refinements of difference between trait, attitude, habit, sentiment, need, etc. Since these are all inside tendencies of some sort, they are for the present occasion all "traits" to me. Nor am I here exploring the question to what extent traits are motivational, cognitive, affective, or expressive. Last of all, and with special restraint, I avoid hammering on the distinction between common (dimensional, nomothetic) traits such as we find in any standard profile, and individual traits (personal dispositions) such as we find in single lives, e.g.,

Jenny's. (Cf. G. W. Allport, 1961, Ch. 15, also 1962.) Nevitt Sanford (1963) has written that by and large psychologists are "unimpressed" by my insisting on this distinction. Well, if this is so in spite of four decades of labor on my part, and in spite of my efforts in the present paper—I suppose I should in all decency cry "uncle" and retire to my corner.

REFERENCES

Adorno, T. W., Frenkel-Brunswik, Else, Levinson, D. J., & Sanford, R. N. *The authoritarian personality.* New York: Harpers, 1950.

Allport, F. H. *Theories of perception and the concept of structure.* New York: Wiley, 1955.

Allport, G. W. What is a trait of personality? *Journal of Abnormal and Social Psychology,* 1931, *25,* 368–372.

Allport, G. W. Review of S. A. Stouffer et al., *The American soldier. Journal of Abnormal and Social Psychology,* 1950, *45,* 168–172.

Allport, G. W. What units shall we employ? In G. Lindzey (Ed.), *Assessment of human motives.* New York: Rinehart, 1958.

Allport, G. W. Religion and prejudice. In *Personality and social encounter.* Boston: Beacon Press, 1960.

Allport, G. W. *Pattern and growth in personality.* New York: Holt, Rinehart & Winston, 1961.

Allport, G. W. The general and the unique in psychological science. *Journal of Personality,* 1962, *30,* 405–422.

Allport, G. W. Behavioral science, religion and mental health. *Journal of Religion and Health,* 1963, *2,* 187–197.

Allport, G. W. (Ed.) *Letters from Jenny.* New York: Harcourt, Brace & World, 1965.

Allport, G. W., & Odbert, H. S. Trait-names: A psycholexical study. *Psychological Monographs,* 1936, *47,* (1, Whole No. 211).

Allport, G. W., & Vernon, P. E. *A study of values.* Boston: Houghton Mifflin, 1931. (Reprinted: With G. Lindzey, 3rd ed., 1960.)

Argyle, M. *Religious behaviour.* Glencoe, Ill.: Free Press, 1959.

Block, J., & Bennett, Lillian. The assessment of communication. *Human Relations,* 1955, *8,* 317–325.

Carr, H. A., & Kingsbury, F. A. The concept of trait. *Psychological Review.* 1938, *45,* 497–524.

Cronbach, L. J., & Meehl, P. E. Construct validity in psychological tests. *Psychological Bulletin,* 1955, *52,* 281–302.

Edwards, A. L. *The social desirability variable in personality assessment and research.* New York: Dryden Press, 1957.

Gibson, J. J. A critical review of the concept of set in contemporary experimental psychology. *Psychological Bulletin,* 1941, *38,* 781–817.

Guthrie, G. M., & McKendry, Margaret S. Interest patterns of Peace Corps volunteers in a teaching project. *Journal of Educational Psychology,* 1963, *54,* 261–267.

Helson, H. *Adaptation-level theory.* New York: Harper & Row, 1964.

Holtzman, W. H. Attitudes of college men toward nonsegregation in Texas schools. *Public Opinion Quarterly,* 1956, *20,* 559–569.

Hunt, J. McV. Traditional personality theory in the light of recent evidence. *American Scientist,* 1965, *53,* 80–96.

La Piere, R. Attitudes vs. actions. *Social Forces, 1934,* 230–237.

Lenski, G. *The religious factor.* Garden City, N.Y.: Doubleday, 1961.

McClelland, D. C. *Personality.* New York: Dryden Press, 1951.

McDougall, W. Tendencies as indispensable postulates of all psychology. In *Proceedings of the XI International Congress on Psychology: 1937,* pp. 157–170. Paris: Alcan, 1938.

Miller, D. R. The study of social relationships: Situation, identity, and social interaction. In S. Koch (Ed.), *Psychology: A study of a science* (Vol. 5, *The process areas, the person, and some applied fields: Their place in psychology and the social sciences,* pp. 639–737). New York: McGraw-Hill, 1963.

Newcomb, T. M., Turner, H. H., & Converse, P. E. *Social psychology: The study of human interaction.* New York: Holt, Rinehart & Winston, 1965.

Sanford, N. Personality: Its place in psychology. In S. Koch (Ed.), *Psychology: A study of a science. Vol. 5. The process areas, the person, and some applied fields: Their place in psychology and in science.* New York: McGraw-Hill, 1963. Pp. 488–592.

Skinner, B. F. *Science and human behavior.* New York: Macmillan, 1953.

Spranger, E. *Lebensformen* (3d ed.). Halle: Niemeyer, 1922. (Translated: P. Pigors, *Types of men.* Halle: Niemeyer, 1928.)

Stone, P. J., Bales, R. F., Namenwirth, J. Z., & Ogilvie, D. M. The General Inquirer: A computer system for content analysis and retrieval based on the sentence as a unit of information. *Behavioral Science,* 1962, *7* (4), 484–498.

Stouffer, S. A., et al. *The American soldier* (2 vols.). Princeton: Princeton University Press, 1949. 2 vols.

Tagiuri, R., & Petrullo, L. *Person perception and interpersonal behavior.* Stanford: Stanford University Press, 1958.

Vernon, P. E. *Personality assessment: A critical survey.* London: Methuen, 1964.

Walker, E. L. Psychological complexity as a basis for a theory of motivation and choice. In D. Levine (Ed.), *Nebraska symposium on motivation: 1964.* Lincoln: University of Nebraska Press, 1964.

Williams, R. M., Jr. *Strangers next door.* Englewood Cliffs, N.J.: Prentice-Hall, 1964.

Wilson, W. C. Extrinsic religious values and prejudice. *Journal of Abnormal and Social Psychology,* 1960, *60,* 286–288.

CHAPTER 6

Operant Reinforcement

Introduction

One of the most influential and also most controversial of psychologists today is Burrhus F. Skinner (1904–   ), whose name is closely associated with behavior modification, or, more precisely, *operant reinforcement*. Skinner, who is perhaps best known for the so-called "Skinner Box," in which animals are placed and are fed only if they respond in desired ways, is a man of unusual breadth and depth, not merely an animal trainer.

A good example on his concerns is freedom, a theme to which he has addressed himself a number of times. This particular selection, now more than 20 years old, gives a good example of his thinking. His well-known utopian novel, *Walden Two* (1948), expands on this theme—that freedom is in danger unless man learns how to control technology, including the technology of human behavior.

Perhaps more than any other living psychologist, Skinner has influenced American college teaching in this field, and he is a direct intellectual descendant of John B. Watson. In addition to other investigations, Skinner pioneered in teaching devices such as programmed instruction.

Interestingly enough, Skinner (like Gordon Allport) objects to being labeled a theorist and would apparently much prefer to be called an experimentalist. You can decide which is appropriate in terms of the following selection.

B.F. SKINNER
Freedom and the control of men

The second half of the twentieth century may be remembered for its solution of a curious problem. Although Western democracy created the conditions responsible for the rise of modern science, it is now evident that it may never fully profit from that achievement. The so-called "democratic philosophy" of human behavior to which it also gave rise is increasingly in conflict with the application of the methods of science to human affairs. Unless this conflict is somehow resolved, the ultimate goals of democracy may be long deferred.

I

Just as biographers and critics look for external influences to account for the traits and achievements of the men they study, so science ultimately explains behavior in terms of "causes" or conditions which lie beyond the individual himself. As more and more causal relations are demonstrated, a practical corollary becomes difficult to resist: it should be possible to *produce* behavior according to plan simply by arranging the proper conditions. Now, among the specifications which might reasonably be submitted to a behavioral technology are these: Let men be happy, informed, skillful, well behaved and productive.

This immediate practical implication of a science of behavior has a familiar ring, for it recalls the doctrine of human

perfectibility of eighteenth- and nineteenth-century humanism. A science of man shares the optimism of that philosophy and supplies striking support for the working faith that men can build a better world and, through it, better men. The support comes just in time, for there has been little optimism of late among those who speak from the traditional point of view. Democracy has become "realistic," and it is only with some embarrassment that one admits today to perfectionistic or utopian thinking.

The earlier temper is worth considering, however. History records many foolish and unworkable schemes for human betterment, but almost all the great changes in our culture which we now regard as worthwhile can be traced to perfectionistic philosophies. Governmental, religious, educational, economic and social reforms follow a common pattern. Someone believes that a change in a cultural practice—for example, in the rules of evidence in a court of law, in the characterization of man's relation to God, in the way children are taught to read and write, in permitted rates of interest, or in minimal housing standards—will improve the condition of men: by promoting justice, permitting men to seek salvation more effectively, increasing the literacy of a people, checking an inflationary trend, or improving public health and family relations, respectively. The underlying hypothesis is always the same: that a different physical or cultural environment will make a different and better man.

B. F. Skinner, "Freedom and the Control of Men." From *American Scholar*, 1955, *25*, 47–65. Reprinted with permission of the author.

The scientific study of behavior not only justifies the general pattern of such proposals; it promises new and better hypotheses. The earliest cultural practices must have originated in sheer accidents. Those which strengthened the group survived with the group in a sort of natural selection. As soon as men began to propose and carry out changes in practice for the sake of possible consequences, the evolutionary process must have accelerated. The simple practice of making changes must have had survival value. A further acceleration is now to be expected. As laws of behavior are more precisely stated, the changes in the environment required to bring about a given effect may be more clearly specified. Conditions which have been neglected because their effects were slight or unlooked for may be shown to be relevant. New conditions may actually be created, as in the discovery and synthesis of drugs which affect behavior.

This is no time, then, to abandon notions of progress, improvement or, indeed, human perfectibility. The simple fact is that man is able, and now as never before, to lift himself by his own bootstraps. In achieving control of the world of which he is a part, he may learn at last to control himself.

II

Timeworn objections to the planned improvement of cultural practices are already losing much of their force. Marcus Aurelius was probably right in advising his readers to be content with a haphazard amelioration of mankind. "Never hope to realize Plato's republic," he sighed, ". . . for who can change the opinions of men? And without a change of sentiments what can you make but reluctant slaves and hypocrites?" He was thinking, no doubt, of contemporary patterns of control based upon punishment or the threat of punishment which, as he correctly observed, breed only reluctant slaves of those who submit and hypocrites of those who discover modes of evasion. But we need not share his pessimism, for the opinions of men can be changed. The techniques of indoctrination which were being devised by the early Christian Church at the very time Marcus Aurelius was writing are relevant, as are some of the techniques of psychotherapy and of advertising and public relations. Other methods suggested by recent scientific analyses leave little doubt of the matter.

The study of human behavior also answers the cynical complaint that there is a plain "cussedness" in man which will always thwart efforts to improve him. We are often told that men do not want to be changed, even for the better. Try to help them, and they will outwit you and remain happily wretched. Dostoevsky claimed to see some plan in it. "Out of sheer ingratitude," he complained, or possibly boasted, "man will play you a dirty trick, just to prove that men are still men and not the keys of a piano. . . . And even if you could prove that a man is only a piano key, he would still do something out of sheer perversity—he would create destruction and chaos—just to gain his point. . . . And if all this could in turn be analyzed and prevented by predicting that it would occur, then man would deliberately go mad to prove his point." This is a conceivable neurotic reaction to inept control. A few men may have shown it, and many have enjoyed Dostoevsky's statement because they tend to show it. But that such perversity is a fundamental reaction of the human organism to controlling conditions is sheer nonsense.

So is the objection that we have no way

of knowing what changes to make even though we have the necessary techniques. That is one of the great hoaxes of the century—a sort of booby trap left behind in the retreat before the advancing front of science. Scientists themselves have unsuspectingly agreed that there are two kinds of useful propositions about nature—facts and value judgments—and that science must confine itself to "what is," leaving "what ought to be" to others. But with what special sort of wisdom is the non-scientist endowed? Science is only effective knowing, no matter who engages in it. Verbal behavior proves upon analysis to be composed of many different types of utterances, from poetry and exhortation to logic and factual description, but these are not all equally useful in talking about cultural practices. We may classify useful propositions according to the degrees of confidence with which they may be asserted. Sentences about nature range from highly probable "facts" to sheer guesses. In general, future events are less likely to be correctly described than past. When a scientist talks about a projected experiment, for example, he must often resort to statements having only a moderate likelihood of being correct; he calls them hypotheses.

Designing a new cultural pattern is in many ways like designing an experiment. In drawing up a new constitution, outlining a new educational program, modifying a religious doctrine, or setting up a new fiscal policy, many statements must be quite tentative. We cannot be sure that the practices we specify will have the consequences we predict, or that the consequences will reward our efforts. This is in the nature of such proposals. They are not value judgments—they are guesses. To confuse and delay the improvement of cultural practices by

quibbling about the word *improve* is itself not a useful practice. Let us agree, to start with, that health is better than illness, wisdom better than ignorance, love better than hate, and productive energy better than neurotic sloth.

Another familiar objection is the "political problem." Though we know what changes to make and how to make them, we still need to control certain relevant conditions, but these have long since fallen into the hands of selfish men who are not going to relinquish them for such purposes. Possibly we shall be permitted to develop areas which at the moment seem unimportant, but at the first signs of success the strong men will move in. This, it is said, has happened to Christianity, democracy and communism. There will always be men who are fundamentally selfish and evil, and in the long run innocent goodness cannot have its way. The only evidence here is historical, and it may be misleading. Because of the way in which physical science developed, history could until very recently have "proved" that the unleashing of the energy of the atom was quite unlikely, if not impossible. Similarly, because of the order in which processes in human behavior have become available for purposes of control, history may seem to prove that power will probably be appropriated for selfish purposes. The first techniques to be discovered fell almost always to strong, selfish men. History led Lord Acton to believe that power corrupts, but he had probably never encountered absolute power, certainly not in all its forms, and had no way of predicting its effect.

An optimistic historian could defend a different conclusion. The principle that if there are not enough men of good will in the world the first step is to create more seems to be gaining recognition. The

Marshall Plan (as originally conceived), Point Four, the offer of atomic materials to power-starved countries—these may or may not be wholly new in the history of international relations, but they suggest an increasing awareness of the power of governmental good will. They are proposals to make certain changes in the environments of men for the sake of consequences which should be rewarding for all concerned. They do not exemplify a disinterested generosity, but an interest which is the interest of everyone. We have not yet seen Plato's philosopher-king, and may not want to, but the gap between real and utopian government is closing.

III

But we are not yet in the clear, for a new and unexpected obstacle has arisen. With a world of their own making almost within reach, men of good will have been seized with distaste for their achievement. They have uneasily rejected opportunities to apply the techniques and findings of science in the service of men, and as the import of effective cultural design has come to be understood, many of them have voiced an outright refusal to have any part in it. Science has been challenged before when it has encroached upon institutions already engaged in the control of human behavior; but what are we to make of benevolent men, with no special interests of their own to defend, who nevertheless turn against the very means of reaching long-dreamed-of goals?

What is being rejected, of course, is the scientific conception of man and his place in nature. So long as the findings and methods of science are applied to human affairs only in a sort of remedial patch-work, we may continue to hold any view of human nature we like. But as the use of science increases, we are forced to accept the theoretical structure with which science represents its facts. The difficulty is that this structure is clearly at odds with the traditional democratic conception of man. Every discovery of an event which has a part in shaping a man's behavior seems to leave so much the less to be credited to the man himself; and as such explanations become more and more comprehensive, the contribution which may be claimed by the individual himself appears to approach zero. Man's vaunted creative powers, his original accomplishments in art, science and morals, his capacity to choose and our right to hold him responsible for the consequences of his choice—none of these is conspicuous in this new self-portrait. Man, we once believed, was free to express himself in art, music and literature, to inquire into nature, to seek salvation in his own way. He could initiate action and make spontaneous and capricious changes of course. Under the most extreme duress some sort of choice remained to him. He could resist any effort to control him, though it might cost him his life. But science insists that action is initiated by forces impinging upon the individual, and that caprice is only another name for behavior for which we have not yet found a cause.

In attempting to reconcile these views it is important to note that the traditional democratic conception was not designed as a description in the scientific sense but as a philosophy to be used in setting up and maintaining a governmental process. It arose under historical circumstances and served political purposes apart from which it cannot be properly understood. In rallying men against tyranny it was necessary that the individual be strengthened, that he be taught that he had rights and could govern himself. To give the common man a new conception of his worth, his dignity, and his power to save himself, both here and hereafter, was often the only resource of the revolutionist. When democratic principles were put into practice, the same doctrines were used as a working formula. This is exemplified by the notion of personal responsibility in Anglo-American law. All governments make certain forms of punishment contingent upon certain kinds of acts. In democratic countries these contingencies are expressed by the notion of responsible choice. But the notion may have no meaning under governmental practices formulated in other ways and would certainly have no place in systems which did not use punishment.

The democratic philosophy of human nature is determined by certain political exigencies and techniques, not by the goals of democracy. But exigencies and techniques change; and a conception which is not supported for its accuracy as a likeness—is not, indeed, rooted in fact at all—may be expected to change too. No matter how effective we judge current democratic practices to be, how highly we value them or how long we expect them to survive, they are almost certainly not the *final* form of government. The philosophy of human nature which has been useful in implementing them is also almost certainly not the last word. The ultimate achievement of democracy may be long deferred unless we emphasize the real aims rather than the verbal devices of democratic thinking. A philosophy which has been appropriate to one set of political exigencies will defeat its purpose if, under other circumstances, it prevents us from applying to human affairs the science of man which probably nothing but democracy itself could have produced.

IV

Perhaps the most crucial part of our democratic philosophy to be reconsidered is our attitude toward freedom—or its reciprocal, the control of human behavior. We do not oppose all forms of control because it is "human nature" to do so. The reaction is not characteristic of all men under all conditions of life. It is an attitude which has been carefully engineered, in large part by what we call the "literature" of democracy. With respect to some methods of control (for example, the threat of force), very little engineering is needed, for the techniques or their immediate consequences are objectionable. Society has suppressed these methods by branding them "wrong," "illegal" or "sinful." But to encourage these attitudes toward objectionable forms of control, it has been necessary to disguise the real nature of certain indispensable techniques, the commonest examples of which are education, moral discourse, and persuasion. The actual procedures appear harmless enough. They consist of supplying information, presenting opportunities for action, pointing out logical relationships, appealing to reason or "enlightened understanding," and so on. Through a masterful piece of misrepresentation, the illusion is fostered that these procedures do not involve the control of behavior; at most, they are simply ways of "getting someone to change his mind." But analysis not only reveals the presence of well-defined behavioral processes, it demonstrates a kind of control no less inexorable, though in some ways more acceptable, than the bully's threat of force.

Let us suppose that someone in whom we are interested is acting unwisely—he is careless in the way he deals with his friends, he drives too fast, or he holds his golf club the wrong way. We could probably help him by issuing a series of commands: don't nag, don't drive over sixty, don't hold your club that way.

Much less objectionable would be "an appeal to reason." We could show him how people are affected by his treatment of them, how accident rates rise sharply at higher speeds, how a particular grip on the club alters the way the ball is struck and corrects a slice. In doing so we resort to verbal mediating devices which emphasize and support certain "contingencies of reinforcement"—that is, certain relations between behavior and its consequences—which strengthen the behavior we wish to set up. The same consequences would possibly set up the behavior without our help, and they eventually take control no matter which form of help we give. The appeal to reason has certain advantages over the authoritative command. A threat of punishment, no matter how subtle, generates emotional reactions and tendencies to escape or revolt. Perhaps the controllee merely "feels resentment" at being made to act in a given way, but even that is to be avoided. When we "appeal to reason," he "feels freer to do as he pleases." The fact is that we have exerted *less* control than in using a threat; since other conditions may contribute to the result, the effect may be delayed or, possibly in a given instance, lacking. But if we have worked a change in his behavior at all, it is because we have altered relevant environmental conditions, and the processes we have set in motion are just as real and just as inexorable, if not as comprehensive, as in the most authoritative coercion.

"Arranging an opportunity for action" is another example of disguised control. The power of the negative form has already been exposed in the analysis of censorship. Restriction of opportunity is recognized as far from harmless. As Ralph Barton Perry said in an article which appeared in the Spring, 1953,

Pacific Spectator, "Whoever determines what alternatives shall be made known to man controls what that man shall choose *from.* He is deprived of freedom in proportion as he is denied access to *any* ideas, or is confined to any range of ideas short of the totality of relevant possibilities." But there is a positive side as well. When we present a relevant state of affairs, we increase the likelihood that a given form of behavior will be emitted. To the extent that the probability of action has changed, we have made a definite contribution. The teacher of history controls a student's behavior (or, if the reader prefers, "deprives him of freedom") just as much in *presenting* historical facts as in suppressing them. Other conditions will no doubt affect the student, but the contribution made to his behavior by the presentation of material is fixed and, within its range, irresistible.

The methods of education, moral discourse, and persuasion are acceptable not because they recognize the freedom of the individual or his right to dissent, but because they make only *partial* contributions to the control of his behavior. The freedom they recognize is freedom from a more coercive form of control. The dissent which they tolerate is the possible effect of other determiners of action. Since these sanctioned methods are frequently ineffective, we have been able to convince ourselves that they do not represent control at all. When they show too much strength to permit disguise, we give them other names and suppress them as energetically as we suppress the use of force. Education grown too powerful is rejected as propaganda or "brain-washing," while really effective persuasion is decried as "undue influence," "demaguery," "seduction," and so on.

If we are not to rely solely upon accident for the innovations which give rise to cultural evolution, we must accept the fact that some kind of control of human behavior is inevitable. We cannot use good sense in human affairs unless someone engages in the design and construction of environmental conditions which affect the behavior of men. Environmental changes have always been the condition for the improvement of cultural patterns, and we can hardly use the more effective methods of science without making changes on a grander scale. We are all controlled by the world in which we live, and part of that world has been and will be constructed by men. The question is this: Are we to be controlled by accident, by tyrants, or by ourselves in effective cultural design?

The danger of the misuse of power is possibly greater than ever. It is not allayed by disguising the facts. We cannot make wise decisions if we continue to pretend that human behavior is not controlled, or if we refuse to engage in control when valuable results might be forthcoming. Such measures weaken only ourselves, leaving the strength of science to others. The first step in a defense against tyranny is the fullest possible exposure of controlling techniques. A second step has already been taken successfully in restricting the use of physical force. Slowly, and as yet imperfectly, we have worked out an ethical and governmental design in which the strong man is not allowed to use the power deriving from his strength to control his fellow men. He is restrained by a superior force created for that purpose—the ethical pressure of the group, or more explicit religious and governmental measures. We tend to distrust superior forces, as we currently hesitate to relinquish sovereignty in order to set up an international police force. But it is only through such counter-control

that we have achieved what we call peace—a condition in which men are not permitted to control each other through force. In other words, control itself must be controlled.

Science has turned up dangerous processes and materials before. To use the facts and techniques of a science of man to the fullest extent without making some monstrous mistake will be difficult and obviously perilous. It is no time for self-deception, emotional indulgence, or the assumption of attitudes which are no longer useful. Man is facing a difficult test. He must keep his head now, or he must start again—a long way back.

V

Those who reject the scientific conception of man must, to be logical, oppose the methods of science as well. The position is often supported by predicting a series of dire consequences which are to follow if science is not checked. A recent book by Joseph Wood Krutch, *The Measure of Man,* is in this vein. Mr. Krutch sees in the growing science of man the threat of an unexampled tyranny over men's minds. If science is permitted to have its way, he insists, "we may never be able really to think again." A controlled culture will, for example, lack some virtue inherent in disorder. We have emerged from chaos through a series of happy accidents, but in an engineered culture it will be "impossible for the unplanned to erupt again." But there is no virtue in the accidental character of an accident, and the diversity which arises from disorder can not only be duplicated by design but vastly extended. The experimental method is superior to simple observation just because it multiplies "accidents" in a systematic coverage of the possibilities. Technology offers many familiar examples. We no longer wait for immunity to disease to develop from a series of accidental exposures, nor do we wait for natural mutations in sheep and cotton to produce better fibers; but we continue to make use of such accidents when they occur, and we certainly do not prevent them. Many of the things we value have emerged from the clash of ignorant armies on darkling plains, but it is not therefore wise to encourage ignorance and darkness.

It is not always disorder itself which we are told we shall miss but certain admirable qualities in men which flourish only in the presence of disorder. A man rises above an unpropitious childhood to a position of eminence, and since we cannot give a plausible account of the action of so complex an environment, we attribute the achievement to some admirable faculty in the man himself. But such "faculties" are suspiciously like the explanatory fictions against which the history of science warns us. We admire Lincoln for rising above a deficient school system, but it was not necessarily something *in him* which permitted him to become an educated man in spite of it. His educational environment was certainly unplanned, but it could nevertheless have made a full contribution to his mature behavior. He was a rare man, but the circumstances of his childhood were rare too. We do not give Franklin Delano Roosevelt the same credit for becoming an educated man with the help of Groton and Harvard, although the same behavioral processes may have been involved. The founding of Groton and Harvard somewhat reduced the possibility that fortuitous combinations of circumstances would erupt to produce other Lincolns. Yet the founders can hardly be condemned for attacking an admirable human quality.

Another predicted consequence of a science of man is an excessive uniformity. We are told that effective control—whether governmental, religious, educational, economic or social—will produce a race of men who differ from each other only through relatively refractory genetic differences. That would probably be bad design, but we must admit that we are not now pursuing another course from choice. In a modern school, for example, there is usually a syllabus which specifies what every student is to learn by the end of each year. This would be flagrant regimentation if anyone expected every student to comply. But some will be poor in particular subjects, others will not study, others will not remember what they have been taught, and diversity is assured. Suppose, however, that we someday possess such effective educational techniques that every student will in fact be put in possession of all the behavior specified in a syllabus. At the end of the year, all students will correctly answer all questions on the final examination and "must all have prizes." Should we reject such a system on the grounds that in making all students excellent it has made them all alike? Advocates of the theory of a special faculty might contend that an important advantage of the present system is that the good student learns *in spite of* a system which is so defective that it is currently producing bad students as well. But if really effective techniques are available, we cannot avoid the problem of design simply by preferring the status quo. At what point should education be deliberately inefficient?

Such predictions of the havoc to be wreaked by the application of science to human affairs are usually made with surprising confidence. They not only show a faith in the orderliness of human behavior; they presuppose an established body of knowledge with the help of which it can be positively asserted that the changes which scientists propose to make will have quite specific results—albeit not the results they foresee. But the predictions made by the critics of science must be held to be equally fallible and subject also to empirical test. We may be sure that many steps in the scientific design of cultural patterns will produce unforeseen consequences. But there is only one way to find out. And the test must be made, for if we cannot advance in the design of cultural patterns with absolute certainty, neither can we rest completely confident of the superiority of the status quo.

VI

Apart from their possibly objectionable consequences, scientific methods seem to make no provision for certain admirable qualities and faculties which seem to have flourished in less explicitly planned cultures; hence they are called "degrading" or "lacking in dignity." (Mr. Krutch has called the author's *Walden Two* an "ignoble Utopia.") The conditioned reflex is the current whipping boy. Because conditioned reflexes may be demonstrated in animals, they are spoken of as though they were exclusively subhuman. It is implied, as we have seen, that no behavioral processes are involved in education and moral discourse or, at least, that the processes are exclusively human. But men do show conditioned reflexes (for example, when they are frightened by all instances of the control of human behavior because some instances engender fear), and animals do show processes similar to the human behavior involved in instruction and moral discourse. When Mr. Krutch asserts that " 'Conditioning' is achieved

by methods which by-pass or, as it were, short-circuit those very reasoning faculties which education proposes to cultivate and exercise," he is making a technical statement which needs a definition of terms and a great deal of supporting evidence.

If such methods are called "ignoble" simply because they leave no room for certain admirable attributes, then perhaps the practice of admiration needs to be examined. We might say that the child whose education has been skillfully planned has been deprived of the right to intellectual heroism. Nothing has been left to be admired in the way he acquires an education. Similarly, we can conceive of moral training which is so adequate to the demands of the culture that men will be good practically automatically, but to that extent they will be deprived of the right to moral heroism, since we seldom admire automatic goodness. Yet if we consider the end of morals rather than certain virtuous means, is not "automatic goodness" a desirable state of affairs? Is it not, for example, the avowed goal of religious education? T. H. Huxley answered the question unambiguously: "If some great power would agree to make me always think what is true and do what is right, on condition of being a sort of clock and wound up every morning before I got out of bed, I should close instantly with the offer." Yet Mr. Krutch quotes this as the scarcely credible point of view of a "protomodern" and seems himself to share T. S. Eliot's contempt for ". . . systems so perfect / That no one will need to be good."

"Having to be good" is an excellent example of an expendable honorific. It is inseparable from a particular form of ethical and moral control. We distinguish between the things we *have* to do to avoid punishment and those we *want* to do for rewarding consequences. In a culture which did not resort to punishment we should never "have" to do anything except with respect to the punishing contingencies which arise directly in the physical environment. And we are moving toward such a culture, because the neurotic, not to say psychotic, by-products of control through punishment have long since led compassionate men to seek alternative techniques. Recent research has explained some of the objectionable results of punishment and has revealed resources of at least equal power in "positive reinforcement." It is reasonable to look forward to a time when man will seldom "have" to do anything, although he may show interest, energy, imagination and productivity far beyond the level seen under the present system (except for rare eruptions of the unplanned).

What we have to do we do with *effort*. We call it "work." There is no other way to distinguish between exhausting labor and the possibly equally energetic but rewarding activity of play. It is presumably good cultural design to replace the former with the latter. But an adjustment in attitudes is needed. We are much more practiced in admiring the heroic labor of a Hercules than the activity of one who works without having to. In a truly effective educational system the student might not "have to work" at all, but that possibility is likely to be received by the contemporary teacher with an emotion little short of rage.

We cannot reconcile traditional and scientific views by agreeing upon *what* is to be admired or condemned. The question is whether anything is to be so treated. Praise and blame are cultural practices which have been adjuncts of the prevailing system of control in Western democracy. All peoples do not engage in

them for the same purposes or to the same extent, nor, of course, are the same behaviors always classified in the same way as subject to praise or blame. In admiring intellectual and moral heroism and unrewarding labor, and in rejecting a world in which these would be uncommon, we are simply demonstrating our own cultural conditioning. By promoting certain tendencies to admire and censure, the group of which we are a part has arranged for the social reinforcement and punishment needed to assure a high level of intellectual and moral industry. Under other and possibly better controlling systems, the behavior which we now admire would occur, but not under those conditions which make it admirable, and we should have no reason to admire it because the culture would have arranged for its maintenance in other ways.

To those who are stimulated by the glamorous heroism of the battlefield, a peaceful world may not be a better world. Others may reject a world without sorrow, longing or a sense of guilt because the relevance of deeply moving works of art would be lost. To many who have devoted their lives to the struggle to be wise and good, a world without confusion and evil might be an empty thing. A nostalgic concern for the decline of moral heroism has been a dominating theme in the work of Aldous Huxley. In *Brave New World* he could see in the application of science to human affairs only a travesty on the notion of the Good (just as George Orwell, in *1984,* could foresee nothing but horror). In a recent issue of *Esquire,* Huxley has expressed the point this way: "We have had religious revolutions, we have had political, industrial, economic and nationalistic revolutions. All of them, as our descendants will discover, were but ripples in an ocean of conservatism—

trivial by comparison with the psychological revolution toward which we are so rapidly moving. *That* will really be a revolution. When it is over, the human race will give no further trouble.'' (Footnote for the reader of the future: This was not meant as a happy ending. Up to 1956 men had been admired, if at all, either for causing trouble or alleviating it. Therefore—)

It will be a long time before the world can dispense with heroes and hence with the cultural practice of admiring heroism, but we move in that direction whenever we act to prevent war, famine, pestilence and disaster. It will be a long time before man will never need to submit to punishment environments or engage in exhausting labor, but we move in that direction whenever we make food, shelter, clothing and labor-saving devices more readily available. We may mourn the passing of heroes but not the conditions which make for heroism. We can spare the self-made saint or sage as we spare the laundress on the river's bank struggling against fearful odds to achieve cleanliness.

.   .   .   .   .

VII

Far from being a threat to the tradition of Western democracy, the growth of a science of man is a consistent and probably inevitable part of it. In turning to the external conditions which shape and maintain the behavior of men, while questioning the reality of inner qualities and faculties to which human achievements were once attributed, we turn from the ill-defined and remote to the observable and manipulable. Though it is a painful step, it has far-reaching consequences, for it not only sets higher standards of human welfare but shows us how to meet them. A change in a theory of human nature cannot change the facts. The achievements of man in science, art, literature, music and morals will survive any interpretation we place upon them. The uniqueness of the individual is unchallenged in the scientific view. Man, in short, will remain man. (There will be much to admire for those who are so inclined. Possibly the noblest achievement to which man can aspire, even according to present standards, is to accept himself for what he is, as that is revealed to him by the methods which he devised and tested on a part of the world in which he had only a small personal stake.)

If Western democracy does not lose sight of the aims of humanitarian action, it will welcome the almost fabulous support of its own science of man and will strengthen itself and play an important role in building a better world for everyone. But if it cannot put its ''democratic philosophy'' into proper historical perspective—if, under the control of attitudes and emotions which it generated for other purposes, it now rejects the help of science—then it must be prepared for defeat. For if we continue to insist that science has nothing to offer but a new and more horrible form of tyranny, we may produce just such a result by allowing the strength of science to fall into the hands of despots. And if, with luck, it were to fall instead to men of good will in other political communities, it would be perhaps a more ignominious defeat; for we should then, through a miscarriage of democratic principles, be forced to leave to others the next step in man's long struggle to control nature and himself.

CHAPTER **7**

Personal Constructs

Introduction

George A. Kelly (1905–1967) and B. F. Skinner probably differ more in their views on personality than any other two theorists discussed in this book. Kelly's is the most interior of all systems, while Skinner's is the most exterior. Kelly, in effect, says that personality is how a person interprets life's events, how he construes reality.

Kelly, an original thinker, seems to have sprung from an unsowed field. In this he is like several other theorists, especially Carl Rogers. His provocative way of thinking and communicating is evident in the selection presented here. It is indeed a pity that Kelly's system seems to be dying out.

A personal note may be of some interest. In planning for the companion volume, *Current Personality Theories* (Itasca, Ill.: F. E. Peacock Publishers, Inc., 1977) I had not seriously considered including a chapter or section on Kelly. However, two analyses, one based on judges and one on a computer-type analysis, showed that Kelly's theory of *personal constructs* was so different from any other that it was in a dimension of its own. Therefore his theory was included rather than more popular examples such as those of Harry Stack Sullivan or Erich Fromm.

You are in for an intellectual treat now—watching a subtle, superior mind at work in this selection.

GEORGE A. KELLY
Man's construction of his alternatives

This paper, throughout, deals with half-truths only. Nothing that it contains is, or is intended to be, wholly true. The theoretical statements propounded are no more than partially accurate constructions of events which, in turn, are no more than partially perceived. Moreover, what we propose, even in its truer aspects, will eventually be overthrown and displaced by something with more truth in it. Indeed, our theory is frankly designed to contribute effectively to its own eventual overthrow and displacement.

Half-truths vs. infallibility

We think this is a good way for psychologists to theorize. When a scientist propounds a theory he has two choices: he can claim that what he says has been dictated to him by the real nature of things, or he can take sole responsibility for what he says and claim only that he has offered one man's hopeful construction of the realities of nature. In the first instance he makes a claim to objectivity in behalf of his theory, the scientist's equivalent of a claim to infallibility. In the second instance he offers only the hope that he may have hit upon some partial truth that may serve as a clue to inventing something better and he invites others to follow this clue to see what they can make of it. In this latter

instance he does not hold up his theoretical proposal to be judged so much in terms of whether or not it is the truth at last—for he assumes from the outset that ultimate truth is not so readily at hand—but in terms of whether his proposition seems to lead toward and give way to fresh propositions, propositions which, in turn, may be more true than anything else has been thus far.

One of the troubles with what are otherwise good theories in the various fields of science is the claim to infallibility that is so often built into their structure. Even those theories which are built upon objective observation or upon firsthand experience make this claim by their failure to admit that what is observed is not revealed but only construed. In fact, the more objectively supported the theory at the time of its inception, the more likely it is to cause trouble after it has served its purpose. A conclusion supported by the facts is likely to be a good one at the time it is drawn. But, because facts themselves are open to reconstruction, such a theory soon becomes a dogmatism that may serve only to blind us to new perceptions of the facts.

Take, for example, the body of theoretical assumptions that Freud propounded out of his experience with psychoanalysis. There was so much truth in what he said—so much new truth. But, like most theories of our times, psychoanalysis, as a theory, was conceived as an absolute truth, and, moreover, it was designed in such a manner that it tended to defy both logical

George A. Kelly, "Man's Construction of His Alternatives." Reprinted with permission from Gardner Lindzey (ed.), *Assessment of Human Motives* (New York: Rinehart & Winston, 1956), pp. 33–61.

examination and experimental validation. As the years go by, Freudianism, which deserves to be remembered as a brave outpost on the early frontier of psychological thought, is condemned to end its days as a crumbling stockade of proprietary dogmatism. Thus, as with other farseeing claims to absolute truth, history will have a difficult time deciding whether Freudianism did more to accelerate psychological progress during the first half of the twentieth century than it did to impede progress during the last half.

This business of absolutism in modern science and the havoc it creates is a matter that has been given a good deal of thought in recent decades. It has been attacked on several fronts. First of all, modern science has itself attacked older dogmatisms through its widespread use of the method of experimentation. But experimentation, if assumed to be a way of receiving direct revelations from nature, can often be found living quite happily side by side with modern dogmatisms of the lowest order.

There is nothing especially revelational about events that happen in an experimental laboratory—other events that happen elsewhere are just as real and are just as worthy of attention. Even the fact that an event took place in a manner predicted by the experimenter gives it no particular claim to being a special revelation from nature. That an experimenter's predictions come true means only that he has hit upon one of many possible systems for making predictions that come true. He may be no more than a wee bit closer to a genuine understanding of things as they really are. Indeed, the fact that he has hit upon one such way of predicting outcomes may even blind him to alternatives which might have proved far more productive in the long run.

Absolutism is coming under other forms of attack. It has been pointed out, for example, that the subject-predicate form of our Indo-European languages has led us to confound objects with what is said about them. Thus every time we open our mouths to say something we break forth with a dogmatism. Each sentence, instead of sounding like a proposal of an idea to be examined in the light of personal experience, echoes through the room like the disembodied rumblings of an oracle. Even as we try to describe a theory of personal constructions of events, one that stands in contrast to theories that claim to spring from events directly, we are caught up in the assumptions and structure of the very language upon which we depend for communication. In view of this fact, we can think of no better way of disclaiming the assumptions of our language than by introducing this paper with the paradoxical statement that we are proposing half-truths only.

Motivation questioned

A second feature of this paper is its outright repudiation of the notion of motivation. Since the topic of the conference series, in which we have been so graciously invited to participate, is "The Assessment of Human Motives," such a repudiation may appear to be in bad taste. It seems a little like being honored with an invitation to preach a sermon in church, and then taking advantage of the solemn occasion in order to present the case for atheism. Yet the present volume on the assessment of human motives may not lose flavor from this kind of seasoning. Perhaps one chapter of heresy may even strengthen the reader's convictions about human motives, just as an occasional rousing speech on atheism might do more than a monotony of sermons to bring a church congregation face to face with its own convictions—or lack of them.

Certainly the repudiation of "motives" as a construct is a major undertaking, not to be ventured into without some thought being given to its consequences. For a period roughly corresponding to the Christian era, metaphysics, including psychology, has conceptualized its spiritual realm in terms of a trichotomy, just as Christianity has envisioned itself in terms of a trinity. The classic trichotomy is variously called by such terms as cognition, conation, and affection; or intellect, will, and emotion; or even, in somewhat more modern terms, thought, action, and feeling. Psychologists keep coming back to this trichotomous division, perhaps because they have never been able to venture beyond it. That we now say we propose to abandon motives will seem to many listeners a kind of unforgivable sin, something like the unforgivable sin of rejecting the Holy Ghost.

In the classic psychological trichotomy, cognition, on the one hand, has been viewed as a realm governed by verbalized rationality, while affection, on the other, has been viewed as a very chaotic, though often pleasant, place where inarticulate irrationality is in command. Conation, the middle category which deals with behavior or determination to act, has been caught between the other two, sometimes believed to be swayed by the rationality of the cognitive mind but at other times suspected of having a secret allegiance to the whimsical irrationality of feeling and emotion.

REPUDIATION OF MOTIVATION AS A CONSTRUCT

Reconciling rationality and irrationality

Because the topic of motivation falls into this disputed area where modern man has had such a difficult time reconciling rationality with irrationality, we propose to start our serious discussion at this particular point. We should like to deal with those matters which are called rational—and therefore by quirk of our language structure assumed actually to be rational—together with those matters which are called irrational—for the same reason—both in the very same psychological terms. In doing so we shall, if our previous experiences repeat themselves, be perceived by some persons to be capitulating to the classic rationalism of Thomas Aquinas and by others as giving hostages to the supposed intuitive irrationality of Freud, Rogers, or Sullivan. Not that we really mind being bracketed with any of these great names; but rather the burden of our comments, it seems to us, rests on other grounds.

This is the risk we take. Why? Why will some see this as conforming to classic rationality and others see it as lapsing into irrationality? We have already mentioned the tendency to confound objects with what is said about them. Some philosophers, Bertrand Russell being possibly the first and foremost, have seen this tendency to confound words and facts as being embedded in the subject-predicate structure of our language. But it involves also the highly questionable *law of the excluded middle,* a law accepted as a basic principle of logic for the past twenty-four hundred years, though now under sporadic attack.

Law of the excluded middle. What this law proposes is that for any proposition there is only one alternative. I call an object a spade. There is only one alternative to calling it a spade—to call it not a spade! I can't say, "to heck with it," or "who cares," or "who brought that up," or that the object cannot be sensibly called either a spade or not a spade; I have to stick with one or the other. Once the object is accused of being a spade it has to plead innocent or guilty, or I have to plead its innocence or guilt in its behalf.

Subject-predicate fallacy. Now, if we combine this dictum with the subject-predicate mode of thought we put ourselves in a stringent position with respect to our world. We call an object a spade. Not only do we therefore imply that it is a spade because we cannot say that it is not a spade, but we put the onus of choosing between the two alternatives on the object itself. We disclaim responsibility for our propositions and try to make the objects we talk about hang themselves on the horns of the dilemmas we invent for dealing with them. If a woman is accused of being a witch, she has to be either a witch or not a witch—it is up to her. The speaker disclaims all responsibility for the dilemma he has imposed upon her.

For centuries Western man has roamed his world impaling every object he has met on the horns of the dilemmas he chose to fashion out of his language. In fact, an individual, if he was very bright and had a vocabulary well stocked with psychological terms, could do a pretty substantial job of impaling himself. Recently so many people have learned to do it in so many ingenious ways that apparently half the world will have to be trained in psychotherapy in order to keep the other half off its own hooks. Yet, even so, it may be that what most of the psychotherapists are doing is lifting people off one set of hooks and hanging them on other more comfortable, more socially acceptable, hooks.

Let us see if we can make this point a little clearer. For example, on occasion I may say of myself—in fact, on occasion I *do* say of myself—"I am an introvert." "I," the subject, "am an introvert," the predicate. The language form of the statement clearly places the onus of being an introvert on the subject—on me. What I actually am, the words say, is an introvert.

The listener, being the more or less credulous person to whom I make the statement, says to himself, "So George Kelly is an introvert—I always suspected he was." Or he may say, "Him an introvert? He's no introvert," a response which implies scarcely less credulity on the part of my listener. Yet the proper interpretation of my statement is that I *construe* myself to be an introvert, or, if I am merely being coy or devious, I am inveigling *my listener into construing* me in terms of introversion. The point that gets lost in the shuffle of words is the psychological fact that I have identified myself in terms of a personal construct—"introversion." If my listener is uncritical enough to be taken in by this quirk of language, he may waste a lot of time either in believing that he must construe me as an introvert or in disputing the point.

In clinical interviewing, and particularly in psychotherapeutic interviewing, when the clinician is unable to deal with such a statement as a personal construction, rather than as fact or fallacy, the hour is likely to come to a close with both parties annoyed with each other and both dreading their next appointment. But more than this, if I say of myself that I am an introvert, I am likely to be caught in my own subject-predicate trap. Even the inner self—my self—becomes burdened with the onus of actually being an introvert or of finding some way to be rid of the introversion that has climbed on my back. What has happened is that I named myself with a name and, having done so, too quickly forgot who invented the name and what he had on his mind at the time. From now on I try frantically to cope with what I have called myself. Moreover, my family and friends are often quite willing to join in the struggle.

A third possibility—relevance. Now, back specifically to the law of the excluded middle. Here, too, we find a failure to take into account a psychological fact, the fact that human thought is essentially constructive in nature and that even the thinking of logicians and mathematicians is no exception. I say that I am an introvert—whatever that is. If I now go ahead and apply the law of the excluded middle I come up with the dilemma that I must continue to claim either to be an introvert or not an introvert—one or the other. But is this˙ necessarily so? May not introversion turn out to be a construct which is altogether irrelevant? If it is not relevant is it any more meaningful to say that I am not an introvert than to say that I am? Yet classical logic fails to make any distinctions between its negatives and its irrelevancies, while modern psychology ought to make it increasingly clear to each of us that no proposition has more than a limited range of relevance, beyond which it makes no sense either to affirm or deny. So we now ought to visualize propositions which are not universal in their range of application but useful only within a restricted range of convenience. For each proposition, then, we see three alternatives, not two: It can be affirmed, it can be denied, or it can be declared irrelevant in the context to which it is applied. Thus we argue, not for the inclusion of the long excluded middle—something between the "Yes" and the "No"—but for a third possibility that is beyond the meaningful range of yes and no.

Apply this more psychological way of thinking to the proposition, "I am an introvert." Instead of lying awake trying to decide whether I am or I am not an introvert, or taking frantic steps, as so many do, to prove that I am not, I simply go off to sleep with the thought that, until the construct of introversion is demonstrated to be of some practical usefulness in my case, there is no point of trying to decide whether I am or not, or what to do about it if I am. Thus we treat the subject-predicate problem and the excluded middle problem in pretty much the same way—we insist on demonstrating relevance before we lose any sleep over a proposition.

Summary. Let us try to summarize our criticisms of the two features of Western thought which went unchallenged for more than two thousand years. First of all, there is the dogmatism of subject-predicate language structure that is often presented under the guise of objectivity. According to this dogmatism, when I say that Professor Lindzey's left shoe is an "introvert," everyone looks at his shoe as if this were something his shoe was responsible for. Or if I say that Professor Cattell's head is "discussive," everyone looks over at him, as if the proposition had popped out of his head instead of out of mine. Don't look at his head! Don't look at that shoe! Look at me; I'm the one who is responsible for the statement. After you figure out what I mean you can look over there to see if you make any sense out of shoes and heads by construing them the way I do. It will not be easy to do this, for it means abandoning one of the most ancient ways of thinking and talking to ourselves.

As far as the law of the excluded middle in this particular context is concerned, whether or not a person has ever heard of this law, or whether he has ever sat down to puzzle out a similar notion on his own, the law is an everyday feature of nearly every educated man's more intellectualized thought processes. The law says, assuming that the term "introvert" ever has meaning, that that shoe, at which we looked a moment ago, has to be construed either as an introvert or as not an introvert; it has simply got to be seen as one or the other. There is no middle ground.

Some people argue against the law of the excluded middle by claiming that the shoe could be a little introvertish, but not completely introvert, or that it could be a little nonintrovertish, though not wholly nonintrovert. This is the notion of shades of gray that can be perceived between black and white. But this notion of reifying the excluded middle by talking about grays is not what we are proposing. In fact, we see this gray thinking as a form of concretism that merely equivocates and fails to get off the ground into the atmosphere of abstraction.

What we are saying, instead, is that "introversion" may well enough be a term that has meaning in some contexts, but that it does not go well with shoes. Since it does not apply to shoes, it makes no more sense to say that Professor Lindzey's left shoe is not an introvert than to say that it is. Thus we see three possibilities, not two, as the law would insist: The shoe is an introvert; the shoe is not an introvert; and the shoe does not fall within the context of the construct of introversion vs. nonintroversion. The third possibility is not a middle proposition in any intermediate sense but rather a kind of outside—beyond-the-pale—kind of proposition.

So much for a summary of this section of our discourse. In spite of our criticisms, let us not say that the inadequacies we have pointed out prevented our language and thought from leading us along a path of progress. Remember that we believe that half-truths

serve to pave the way toward better truths. Time spent with a half-truth is not necessarily wasted; it may have been exceedingly profitable. In order to appreciate a half-truth one has to examine two things; what it replaced and what it led up to. Let us see what the kind of thing we have been criticizing actually replaced. Let us compare it with more primitive modes of language and thought.

**From magic to fallacy
in two thousand years**

Western thinking, which has pretty much overrun the world recently, takes the very practical view that a word is beholden to the object it is used to describe. The object determines it. This is a moderate improvement over the so-called magical way of thinking which has it that the object is beholden to the word. The improvement has been the basis of scientific thinking, particularly the experimentalism that has psychologists and others bubbling with so much excitement these days.

Let us see how the improvement works. Say the word and the object will jump out at you—that is magical thinking—very bad! Prod the object and the word will jump out at you—that is objective thinking; very good! Worth publishing! Say "Genie, come genie" and hope that a genie will pop out of the bottle—that is magical; no good! Kick the bottle until either a genie pops out or does not pop out—now that is *science!*

But there is something a person can do besides shouting, "Genie, come genie," or kicking the bottle through a series of statistically controlled experiments. He can ask himself, and the other people who have worked themselves up over the genie business, just what they are trying to get at. This is what the skilled psychotherapist does in dealing with the thoughts of man. His approach is based on the notion that "genie" is a construct someone erected in order to find his way through a maze of events. It is not a substitute for experimentation but a useful prelude to it. It is a proper substitute, however, for random measurement of verbalizations.

Meaning and the man

This is the way we see the matter: Magical thinking has it that the object is beholden to the word—when the word is spoken, the object must produce itself. So-called objective thinking, under which it has been possible to make great scientific progress, says that the word is beholden to the object—kick the bottle to validate the word. If, however, we build our sciences on a recognition of the psychological nature of thought we take a third position—the word is beholden to the person who utters it, or, more properly speaking, to the *construction* system, that complex of personal constructs of which it is a part.

This concern with personal meaning should prove no less valuable to the scientist than it has to the psychotherapist. It stems from the notion that, when a person uses a word, he is expressing, in part, his own construction of events. One comes to understand the communication, therefore, not by assuming the magical existence of the word's counterpart in reality and then invoking that counterpart by incantation; nor does he understand it by scrounging through a pile of accumulated facts to see if one of them will own up to the word; rather, he understands the communication by examining the personal construction system within which the word arose and within which it came to have intimate meaning for the individual who attempted to communicate.

Now what happens to motivation?

How does this apply to motives? We have already said that we do not even use the term as a part of our own construction system, yet it enters our system, perforce, as a matter to be construed. If a person catches his friends in the act of using such a term as "motives," how does he act? Does he put his fingers in his ears? Does he start kicking the bottle of reality to see if it produces the phenomenon? If it fails, shall he accuse his friends of irrationality? We think not.

Again, if we so much as start to inquire into motivation as a construct, do we not thereby reify it? Or if we deal with a realm which so many believe is essentially irrational in nature, are we not capitulating ourselves to irrationality? And if we attempt to think rationally about the behavior of an individual who is acting irrationally, are we not closing our eyes to an irrationality that actually exists? Are we not hiding behind a safe intellectualism? All of these questions rise out of the long-accepted assumptions of a subject-predicate mode of thought that tries to make reality responsible for the words that are used to construe it. Because of the currency of this kind of interpretation we run the risk we mentioned a few moments ago—the risk of being bracketed with either the classic rationalists or the modern intuitionists.

Actually we are neither. Our position is that of a psychology of personal constructs (Kelly, 1955), a psychologist's system for construing persons who themselves construe in all kinds of other ways. Thus I, Person A, employ Construct A', a component construct within my own construction system, to understand

Construct B', a component construct within Person B's construction system. His B' is not a truth revealed to him by nature. Nor is my A' revealed to me by his human nature. Construct A' is my responsibility, just as B' is his. In each instance the validity of the construct rests, among other things, upon its prophetic effectiveness, not upon any claim to external origin, either divine or natural.

Now let us hope we are in a safe position to deal with the assessment of human motives without appearing either to reify them or to talk nonsense. Our discussion might as well start where our thinking started.

REPUDIATION OF THE MOTIVATION CONSTRUCT FOR DIAGNOSIS

Some twenty years or more ago a group of us were attempting to provide a traveling psychological clinic service to the schools in the State of Kansas. One of the principal sources of referrals was, of course, teachers. A teacher complained about a pupil. This word-bound complaint was taken as prima-facie grounds for kicking the bottle—I mean, examining the pupil. If we kicked the pupil around long enough and hard enough we could usually find some grounds to justify any teacher's complaint. This procedure was called in those days, just as it is still called, "diagnosis." It was in this manner that we conformed to the widely accepted requirements of the scientific method— we matched hypothesis with evidence and thus arrived at objective truth. In due course of time we became quite proficient in making something out of teachers' complaints, and we got so we could adduce some mighty subtle evidence. In short, we began to fancy ourselves as pretty sensitive clinicians.

Now, as every scientist and every clinician knows and is fond of repeating, treatment depends upon diagnosis. First you find out what is wrong—really wrong. Then you treat it. In treatment you have several alternatives; you can cut it out of the person, or you can remove the object toward which the child behaves improperly, or you can remove the child from the object, or you can alter the mechanism he employs to deal with the object, or you can compensate for the child's behavior by taking up a hobby in the basement, or teach the child to compensate for it, or, if nothing better turns up, you can sympathize with everybody who has to put up with the youngster. But first, always first, you must kick the bottle to make it either confirm or reject your diagnostic hunches. So in Kansas we diagnosed pupils, and having impaled ourselves and our clients with our diagnoses, we cast about more or less frantically for ways of escape.

After perseverating in this classical stupidity—the treatment-depends-on-objective-diagnosis stupidity—for more years than we like to count, we began to suspect that we were being trapped in some pretty fallacious reasoning. We should have liked to blame the teachers for getting us off on the wrong track. But we have verified their complaints, hadn't we? We had even made "differential diagnoses," a way of choosing up sides in the name-calling games commonly played in clinical staff meetings.

Two things became apparent. The first was that the teacher's complaint was not necessarily something to be verified or disproved by the facts in the case, but was, rather, a construction of events in a way that, within the limits and assumptions of her personal construction system, made the most sense to her at the moment. The second was the realization that, in assuming diagnosis to be the independent variable and treatment the dependent variable, we had got the cart before the horse. It would have been better if we had made our diagnoses in the light of changes that do occur in children or that can be made to occur, rather than trying to shape those changes to independent but irrelevant psychometric measurements or biographical descriptions.

"Laziness"

What we should like to make clear is that both these difficulties have the same root—the traditional rationale of science that leads us to look for the locus of meaning of words in their objects of reference rather than in their subjects of origin. We hear a word and look to what is talked about rather than listen to the person who utters it. A teacher often complained that a child was "lazy." We turned to the child to determine whether or not she was right. If we found clear evidence that would support a hypothesis of laziness, then laziness was what it was—nothing else—and diagnosis was complete. Diagnosis having been accomplished, treatment was supposed to ensue. What does one do to cure laziness? While, of course, it was not quite as simple as this, the paradigm is essentially the one we followed.

Later we began to put "laziness" in quotes. We found that a careful appraisal of the teacher's construction system gave us a much better understanding of the meaning of the complaint. This, together with some further inquiry into the child's outlook, often enabled us to arrive at a vantage point from which we could deal with the problem in various ways. It occurred to us that we might, for example, help the teacher reconstrue the child in terms other than "laziness"—terms which gave her more latitude for exercising her own particular creative talents in dealing with him. Again, we might help the child deal with the teacher and in this way alleviate her discomfort. And, of course, there was sometimes the possibility that a broader reorientation of the child toward himself and school matters in general would prove helpful.

We have chosen the complaint of "laziness" as our example for a more special reason. "Laziness" happens to be a popular motivational concept that has widespread currency among adults who try to get others to make something out of themselves. Moreover, our disillusionment with motivational conceptualization in general started with this particular term and arose out of the specific context of school psychological services.

Our present position regarding human motives was approached by stages. First we realized that even when a hypothesis of laziness was confirmed there was little that could be said or done in consequence of such a finding. While this belief originally appeared to be less true of other motivational constructs, such as appetite or affection, in each instance the key to treatment, or even to differential prediction of outcomes, appeared to reside within the framework of other types of constructs.

Another observation along the way was that the teachers who used the construct of "laziness" were usually those who had widespread difficulties in their classrooms. Soon we reached the point in our practice where we routinely used the complaint of "laziness" as a point of departure for reorienting the teacher. It usually happened that there was more to be done with her than there was to be done with the child. So it was, also, with other complaints cast in motivational terms. In general, then, we found that the most practical approach to so-called motivational problems was to try to reorient the people who thought in such terms. Complaints about motivation told us much more about the complainants than it did about their pupils.

This generalization seems to get more and more support from our clinical experience. When we find a person who is more interested in manipulating people for his own purposes, we usually find him making complaints about their motives. When we find a person who is concerned about motives, he usually turns out to be one who is threatened by his fellow men and wants to put them in their place. There is no doubt that the construct of motives is widely used, but it usually turns out to be a part of the language of complaint about the behavior of other people. When it appears in the language of the client himself, as it does occasionally, it always—literally always—appears in the context of a kind of rationalization apparently designed to appease the therapist, not in the spontaneous utterances of the client who is in good rapport with his therapist.

One technique we came to use was to ask the teacher what the child would do if she did not try to motivate him. Often the teacher would insist that the child would do nothing—absolutely nothing—just sit! Then we would suggest that she try a nonmotivational approach and let him "just sit." We would ask her to observe how he went about "just sitting." Invariably the teacher would be able to report some extremely interesting goings on. An analysis of what the "lazy" child did while he was being lazy often furnished her with her first glimpse into the child's world and provided her with her first solid grounds for communication

with him. Some teachers found that their laziest pupils were those who could produce the most novel ideas; others, that the term "laziness" had been applied to activities that they had simply been unable to understand or appreciate.

Construed alternatives

It was some time later that we sat down and tried to formulate the general principles that undergirded our clinical experiences with teachers and their pupils. The more we thought about it, the more it seemed that our problems had always resolved themselves into questions of what the child would do if left to his own devices rather than questions about the amount of his motivation. These questions of what the child would do seemed to hinge primarily on what alternatives his personal construction of the situation allowed him to sense. While his construed alternatives were not necessarily couched in language symbols, nor could the child always clearly represent his alternatives, even to himself, they nonetheless set the outside limits on his day-to-day behavior. In brief, whenever we got embroiled in questions of motivation we bogged down, the teachers bogged down, and the children continued to aggravate everybody within earshot. When we forgot about motives and set about understanding the practical alternatives which children felt they were confronted by, the aggravations began to resolve themselves.

What we have said about our experiences with children also turned up in our psychotherapeutic experiences with adults. After months or, in some cases, years of psychotherapy with the same client, it did often prove to be possible to predict his behavior in terms of motives. This, of course, was gratifying; but predictive efficiency is not the only criterion of a good construction, for one's understanding of a client should also point the way to resolving his difficulties. It was precisely at this point that motivational constructs failed to be of practical service, just as they had failed to be of service in helping children and teachers get along with each other. Always the psychotherapeutic solution turned out to be a reconstruing process, not a mere labeling of the client's motives. To be sure, there were clients who never reduced their reconstructions to precise verbal terms, yet still were able to extricate themselves from vexing circumstances. And there were clients who got along best under conditions of support and reassurance with a minimum of verbal structuring on the part of the therapist. But even in these cases, the solutions were not worked out in terms of anything that could properly be called motives, and the evidence always pointed to some kind of reconstruing process that enabled the client to make his choice between new sets of alternatives not previously open to him in a psychological sense.

APPROACH TO A NEW PSYCHOLOGICAL THEORY

Now, perhaps, it is time to launch into the third phase of our discussion. We started by making some remarks of a philosophical nature and from there we dropped back to recall some of the practical experiences that first led us to question the construct of motivation. Let us turn now to the formulation of psychological theory and to the part that motivation plays in it.

A half century ago William McDougall published his little volume, *Physiological Psychology* (1905). In the opening pages

he called his contemporary psychologists' attention to the fact that the concept of *energy* had been invented by physicists in order to account for movement of objects, and that some psychologists had blandly assumed that they too would have to find a place for it in their systems. While McDougall was to go on in his lifetime to formulate a theoretical system based on instinctual drives and thus, it seems to us, failed to heed his own warning, what he said about the construct of energy still provides us with a springboard for expounding a quite different theoretical position.

The physical world presented itself to preclassical man as a world of solid objects. He saw matter as an essentially inert substance, rather than as a complex of related motion. His axes of reference were spatial dimensions—length, breadth, depth—rather than temporal dimensions. The flow of time was something he could do very little about, and he was inclined to take a passive attitude toward it. Even mass, a dimension which lent itself to more dynamic interpretations, was likely to be construed in terms of size equivalents.

Classical man, as he emerged upon the scene, gradually became aware of motion as something that had eluded his predecessors. But for him motion was still superimposed upon nature's rocks and hills. Inert matter was still the phenomenon, motion was only the epiphenomenon. Action, vitality, and energy were the breath of life that had to be breathed into the inertness of nature's realities. In Classical Greece this thought was magnificently expressed in new forms of architecture and sculpture that made the marble quarried from the Greek islands reach for the open sky, or ripple like a soft garment in the warm Aegean breeze. But motion, though an intrinsic feature of the Greek idiom, was always something superimposed, something added. It belonged to the world of the ideal and not to the hard world of reality.

The construct of motivation implies that man is essentially inert

Today our modern psychology approaches its study of man from the same vantage point. He is viewed as something static in his natural state, hence something upon which motion, life, and action have to be superimposed. In substance he is still perceived as like the marble out of which the Greeks carved their statues of flowing motion and ethereal grace. He comes alive, according to most of the psychology of our day, only through the application of special enlivening forces. We call these forces by such names as "motives," "incentives," "needs," and "drives." Thus, just as the physicists had to erect the construct of energy to fill the gap left by their premature assumption of a basically static universe, so psychology has had to burden itself with a construct made necessary by its inadequate assumption about the basic nature of man.

We now arrive at the same point in our theoretical reasoning at which we arrived some years earlier in appraising our clinical experience. In each instance we find that efforts to assess human motives run into practical difficulty because they assume inherently static properties in human nature. It seems appropriate, therefore, at this juncture to re-examine our implied assumptions about human nature. If we then decide to base our thinking upon new assumptions we can next turn to the array of new constructs that may be erected for the proper

elaboration of the fresh theoretical position.

In this theory the construct of motivation is redundant in explaining man's activity

There are several ways in which we can approach our problem. We could, for example, suggest to ourselves, as we once suggested to certain unperceptive classroom teachers, that we examine what a person does when he is not being motivated. Does he turn into some kind of inert substance? If not—and he won't—should we not follow up our observation with a basic assumption that any person is motivated, motivated for no other reason than that he is alive? Life itself could be defined as a form of process or movement. Thus, in designating man as our object of psychological inquiry, we should be taking it for granted that movement is an essential property of his being, not something that has to be accounted for separately. We should be talking about a form of movement—man—not something that has to be motivated.

Pursuant to this line of reasoning, motivation ceases to be a special topic of psychology. Nor, on the other hand, can it be said that motivation constitutes the whole of psychological substance, although from the standpoint of another theoretical system it might be proper to characterize our position so. *Within our system,* however, the term "motivation" can appear only as a redundancy.

How can we further characterize this stand with respect to motivation? Perhaps this will help: Motivational theories can be divided into two types, push theories and pull theories. Under push theories we find such terms as drive, motive, or even stimulus. Pull theories use such constructs as purpose, value, or need. In terms of a well-known metaphor, these are the pitchfork theories on the one hand and the carrot theories on the other. But our theory is neither of these. Since we prefer to look to the nature of the animal himself, ours is probably best called a jackass theory.

Thus far our reasoning has led us to a point of view from which the construct of "human motives" appears redundant—redundant, that is, as far as accounting for human action is concerned. But traditional motivational theory is not quite so easily dismissed. There is another issue that now comes to the fore. It is the question of what directions human actions can be expected to take.

The construct of motivation is not needed to explain directionality of movement

We must recognize that the construct of "motive" has been traditionally used for two purposes; to account for the fact that the person is active rather than inert, and also for the fact that he chooses to move in some directions rather than in others. It is not surprising that, in the past, a single construct has been used to cover both issues; for if we take the view that the human organism is set in motion only by the impact of special forces, it is reasonable to assume also that those forces must give it direction as well as impetus. But now, if we accept the view that the organism is already in motion simply by virtue of its being alive, then we have to ask ourselves if we do not still require the services of "motives" to explain the directionality of the movement. Our answer to this question is "No." Let us see why.

Here, as before, we turn first to our experiences as a clinician to find the earliest inklings of a new theoretical position. Specifically, we turn to experiences in psychotherapy.

Clinical experience. When a psychologist undertakes psychotherapy with a client he can approach his task from any one of a number of viewpoints. He can, as many do, devote most of his attention to a kind of running criticism of the mistakes the client makes, his fallacies, his irrationalities, his misperceptions, his resistances, his primitive mechanisms. Or, as others do, he can keep measuring his client; so much progress today, so much loss yesterday, gains in this respect, relapses in that. If he prefers, he can keep his attention upon his own role, or the relation between himself and his client, with the thought that it is not actually given to him ever to know how the client's mind works, nor is it his responsibility to make sure that it works correctly, but only that he should provide the kind of warm and responsive human setting in which the client can best solve his own problems.

Any one of these approaches may prove helpful to the client. But there is still another approach that, from our personal experience, can prove most helpful to the client and to the psychotherapist. Instead of assuming, on the one hand, that the therapist is obliged to bring the client's thinking into line, or, on the other, that the client will mysteriously bring his own thinking into line once he has been given the proper setting, we can take the stand that client and therapist are conjoining in an exploratory venture. The therapist assumes neither the position of judge nor that of the sympathetic bystander. He is sincere about this; he is willing to learn along with his client. He is the client's fellow researcher who seeks first to understand, then to examine, and finally to assist the client in subjecting alternatives to experimental test and revision.

The psychologist who goes at psychotherapy this way says to himself, "I am about to have the rare opportunity of examining the inner workings of that most intricate creation in all of nature, a human personality. While many scholars have written about the complexity of this human personality, I am now about to see for myself how one particular personality functions. Moreover, I am about to have an experienced colleague join me in this venture, the very person whose personality is to be examined. He will help me as best he can, but there will be times when he cannot help, when he will be as puzzled and confused as I am."

When psychotherapy is carried out in this vein the therapist, instead of asking himself continually whether his client is right or not, or whether he himself is behaving properly, peers intently into the intimate psychological processes which the unusual relation permits him to see. He inquires rather than condemns. He explores rather than rejects or approves. How does this creature, man, actually think? How does he make choices that seem to be outside the conventionalized modes of thought? What is the nature of his logic—quite apart from how logicians define logic? How does he solve his problems? What ideas does he express for which he has no words?

Conventional psychological concepts. Out of this kind of experience with psychotherapy we found ourselves becoming increasingly impatient with certain standard psychotherapeutic concepts. "Insight" was one of the first to have a hollow sound. It soon became apparent that, in any single case, there was any number of different possible insights that could be used to structure the same facts, all of them more or less true. As one acquires a variety of psychotherapeutic experience he begins to be amazed by how sick or deviant some clients can be and still surmount their difficulties, and how well or insightful others can be and yet fall apart at every turn. Certainly the therapist who approaches his task primarily as a scientist is soon compelled to concede that unconventional insights often work as well or better than the standardized insights prescribed by some current psychological theory.

Another popular psychotherapeutic concept that made less and less sense was "resistance." To most therapists resistance is a kind of perverse stubbornness in the client. Most therapists are annoyed by it. Some accuse the client of resisting whenever their therapeutic efforts begin to bog down. But our own experiences with resistance were a good deal like our experiences with laziness—they bespoke more of the therapist's perplexity than of the client's rebellion. If we have been dependent entirely on psychotherapeutic experiences with our own clients we might have missed this point; it would have been too easy for us, like the others, to blame our difficulties on the motives of the client. But we were fortunate enough to have opportunities also for supervising therapists, and here, because we were not ourselves quite so intimately involved, it was possible to see resistance in terms of the therapist's naiveté.

When the so-called resistance was finally broken through—to use a psychotherapist's idiom—it seemed proper, instead of congratulating ourselves on our victory over a stubborn client, to ask ourselves and our client just what had happened. There were, of course, the usual kinds of reply, "I just couldn't say that to you then," or "I knew I was being evasive, but I just didn't know what to do about it," etc.

But was this stubbornness? Some clients went further and expressed it this way, "To have said then what I have said today would not have meant the same thing." This may seem like a peculiar remark, but from the standpoint of personal construct theory it makes perfectly good sense. A client can express himself only within the framework of his construct system. Words alone do not convey meaning. What this client appears to be saying is this: When he has the constructs for expressing himself, the words that he uses ally themselves with those constructs and they make sense when he utters them. To force him to utter words which do not parallel his constructs, or to mention events which are precariously construed, is to plunge him into a chaos of personal nonsense, however much it may clarify matters for the therapist. In short, our experience with psychotherapy led us to believe that it was not orneriness that made the client hold out so-called important therapeutic material, but a genuine inability to express himself in terms that would not appear, from his point of view, to be utterly misconstrued.

Perhaps these brief recollections of therapeutic experiences will suffice to show how we began to be as skeptical of motives as direction-finding devices as we were skeptical of them as action-producing forces. Over and over again, it appeared that our clients were making their choices, not in terms of the alternatives we saw open to them, but in terms of the alternatives they saw open to them.

It was their network of constructions that made up the daily mazes that they ran, not the pure realities that appeared to us to surround them. To try to explain a temper tantrum or an acute schizophrenic episode in terms of motives only was to miss the whole point of the client's system of personal dilemmas. The child's temper tantrum is, for him, one of the few remaining choices left to him. So for the psychotic; with his pathways structured the way they are in his mind, he has simply chosen from a particular limited set of alternatives. How else can he behave? His other alternatives are even less acceptable.

We have not yet fully answered the question of explaining directionality. We have described only the extent to which our therapeutic experiences led us to question the value of motives. But, after all, we have not yet found, from our experience, that clients do what they do because there is nothing else they can do. We have observed only that they do what they do because their choice systems are definitely limited. But, even by this line of reasoning, they do have choices, often bad ones, to be sure, but still choices. So our question of directionality of behavior is narrowed down by the realization that a person's behavior must take place within the limited dimensions of his personal construct system. Yet, as long as his system does have dimensions, it must provide him with some sets of alternatives. And so long as he has some alternatives of his own making we must seek to explain why he chooses some of them in preference to others.

"Neurotic paradox." Before we leave off talking about clinical experience and take up the next and most difficult phase of our discussion, it will do no harm to digress for a few moments and talk about

the so-called neurotic paradox. O. H. Mowrer has described this as "the paradox of behavior which is at one and the same time self-perpetuating and self-defeating" (1950, p. 486). We can state the paradox in the form of a question, "Why does a person sometimes persist in unrewarding behavior?" Reinforcement theory finds this an embarrassing question, while contiguity theory, to which some psychologists have turned in their embarrassment, finds the converse question equally embarrassing, "Why does a person sometimes *not* persist in unrewarding behavior?"

From the standpoint of the psychology of personal constructs, however, there is no neurotic paradox. Or, to be more correct, the paradox is the jam which certain learning theorists get themselves into rather than the jam their clients get themselves into. Not that clients stay out of jams, but they have their own ingenious ways of getting into them and they need no assistance from us psychologists. To say it another way, the behavior of a so-called neurotic client does not seem paradoxical to him until he tries to rationalize it in terms his therapist can understand. It is when he tries to use his therapist's construction system that the paradox appears. Within the client's own limited construction system he may be faced with a dilemma but not with a paradox.

Perhaps this little digression into the neurotic paradox will help prepare the ground for the next phase of our discussion. Certainly it will help if it makes clear that the criteria by which a person chooses between the alternatives, in terms of which he has structured his world, are themselves cast in terms of constructions. Not only do men construe their alternatives, but they construe also criteria for choosing between them. For us psychologists who try to understand what is going on in the minds of our clients it is not as simple as saying that the client will persist in rewarding behavior, or even that he will vacillate between immediate and remote rewards. We have to know what this person construes to be a reward, or, still better, we can bypass such motivational terms as "reward," which ought to be redefined for each new client and on each new occasion, and abstract from human behavior some psychological principle that will transcend the tedious varieties of personalized motives.

If we succeed in this achievement we may be able to escape that common pitfall of so-called objective thinking, the tendency to reify our constructs and treat them as if they were not constructs at all, but actually all the things that they were originally only intended to construe. Such a formulation may even make it safer for us to write operational definitions for purposes of research, without becoming lost in the subject-predicate fallacy. In clinical language it may enable us to avoid concretistic thinking—the so-called brain-injured type of thinking—which is what we call operationalism when we happen to find it in a client who is frantically holding on to his mental faculties.

Now we have been procrastinating long enough. Let us get on to the most difficult part of our discussion. We have talked about experiences with clients who, because they hoped we might be of help to them, honored us with invitations to the rare intimacies of their personal lives and ventured to show us the shadowy processes by which their worlds were ordered. We turned aside briefly in our discussion to talk about the neurotic paradox, hoping that what we could point to there would help the listener anticipate what needed to come next. Now we turn again to a more theoretical form of discourse.

Man links the past with the future— Anticipation

If man, as the psychologist is to see him, exists primarily in the dimensions of time, and only secondarily in the dimensions of space, then the terms which we erect for understanding him ought to take primary account of this view. If we want to know why man does what he does, then the terms of our whys should extend themselves in time rather than in space; they should be events rather than things; they should be mileposts rather than destinations. Clearly, man lives in the present. He stands firmly astride the chasm that separates the past from the future. He is the only connecting link between these two universes. He, and he only, can bring them into harmony with each other. To be sure, there are other forms of existence that have belonged to the past and, presumably, will also belong to the future. A rock that has rested firm for ages may well exist in the future also, but it does not link the past with the future. In its mute way it links only past with past. It does not anticipate; it does not reach out both ways to snatch handfuls from each of the two worlds in order to bring them together and subject them to the same stern laws. Only man does that.

If this is the picture of man, as the psychologist envisions him—man, a form of movement; man, always quick enough, as long as he is alive, to stay astride the darting present—then we cannot expect to explain him either entirely in terms of the past or entirely in terms of the future. We can explain him, psychologically, only as a link between the two. Let us, therefore, formulate our basic postulate for a

psychological theory in the light of this conjunctive vision of man. We can say it this way: *A person's processes are psychologically channelized by the ways in which he anticipates events.*

The nature of personal constructs

Taking this proposition as a point of departure, we can quickly begin to sketch a theoretical structure for psychology that will, undoubtedly, turn out to be novel in many unexpected ways. We can say next that man develops his way of anticipating events by construing, by scratching out his channels of thought. Thus he builds his own maze. His runways are the constructs he forms, each a two-way street, each essentially a pair of alternatives between which he can choose.

Another person, attempting to enter this labyrinth, soon gets lost. Even a therapist has to be led patiently back and forth through the system, sometimes for months on end, before he can find his way without the client's help, or tell to what overt behavior each passageway will lead. Many of the runways are conveniently posted with word signs, but most of them are dark, cryptically labeled, or without any word signs at all. Some are rarely traveled. Some the client is reluctant to disclose to his guest. Often therapists lose patience and prematurely start trying to blast shortcuts in which both they and their clients soon become trapped. But worst of all, there are therapists who refuse to believe that they are in the strangely structured world of man; they insist only that the meanderings in which they are led are merely the play of whimsical motives upon their blind and helpless client.

Our figure of speech should not be taken too literally. The labyrinth is conceived as a network of constructs, each of which is essentially an abstraction and, as such, can be picked up and laid down over many different events in order to bring them into focus and clothe them with personal meaning. Moreover, the constructs are subject to continual revision, although the complex interdependent relation between constructs in the system often makes it precarious for the person to revise one construct without taking into account the disruptive effect upon major segments of the system.

In our efforts to communicate the notion of a personal construct system we repeatedly run into difficulty because listeners identify personal constructs with the classic view of a concept. Concepts have long been known as units of logic and are treated as if they existed independently of any particular person's psychological processes. But when we use the notion of "construct" we have nothing of this sort in mind; we are talking about a psychological process in a living person. Such a construct has, for us, no existence independent of the person whose thinking it characterizes. The question of whether it is logical or not has no bearing on its existence, for it is wholly a psychological rather than a logical affair. Furthermore, since it is a psychological affair, it has no necessary allegiance to the verbal forms in which classical concepts have been traditionally cast. The personal construct we talk about bears no essential relation to grammatical structure, syntax, words, language, or even communication; nor does it imply consciousness. It is simply a psychologically construed unit for understanding human processes.

We must confess that we often run into another kind of difficulty. In an effort to understand what we are talking about, a listener often asks if the personal construct is an intellectual affair. We find that, willy-nilly, we invite this kind of question because of our use of such terms as thought and thinking. Moreover, we are speaking in the terms of a language system whose words stand for traditional divisions of mental life, such as "intellectual."

Let us answer this way. A construct owes no special allegiance to the intellect, as against the will or the emotions. In fact, we do not find it either necessary or desirable to make that classic trichotomous division of mental life. After all, there is so much that is "emotional" in those behaviors commonly called "intellectual," and there is so much "intellectualized" contamination in typical "emotional" upheavals that the distinction becomes merely a burdensome nuisance. For some time now we have been quite happy to chuck all these notions of intellect, will, and emotion; so far, we cannot say we have experienced any serious loss.

Now we are at the point in our discourse where we hope our listeners are ready to assume, either from conviction or for the sake of argument, that man, from a psychological viewpoint, makes of himself a bridge between past and future in a manner that is unique among creatures, that, again from a psychological viewpoint, his processes are channelized by the personal constructs he erects in order to perform this function, and, finally, that he organizes his constructs into a personal system that is no more conscious than it is unconscious and no more intellectual than it is emotional. This personal construct system provides him with both freedom of decision and limitation of action—freedom, because it permits him to deal with the meanings of events rather than forces him to be helplessly pushed about by them, and limitation, because he can never make choices outside the world of alternatives he has erected for himself.

The choice corollary

We have left to the last the question of what determines man's behavioral choices between his self-construed alternatives. Each choice that he makes has implications for his future. Each turn of the road he chooses to travel brings him to a fresh vantage point from which he can judge the validity of his past choices and elaborate his present pattern of alternatives for choices yet to be made. Always the future beckons him and always he reaches out in tremulous anticipation to touch it. He lives in anticipation; we mean this literally; *he lives in anticipation!* His behavior is governed, not simply by *what* he anticipates—whether good or bad, pleasant or unpleasant, self-vindicating or self-confounding—but by *where* he believes his choices will place him in respect to the remaining turns in the road. If he chooses this fork in the road, will it lead to a better vantage point from which to see the road beyond or will it be the one that abruptly brings him face-to-face with a blank wall?

What we are saying about the criteria of man's choices is *not* a second theoretical assumption, added to our basic postulate to take the place of the traditional beliefs in separate motives, but is a natural outgrowth of that postulate—a corollary to it. Let us state it so. *A person chooses for himself that alternative in a dichotomized construct through which he anticipates the greater possibility for extension and definition of his system.*

Such a corollary appears to us to be implicit in our postulate that a person's processes are psychologically channelized by the ways in which he anticipates

events. For the sake of simplification we have skipped over the formal statement of some of the intervening corollaries of personal construct theory: the corollary that deals with construing, the corollary that deals with the construct system, and the corollary that deals with the dichotomous nature of constructs. But we have probably covered these intervening ideas well enough in the course of our exposition.

What we are saying in this crucial *Choice Corollary* gives us the final ground for dismissing motivation as a necessary psychological construct. It is that if a person's processes are channelized by the ways in which he anticipates events he will make his choices in such a way that he apparently defines or extends his system of channels, for this must necessarily be his comprehensive way of anticipating events.

At the risk of being tedious, let us recapitulate again. We shall be brief. Perhaps we can condense the argument into three sentences. First we saw no need for a closet full of motives to explain the fact that man was active rather than inert; there was no sense in assuming that he was inert in the first place. And now we see no need to invoke a concept of motives to explain the directions that his actions take; the fact that he lives in anticipation automatically takes care of that. Result: no catalogue of motives to clutter up our system and, we hope, a much more coherent psychological theory about living man.

Footnotes

At this point our discourse substantially concludes itself. What we have left to offer are essentially footnotes that are intended to be either defensive or provocative, perhaps both. Questions naturally arise the moment one begins to pursue the implications of this kind of theorizing. One can scarcely take more than a few steps before one begins to stumble over a lot of ancient landmarks that remain to serve no purpose except to get in the way. Perhaps it is only fair that we spotlight some of these relics in the hope of sparing our listeners some barked intellectual shins.

Is this a dynamic theory? This is the kind of question our clinical colleagues are likely to ask. We are tempted to give a flat "No" to that question. No, this is not what is ordinarily called a dynamic theory; it intentionally parts company with psychoanalysis, for example— respectfully, but nonetheless intentionally. However, if what is meant by a "dynamic theory" is a theory that envisions man as active rather than inert, then this is an all out dynamic theory. It is so dynamic that it does not need any special system of dynamics to keep it running! What must be made clear, or our whole discourse falls flat on its face, is that we do not envision the behavior of man in terms of the external forces bearing upon him; that is a view we are quite ready to leave to the dialectic materialists and to some of their unwitting allies who keep chattering about scientific determinism and other subject-predicate forms of nonsense.

Is this rationalism revisited? We anticipated this question at the beginning of our discussion. We are tempted to answer now by claiming that it is one of the few genuine departures from rationalism, perhaps the first in the field of psychology. But here is a tricky question, because it is not often clear whether one is referring to extrapsychological rationalism or to an essential-psychological rationalism that is often imperfect when judged by classical standards and

often branded as "irrationality," or whether the question refers simply to any verbalized structure applied to the behavior of man in an effort to understand him.

Certainly ours is not an extrapsychological rationalism. Instead, it frankly attempts to deal with the essential rationalism that is actually demonstrated in the thinking of man. In doing so it deals with what is sometimes called the world of the irrational and nonrational.

But, in another sense, our interpretation, in its own right and quite apart from its subject matter, is a psychologist's rationale designed to help him understand how man comes to believe and act the way he does. Such a rationale approaches its task the way it does, not because it believes that logic has to be as it is because there is no other way for it to be, not because it believes that man behaves the way he does because there is no other way for him to react to external determining forces, nor even because the rationale's own construction of man provides him with no alternatives, but, rather, because we have the hunch that the way to understand all things, even the ramblings of a regressed schizophrenic client, is to construe them so that they will be made predictable. To some persons this approach spells rationalism, pure and simple, probably because they are firmly convinced that the nether world of man's motives is so hopelessly irrational that anyone who tries to understand that world sensibly must surely be avoiding contact with man as he really is.

Finally, there is the most important question of all; how does the system work? That is a topic to be postponed to another time and occasion. Of course, we think it does work. We use it in psychotherapy and in psychodiagnostic planning for psychotherapy. We also find a place for it in dealing with many of the affairs of everyday life. But there is no place here for the recitation of such details. We hope only that, so far as we have gone, we have been reasonably clear, and a mite provocative, for only by being both clear and provocative can we give our listeners something they can set their teeth into.

REFERENCES

Kelly, G. A. *The psychology of personal constructs.* New York: W. W. Norton, 1955.

McDougall, W. *Physiological psychology.* London: Dent, 1905.

Mowrer, O. H. *Learning theory and personality dynamics.* New York: Ronald Press, 1950.

CHAPTER 8

Existential Theory

Introduction

Ludwig Binswanger (1881–1966), a psychiatrist, was perhaps the most representative of the relatively small but highly influential group which represents an existentialist protest against Freudian doctrines. The existentialists know who they are and what they stand for, but from the viewpoint of an outsider they seem to have little in common, and they appear to (and actually do) contradict themselves relative to their philosophical positions.

What can be said about existential psychiatry that is generally true? First, it is a here-and-now point of view. Second, the individual is seen as responsible, having freedom of expression. Third, it is a point of view of individuals and not of people; each individual is seen as unique. Fourth, it is a somewhat tragic or sad point of view, stressing futility and man's doleful alternatives: The past represents regret, and the future represents fear. Fifth, it points out man's aloneness, his close relation to eternity, his direct contact with reality, his ineffable personhood.

If these views of an outside observer seem to add up to mere words, then the essence of existential psychology has not been captured for you. It is probably much harder to understand the existential point of view than any other, and yet it is a relatively simple position. You will see that this is true in the following selection. Paradoxically, this is just about the clearest statement made by Binswanger, but it probably tells less about existentialism than his more obscure pieces.

LUDWIG BINSWANGER
The differentiation between human existence and animal being

In "The Case of Ellen West," my first study planned as an example of existential analysis as applied to psychiatry, conditions were particularly favorable for existential analysis. In this case I had at my disposal an unusual abundance of spontaneous and immediately comprehensible verbal manifestations such as self-descriptions, dream accounts, diary entries, poems, letters, autobiographical drafts, whereas usually, and especially in cases of deteriorated schizophrenics, we have to obtain the material for existential analysis by persistent and systematic exploration of our patients over months and years. First and foremost it is our task to assure ourselves, over and over again, of what our patients really mean by their verbal expressions. Only then can we dare to approach the scientific task of discerning the "worlds" in which the patients are or, in other words, to understand how all partial links of the existential structure become comprehensible through the total structure, just as the total structure constitutes itself, without incongruity, from the partial links. In this, as in any other scientific investigation, there do occur errors, dead ends, premature interpretations; but, also as in any other, there are ways and means of correcting and rectifying these errors. It is one of the most impressive

achievements of existential analysis to have shown that even in the realm of subjectivity "nothing is left to chance," but that a certain organized structure can be recognized from which each word, each idea, drawing, action, or gesture receives its peculiar imprint—an insight of which we make continuous use in existential analytical interpretations of the Rorschach test and recently also in the Word Association Test. It is always the same world-design which confronts us in a patient's spontaneous verbal manifestations, in the systematic exploration of his Rorschach and Word Association responses, in his drawings, and also, frequently, in his dreams. And only after having encompassed these worlds and brought them together can we understand the form of our patient's existence in the sense of what we call "neurosis" or "psychosis." Only then may we dare to attempt to understand single, partial links of those forms of world and existence (clinically evaluated as symptoms) from the modes and ways of the patient's total being-in-the-world.

Naturally, the connections of the life-history, too, here play an important part but, as we shall soon realize, by no means in the same way as in psychoanalysis. Whereas for the latter they are the goal of the investigation, for existential analysis they merely provide material for that investigation.

The following examples will illustrate the kind of world-designs with which we have to deal in psychopathology; but the

Ludwig Binswanger, "The Differentiation between Human Existence and Animal Being." Reprinted from Rollo May, Ernest Angel, and H. F. Ellenberger (eds.), *Existence* (New York: Basic Books, 1956), pp. 201–213.

number of such deviations is infinite. We are still at the beginning of describing and investigating them.

For my first clinical illustration I shall report the case of a young girl who at the age of five experienced a puzzling attack of anxiety and fainting when her heel got stuck in her skate and separated from her shoe. Ever since, the girl—now twenty-one years of age—suffered spells of irresistible anxiety whenever a heel of one of her shoes appeared to loosen or when someone touched the heel or only spoke of heels. (Her own had to be nailed to her soles.) On such occasions, if she could not get away in time, she would faint.

Psychoanalysis proved clearly and convincingly that hidden behind the fear of loose or separating heels were birth phantasies, both about being born herself and therefore separated from mother and about giving birth to a child of her own. Of the various disruptions of continuity which psychoanalysis revealed as being frightening to the girl, the one between mother and child was fundamental and most feared. (I am omitting completely, in this context, the masculine component.) Before the period of Freud, one would have stated that the skating accident, harmless as it was per se, had "caused" the "heel phobia." Freud demonstrated subsequently that the pathogenic effect is produced by phantasies connected with and preceding such an accident. Yet in both periods still another explanation would be drawn upon to account for the fact that a specific event or phantasy had such a far-reaching effect precisely upon this person—namely, the explanation of "constitution" or "predisposition." For each of us has experienced the "birth trauma," but some lose their heels without developing a hysterical phobia.

We do not, of course, propose to

unfold, let alone solve, the problem of "predisposition" in all its aspects; but I dare say that we can throw some more light on it when we view it from an "anthropological"[1] angle. In later studies we were able to demonstrate that we could reach even *behind* the phantasies insofar as we could trace and investigate the world-design which made possible those phantasies and phobias in the first place.

What serves as a clue to the world-design of our little patient is the category of *continuity,* of continuous connection and containment. This entails a tremendous constriction, simplification, and depletion of the "world content," of the extremely complex totality of the patient's contexts of reference. Everything that makes the world significant is submitted to the rule of that *one* category which alone supports her "world" and being. This is what causes the great anxiety about any disruption of continuity, any gap, tearing or separating, being separated or torn. This is why separation from the mother, experienced by everyone as the arch-separation in human life, had to become so prevalent that any event of separation served to symbolize the fear of separation from the mother and to invite and activate those phantasies and daydreams.

We should, therefore, not explain the emergence of the phobia by an overly strong "pre-oedipal" tie to the mother, but rather realize that such an overly strong filial tie is only possible on the premise of a world-design exclusively based on connectedness, cohesiveness, continuity. Such a way of experiencing "world"—which always implies such a "key"—does not have to be "con-

---

[1] ["Anthropology" as used by Binswanger is equivalent to "psychology as the study of man."—R. C.]

scious"; but neither must we call it "unconscious" in the psychoanalytical sense, since it is outside the contrast of these opposites. Indeed, it does not refer to anything psychological but to something which only makes possible the psychic fact. At this point we face what is actually "abnormal" in this existence—but we must not forget that where the world-design is narrowed and constricted to such a degree, the self, too, is constricted and prevented from maturing. Everything is supposed to stay as it was before. If, however, something new does happen and continuity is disrupted, it can only result in catastrophe, panic, anxiety attack. For then the world actually collapses, and nothing is left to hold it up. The inner or existential maturation and the genuine time-orientation toward the future are replaced by a preponderance of the past, of "already having-been-in." The world must stop here, nothing must happen, nothing must change. The context must be preserved as it has always been. It is this type of temporal orientation that permits the element of *suddenness* to assume such enormous significance; because suddenness is the time quality that explodes continuity, hacks it and chops it to pieces, throws the earlier existence out of its course, and exposes it to the Dreadful,[2] to the naked horror. This is what in psychopathology we term, in a most simplifying and summarizing manner, anxiety attack.

Neither the loss of the heel nor the womb and birth phantasies are "explanations" of the emergence of the phobia. Rather, they became so significant because holding on to mother meant to this child's existence—as is natural for the small child—having a hold on the world. By the same token, the skating incident assumed its traumatic significance because, in it, the world suddenly changed its face, disclosed itself from the angle of suddenness, of something totally different, new, and unexpected. For that there was no place in this child's world; it could not enter into her world-design; it stayed, as it were, always outside; it could not be mastered. In other words, instead of being accepted by the inner life so that its meaning and content could be absorbed, it appeared and reappeared over and over again without having any meaning for the existence, in an ever-recurring invasion by the Sudden into the motionlessness of the world-clock. This world-design did not manifest itself[3] before the traumatic event occurred; it did only on the *occasion* of that event. Just as the a priori or transcendental forms of the human mind make experience only into what experience is, so the form of that world-design had first to produce the condition of the possibility for the ice-skating incident in order for it to be experienced as traumatic.

It should be mentioned that this case is not at all an isolated one. We know that anxiety can be tied to various types of disruption of continuity; *e.g.,* it may appear as horror at the sight of a loose button hanging on a thread or of a break in the thread of saliva. Whatever the life-historical events are to which these anxieties refer, we are always dealing here with the same depletion of being-in-the-world, narrowed down to include only the

---

[2] [This adjective used as a noun, "the Dreadful," signifies the abstract quintessence of all that is dreadful, the epitome of dreadfulness. This and similar expressions which follow in this essay—such as "the Sudden," "the Uncanny," "the Horrid"—have been capitalized to indicate that the adjective has the substantive quality of a noun.—Editors]

---

[3] [Binswanger is here using Kantian expression.—Editors]

category of continuity. In this peculiar world-design, with its peculiar being-in-the-world and its peculiar self, we see in existential terms the real key to the understanding of what is taking place. Like the biologist and neuropathologist, we do not stop at the single fact, the single disturbance, the single symptom, but we keep searching for an embracing whole within which the fact can be understood as a partial phenomenon. But this whole is neither a functional whole—a "Gestalt-circle"—nor a whole in the sense of a complex. Indeed, it is no objective whole at all but a whole in the sense of the unity of a world-design.

We have seen that we cannot progress far enough in our understanding of anxiety if we consider it only as a psychopathological symptom per se. In short, we must never separate "anxiety" from "world," and we should keep in mind that anxiety always emerges when the world becomes shaky or threatens to vanish. The emptier, more simplified, and more constricted the world-design to which an existence has committed itself, the sooner will anxiety appear and the more severe will it be. The "world" of the healthy with its tremendously varied contexture of references and compounds of circumstance can never become entirely shaky or sink. If it is threatened in one region, other regions will emerge and offer a foothold. But where the "world," as in the present case and in numerous others, is so greatly dominated by one or a few categories, naturally the threat to the preservation of that one or those few categories must result in a more intensified anxiety.

Phobia is always an attempt at safeguarding a restricted, impoverished "world," whereas anxiety expresses the loss of such a safeguard, the collapse of the "world," and thus the delivery of the

existence to nothingness—the intolerable, dreadful, "naked horror." We then must strictly differentiate between the historically and situationally conditioned *point of breakthrough* of anxiety and the existential *source* of anxiety. Freud made a similar distinction when he differentiated between phobia as a symptom and the patient's own libido as the real object of anxiety. However, in our concept the theoretical construct of libido is replaced by the phenomenological-ontological structure of existence as being-in-the-world. We do not hold that man is afraid of his own libido, but we state that existence as being-in-the-world is, as such, determined by uncanniness and nothingness. The source of anxiety is existence itself.

Whereas in the preceding instance we had to deal with a static "world," as it were, a world in which nothing was supposed to "come to pass" or happen, in which everything had to remain unchanged and no separating agent was to interfere with its unity, we shall in the following example meet a torturously heterogeneous, disharmonious "world," again dating from early childhood. The patient, displaying a pseudo-neurotic syndrome of polymorphous schizophrenia, suffered from all sorts of somato-, auto-, and allopsychic phobias.[4] The "world" in which that which is—everything-that-is—was accessible to him was a world of push and pressure, loaded with energy to the point of bursting. In that world no step could be made without running the danger of being knocked against or knocking against something, whether in real life or in phantasy. The temporality of this world was one of

---

[4] [A reference to concepts by Wernicke, meaning simply phobias relative to the patient's own body, to his own psyche, and to the external world.—Translator]

urgency, its spatiality therefore one of horribly crowded narrowness and closeness, pressing upon "body and soul" of the existence. This came clearly to light in the Rorschach test. At one point the patient saw pieces of furniture "on which one might knock one's shin"; at another, "a drum that strikes one's leg"; at a third, "lobsters which squeeze you," "something you get scratched with"; and finally, "centrifugal balls of a flywheel which hit me in the face, me of all people, although for decades they had stayed fixed with the machine; only when I get there something happens."

As the world of things behaves, so does the world of one's fellow men; everywhere lurk danger and disrespect, mobs or jeering watchers. All this, of course, points to the borderline of delusions of "reference" or "encroachment."

It is very instructive to observe the patient's desperate attempts to control this disharmonious, energy-crammed, threatening world, to harmonize it artificially, and to belittle it in order to avoid the constantly imminent catastrophe. He does this by keeping himself at the greatest possible distance from the world, rationalizing this distance completely—a process which, here as everywhere, is accompanied by the devaluation and depletion of the world's abundance of life, love, and beauty. This is particularly demonstrated in his Word Association Test. His Rorschach responses, too, bear witness to the artificial rationalization of his world, to its symmetrization and mechanization. Whereas in our first case everything-that-is was only accessible in a world reduced to the category of continuity, in this case it is a world reduced to the mechanical category of push and pressure. We are therefore not surprised to see that in this existence and its world there is no

steadiness, that its stream of life does not flow quietly along, but that everything occurs by jerks and starts, from the simplest gestures and movements to the formulation of lingual expression and the performance of thinking and volitional decisions. Everything about the patient is jagged and occurs abruptly, while between the single jerks and pushes emptiness prevails. (The reader will notice that we are describing in existential-analytical terms what could clinically be called schizoid and autistic.) Again, very typical is the patient's behavior in the Rorschach test. He feels a desire to "fold up the cards and file them away with a final effort," just as he would like to fold up and file away the world as such with a final effort, or else he would not be able to control it any more.

But these final efforts exhaust him to such a degree that he becomes increasingly inactive and dull. If in the first case it was continuity of existence that had to be preserved at all costs, in the present case it is its dynamic *balance.* Here, too, a heavy phobic armor is employed in the interest of that preservation. Where it fails, even if only in phantasy, anxiety attacks and complete desperation take over. . . .

Whereas the above case permitted us a view of the kind of world in which "delusions of reference and encroachment"[5] become possible, a third case, that of Lola Voss, gave us some insight into the world-structure which makes possible delusions of persecutions. It offered us the rare opportunity to watch the appearance of severe hallucinatory delusions of persecutions, preceded by a pronounced phobic phase.

---

[5] The Swiss School differentiates between delusions characterized by ideas of reference and being encroached upon, on the one hand, and of persecutions, on the other.

This expressed itself in a highly complicated superstitious system of consulting an oracle of words and syllables, whose positive or negative dicta guided the patient in the commission or omission of certain acts. She would feel compelled to break up the names of things into syllables, to recombine these syllables in accordance with her system and, depending on the results of these combinations, to make contact with the persons or things in question or to avoid them like the plague. Again, all this served as a safeguarding for the existence and its worlds against catastrophe. But in this case, catastrophe was not felt to be in the disruption of the world's continuity nor in the disturbance of its dynamic balance, but in the invasion by the unspeakably Uncanny and Horrid. This patient's "world" was not dynamically loaded with conflicting forces which had to be artificially harmonized; hers was not a world-design reduced to push and pressure but one reduced to the categories of familiarity and strangeness—or uncanniness. The existence was constantly threatened by a prowling, as yet impersonal, hostile power. The incredibly thin and flimsy net of artificial syllable-combinations served as a safeguard against the danger of being overwhelmed by that power and against the unbearable threat of being delivered to it.

It was very informative to observe how, simultaneously with the disappearance of these safeguards, a new, quite different, because now quite unintended, safeguard made its appearance, namely the actual delusions of persecution.

The place of the impersonal power of the bottomless Uncanny was now taken by the secret conspiracy of personalized enemies. Against these the patient could now consciously defend herself—with accusations, counterattacks, attempts at escape—all of which seemed like child's play compared with the constantly helpless state of being threatened by the horrible power of the incomprehensible Uncanny. But such gain in the security of existence was accompanied by the patient's complete loss of existential freedom, her complete yielding to the idea of hostility on the part of her fellow men, or, in psychopathological terms, by delusions of persecution.

I am reporting this case in order to demonstrate that we cannot understand these delusions if we begin our investigation with a study of the delusions themselves. Rather should we pay close attention to what *precedes* the delusions—be it for months, weeks, days, or only hours. We would then surely find that the delusions of persecution, similarly to the phobias, represent a protection of the existence against the invasion of something inconceivably Frightful, compared with which even the secret conspiracies of enemies are more tolerable; because the enemies, unlike the incomprehensible Frightful, can be "taken at something"[6]—be it perceiving, anticipating, repelling, battling them.

In addition, the case of Lola Voss can show that we are no longer constrained by the bothersome contrast of psychic life with which we can empathize and that with which we cannot, but that we have at our disposal a method, a scientific tool, with which we can bring closer to a systematic scientific understanding even the so-called incomprehensible life of the psyche.

Of course, it still depends upon the imagination of the single researcher and physician how truly he is able to reex-

---

[6] [A Heideggerian concept which, in this context, serves to emphasize that these enemies can be "handled" by the patient.—Translator]

perience and resuffer, by virtue of his own experiential abilities, all the potential experience which existential-analytical research methodically and planfully opens to his insight.

In many cases, however, it does not suffice to consider only *one* world-design, as we have done so far for the sake of simplicity of presentation. Whereas this serves our purpose in the morbid depressions, as in mania and melancholia, in our investigations of what is clinically known as schizophrenic processes we cannot neglect the bringing into focus and the describing of the various worlds in which our patients live in order to show the changes in their "being-in-the-world" and "beyond-the-world." In the case of Ellen West, for instance, we saw the existence in the shape of a jubilant bird soaring into the sky—a flight in a world of light and infinite space. We saw the existence as a standing and walking on the ground in the world of resolute action. And, finally, we saw it in the form of a blind worm crawling in muddy earth, in the moldering grave, the narrow hole. Above all, we saw that "mental illness" really means for the "mind," how the human mind really reacts under such conditions, how its forms actually change. In this case it was a change to a precisely traceable narrowing-down, to a depletion or excavation of existence, world, and beyond-world to the point where, finally, of all the spiritual riches of the patient's world, of its abundance in love, beauty, truth, kindness, in variety, growth, and blossoming, "nothing was left except the big unfilled hole." What did remain was the animalistic compulsion to cram down food, the irresistible instinctual urge to fill the belly to the brim. All this could be demonstrated not only in the modes and changes of spatiality, of the hue, materiality, and

dynamics of the various worlds, but also in the modes and changes of temporality, up to the state of the "eternal emptiness" of so-called autism. . . .

Apart from the deepening of our understanding of psychoses and neuroses, existential analysis is indispensable to psychology and characterology. As to characterology, I shall confine myself here to the analysis of miserliness. It has been said that miserliness consists in persisting in the state of potentiality, in "a fight against realization," and that only from this angle can the bondage to money be understood. But this is still too rationalistic an interpretation. One has rather to analyze the miser's world-design and existence; in short, to explore what world-design and what world-interpretation lie at the root of miserliness, or in what way that-which-is is accessible to the stingy.

Viewing the behavior of the miser and his description in literature (as by Molière and Balzac) we find that he is primarily interested in *filling,* namely the filling of cases and boxes, stockings and bags with "gold," and only consequently in refusing to spend and in retaining. "Filling" is the a priori or transcendental tie that allows us to combine feces and money through a common denominator. It is only this that provides psychoanalysis with the empirical possibility of considering money-addiction as "originating" from the retention of feces. But by no means is the retaining of feces the "cause" of stinginess.

The above-mentioned empty spaces, however, are designed not only to be filled but, in addition, to hide their content from the eyes and hands of fellow men. The miser "sits" or "squats" on his money "like the hen on her egg." (We can learn a great deal from such phrases of idiomatic language since language has always proceeded, to a high degree, phenomenologically rather than discursively.) The pleasure of spending money, of giving it out—possible only in sympathetic contact with one's fellow men—is replaced by the pleasure of secret viewing, rummaging, touching and mental touching, and counting the gold. Such are the secret orgies of the miser, to which may be added the lust for the glittering, sparkling gold as such as the only spark of life and love which is left to the miser. The prevalence of filling-up and its worldly correlate, the cavity, points to something "Moloch-like"[7] in such a world and existence. This, naturally, carries with it (according to the unitary structure of being-in-the-world) also a certain Moloch-like form of the self-world, and in this case particularly of the body-world and of body-consciousness, as rightly emphasized by psychoanalysis. As to temporality, the very saying that one can be "stingy with one's time" proves that the miser's time is here spatialized in a Moloch-like sense, insofar as small portions of time are eagerly and constantly being saved, accumulated, and jealously guarded. From this follows the inability to give "of one's time." Of course all this implies at the same time the loss of the possibility of true or existential temporalization, of maturation of personality. The miser's relation to death which here, as in all existential-analytical investigations, is of the greatest importance, can in this context not be discussed. It is closely linked to his relations to his fellow men and linked also to his profound lack of love.

In the same way in which we investigate and understand a characterological trait,

we investigate and understand what in psychiatry and psychopathology is so summarily termed feelings and moods. A feeling or a mood is not properly described as long as one does not describe how the human existence that has it, or is in it, is in-the-world, "has" world and exists. (See in my studies on *The Flight of Ideas* the description of the optimistic moods and the feelings of exhilarant gaiety.) What has to be considered here is, in addition to temporality and spatiality, the shade, the lighting, the materiality and, above all, the dynamics of the given world-design. All this can be examined again through the medium of individual verbal manifestations as well as through metaphors, proverbs, idiomatic phrases in general, and through the language of writers and poets. Indeed, idiomatic language and poetry are inexhaustible sources for existential analysis. . . .

Existential analysis is not a psychopathology, nor is it clinical research nor any kind of objectifying research. Its results have first to be recast by psychopathology into forms that are peculiar to it, such as that of a psychic organism, or even of a psychic apparatus, in order to be projected onto the physical organism.[8] This cannot be achieved without a greatly simplifying reduction whereby the observed existential-analytical phenomena are largely divested of their phenomenal contents and reinterpreted into functions of the psychic

---

[7] [The author here refers not to the cruel aspects of Moloch-worship but to the hollowness of the idol which had to be filled.—Editors]

[8] We are speaking here of the role of psychopathology within the total frame of psychiatric medical research. We do not neglect the fact that in the psychoanalytical investigation, as well as in every purely "understanding" psychopathology, germs of existential-analytical views can always be found. But they indicate neither a methodical scientific procedure nor a knowledge of why and in what way existential analysis differs from the investigation of life-historical connections and from an "empathic" or "intuitive" entering into the patient's psychic life.

organism, psychic "mechanisms," etc. However, psychopathology would be digging its own grave were it not always striving to test its concepts of functions against the phenomenal contents to which these concepts are applied and to enrich and deepen them through the latter. Additionally, existential analysis satisfies the demands for a deeper insight into the nature and origin of psychopathological symptoms. If in these symptoms we recognize "facts of communication"— namely, disturbances and difficulties in communication—we should do our utmost to retrace their causes—retrace them, that is, to the fact that the mentally ill live in "worlds" different from ours. Therefore, knowledge and scientific description of those "worlds" become the main goal of psychopathology, a task which it can perform only with the help of existential analysis. The much-discussed *gap* that separates our "world" from the "world" of the mentally ill and makes communication between the two so difficult is not only scientifically explained but also scientifically bridged by existential analysis. We are now no longer stopped at the so-called borderline between that psychic life with which we can, and that with which we cannot, empathize. Quite a number of case reports show that our method has succeeded beyond earlier hopes in communicating with patients, in penetrating their life-history, and in understanding and describing their world-designs even in cases where all this seemed impossible before. This applies, in my experience, particularly to cases of hypochondriacal paranoids who are otherwise hardly accessible. Thus we also comply here with a *therapeutic* demand.

This insight—that the world-designs as such distinguish the mentally ill from the healthy and hamper communication with the former—also throws new light on the problem of the projection[9] of psychopathological symptoms onto specific brain processes. Now it cannot be so important to localize single psychic symptoms in the brain but rather, primarily, to ask where and how to localize the fundamental psychic disturbance which is recognizable by the change of "being-in-the-world" as such. For indeed, the "symptom" (*e.g.,* of flight of ideas, of psychomotor inhibition, neologism, stereotypy, etc.) proves to be the expression of a spreading change of the soul, a change of the total form of existence and the total style of life.

---

[9] [The German term "projection" is used here in the sense of localizing or assigning.—Translator]

CHAPTER 9

Sociological Theory

Introduction

George H. Mead (1863–1931), the author of this selection from his classic book, *Mind, Self and Society,* did not write these words! They were actually written by students of Mead who took notes at his lectures in the Sociology Department of the University of Chicago. This will account for the unusual style of the selection; Mead, apparently in a formless way, repeats the same concepts over and over again.

The reader who can go over this material slowly (perhaps it should be listened to, while being read aloud) will have the intellectual treat of listening to an absolutely original concept being taken up and worked through by the force of logic, by examples, and by appeals to reason. The result is a well-organized conceptualization of how the self develops, and how a sense of community and the existence of myriad social organizations are instilled in the minds of individuals through the mechanisms of symbolic communications, first in terms of gestures and then through the medium of language, which is what separates humans from infrahuman organisms.

From my own point of view, the fullest comprehension of human personality comes from understanding the concepts of all personality theorists. Mead's viewpoints are so unique that an understanding of his ideas is essential for a complete understanding of the nature of human nature. It is hoped that you will be led to sample all the original writings of the various personality theorists presented in this book.

GEORGE H. MEAD
Language and the development of the self

The primitive situation is that of the social act which involves the interaction of different forms[1] to each other, in carrying out the social process. Within that process one can find what we term the gestures, those phases of the act which bring about the adjustment of the response of the other form. These phases of the act carry with them the attitude as the observer recognizes it, and also what we call the inner attitude. The animal may be angry or afraid. There are such emotional attitudes which lie back of these acts, but these are only part of the whole process which is going on. Anger expresses itself in attack; fear expresses itself in flight. We can see, then, that the gestures mean these attitudes on the part of the form, that is, they have that meaning for us. We see that an animal is angry and is going to attack. We know that that is in the action of the animal, and is revealed by the attitude of the animal. We cannot say that the animal means it in the sense that he has a reflective determination to attack. A man may strike another before he means it; a man may jump and run away from a loud sound behind his back before he knows what he is doing. If he has the idea in his mind, then the gesture not only means this to the observer but it also means the idea

George H. Mead, "Language and the Development of the Self." Reprinted from George H. Mead, *Mind, Self, and Society* (Chicago: University of Chicago Press, 1934), pp. 179–189. © 1934 University of Chicago Press. All rights reserved.
[1] The term *form* is used throughout this passage in the sense of *organism* or *individual*.

which the individual has. In one case the observer sees that the attitude of the dog means attack, but he does not say that it means a conscious determination to attack on the part of the dog. However, if somebody shakes his fist in your face you assume that he has not only a hostile attitude but that he has some idea behind it. You assume that it means not only a possible attack, but that the individual has an idea in his experience.

When, now, that gesture means this idea behind it and it arouses that idea in the other individual, then we have a significant symbol. In the case of the dogfight we have a gesture which calls out appropriate response; in the present case we have a symbol which answers to a meaning in the experience of the first individual and which also calls out that meaning in the second individual. Where the gesture reaches that situation it has become what we call "language." It is now a significant symbol and it signifies a certain meaning.

The gesture is that phase of the individual act to which adjustment takes place on the part of other individuals in the social process of behavior. The vocal gesture becomes a significant symbol (unimportant, as such, on the merely affective side of experience) when it has the same effect on the individual making it that it has on the individual to whom it is addressed or who explicitly responds to it, and thus involves a reference to the self of the individual making it. The gesture in general, and the vocal gesture in particular, indicates some object or other within the field of social behavior, an object of common interest to all the individuals involved in the given social act thus directed toward or upon that object. The function of the gesture is to make adjustment possible among the individuals implicated in any given social act with reference to the object or objects with which that act is concerned; and the significant gesture or significant symbol affords far greater facilities for such adjustment and readjustment than does the non-significant gesture, because it calls out in the individual making it the same attitude toward it (or toward its meaning) that it calls out in the other individuals participating with him in the given social act, and thus makes him conscious of their attitude toward it (as a component of his behavior) and enables him to adjust his subsequent behavior to theirs in the light of that attitude. In short, the conscious or significant conversation of gestures is a much more adequate and effective mechanism of mutual adjustment within the social act— involving, as it does, the taking, by each of the individuals carrying it on, of the attitudes of the others toward himself— than is the unconscious or nonsignificant conversation of gestures.

When, in any given social act or situation, one individual indicates by a gesture to another individual what this other individual is to do, the first individual is conscious of the meaning of his own gesture—or the meaning of his gesture appears in his own experience— insofar as he takes the attitude of the second individual toward that gesture, and tends to respond to it implicitly in the same way that the second individual responds to it explicitly. Gestures become significant symbols when they implicitly arouse in an individual making them the same responses which they explicitly

arouse, or are supposed to arouse, in other individuals, the individuals to whom they are addressed; and in all conversations of gestures within the social process, whether external (between different individuals) or internal (between a given individual and himself), the individual's consciousness of the content and flow of meaning involved depends on his thus taking the attitude of the other toward his own gestures. In this way every gesture comes within a given social group or community to stand for a particular act or response, namely, the act or response which it calls forth explicitly in the individual to whom it is addressed, and implicitly in the individual who makes it; and this particular act or response for which it stands is its meaning as a significant symbol. Only in terms of gestures as significant symbols is the existence of mind or intelligence possible; for only in terms of gestures which are significant symbols can thinking—which is simply an internalized or implicit conversation of the individual with himself by means of such gestures—take place. The internalization in our experience of the external conversations of gestures which we carry on with other individuals in the social process is the essence of thinking; and the gestures thus internalized are significant symbols because they have the same meanings for all individual members of the given society or social group, i.e., they respectively arouse the same attitudes in the individuals making them that they arouse in the individuals responding to them: otherwise the individual could not internalize them or be conscious of them and their meanings. As we shall see, the same procedure which is responsible for the genesis and existence of mind or consciousness—namely, the taking of the attitude of the other toward one's self, or toward one's own behavior—also necessarily involves the genesis and existence at the same time of significant symbols, or significant gestures.

In the case of the vocal gesture the form hears its own stimulus just as when this is used by other forms, so it tends to respond also to its own stimulus as it responds to the stimulus of other forms. That is, birds tend to sing to themselves, babies to talk to themselves. The sounds they make are stimuli to make other sounds. Where there is a specific sound that calls out a specific response, then if this sound is made by other forms it calls out this response in the form in question. If the sparrow[2] makes use of this particular sound then the response to that sound will be one which will be heard more frequently than another response. In that way there will be selected out of the sparrow's repertoire those elements which are found in the song of the canary, and gradually such selection would build up in the song of the sparrow those elements which are common to both, without assuming a particular tendency of imitation. There is here a selective process by which is picked out what is common. "Imitation" depends upon the individual influencing himself as others influence him, so that he is under the influence not only of the other but also of himself insofar as he uses the same vocal gesture.

The vocal gesture, then, has an importance which no other gesture has. We cannot see ourselves when our face assumes a certain expression. If we hear ourselves speak we are more apt to pay attention. One hears himself when he is irritated using a tone that is of an irritable quality, and so catches himself. But in the facial expression of irritation the stimulus is not one that calls out an expression in the individual which it calls out in the other. One is more apt to catch himself up and control himself in the vocal gesture than in the expression of the countenance.

It is only the actor who uses bodily expression as a means of looking as he wants others to feel. He gets a response which reveals to him how he looks by continually using a mirror. He registers anger, he registers love, he registers this, that, or the other attitude, and he examines himself in a glass to see how he does so. When he later makes use of the gesture it is present as a mental image. He realizes that that particular expression does call out fright. If we exclude vocal gestures, it is only by the use of the mirror that one could reach the position where he responds to his own gestures as other people respond. But the vocal gesture is one which does give one this capacity for answering to one's own stimulus as another would answer.

If there is any truth in the old axiom that the bully is always the coward, it will be found to rest on the fact that one arouses in himself that attitude of fear which his bullying attitude arouses in another, so that when put into a particular situation which calls his bluff, his own attitude is found to be that of the others. If one's own attitude of giving way to the bullying attitude of others is one that arouses the bullying attitude, he has in that degree aroused the attitude of bullying in himself. There is a certain amount of truth in this when we come back to the effect upon one's self of the gesture of which he makes use. Insofar as one calls out the attitude in himself that one calls out in others, the response is picked out and strengthened. That is the only basis for what we call imitation. It is not imitation in the sense of simply doing

---

[2] When you put a sparrow and a canary together in neighboring cages and the call of one calls out a series of notes in the other.

what one sees another person doing. The mechanism is that of an individual calling out in himself the response which he calls out in another, consequently giving greater weight to those responses than to the other responses, and gradually building up those sets of responses into a dominant whole. That may be done, as we say, unconsciously. The sparrow does not know it is imitating the canary. It is just a gradual picking up of the notes which are common to both of them. And that is true wherever there is imitation.

So far as exclamatory sounds are concerned (and they would answer in our own vocal gestures to what is found in those of animals), the response to these does not enter into immediate conversation, and the influence of these responses on the individual are comparatively slight. It seems to be difficult to bring them into relationship with significant speech. We are not consciously frightened when we speak angrily to someone else, but the meaning of what we say is always present to us when we speak. The response in the individual to an exclamatory cry which is of the same sort as that in the other does not play any important part in the conduct of the form. The response of the lion to its roar is of very little importance in the response of the form itself, but our response to the meaning of what we say is constantly attached to our conversation. We must be constantly responding to the gesture we make if we are to carry on successful vocal conversation. The meaning of what we are saying is the tendency to respond to it. You ask somebody to bring a visitor a chair. You arouse the tendency to get the chair in the other, but if he is slow to act you get the chair yourself. The response to the vocal gesture is the doing of a certain thing, and you arouse that same tendency in yourself. You are always replying to yourself, just as other people reply. You assume that in some degree there must be identity in the reply. It is action on a common basis.

I have contrasted two situations to show what a long road speech or communication has to travel from the situation where there is nothing but vocal cries over to the situation in which significant symbols are utilized. What is peculiar to the latter is that the individual responds to his own stimulus in the same way as other people respond. Then the stimulus becomes significant; then one is saying something. As far as a parrot is concerned, its "speech" means nothing, but where one significantly says something with his own vocal process he is saying it to himself as well as to everybody else within reach of his voice. It is only the vocal gesture that is fitted for this sort of communication, because it is only the vocal gesture to which one responds or tends to respond as another person tends to respond to it. It is true that the language of the hands is of the same character. One sees one's self using the gestures which those who are deaf make use of. They influence one the same way as they influence others. Of course, the same is true of any form of script. But such symbols have all been developed out of the specific vocal gesture, for that is the basic gesture which does influence the individual as it influences others. Where it does not become significant is in the vocalization of the two birds. Nevertheless, the same type of process is present, the stimulus of the one bird tending to call out the response in another bird which it tends to call out, however slightly, in the bird itself.

When we speak of the meaning of what we are doing we are making the response itself that we are on the point of carrying out a stimulus to our action. It becomes a stimulus to a later stage of action which is to take place from the point of view of this particular response. In the case of the boxer the blow that he is starting to direct toward his opponent is to call out a certain response which will open up the guard of his opponent so that he can strike. The meaning is a stimulus for the preparation of the real blow he expects to deliver. The response which he calls out in himself (the guarding reaction) is the stimulus to him to strike where an opening is given. This action which he has initiated already in himself thus becomes a stimulus for his later response. He knows what his opponent is going to do, since the guarding movement is one which is already aroused, and becomes a stimulus to strike where the opening is given. The meaning would not have been present in his conduct unless it became a stimulus to strike where the favorable opening appears.

Such is the difference between intelligent conduct on the part of animals and what we call a reflective individual. We say the animal does not think. He does not put himself in a position for which he is responsible; he does not put himself in the place of the other person and say, in effect, "He will act in such a way and I will act in this way." If the individual can act in this way, and the attitude which he calls out in himself can become a stimulus to him for another act, we have meaningful conduct. Where the response of the other person is called out and becomes a stimulus to control his action, then he has the meaning of the other person's act in his own experience. That is the general mechanism of what we term "thought," for in order that thought may exist there must be symbols, vocal gestures generally, which arouse in the individual himself the response which he is calling out in the other, and such that

from the point of view of the response he is able to direct his later conduct. It involves not only communication in the sense in which birds and animals communicate with each other, but also an arousal in the individual himself of the response which he is calling out in the other individual, a taking of the role of the other, a tendency to act as the other person acts. One participates in the same process the other person is carrying out and controls his action with reference to that participation. It is that which constitutes the meaning of an object, namely, the common response in one's self as well as in the other person, which becomes, in turn, a stimulus to one's self.

If you conceive of the mind as just a sort of conscious substance in which there are certain impressions and states, and hold that one of those states is a universal, then a word becomes purely arbitrary—it is just a symbol. You can then take words and pronounce them backwards, as children do; there seems to be absolute freedom of arrangement and language seems to be an entirely mechanical thing that lies outside of the process of intelligence. If you recognize that language is, however, just a part of a cooperative process, that part which does lead to an adjustment to the response of the other so that the whole activity can go on, then language has only a limited range of arbitrariness. If you are talking to another person you are, perhaps, able to scent the change in his attitude by something that would not strike a third person at all. You may know his mannerism, and that becomes a gesture to you, a part of the response of the individual. There is a certain range possible within the gesture as to what is to serve as the symbol. We may say that a whole set of separate symbols with one meaning are acceptable; but they always are gestures, that is, they are always parts of the act of the individual which reveal what he is going to do to the other person so that when the person utilizes the clew he calls out in himself the attitude of the other. Language is not ever arbitrary in the sense of simply denoting a bare state of consciousness by a word. What particular part of one's act will serve to direct cooperative activity is more or less arbitrary. Different phases of the act may do it. What seems unimportant in itself may be highly important in revealing what the attitude is. In that sense one can speak of the gesture itself as unimportant, but it is of great importance as to what the gesture is going to reveal. This is seen in the difference between the purely intellectual character of the symbol and its emotional character. A poet depends upon the latter; for him language is rich and full of values which we, perhaps, utterly ignore. In trying to express a message in something, less than ten words, we merely want to convey a certain meaning, while the poet is dealing with what is really living tissue, the emotional throb in the expression itself. There is, then, a great range in our use of language; but whatever phase of this range is used is a part of a social process, and it is always that part by means of which we affect ourselves as we affect others and mediate the social situation through this understanding of what we are saying. That is fundamental for any language; if it is going to be language one has to understand what he is saying, has to affect himself as he affects others.

The fundamental difference between the game and play is that in the latter the child must have the attitude of all the others involved in that game. The attitudes of the other players which the participant assumes organize into a sort of unit, and it is that organization which controls the response of the individual. The illustration used was of a person playing baseball. Each one of his own acts is determined by his assumption of the action of the others who are playing the game. What he does is controlled by his being everyone else on that team, at least insofar as those attitudes affect his own particular response. We get then an "other" which is an organization of the attitudes of those involved in the same process.

The organized community or social group which gives to the individual his unity of self may be called "the generalized other." The attitude of the generalized other is the attitude of the whole community. Thus, for example, in the case of such a social group as a ball team, the team is the generalized other insofar as it enters—as an organized process or social activity—into the experience of any one of the individual members of it.

If the given human individual is to develop a self in the fullest sense, it is not sufficient for him merely to take the attitudes of other human individuals toward himself and toward one another within the human social process, and to bring that social process as a whole into his individual experience merely in these terms: he must also, in the same way that he takes the attitudes of other individuals toward himself and toward one another, take their attitudes toward the various phases or aspects of the common social activity or set of social undertakings in which, as members of an organized society or social group, they are all engaged; and he must then, by generalizing these individual attitudes of that organized society or social group itself, as a whole, act toward different social projects which at any given time it is carrying out, or toward the various larger phases of the general social process which constitutes its life and of which these projects are specific manifestations. This getting of the broad activities of any given social whole or organized society as such within the experiential field of any one of the individuals involved or included in that whole is, in other words, the essential basis and prerequisite of the fullest development of that individual's self: only insofar as he takes the attitudes of the organized social group to which he belongs toward the organized, cooperative social activity or set of such activities in which that group as such is engaged, does he develop a complete self or possess the sort of complete self he has developed. And on the other hand, the complex cooperative processes and activities and institutional functionings of organized human society are also possible only insofar as every individual involved in them or belonging to that society can take the general attitudes of all other such individuals with reference to these processes and activities and institutional functionings, and to the organized social whole of experiential relations and interactions thereby constituted—and can direct his own behavior accordingly.

It is in the form of the generalized other that the social process influences the behavior of the individuals involved in it and carrying it on, i.e., that the community exercises control over the conduct of its individual members; for it is in this form that the social process or community enters as a determining factor into the individual's thinking. In abstract thought the individual takes the attitude of the generalized other toward himself, without reference to its expression in any particular other individuals; and in concrete thought he takes that attitude insofar as it is expressed in the attitudes toward his behavior of those other individuals with

whom he is involved in the given social situation or act. But only by taking the attitude of the generalized other toward himself, in one or another of these ways, can he think at all; for only thus can thinking—or the internalized conversation of gestures which constitutes thinking—occur. And only through the taking by individuals of the attitude or attitudes of the generalized other toward themselves is the existence of a universe of discourse, as that system of common or social meanings which thinking presupposes at its context, rendered possible.

The self-conscious human individual, then, takes or assumes the organized social attitudes of the given social group or community (or of some one section thereof) to which he belongs, toward the social problems of various kinds which confront that group or community at any given time, and which arise in connection with the correspondingly different social projects or organized cooperative enterprises in which that group or community as such is engaged; and as an individual participant in these social projects or cooperative enterprises, he governs his own conduct accordingly. In politics, for example, the individual identifies himself with an entire political party and takes the organized attitudes of that entire party toward the rest of the given social community and toward the problems which confront the party within the given social situation; and he consequently reacts or responds in terms of the organized attitudes of the party as a whole. He thus enters into a special set of social relations with all the other individuals who belong to that political party; and in the same way he enters into various other special sets of social relations, with various other classes of individuals respectively, the individuals of each of these classes being the other members of some one of the particular organized subgroups (determined in socially functional terms) of which he himself is a member within the entire given society or social community. In the most highly developed, organized, and complicated human social communities—those evolved by civilized man—these various socially functional classes or subgroups of individuals to which any given individual belongs (and with the other individual members of which he thus enters into a special set of social relations) are of two kinds. Some of them are concrete social classes or subgroups, such as political parties, clubs, corporations, which are all actually functional social units, in terms of which their individual members are directly related to one another. The others are abstract social classes or subgroups, such as the class of debtors and the class of creditors, in terms of which their individual members are related to one another only more or less indirectly, and which only more or less indirectly function as social units, but which afford or represent unlimited possibilities for the widening and ramifying and enriching of the social relations among all the individual members of the given society as an organized and unified whole. The given individual's membership in several of these abstract social classes or subgroups makes possible his entrance into definite social relations (however indirect) with an almost infinite number of other individuals who also belong to or are included within one or another of these abstract social classes or subgroups cutting across functional lines of demarcation which divide different human social communities from one another, and including individual members from several (in some cases

from all) such communities. Of these abstract social classes or subgroups of human individuals the one which is most inclusive and extensive is, of course, the one defined by the logical universe of discourse (or system of universally significant symbols) determined by the participation and communicative interaction of individuals; for of all such classes or subgroups, it is the one which claims the largest number of individual members, and which enables the largest conceivable number of human individuals to enter into some sort of social relation, however indirect or abstract it may be, with one another—a relation arising from the universal functioning of gestures as significant symbols in the general human social process of communication.

I have pointed out, then, that there are two general stages in the full development of the self. At the first of these stages, the individual's self is constituted simply by an organization of the particular attitudes of other individuals toward himself and toward one another in the specific social acts in which he participates with them. But at the second stage in the full development of the individual's self that self is constituted not only by an organization of these particular individual attitudes, but also by an organization of the social attitudes of the generalized other or the social group as a whole to which he belongs. These social or group attitudes are brought within the individual's field of direct experience, and are included as elements in the structure or constitution of his self, in the same way that the attitudes of particular other individuals are; and the individual arrives at them, or succeeds in taking them, by means of further organizing, and then generalizing, the attitudes of particular other individuals in terms of their organized social bearings and implications. So the self reaches its full development by organizing these individual attitudes of others into the organized social or group attitudes, and by thus becoming an individual reflection of the general systematic pattern of social or group behavior in which it and the others are all involved—a pattern which enters as a whole into the individual's experience in terms of these organized group attitudes which, through the mechanism of his central nervous system, he takes toward himself, just as he takes the individual attitudes of others.

The game has a logic, so that such an organization of the self is rendered possible: there is a definite end to be obtained; the actions of the different individuals are all related to each other with reference to that end so that they do not conflict; one is not in conflict with himself in the attitude of another man on the team. If one has the attitude of the person throwing the ball he can also have the response of catching the ball. The two are related so that they further the purpose of the game itself. They are interrelated in a unitary, organic fashion. There is a definite unity, then, which is introduced into the organization of other selves when we reach such a stage as that of the game, as over against the situation of play where there is a simple succession of one role after another, a situation which is, of course, characteristic of the child's own personality. The child is one thing at one time and another at another, and what he is at one moment does not determine what he is at another. That is both the charm of childhood as well as its inadequacy. You cannot count on the child; you cannot assume that all the things he does are going to determine what he will do at any moment. He is not organized into a whole. The child has no definite character, no definite personality.

The game is then an illustration of the situation out of which an organized personality arises. Insofar as the child does take the attitude of the other and allows that attitude of the other to determine the thing he is going to do with reference to a common end, he is becoming an organic member of society. He is taking over the morale of that society and is becoming an essential member of it. He belongs to it insofar as he does allow the attitude of the other that he takes to control his own immediate expression. What is involved here is some sort of an organized process. That which is expressed in terms of the game is, of course, being continually expressed in the social life of the child, but this wider process goes beyond the immediate experience of the child himself. The importance of the game is that it lies entirely inside of the child's own experience, and the importance of our modern type of education is that it is brought as far as possible within this realm. The different attitudes that a child assumes are so organized that they exercise a definite control over his response, as the attitudes in a game control his own immediate response. In the game we get an organized other, a generalized other, which is found in the nature of the child itself, and finds its expression in the immediate experience of the child. And it is that organized activity in the child's own nature controlling the particular response which gives unity, and which builds up his own self.

What goes on in the game goes on in the life of the child all the time. He is continually taking the attitudes of those about him, especially the roles of those who in some sense control him and on whom he depends. He gets the function of the process in an abstract sort of a way at first. It goes over from the play into the game in a real sense. He has to play the game. The morale of the game takes hold of the child more than the larger morale of the whole community. The child passes into the game and the game expresses a social situation in which he can completely enter; its morale may have a greater hold on him than that of the family to which he belongs or the community in which he lives. There are all sorts of social organizations, some of which are fairly lasting, some temporary, into which the child is entering, and he is playing a sort of social game in them. It is a period in which he likes "to belong," and he gets into organizations which come into existence and pass out of existence. He becomes a something which can function in the organized whole, and thus tends to determine himself in his relationship with the group to which he belongs. That process is one which is a striking stage in the development of the child's morale. It constitutes him a self-conscious member of the community to which he belongs.

Such is the process by which a personality arises. I have spoken of this as a process in which a child takes the role of the other, and said that it takes place essentially through the use of language. Language is predominantly based on the vocal gesture by means of which cooperative activities in a community are carried out. Language in its significant sense is that vocal gesture which tends to arouse in the individual the attitude which it arouses in others, and it is this perfecting of the self by the gesture which mediates the social activities that gives rise to the process of taking the role of the other. The latter phrase is a little unfortunate because it suggests an actor's attitude which is actually more sophisticated than that which is involved in our own experience. To this degree it does not correctly describe that which I have in mind. We see the process most definitely in a primitive form in those situations where the child's play takes different roles. Here the very fact that he is ready to pay out money, for instance, arouses the attitude of the person who receives money; the very process is calling out in him the corresponding activities of the other person involved. The individual stimulates himself to the response which he is calling out in the other person, and then acts in some degree in response to that situation. In play the child does definitely act out the role which he himself has aroused in himself. It is that which gives, as I have said, a definite content in the individual which answers to the stimulus that affects him as it affects somebody else. The content of the other that enters into one personality is the response in the individual which his gesture calls out in the other.

We may illustrate our basic concept by a reference to the notion of property. If we say "This is my property, I shall control it," that affirmation calls out a certain set of responses which must be the same in any community in which property exists. It involves an organized attitude with reference to property which is common to all the members of the community. One must have a definite attitude of control of his own property and respect for the property of others. Those attitudes (as organized sets of responses) must be there on the part of all, so that when one says such a thing he calls out in himself the response of the others. He is calling out the response of what I have called a generalized other. That which makes society possible is such common responses, such organized attitudes, with reference to what we term property, the cults of religion, the process of education, and the relations of the family. Of course, the wider the society the more definitely universal these objects must be. In any case there must be a definite set of responses, which we may speak of as abstract, and which can belong to a very large group. Property is in itself a very abstract concept. It is that which the individual himself can control and nobody else can control. The attitude is different from that of a dog toward a bone. A dog will fight any other dog trying to take the bone. The dog is not taking the attitude of the other dog. A man who says "This is my property" is taking an attitude of the other person. The man is appealing to his rights because he is able to take the attitude which everybody else in the group has with reference to property, thus arousing in himself the attitude of others.

What goes to make up the organized self is the organization of the attitudes which are common to the group. A person is a personality because he belongs to a community, because he takes over the institutions of that community into his own conduct. He takes its language as a medium by which he gets his personality, and then through a process of taking the different roles that all the others furnish he comes to get the attitude of the members of the community. Such, in a certain sense, is the structure of a man's personality. There are certain common responses which each individual has toward certain common things, and insofar as those common responses are awakened in the individual when he is affecting other persons he arouses his own self. The structure, then, on which the self is built is this response which is common to all, for one has to be a member of a community to be a self. Such responses are abstract attitudes, but they constitute just what we term a man's character. They give him what we term his prin-

ciples, the acknowledged attitudes of all members of the community toward what are the values of that community. He is putting himself in the place of the generalized other, which represents the organized responses of all the members of the group. It is that which guides conduct controlled by principles, and a person who has such an organized group of responses is a man who we say has character, in the moral sense.

It is a structure of attitudes, then, which goes to make up a self, as distinct from a group of habits. We all of us have, for example, certain groups of habits, such as the particular intonations which a person uses in his speech. This is a set of habits of vocal expression which one has but which one does not know about. The sets of habits which we have of that sort mean nothing to us; we do not hear the intonations of our speech that others hear unless we are paying particular attention to them. The habits of emotional expression which belong to our speech are of the same sort. We may know that we have expressed ourselves in a joyous fashion but the detailed process is one which does not come back to our conscious selves. There are whole bundles of such habits which do not enter into a conscious self, but which help to make up what is termed the unconscious self.

After all, what we mean by self-consciousness is an awakening in ourselves of the group of attitudes which we are arousing in others, especially when it is an important set of responses which go to make up the members of the community. It is unfortunate to fuse or mix up consciousness, as we ordinarily use that term, and self-consciousness. Consciousness, as frequently used, simply has reference to the field of experience, but self-consciousness refers to the ability to call out in ourselves a set of definite responses which belong to the others of the group. Consciousness and self-consciousness are not on the same level. A man alone has, fortunately or unfortunately, access to his own toothache, but that is not what we mean by self-consciousness.

I have so far emphasized what I have called the structures upon which the self is constructed, the framework of the self, as it were. Of course we are not only what is common to all: each one of the selves is different from everyone else; but there has to be such a common structure as I have sketched in order that we may be members of a community at all. We cannot be ourselves unless we are also members in whom there is a community of attitudes which control the attitudes of all. We cannot have rights unless we have common attitudes. That which we have acquired as self-conscious persons makes us such members of society and gives us selves. Selves can only exist in definite relationships to other selves. No hard-and-fast line can be drawn between our own selves and the selves of others, since our own selves exist and enter as such into our experience only insofar as the selves of others exist and enter as such into our experience also. The individual possesses a self only in relation to the selves of the other members of his social group; and the structure of his self expresses or reflects the general behavior pattern of this social group to which he belongs, just as does the structure of the self of every other individual belonging to this social group.

CHAPTER 10

Constitutional Theory: Sheldon

Introduction

Physiognomists deal with the body and the personality. Since body measurements are objective, the general research procedure, as in William H. Sheldon's (1899–1977) early research reported here, is to make mathematical correlations between physical measurements and ratings of personality traits.

If there is a correlation between appearance and personality, the relationship may be mediated by society—not by biology. If in a particular society fat people are considered attractive and thin people ugly, a fat child is likely to develop a favorable personality, not as a direct result of the fatness but rather because of positive social attitudes toward obesity. Social reactions to one's appearance, whether it be height or weight, color of skin, or other aspects, may affect one's personality.

Sheldon apparently was not discouraged by the low findings of this research, since he went on to conduct considerably more complex investigations and wrote several large books on the general topic of physiognomy and personality. However, he has been a lone voice; generally, few in the field of applied personality accept the notion that there is any worthwhile degree of correlation between personality and body size or shape.

Constitutional Theory

WILLIAM H. SHELDON
Social traits and morphologic types

Since there is some statistical evidence in support of the existence of a relationship between morphological index and intelligence, it seems at least possible that relationships may exist between this morphological index and other samplings of behavior. It is conceivable certainly that bodily proportions and relative activity of the vegetative system might influence certain forms of social behavior much more markedly than these conditions could influence general intelligence.

There are many common prejudices in support of such a notion. Fat men are often referred to as generally sociable and good-natured. Thin, alert, quick-moving men are sometimes regarded with suspicion; it is frequently assumed that the latter are selfish, aggressive, or unsociable. The former usually belong in the macrosplanchnic classification, and the latter are the generally microsplanchnic. There is furthermore some good clinical evidence that certain general psychological types are closely related to distinctive types of physique. Kretschmer found a close association between the asthenic physique and dementia praecox symptoms; also between the pyknic physique and a manic-depressive condition.[1] Clearly Kretschmer's asthenic physique is almost identical with the late

Sante Naccarati's microsplanchnic, while the pyknic (fat man) is pretty sure to be a macrosplanchnic.

In order to experiment with the possibility of finding relations between physical and social traits, a form of rating scale was adapted to the measurement of certain social traits among college students. Five traits were selected which have been widely used in rating scales, and have been commonly associated with physical attributes. These were *sociability, perseverance, leadership, aggressiveness,* and *emotional excitability.*

OBTAINING MEASUREMENTS OF SOCIAL TRAITS

The process of obtaining measurements of social traits by a rating scale method may well be described as consisting of about five fairly definite steps: (1) selection and description of the traits to be measured, (2) selection of the subjects to be measured, (3) selection of raters, (4) getting the cooperation of these raters, and (5) the process of rating, i.e., of obtaining and recording ratings.

1. *The description of the traits.* In this study the following typed descriptions of the traits used were placed in the hands of the raters:

1. Sociability. Consider (this man's) general sociability, his good-naturedness and likeableness; how easily and pleasantly he gets along with people. Is he above or below the average fraternity man in popularity and general likeableness?

William H. Sheldon, "Social Traits and Morphologic Types." Reprinted from the *Journal of Personnel Research*, 1927, 5, 47–55. Reprinted with permission of *Personnel Journal*, © March 1927.

[1] Kretschmer, E. *Physique and Character.* New York: Harcourt Brace, 1925.

2. *Perseverance.* Consider his perseverance and determination; his tenacity of purpose. Is he of the sort who sticks to a project with great tenaciousness, or does he tend to "go from one thing to another?" How determined is he?

3. *Leadership.* Consider his leadership ability. Does he appear to dominate his group, (i.e., the other freshmen in the fraternity), and to influence their thinking and activities? To what extent does he seem to influence his associates?

4. *Aggressiveness.* Consider his personal aggressiveness. Does he generally push himself forward, as in fraternity meetings, discussions and arguments, social gatherings, etc.? How self-assertive and aggressive is he?

5. *Emotional excitability.* Consider his emotional excitability. Does he get excited easily, express himself violently, raise his voice, or lose his temper? Does he get angry and flushed and "wrought up" easily? How excitable is he?

2. *Selection of subjects.* The rating was limited to freshmen who had joined fraternities, as each of these men was presumably well known to a definite group of older students who were available as raters. Moreover it was possible to rate these men in convenient small groups, thus making each rating definitely comparative.

All but three of the fraternities on the campus were included in the experiment, but about 40 of the freshmen who for one reason or another were not at the time well known to their respective fraternities, were omitted. Ratings were obtained on

	Rating
Name.........................	1. ....
	2. ....
	3. ....
	4. ....
	5. ....
Name.........................	1. ....
	2. ....
	3. ....
	4. ....
	5. ....
Name.........................	1. ....
	2. ....
	3. ....
	4. ....
	5. ....
Name.........................	1. ....
	2. ....
	3. ....
	4. ....
	5. ....
Name.........................	1. ....
	2. ....
	3. ....
	4. ....
	5. ....

FIGURE 10.1. Rating card

155 of the freshmen whose morphological measurements had previously been taken.

3. *Selection of raters.* At each fraternity five men were selected as raters. In choosing these men the first criterion was that they be upperclassmen who knew the freshmen; second, that they be if possible men whom the writer already knew (through university personnel work, classroom work, student activities, etc.); third, that they be entirely willing to serve in the experiment. These men were asked for three quarters of an hour of their time, and they retired with the writer to some room in the fraternity house to make the ratings.

4. *Getting cooperation.* In order to accomplish this purpose, I proceeded in much the manner of introducing the subject of rating scales to a small class of students. In a 15-minute talk, the general history, chief uses, and most common shortcomings of rating scales were explained. I especially stressed and illustrated the so-called "halo error," and the error of avoiding the lower extremes of the scale (rating too high). These students were well aware that a good deal of careless rating scale work had been carried on. Many of them had been called upon to make ratings with very inadequate instructions, and often without knowledge of the nature of the problem involved. They had to be interested in rating scales, and one way of accomplishing this was to teach them as much as possible about rating scales in the time available.

All of the students used as raters were at least reasonably coöperative. Some were really enthusiastic. In one fraternity I was unable to get five satisfactory raters; in two it turned out that there was a good deal of internal disagreement with regard to freshmen and other matters. These three fraternities were omitted.

5. *Obtaining and recording ratings.*

Following the preliminary discussion of rating scales, each of the five raters was provided with a card on which were printed the names of the freshmen to be rated. Opposite each name was a column of serial numbers, from 1 to 5; these numbers represented the five traits. Trait number 1 was sociability; number 2, perseverance, etc. The card appeared as in Figure 10.1. If more than five freshmen were to be rated, more than one card was provided. Next, each rater was supplied with the sheet on which was printed the description of traits mentioned above. At the bottom of this sheet the following instructions appeared:

These ratings are to be made on a scale of ten. If a man is extremely high in a particular trait, he should be given a rating of *nine* or *ten* in that trait; if he is extremely low, a rating of *one* or *two*. If he is about average, for fraternity men of your acquaintance, he should receive a rating of about *five*.

As soon as the instructions were thoroughly understood, the raters were told to consider the first trait, sociability. They read the description of that trait, and when each rater was sure that he understood what was meant by sociability as well as he *could* understand it *from the description given,* he proceeded to rate each of his freshmen on that trait. This procedure was followed for each of the five traits. The raters were cautioned, after rating each trait, to try to keep their average rating at above five, to forget about every other trait except the one being rated, and that high ratings were not necessarily favorable ratings.

The distinctive feature of this method was its fairly successful avoidance of the common error of rating indiscriminately high or indiscriminately average. Instructions were thoroughly standard for the different rating groups, and careless rating was held at a minimum. One serious error in such ratings would evi-

TABLE 10.1. Reliability coefficients of two ratings of the same men

	Socia-bility	Perse-verance	Leader-ship	Aggres-siveness	Emotional excitability
r_{12}	0.93	0.89	0.85	0.90	0.82

$N = 28$

dently arise from different interfraternity standards of judgment. This was unavoidable and undoubtedly played some part in the results. However, it was corrected for statistically in the following manner: A freshman's rating on a given trait was considered to be the sum of the five ratings given him by his fraternity brothers. He thus really had one rating, made on a basis of 50. If the average of the ratings made by his fraternity on that trait exceeded the average for the entire group of raters, his rating was lowered by the amount of this deviation—and, of course, vice versa. A simple formula illustrates this correction:

$$Rc = R + (Mg - Mf)$$

When Rc = Corrected rating
R = Original rating of a man by his fraternity
Mf = Mean of the ratings made by this fraternity on that trait
Mg = Mean of the ratings by the whole group on that trait

RELIABILITY OF THE RATINGS

A check on the reliability of these social ratings was attempted by asking five of the fraternities to rerate their freshman, about a month after the original rating had been made. Twenty-eight freshmen were thus rerated, and these new ratings were correlated with the original ratings for each of the traits. These correlations appear in Table 10.1.

The average correlation for the 5 traits is 0.88, which is about as high as the coefficient of reliability for most intelligence tests.

The remainder of the present section of this study will be devoted to correlation (1) between these social ratings and morphologic measurements; and (2) between the social ratings and intelligence criteria.

SOCIAL RATINGS AND MORPHOLOGIC MEASUREMENTS

These correlations appear in Table 10.2.

TABLE 10.2. Correlations of morphologic measurements and social ratings

	Socia-bility	Perse-verance	Leader-ship	Aggres-siveness	Emotional excitability
Morphologic index	−0.217	0.011	−0.138	−0.076	−0.004
Length of lower extremities.	−0.072	−0.006	0.005	0.141	0.059
Length of upper extremities	−0.003	−0.024	0.023	0.031	0.072
Sternum length	0.053	0.055	0.145	0.113	0.034
Xipho-epigastric	−0.092	−0.023	0.071	0.003	0.057
Transverse thoracic diameter	0.001	−0.009	0.114	0.168	0.112
Anterior-posterior thoracic diameter. ...	−0.008	−0.025	0.024	0.077	0.039
Transverse epigastric diameter	0.029	−0.111	0.084	0.240	0.041
Anterior-posterior epigastric diameter ..	0.005	−0.046	0.009	0.063	0.039
Transverse pelvic diameter	−0.084	0.036	0.026	0.086	0.029
Height........................	0.002	−0.065	0.049	0.133	0.093
Weight	0.131	0.028	0.024	0.073	0.079

There are no high correlations in the group. Of the 60 correlations, 12 are above 0.10, 2 are above 0.20, and 18 are negative. Thirty-three of the group are lower than their probable errors; only three are above three times their probable errors, and but one is four times its probable error (that between aggressiveness and transverse epigastric diameter). These are not very high correlations. Yet a few of them appear to merit further consideration.

Sociability shows a negative correlation (- 0.217) with morphological index, and a positive one with weight (0.131). This seems to support to some slight extent the popular notion that fat or "heavy-set" men are more sociable than thin men. Yet there is no correlation higher than 0.09 between sociability and any single physical measurement. Whatever relation exists here certainly is not due to the preponderance of any particular part of the anatomy over the rest.

The trait *Aggressiveness* shows the greatest number of relatively high correlations with the physical measurements. Here 5 of the 12 correlations are higher than 0.10. The correlation of 0.240 between this trait and transverse epigastric diameter is the highest in the entire group. Incidentally, this same physical trait shows a higher average correlation (0.10) with all five of the social traits than does any other of the measurements. Aggressiveness appears to go with bigness of frame rather than with any special morphologic trait. It correlates positively with long legs (0.141), with a long sternum (0.113), with a wide chest (0.168), with a wide "middle" (0.240), with height (0.133), and with weight (0.073). Weight apparently is less a factor here than general bigness of stature. There seems to be some slight evidence that macrosplanchnics are more aggressive than microsplanchnics.

In the column headed *Leadership* three correlations are over ±0.10. The correlation with morphologic index is −0.138. The large-bodied fellows (macrosplanchnics) are somewhat higher in both sociability and leadership, apparently to about the same degree that they are lower in scholarship and intelligence. The correlation of 0.145 between leadership and sternum length is probably not entirely due to chance, as this measurement correlates positively with all five of the social traits.

Emotionality correlates uniformly low with almost all of these measurements.

TABLE 10.3. Intercorrelations of social traits

	Socia-bility	Perse-verance	Leader-ship	Aggres-siveness	Emotional excitability
Sociability..........................					
Perseverance......................	0.043				
Leadership	0.471	0.339			
Aggressiveness	0.147	−0.041	0.520		
Emotional excitability..............	−0.011	−0.225	0.158	0.517	

TABLE 10.4. Correlations of social traits and intelligence

	Socia-bility	Perse-verance	Leader-ship	Aggres-siveness	Emotional excitability
Grades	−0.181	0.298	0.190	0.049	−0.083
Psychological test	−0.276	0.171	0.060	0.084	0.009

There is one coefficient of 0.112 between this trait and transverse thoracic diameter; the rest are below 0.10. It is of interest to note that the three traits leadership, aggressiveness, and emotionality show uniformly positive correlations with all of the measurements, and all three correlate negatively with the morphologic index. Evidently these traits are associated slightly with general bigness of body, and also to some slight extent with compactness, or predominance of the torso over the extremities. Perseverance shows almost the opposite tendency.

Eight of the twelve correlations between *Perseverance* and physical measurements are negative, but they are very low.

In order to throw further light on these relationships, the intercorrelations of the five social traits are given in Table 10.3.

These correlations are for the most part about as would be expected. Sociability shows practically no relationship with perseverance, a rather close relationship with leadership, a lower one with aggressiveness, and none with emotionality. Perseverance correlates 0.34 with leadership, and -0.23 with emotionality. Leadership and aggressiveness are rather closely related, and the former correlates 0.16 with emotionality. The correlation of 0.52 between aggressiveness and emotionality is surprisingly high. It remains 0.52 when leadership is partialed out. Likewise the leadership-aggressiveness correlation of 0.52 remains the same when emotionality is partialed out, but the leadership-emotionality relationship of 0.16 changes to -0.15 when aggressiveness is partialed out. The halo error is certainly not apparent. Leadership is the only trait which correlates positively with all the others, and none of the high correlations of the table was significantly changed by partialing.

SOCIAL RATINGS AND INTELLIGENCE CRITERIA

The correlations in this group are given in Table 10.4.

The negative correlations between intelligence and sociability are to be expected, and are consistent with the fact that morphologic index was positively related to the former and negatively to the latter. It is well known that there is some slight negative relationship between popularity and the orthodox criteria of intelligence, especially around a fraternity house. A rather interesting point here arises from the fact that the negative relationship with the test results is distinctly higher than with scholarship. This contradicts the common student rationalization to the effect that the "popular" men are just as intelligent but are less interested in grades.

The highest correlation in this group is between perseverance and grades (0.30). No doubt a knowledge of past scholarship performance entered into these ratings to some extent, and of course the same could be said of the positive relationship between perseverance and psychological test scores.

A somewhat surprising correlation is that between leadership and grades (0.19). Leadership correlates positively (0.47) with sociability and positively with scholarship, although these two latter traits are negatively related. With sociability held constant, leadership and scholarship correlate 0.32, which is pretty significantly high. This would imply rather strongly that, while scholarship is something of a handicap to general sociability and popularity, it is a decided asset in college leadership.

Aggressiveness correlates positively with both of the intelligence criteria, but the correlations are low. In this case, partialing out leadership reduces each of these correlations to a point well below its probable error.

Emotionality correlates –0.08 with scholarship, and about zero with psychological test scores. When perserverance is partialled out, the emotionality-scholarship correlation reduces to –0.018. There does not appear to be much relationship between emotionality and intelligence.

The correlation between psychological test scores and scholarship, for the group of subjects used in this experiment, was 0.395 ($N = 304$). This is not far from the average correlation between these two traits as reported at the University of Chicago and elsewhere.

SUMMARY

In summarizing the results of this section of the study, the following conclusions appear justifiable:

1. Certain relationships were found between morphologic measurements and social traits. These are slight, as measured by the coefficient or correlation, but they are too high and too numerous to be due to chance.

2. These relationships are not traceable to the influence of some one or two relatively close relationships spreading to intercorrelated traits.

3. The three social traits which correlated most closely with these measurements were aggressiveness, leadership, and sociability, in that order. Intercorrelations and partial correlations show that leadership is closely related both to sociability and to aggressiveness, while there is little or no relation between the latter two. It seems probable that the two traits sociability and aggressiveness were the most clearly defined and useful in this study.

4. There is a slight tendency for the breadth, or transverse diameter, measurements to correlate more definitely with the social traits than do the other measurements. On the whole, the factor of general size, or bigness, seems to be related positively to at least sociability, leadership, and aggressiveness.

5. Both psychological test scores and scholarship correlate negatively with sociability. The more intelligent students are likely to be lower than average in popularity. This is more strikingly true when intelligence is measured by psychological test results, than when measured by scholarship.

6. There is, however, a positive relationship between leadership and scholarship. It appears that, while scholarship is something of a handicap in general sociability and popularity, it is a decided asset in college leadership. While the popular man is in general likely to be below average in scholarship, those who are most respected and copied (the most extremely popular) are likely to be above average.

CHAPTER 11

Constitutional Theory: Fisher

Introduction

Students of personality have conducted innumerable investigations to check hypotheses about how humans develop and how they maintain their personalities. One of the most imaginative and persistent investigators in this field is Seymour Fisher (1922–   ) whose *Body Experience in Fantasy and Behavior* (1970) and his co-authored book with S. E. Cleveland, *Body Image and Personality* (1968), represent excellent summaries of the experimental approach in constitutional psychology.

This somewhat difficult paper is representative of reports of dozens of studies that Fisher has conducted. In a most ingenious manner he tries to determine how males and females regard their respective sexes in terms of power and superiority and how this relates to the left and right sides of the body. A close study of this research report will repay the necessary effort. Not only are the results of value and interest, especially in these days of women's rights, but the methodology and the statistical manipulations can be of value to the nascent student of personality.

SEYMOUR FISHER

Sex designations of right and left body sides and assumptions about male-female superiority

There is considerable literature which speculates about the symbolic meaning of right and left and more specifically about the significance of the right and left sides of one's body. It is typically suggested that the right side of one's body is perceived as stronger and "better" than the left. Sometimes the difference between the two sides is depicted in terms of the right being associated with masculinity and the left with femininity. These speculations are variously derived from observations of schizophrenics and patients with organic brain pathology who develop delusions in which their right ٬and left sides have different identities (Fenichel, 1945; Schilder, 1935); from folklore and myths (Hertz, 1960) in which right and left are given dramatic symbolic meaning; and from semantic analyses of words denoting right and left in different languages (Blau, 1946). Empirical support for such speculations has been fragmentary. It is true that experimental evidence exists that individuals vary considerably in the degree to which they are aware of a differentiation between their right and left body sides (Fisher, 1958, 1960). It is also true that clear-cut right-left gradients of GSR reactivity have

been measured which are significantly linked with such variables as degree of personal disorganization (Fisher & Cleveland, 1959), body-image disturbance (Fisher & Abercrombie, 1958), and qualities portrayed in figure-drawing productions (Fisher, 1959). One must add that there are a few studies which indicate that the right-left directionality ascribed to moving stimuli may reflect trait characteristics (Fisher, 1961; Thurstone, 1952). However, in general it must be accepted that our empirical knowledge about the nature of the evaluative distinctions we make between the right and left sides of our bodies is quite limited.

The present study is concerned with the relative sex-role characteristics which the individual ascribes to the right and left sides of his body. It is assumed that persons do differ in the degree to which they attribute male and female qualities to their two body sides. Further, it is assumed, in keeping with the usual speculative formulation, that the right side of the body is perceived as stronger and more powerful than the left. In this context the specific hypothesis was formulated that the greater the degree to which an individual ascribes his own sex characteristics to his right side and those of the opposite sex to his left side the more likely he is to perceive his own sex as relatively superior to the opposite sex. That is, if one identifies the presumed "strong" side of one's body with one's own sex and the "weak" side with the

Note: This study was partially supported by Grant M5761 from the United States Public Health Service.

opposite sex, this may be taken as an indication that a corresponding differentiation is made in the power status of the two sexes.

It should be emphasized at this point that the hypothesis is intended at a more general level to provide an element of support for a view expressed elsewhere (Fisher & Cleveland, 1958) that the value one assigns to a given body region reflects a projection upon the body scheme of a related attitude which has been adopted in relation to an issue or object which is of special significance in one's environs. In this instance, the perception of a particular power difference between the sexes is considered to be reflected in the assignment of differential sex attributes to the right and left body sides. Initial studies have already shown promise in demonstrating correlations between the individual's values and attitudes and the patterning of his body scheme. Thus, it has been observed that the qualities one assigns to one's body-boundary regions are linked with intensity of achievement motivation (Fisher, 1963). Also, evidence exists that an individual's perception of his own height may be influenced by the degree to which he feels inferior or depreciated (Popper, 1958). Even further, it has been demonstrated that the size ascribed by an individual to his arm may be a function of whether it is passive or pointing at a meaningful target (McFarland, Wapner, & Werner, 1960).

PROCEDURE

The degree to which the subject links masculinity or femininity with each of his body sides was measured by means of a previously used semiprojective technique (Fisher, 1960). He was asked to place one narrow paper cylinder on the middle finger of his right hand and an identical cylinder on the corresponding finger of his left hand. He was told to imagine that each cylinder represented a puppet. He was to assign a name to each and compose a brief story in which the two characters he had named interacted in some manner. Four sets of characters and accompanying stories were first obtained spontaneously and without directive instructions. Then, one story was secured with the instruction to name and imagine an interaction between two characters "from some culture other than the United States." Finally, a story was obtained with the instruction to imagine "two people who are involved in a very dramatic situation." The special instructions given for the last two stories were adopted because preliminary trials indicated that it was difficult to motivate most subjects to create more than three or four stories completely spontaneously.

Scoring of the subject's productions was confined entirely to the sexes of the names he assigned to the total of 12 story characters he created. The masculine or feminine designation of the name applied to a body side was the basic scoring unit. For male subjects a score was tabulated which equaled the number of instances in which simultaneously a male name was applied to the right hand and a female name to the left. The analogous score derived for the female subjects was equal to the frequency with which there was simultaneously a female name applied to the right hand and a male name to the left. This scoring procedure was intended to reflect the specific fact of having assigned one's own sex to the right or "strong" side and the opposite sex to the left or "weak" side. When both right and left were simultaneously labeled as being of the same sex, the names were not included in the score total. This was also true for response patterns in which the right was identified with the opposite sex and the left with one's own sex. It should be parenthetically noted that subjects often expressed overt conflict and indecision about whether to choose a male or female name for a given body side. Some would debate for as long as several minutes before reaching a decision. The stories which were related by the subjects about each pair of puppets were not analyzed. These stories were obtained simply to insure that the subjects would experience some degree of ego involvement and not see the task as one merely requiring the assignment of names to right and left.

Of course, underlying the entire procedure was the assumption that each puppet took on special meaning for the subject in terms of its right versus left placement. The tenability of this assumption will be shown at a later point in terms of the fact that any but a right-left perspective on the data fails to explain the results obtained.

The hypothesis under consideration required a measure of the subject's concept of the relative power status of the male versus the female. The technique adopted to secure this measure was based on judgments of male and female pictures, and may generally be compared to analogous procedures involving ratings of faces which have variously been used to tap prejudice (Sherif, 1935) and emotional states (Murray, 1933). Each subject was presented with a series of 40 paired pictures of faces (front view). Twenty of the pictures involved male-female pairs. Ten involved male-male and ten female-female pairs. The subjects were given the following instructions:

You will be looking at a number of pairs of pictures. Each pair is presented on a card that is numbered. Also, each picture is identified by a letter. Study each pair and try to imagine from the pictures what sort of person each of the pictured persons is. Then, imagine that they were to meet each other and set up a personal relationship. If this happened, which of each pair would probably turn out to be the dominant one, the one who took leadership?

On the sheet of paper you have indicate next to each number the letter of the person you think would be the dominant one. Consider this to be a guessing game. Don't worry about whether you are right or wrong.

It was assumed that the greater the degree to which a subject designated one sex as likely to be dominant over the other sex in his judgments of the 20 pairs involving a male and a female figure, the more he was indicating his assumption of relative superiority for that sex.

The pictures used were taken from a college yearbook in which poses and photography were standard for all. Male and female pairs were randomly composed from a pool of pictures, but a few were eliminated in which one of the pair seemed obviously to have a more aggressive expression than the other. In half of the pictured pairs the male was on the right and in half the male was on the left. The male-male and female-female pairs were introduced into the series in order to conceal from the subject that his judgments were to be analyzed with relation to male-female differences. The 40 pictures were presented in a randomized order which was the same for all subjects.

Subjects

The subjects consisted of 50 males and 54 female college students who were recruited by payment of a fee. The median age in both groups was 20. To control for handedness all subjects were righthanded. In order to qualify as righthanded, a subject had to indicate that he wrote and ate with his right hand and also considered it to be stronger than the left. All the procedures were administered on an individual basis.

RESULTS

In the male group the median number of instances in which the right-hand puppet was designated male at the same time that the left was designated female was 0 (range 0–4). In the female group the median for labeling of right as female and left simultaneously as male was 1 (range: 0–5).

As for the picture superiority judgments, it was found that the median tendency in the male group was to choose 11 males as superior to females (range: 5–19). The corresponding median in the female group was 12 (range: 7–17).

TABLE 11.1. Chi square analysis of relationship of right and left puppet sex scores to judgments of male-female superiority

Number of male pictures judged superior	Males: Male puppet right and female left"			Females: Female puppet right and male left"		
	H	L	x^2	H	L	x^2
H	20	8	3.5*	9	17	4.7**
L	10	12		18	10	

" H = above median, L = at median or below.
* $p < .05$, one-tailed test.
** $p < .02$, one-tailed test.

As is apparent in Table 11.1, the results are supportive of the hypothesis in both sex groups. Thus, male subjects with above median frequency of puppet designation patterns in which the male is on the right and the female on the left exceed those at or below the median in this respect with regard to the frequency with which they judge males to be superior to females ($x^2 = 3.5$, $p < .05$, one-tailed test). Relatedly, one finds that female subjects who are above the median in labeling the right hand as female and

the left as male surpass those at the median or below in this respect in ascribing relative superiority to female pictures ($x^2 = 4.7$, $p < .02$, one-tailed test).

Since there were also puppet designations in which simultaneously the right puppet was identified with the opposite sex and the left puppet with the subject's own sex, the question does arise as to how the results would be influenced if such designations were balanced against those in which the right puppet is identified with the subject's own sex and the left with the opposite sex. It could be. argued, for example, that if a male subject gives two stories in which the right puppet is male and the left female he should not be classified as perceiving his right side as masculine if he simultaneously gives as many or more stories in which the obverse sex designations of the right and left puppets occur. An analysis was therefore undertaken of all cases in which both types of right-left puppet response patterns were present. This involved 44 males and 51 females. In each sex group, whenever the number of responses depicting the same sex on the left and the opposite sex on the right equaled or exceeded the number in which the same sex was on the right and the opposite sex on the left, a score was derived by subtracting the first mentioned from the second. If the first was less than the second, no change was made in the second. These derived scores were related to the picture judgments by means of chi-square. It was found that in the male group those who were above the median in labeling the right puppet as male and the left as female exceeded those who were at or below the median in this respect in choosing males as superior to females ($x^2 = 3.0$, $p < .05$, one-tailed test). However, in the female group those who were above the median in portraying the right puppet as female and the left as male were significantly more inclined than those at or below the median in this respect to perceive females as superior to males ($x^2 = 2.7$, $p < .05$, one-tailed test). Thus, although the hypothesis under consideration was phrased specifically in terms of a count of puppet response patterns in which one's own sex is on the right and the opposite sex on the left, it is generally supported by the more complex scoring procedure just described.

It seemed important to establish that the overall results were unique to the matter of right-left differentiation and could not be duplicated merely by counting the gross frequency with which male and female names were applied to puppets. Therefore, in each sex group the total number of male puppet names was related to the picture judgment scores; and the same was done for the total number of female puppet names. In all four of these comparisons the chi-square values proved to be of a chance order.

DISCUSSION

The results provide considerable support for the hypothesis. It is apparent that the specific equation of right-side puppets with one's own sex and left-side puppets with the opposite sex is indicative of a trend to place one's sex as relatively high in the male-female power relationship. It has been assumed that the sex roles applied to the puppets reflect attitudes that the individual has developed with regard to the right and left sides of his body. While there has been no direct demonstration of such a relationship, the fact of its probability has been enhanced by showing that only a data analysis based on a right-left differentiation of response provides support for the hypothesis. It

could, of course, be argued that similar results might have been obtained by the use of puppets in right-left positions which were not attached to one's body in any fashion. That is, the mere matter of right-left differentiation rather than right-left differentiation of one's body areas might be viewed as the prime parameter. However, while it would be interesting to repeat the present study with puppets in right-left positions that were not attached to the body, it would not in any way invalidate the present data interpretations if a similar pattern of results appeared. One must consider that right and left have meaning only with reference to one's body as an axis or marker. Presumably, the same or similar right-left differentiations in the body scheme would be tapped in making right-left judgments about objects "out there" as upon one's own body. Indeed, Gerstmann (1942), Benton (1959), and Critchley (1953) have called attention to the intimate connection between the ability to discriminate the right-left sectors of one's body and to perceive accurately the right-left dimensions of non-self-objects.

At a general level, the results provide another increment of support for the view that the body scheme is an expression in body terms of attitudes about significant issues and objects in one's environs. This view suggests that one's body is unique as a perceptual object because it is part of the perceiver. As such, it is closer to the perceiver and likely to elicit a higher level of ego involvement from him than most other perceptual objects. In this unique position it easily becomes, as do other highly ego-involving objects, a target upon which the individual projects feelings, values, and attitudes. Thus, one body sector may be assigned values related to attitudes about incorporation. Another sector may be linked with feelings related to the expression of anger. While in the present instance, values have apparently been assigned to the right and left sides as a function of assumptions about male-female power relationships. Of course, this model regarding the body scheme is speculative, but it offers abundant opportunity for the formulation of testable hypotheses.

REFERENCES

Benton, A. L. *Right-left discrimination and finger localization.* New York: Hoeber-Harper, 1959.

Blau, A. The master hand: A study of the origin of right and left sidedness and its relation to personality and language. *Research Monographs of the American Orthopsychiatric Association,* 1946, *5.*

Critchley, M. *The parietal lobes.* London: Edward Arnold, 1953.

Fenichel, O. *The psychoanalytic theory of neurosis.* New York: Norton, 1945.

Fisher, S. Body image and asymmetry of body reactivity. *Journal of Abnormal and Social Psychology,* 1958, *57,* 292–298.

Fisher, S. Body reactivity gradients and figure drawing variables. *Journal of Consulting Psychology,* 1959, *11,* 54–59.

Fisher, S. Right-left gradients in body image, body reactivity and perception. *Genetic Psychology Monographs,* 1960, *61,* 197–228.

Fisher, S. Achievement themes and directionality of autokinetic movement. *Journal of Abnormal and Social Psychology,* 1961, *63,* 64–68.

Fisher, S. A further appraisal of the body boundary concept. *Journal of Consulting Psychology,* 1963, *27,* 62–74.

Fisher, S., & Abercrombie, J. The relationship of body image distortions to body reactivity gradients. *Journal of Personality,* 1958, *26,* 320–329.

Fisher, S., & Cleveland, S. E. *Body image and personality.* Princeton, N.J.: Van Nostrand, 1958.

Fisher, S., & Cleveland, S. E. Right-left reactivity patterns in disorganized states. *Journal of Nervous and Mental Disease,* 1959, *128,* 396–400.

Gerstmann, J. Problem of imperception of disease and of impaired body territories with organic lesions: Relation to body schema and its disorders. *Archives of Neurology and Psychiatry,* 1942, *48,* 890–913.

Hertz, R. *Death and the right hand.* New York: Free Press of Glencoe, 1960.

McFarland, J. H., Wapner, S., & Werner, H. *Factors affecting body image as measured by perceived arm length.* Paper presented at meeting of the Eastern Psychological Association, New York, 1960.

Murray, H. A. The effect of fear upon estimates of the maliciousness of other personalities. *Journal of Social Psychology,* 1933, *4,* 310–329.

Popper, J. M. *Motivational and social factors in children's perceptions of height.* Doctoral dissertation, Stanford University, 1958. Ann Arbor: University microfilms 00-25383, 1958.

Schilder, P. *The image and appraisal of the human body.* London: Kegan Paul, Trench, Trubner, 1935.

Sheriff, M. An experimental study of stereotypes. *Journal of Abnormal and Social Psychology,* 1935, *29,* 371–375.

Thurstone, L. L. *Progress report on a color film.* University of Chicago, Psychometric Laboratory, 1952 (No. 80).

CHAPTER **12**

Constitutional Theory: Goldstein

Introduction

Kurt Goldstein (1878–1965), a neurologist, became interested in the struggles of brain-injured individuals to achieve an orderly way of living, despite their handicaps. As a result of his clinical observations of thousands of patients, he developed the concept that people strive always for self-actualization in a unitary (holistic) manner. This view contrasts with perceptions of people as an agglomeration of parts. Goldstein's view of personality might be likened to the flower's differentiation from the seed, a whole entity having unity, rather than being similar to an automobile as a collection of parts which function together.

This organismic, holistic view of Goldstein's has not achieved the recognition it deserves. He viewed the body-mind issue as unreal: One is not body and mind, but rather body/mind. This selection makes the point that the individual is not cognition and affection and behavior, but rather thinking/feeling/acting—a unit. In his view, emotions are not to be seen as disturbers but rather as part of the totality of the united individual.

KURT GOLDSTEIN

On emotions: Considerations from the organismic point of view

Emotions are usually regarded as conditions, the psychological causes of which have a disorganizing effect on the activity the organism may be engaged in at the time. Behavior is disturbed, and effective adjustment is said to be more or less impeded. The condition includes changes in observable behavior, certain visceral phenomena, and a definite affective experience. These characteristics are often attributed to a weakening or loss of cerebral control.

My conception of anxiety, as explained in my book *The Organism* (1939) might seem to be in agreement with these assumptions. In fact it is not. The description of anxiety as a state of disorganization does not imply that all emotions must be so characterized. As a matter of fact, not all can be considered simply as disordered conditions, as states of negative value for the organism's performances. This point has been stressed by R. W. Leeper in a recent paper (1948). He states that all of the current discussions of emotion emphasize the disorganization of response. But he asks what is meant by the terms order and disorder and says: "The criterion of organization is not a matter of whether there is some interference with preceding activities or with inconsistent subordinate activities. It is the question whether this interference is relatively chaotic and haphazard, or whether these suppressions and changes of subordinate activities are harmonious with some main function which is being served" (p. 12). I agree with this, but there remains the question of what is meant by "main function." I have pointed out that order and disorder can be defined only in relation to the structure of the organism and the task before it at a given moment. Disorder is a state in which the individual, owing to external or internal conditions, cannot come to terms with the task in such a way that self-realization takes place. Order is the state in which that is the case. Thus order and disorder are not simply different forms of functional organization; they can be defined only in terms of their relationship to the basic trend of the organism, that of self-realization. Whether there is order or disorder can be judged only from the positive or negative value which the condition holds for the organism's self-realization. Hence, the same objective condition may imply organization or disorganization for one individual, but not for another, or for the same individual under one set of conditions, not under another. Only if we apply this criterion shall we be able to decide whether an emotion is disturbing or not, and to discover the meaning of emotion in the totality of behavior of men.

In anxiety disorganization is clearly apparent. It is, as we have said, the experience of the "catastrophic situation," of danger of going to pieces, of "losing

Kurt Goldstein: "On Emotions: Considerations from the Organismic Point of View." Reprinted from *Journal of Psychology*, 1951, *31*, 37–49. Reprinted with permission of the Journal Press.

one's existence." We shall see later that even here the organism must not be altogether in disorder, that even here the emotion is not simply a negative phenomenon but has some positive effect for the life of the individual. Nevertheless, disorder is here such a paramount feature that we may well say it characterizes the emotion.

There is another emotion which may appear as disorganization. This emotion is ecstasy. Here, also, is danger of losing contact with the world. But the individual is in a condition which is of great positive value for its life. What appears like disorder represents a particular kind of order and self-realization.

There are other emotions in which disorganization is not at all a prominent feature. The individual, in spite of the emotion, is not hindered from acting in accordance with the requirements of the task before him. Thus emotion and ordered behavior are in no way incompatible; the experience of "emotional upset" may become even the origin of particularly fruitful activity relevant to the individual's self-realization. That occurs, for instance, in fear. Fear has some similarity with anxiety, but there is an essential difference. Fear can inspire purposeful activity, thus helping in the maintenance of ordered behavior and allowing for self-realization in a dangerous situation. In this way, even though experienced as disturbance, emotion may not really be a state of disorganization, but rather one of reorganization with special significance within the totality of behavior.

Emotions are usually considered as factors adding something to behavior, to thinking, acting, *etc.* According to Munn (1946): "Emotions disturb or upset whatever activities are in progress at the time of arousal . . . Emotions are what

produces this disturbance" (p. 263). Are emotions *something outside of behavior,* acting on it, or *do they belong to behavior,* as characteristic aspects of it? Our previous discussion of the structure of anxiety has shown that anxiety is not something additional to behavior, but is an aspect of a definite kind of behavior.

I would like to demonstrate the inherent character of emotions in another example. If, given a problem, we achieve the solution immediately, we may experience a feeling of comfort and satisfaction. But if this easy solution occurs in a situation where we want to show what we are able to do, we may feel cheated, disappointed, and angry because the task was too easy and we could not show our ability. If the problem is very difficult and we are not able to solve it satisfactorily, we feel tense and dissatisfied, especially if success would be important for us in that situation. If unsuccessful, we may find ourselves in a condition of anxiety. If we have great difficulty in solving the problem, but, in spite of that, are ambitious and eager to tackle difficult tasks, the very difficulty may induce a feeling of adventure, elation, and courage. When achievement of the correct solution is less important to us, we may feel at ease even in failure. The same holds true when we think that failure cannot be ascribed to our personal inadequacy since it is generally impossible to find the correct solution, or when we take an over-all attitude of callousness or resignation towards the world. If we resent the very fact of being asked to solve a given problem, defiance may be the result, and failure may even give us satisfaction.

Thus we see that success or failure in the solution of the same problem may go along with very different emotions. Such examples lead us to suspect that there is no behavior without emotion, and that there is no one-to-one correlation between the objective situation and the emotions induced by it. In order to understand what emotions will arise we need to consider the implications of the situation with regard to the organism's potential for self-realization.

I have shown that all phenomena which we may separate in human behavior are abstractions. Behavior is always an entity and concerns the whole personality. Only abstractively can we separate such "aspects" as "bodily processes" on the one hand and "conscious phenomena," states of awareness as "feelings" and "attitudes" on the other hand. In normal human behavior these "aspects" are integrated and organized for optimal self-realization under the given conditions. Emotions *qua* phenomena of awareness are inherent in the entity of behavior in the same way as are "thinking" or "bodily processes," *etc*. At the very moment when emotions come to the foreground, phenomena belonging to other "aspects" are correspondingly modified. The individual is more or less aware of being driven by emotion, and his behavior is changed in its entirety. Optimum self-realization under the given conditions determines qualitative and quantitative differences of emotions. In the example above a definite emotion belongs to each variation. Each of these corresponds to a definite relationship between individual, environmental situation and internal conditions. The latter in turn depend upon the effect of *environmental stimuli* on the individual and the *aftereffects* of previous experiences. Hence a given emotion may be determined by a preceding emotional state, e.g., a mood prevailing at the time of stimulation, of previous emotions as they are aroused by those in progress. In

The Organism (p. 307) I have dealt more generally with the structure of aftereffects of phenomena belonging to different "aspects" of human behavior. I concluded there that phenomena of each "aspect" assert direct aftereffects only on phenomena belonging to the same "aspect," and affect other "aspects" only indirectly by changing the total behavior. This applies to emotions too. Previous emotions exert *direct* aftereffects only on present *emotions*.

The kind and intensity of emotion dominant in a particular situation depend upon how much the present situation stimulates feelings and how much the aftereffect of previous experiences modifies them both qualitatively and quantitatively. All these factors have to be carefully considered if we want to understand the rôle which a given emotion plays in a particular behavior sequence. A person in a gay mood confronted with something which would ordinarily produce sadness may not be affected as long as the situation allows for continuation of that self-realization which fitted the situation in which he lives. However, if anything in the present situation arouses previous sadness, the factors which produce sadness may become so strong that his mood will change correspondingly.

We usually say that an individual is acting without affect when the emotional situation allows action and self-realization adequate to the demands of the situation. If the latter are disturbed in the presence of emotion, we speak about emotional influences on behavior. Such observations are the basis for the distinction between *unemotional* ("normal") and *emotional* ("disturbed") behavior. To quote Woodworth (1940): "Activity is unemotional in proportion as it consists in observing and managing the situation (p. 438) . . . The difference between emotional and unemotional activity depends on the degree to which the individual keeps his head, that is, on the degree to which the brainy life of relation dominates his whole activity (p. 437) . . . It depends on how free the lower centers are at any time from domination by the central cortex" (p. 438). I shall not discuss here whether this physiological explanation gives us real insight into the rôle played by emotions in the totality of behavior. However that may be, the problem remains—in such an interpretation of the phenomena—why, in a certain situation, the brain centers lose their dominance, and whether it is really justified to say that there are ever activities without experienced emotion. Is the feeling of quietness and satisfaction in adequate activities not affect? I think it is very doubtful whether there exist actions without emotion. The emotions may be in the background, but they belong to the behavior, as in general the condition in the background belongs to normal "figure" formation. Is it not influence of emotions if they guarantee constant and objectively correct performance? I agree with Guenther Stern (private communication) when he states that experiences and activities are always accompanied by emotions, that experience is always pervaded by a certain "tonality." "Yet, in everyday life, the tempting and threatening qualities matter most. They are the first sense matters, whereby we do not mean only that sense data are saturated with mood qualities, but that their embodiment in object-like data represents the second stage." Certainly sense data are not under all conditions primary. This is the case only in a special kind of situation in which "personal" factors are to a degree kept ineffective. This does not mean that all

relation of the personality to the activity in progress is eliminated. Without all such relation, activity would not go on. The impression of lack of "personal" influence originates from the *constancy of affect,* from the fact that the activity is not disrupted by "personal" events. For instance, if confronted with a scientific problem to be solved, we may appear "detached," *i.e.,* not under the influence of emotion. But that must not mean that we are without any emotion. The situation is essentially similar to that in reflexes which are guaranteed by the constant condition of the excitation in the rest of the organism. Reflexes appear as a reaction to stimuli under a very special condition of the organism, *i.e.,* the abstract attitude or special experimental condition which keeps the excitation level of the organism constant except for the part where the reflex activity takes place. The same is true of "emotionless" behavior. Such behavior is possible as a function of the abstract attitude which allows the individual to exclude subjective influences detrimental to the task at hand. This constancy of emotion belongs as a prerequisite to scientific activity as various specific emotions belong to other activities. Only with the help of the abstract attitude can objective activity take place "in proportion as it consists in observing and managing the solution" (Woodworth, 1940, p. 438). However, these activities are not sufficiently characterized in terms of "managing the solution." The whole personality is always involved, feelings and emotions providing an adequate background for the activity in progress. This is true of that kind of self-realization in which the objective world is in the foreground. Whether or not that represents the highest form of self-realization is a problem. It certainly is not the most "natural" one. I again agree with Stern when he says: "It is not the mood character of the world that is puzzling, but, on the contrary, the fact that in certain so-called theoretical acts the world seems to shake off that character ... that man is able to disregard it and handle the world unemotionally in a rational way." I would like to add, he is not only able to do that, but *this very ability is the basic presupposition for a very important form of self-realization, because it alone guarantees "security."* According to some authors, this type of self-realization is the "normal" one, "security"—the effect of stability in action and experience—being considered the most basic goal of the individual. This viewpoint overlooks the enormous significance of the experience of variety which accompanies emotions in human life, the individual and social. Even "emotionless" activity would not exist or receive so much attention, were it not ultimately directed by a definite emotion: by the craving for security and the drive to obtain it.

We have so far considered emotions qua *inherent aspects of behavior.* But let us not overlook the fact that emotions are not only inherent characteristics, they also serve a special *purpose.* Our previous description of purpose of the constant emotional background in "emotionless" activities points already in this direction. This "constant" state of emotion is apparently a deliberately produced means to guarantee this type of behavior. The self-realization underlying such behavior is not a passive process; it is an expression of personal action and decision. The individual wants to be put before a task in which he can realize himself. He searches for the task. Now each task implies a conflict between organism and world, and definite emotions accompany it, always

somewhat disturbing the activity. But, in addition, emotions may come to the fore which help the individual to overcome the difficulties of his endeavor. It is not only the little boy in the children's story who went out into the world to learn the nature of fright. The grown-up acts very much like him in his natural adventurous aim to conquer the outer and inner world. Thus we see emotions have *both detrimental and facilitating effects.* From this originates the ambivalence of functional value of emotions. They are both helpful and disturbing. The goal cannot be reached without some risk and insecurity. This is the case particularly in those activities which are most important for human existence.

If this ambiguity is eliminated to a high degree, as in "emotionless behavior," in the abstract attitude, then the world becomes more "secure," but, at the same time, life becomes progressively more rigid and loses in freedom, vitality, and colorfulness. It becomes more and more drab. *The presence of emotions represents the colorfulness of human life.* It makes the individual feel that it is *he* who experiences, that it is *he* who acts, that *he* is. Life goes on close to the center of the personality, the ego. The individual feels himself as being within the world. In "emotionless" actions, on the other hand, the ego is more or less eliminated and activity more or less detached.

Certain emotions are more dangerous than others. That becomes evident, for instance, when we compare the effect of similar emotions in greater or lesser intensity, *e.g.,* anxiety and fear (Goldstein, 1939). In anxiety the emotion is so strong, the organism is so highly altered in its function, that the abstract attitude can no longer be assumed by the individual. In danger of going to pieces and being unable to act at all the individual must be protected if he is to survive. This means going back to a lower level of coming to terms with the world, thus depriving the personality of important characteristics; but at least it guarantees mere existence. In fear also, the individual experiences strong affect, but not so intensely as to become unable to realize the danger—that is, the danger of impending anxiety—and he can build up protective mechanisms with the help of the preserved abstraction. Fear sharpens the senses and allows us to observe things and events which we may never see in the "emotionless" condition. In fear we gain a new insight into the structure of the world and the nature of man. Fear induces special effort in activity and discloses at the same time danger to human life and the basic significance of the emotion of courage for human existence. In fear, *the positive character of emotion* becomes particularly evident.

As far as I can see it was especially Jean Paul Sartre who considered *emotions as meaningful performances*. "They are mobilized by man in certain situations for definite purposes." I agree with that and also when he states that in emotion we live in *another world*. It corresponds to my general concept of the relation between specific activities and a definite world (Goldstein, 1939, p. 310). I could show that the "usual world" depends upon behavior in the abstract attitude, and that with "concrete" behavior there goes parallel another "world" in which things and events are related to each other in a more direct, concrete, and personal way. We tend to act in response to objects rather than to think about them. The situation is similar with regard to "emotional" and "emotionless" behavior: to each belongs a particular "world." When under the influence of emotions, the world in which we live shows, in general, some of the charac-

teristics of the "concrete" world. To be sure, they manifest themselves in different ways, in accordance with the special character of the emotion in a given situation. Sartre (1948) writes:

In normal and adapted action, the objects "to be realized" appear as having to be realized in certain ways. The means themselves appear as potentialities which demand existence. This apprehension of the means as the only possible way to reach the end can be called a pragmatistic intuition of the determinism of the world around us . . . the world of our desires, our needs and our acts. . . . (p. 57)

Our normal world[1] can be modified when the demands on us arising from it become too difficult, "when the paths traced out become too difficult, or when we see no path, we can no longer live in so urgent and difficult a world. All the ways are barred. However, we must act. So we try to change the world" (Sartre, 1948, p. 158). That is the transformation of the world in emotion. In this changed world we try ". . . to live as if the connections between things and their potentialities were not ruled by deterministic processes, but by magic (p. 59) . . . Magical behavior aims at denying an object of the external world, and will go so far as to annihilate itself in order to annihilate the object with it" (p. 64), *i.e.*, the object with which we cannot cope. "The impossibility of finding a solution to the problem objectively apprehended as a quality of the world serves as motivation for the new unreflective consciousness which now perceives the world otherwise and with a new aspect, and which requires new behavior—through which this aspect is perceived—and which serves as 'hyle' for the new intention" (p. 60). Thus emotions save the individual in an unstable situation. That is their purpose.

_____
[1] That is, the normal world in which we act.

I agree with Sartre that an individual, when faced with a situation too difficult to be handled adequately, goes over into another "world," and that under anxiety, the individual lives—in Sartre's words— "a lesser existence, lesser presence" (Goldstein, 1949, p. 60). That corresponds to my characterization of this level as a "shrunken range of behavior," as a "level of existence within which a number of potential activities of human beings can no longer be realized." Thus the individual is reduced severely in self-realization.

However, this level to which the individual is reduced is not necessarily the magic level, as Sartre believes. There may be conditions where living in a magic world is the only possibility for at least a certain kind of self-realization. Whether that is the case in all situations of anxiety, and particularly whether the appearance of a magic attitude can be understood as reaction of the individual to anxiety *alone* appears doubtful. If in a condition of great danger the individual evades the given world and passes over onto a new plane of "existence," this new world must not be a magic world, it can simply be a *restricted, abnormally concrete world,* as I have shown for individuals with brain damage whose existence is constantly endangered by catastrophic situations. This new level is a means to guarantee some kind of existence in a state of abnormal relation between the person and the outer world due to the change of the individual by pathology. Anxiety occurs here as the effect of catastrophes, of failure; it belongs to the breakdown of organismic life and disappears as soon as failure disappears. That takes place if and to the degree as the "new" level of existence has been achieved. *But are we allowed to speak here of a purpose of the emotion of anxiety?* If we mean by purpose some impulse by which activity is

inspired adequate to the "nature" of the organism, certainly not. The effect is not suited to realize essential capacities of the individual, and his lower level cannot be considered the purposeful intention of it. That corresponds to the observation that the individual does not try to achieve it. What he tries is to find a way out of the disastrous situation. He tries to reach an adjustment to the outer world which allows some kind of reaction without permanent disturbance by catastrophes. That is the case in an environment in which he has not to use—to fulfill the demands of the environment—the "abstract attitude," and in which he can be successful in concrete behavior (Goldstein, 1939, p. 38). The individual's activity is not purposeless, insofar as a condition is reached in which at least some activities are possible. But that is achieved in a passive way. Active shifting to another level would not even be possible for the patients, because they are deprived of the capacity to do that due to their pathology. The passive character of this shifting becomes apparent also by the fact that the new level can be preserved only if the organism is protected otherwise, that is, if he can, with the help of other human beings, live in a definite environment from which no demands arise he cannot cope with. Left to his own devices, the patient would soon "break down." Thus we cannot describe the individual's shift onto a new plane of existence as the "purpose" of anxiety. It is not at all fruitful for the individual in the sense of self-realization. It may therefore not even be justified to say that the individual now lives in another "world." The environment to which he is reduced in order to live at all *does not belong to the realm of the various forms of "world" of normal human existence* (Goldstein, 1947, p. 67). With our interpretation of the effect of anxiety, a discrepancy in Sartre's concept can be avoided, namely, that he on the one hand considers emotions purposeful, and on the other one states they are "not effective." That appears contradictory: effectiveness and purpose do belong together. If one denies purposefulness of anxiety, as we do, it is understandable that it is not effective. Other emotions which are purposeful are effective, too. That is, for instance, the case in fear. In fear the individual's natural "world" does not disappear; even though it does undergo some change, it is essentially preserved. *The behavior in anxiety is thus not on the same level as that under other conditions of emotion.* It might serve to avoid confusion if we would not label that condition emotion but designate it as the *inner experience of catastrophe!*

Fear is a real emotion. *It* has positive value for behavior. It has a purpose, the purpose of enabling the individual to achieve optimal self-realization under the given conditions, and it is effective. G. Stern has indicated the different ways in which the relation between emotion and activity has been considered, *e.g.,* the relationship between sadness and crying. According to Stern, it is not true that we cry *because* we are sad—as the layman would think. Nor do we become sad because we cry, as William James would have assumed. Nor do we cry in order to become sad, as Sartre might say. It would seem to me that we best describe the phenomenon as a condition of the organism *to which the feeling of sadness belongs in the same way as crying.* Both sadness and crying originate in the individual on the one hand as a disturbing occurrence, on the other one as an *aid in overcoming the difficulties of the situation which have produced them.* The organism, we might say, *gives in* to sadness and thus manages to establish a more adequate relationship with the world in spite of it. As a consequence of this giving in, the individual is able to handle the difficulties better than in permanent conflict in passive sadness. He tries to bear something disagreeable and can so organize a situation in a way in which he can handle the disturbing character of the original condition, that condition from which sadness originated. To be sure, that will be possible only with limitation of self-realization, but will make possible that it essentially remain preserved. I have shown on another occasion (Goldstein, 1947, p. 439) that this is the way in which the organism tends to overcome difficulties in general if he cannot eliminate them altogether. A new state becomes organized which allows for self-realization even though in a somewhat restricted fashion. On this new plane emotions are effective. Here, giving in somewhat and not simply fighting them, has some positive value. Indeed, such a selective procedure is possible only with the help of the highest function of human nature, that of abstraction, which induces self-control in the interest of higher goals. At random, it might be mentioned, here lies the basis of all success in psycho-therapy.

Thus we can see again that *emotions are part and parcel of behavior.* Behavior is determined by the trend towards self-realization. Depending on various external and internal conditions with which the organism has to cope at the time, self-realization expresses itself in different activities which belong to different "worlds." There is always a tendency towards "optimal" adjustment of the personality and the world in which the individual has to live. The difficulties encountered—the opposing forces of physical and social world, the inner conflicts—produce different kinds of reactions. A definite emotion is coordinated with each reaction, *i.e.,* always that emotion which fits in best with optimal self-realization under the given conditions. But there remains a lack, and emotions are also, in a sense, the expression of this lack. But emotions are *not simply a part of the changed situation; rather, the individual can and does bring himself into these emotional conditions because they make for better self-realization.* All these emotional conditions belong to human existence; they correspond to the different "worlds" of man.

Thus: *no action occurs without emotion.* The quantitative and qualitative differences of emotions correspond to the different ways of self-realization. In everyday life various emotions arise which more or less disturb and/or facilitate action. The human being assumes, and has to assume, different attitudes in order to realize all his capacities. The rôle played by the emotions differs with these different attitudes. In activity induced by the abstract attitude, particularly in the scientific approach to the world, emotions are kept at bay. They are "in the background" or, more correctly, they are kept relatively constant. This state comes into being in the search for security, and the feeling of security is part of it. Yet, there appears at the same time the joy in activity, the experience of satisfaction of creative power, and the freedom to overcome difficulties. Nevertheless, under the influence of the abstract attitude there manifests itself only a restricted aspect of the world and of the person, of human nature in general. Another, and a very important one appears in "emotional" activity, revealing the colorfulness of human nature and its world. Here security is reduced. The adventurous character of man is active, wanting to face and overcome the difficulties of life which oppose his self-realization. Emotions here are a deliberate means to come to terms

with particular situations. Under these conditions we are justified in speaking of the "purpose" of emotions.

When emotion is so strong that the individual is no longer able to bear the disturbance accompanying it, as, *e.g.,* in the condition of anxiety, then there is no other means to meet the emotion than to escape to a lower level of existence. An essential part of the human world is lost. These are the only states of emotion where disturbance is in the foreground. Here emotion has *no* purpose; insofar as it is not desired, it is not effective in terms of the individual's "adequate" activities. All other emotions have some positive character, some purpose; they imply both positive and negative value for behavior and self-realization. When we are sad, the negative side is, characteristically, in the foreground. The opposite is the case in joy.

We should now proceed to show the fruitfulness of this view in a systematic analysis of the various kinds of emotions. However, I shall discuss only one kind: *joy*—as an example for indicating the general direction which such analysis should take. The discussion of joy will demonstrate again the complexity of the structure of what we call emotion.

To characterize joy as a disturbance of behavior would immediately appear to be wrong. Joy brings about disturbance, to be sure, if we compare it with behavior in an "emotionless" state. But this negative value is outweighed by its great positive value for self-realization. Sartre has characterized joy as a condition in which we anticipate an "instantaneous totality" which, in fact, is only partially realized. "The behavior is accompanied by the certainty that the possessions[2] will be realized sooner or later" (Munn, 1946, p. 69). It is true that in joy we transcend the

---

[2] E.g., meeting a beloved person.

immediate reality, but we remain in the world in which we are living and acting. I cannot agree with Sartre that we shift onto a magic plane. We are not so deceived as to consider the world already perfect, but we expect and hope that it will be so in the future. This experience we owe to the capacity of abstraction which implies the category of possibility, a category of paramount significance in human experience. Individuals who are impaired in this capacity, due to brain damage, and cannot take the attitude toward something merely possible, do not experience joy in this sense. They experience an affect which may appear on the surface like joy, but should be distinguished from it. It is the experience of pleasure by relief of tension (Goldstein, 1939, p. 195). It corresponds to the agreeable feeling which we experience on return to a state of equilibrium after the latter has been disturbed, or to the feeling of being freed from distress. It is a passive experience and lacks the feeling of activity and freedom so characteristic of joy. Pleasure lasts only until a new situation stimulates new activity. In joy, on the other hand, we have the experience of infinite continuation. The two emotions play essentially different rôles with regard to self-realization, and they belong to different "worlds." Pleasure may be a necessary state of respite. But it is a phenomenon of "standstill," *it is akin to death*. It separates us from the world while in joy we experience "existence" of ourself and the world. Pleasure is equilibrium, elimination of danger, quietness. In joy there is disequilibrium at both "higher" and "lower" levels than "normal" behavior. It is, however, a *productive disequilibrium* leading forward to fruitful activity and self-realization. There is, of course, the danger of complete loss of equilibrium, *i.e.*, the disintegration of the personality which in turn may produce a state of anxiety as in pathological conditions. But man enjoys this danger, it corresponds to the tension which is part of living to its very apex. This example shows how behavior in emotion mirrors the complexity and ambiguity of human nature and the world belonging to it.

Our discussion has led us to realize not only how pertinent emotions are for human behavior, that they are inherent in it, but it also points to an *essential character of man, his not being primarily concerned with security*. The search for security is neither the only nor the highest form of self-realization of man. At least there are other forms which do not lack emotion, when we live in insecurity, when we take over insecurity deliberately, because only then we can realize ourselves in the highest form. There we are correct to speak of purpose of emotions.

REFERENCES

Goldstein, K. *The organism*. New York: American Book Co., 1939.

Goldstein, K. *Human nature in the light of psychopathology*. Cambridge: Harvard University Press, 1947.

Goldstein, K. The idea of disease and therapy. *Review of Religion*, 1949, *13*, 229–240.

Leeper, R. W. A motivational theory of emotion to replace emotion and disorganized response. *Psychological Review*, 1948, *55*, 2–21.

Munn, N. L. *Psychology*. Boston: Houghton Mifflin, 1946.

Sartre, J. P. *The emotions: Outline of a theory*. New York: Philosophical Library, 1948.

Woodworth, R. S. *Psychology*. New York: Holt, 1940.

CHAPTER **13**

Soviet Personality Theory: Makarenko

Introduction

Following the 1917 Soviet Revolution and the ending of World War I in 1919, Russia was in a virtual state of chaos in practically all respects. One of the major problems of the new state was its young people, many of whom, made homeless and parentless by the revolution and the war, formed themselves into raiding gangs.

In the early 1920s Anton Makarenko (1888–1939), a teacher who had been active in revolutionary activities, was offered the task of heading a rehabilitation institution for such children. He was extraordinarily successful in his efforts to rehabilitate these youths. A fascinating autobiographical account of Makarenko's work at the Gorki colony is found in his book *The Road to Life: An Epic in Education* (1955).

This selection from *The Collective Family* illustrates Makarenko's relaxed style. More of an activist than a theoretician, he formulated a dictum about how to bring up children—"Make the maximum possible demands with the maximum possible respect"—which dominates Soviet adult-child relationships today.

A. S. MAKARENKO
The parent as upbringer

Perhaps this book is too daring?

In molding their children, modern parents mold the future history of our country and, consequently, the history of the world as well. Can I shoulder the burden of so tremendous a subject? Have I the right or the courage to tackle even its main problems?

Fortunately, no such daring is required of me. Our Revolution has its great books, but it has even more great deeds. The books and deeds of the Revolution—these are the teachers of the new man. Every thought, every movement, every breath of our life vibrates with the glory of the new citizen of the world. Is it possible not to sense that vibration, is it possible not to know how we should educate our children?

But there is also a humdrum side to our life, and this humdrum side gives rise to a complicated set of trivialities. Amid the trivialities one is apt to lose sight of the man. It happens sometimes that our parents seek the truth among these trivialities, forgetting that ready to their hand lies the great philosophy of the Revolution.

To help parents look about them, to help them think, to open their eyes—such is the modest aim of this book.

Our youth is a world phenomenon which defies comparison, a phenomenon whose greatness and significance we are, perhaps, incapable of comprehending. Who gave it birth, who taught it, educated it, entrusted it with the cause of the Revolution? Whence came these tens of millions of craftsmen, engineers, airmen, combine operators, commanders, scientists? Can it be that we, we old people, created this youth? But when? How did we fail to notice it? Was it not we who grumbled at our schools and universities, grumbled, more often than not, unthinkingly, for want of something better to do; was it not we who considered our People's Commissariats for Education only fit to be grumbled at? And meanwhile the family seemed to be creaking at every joint, more chilled by emotional currents than warmed by love. And anyhow there was no time. We built, we fought, then built again, and we are still building now, we do not down tools for an instant.

But look! In the incredible vastness of the Kramatorsk workshops, in the immense expanse of the Stalingrad Tractor Works, in the Stalino, Makeyevka and Gorlovka mines, in airplanes, in tanks, in submarines, in laboratories, over microscopes, above the wastes of the Arctic, at every possible kind of steering gear and regulator, at entrances and exits—everywhere there are tens of millions of new, young and terribly interesting people.

They are modest. Some of them are not very refined in their conversation, sometimes their humor is rough. . . . There is no denying that.

But they are the masters of life, they are calm and confident; unhesitatingly, without hysterics and posing, without boastfulness and without complaining, at absolutely unforeseeable speed—they are doing the job. And just show them one of the sights, which even we are already beginning to forget about, such as, for instance: N. A. Pastukhov & Sons, Engineering Works—and you will be surprised at the subtle humor of their reactions!

And against the background of this historical miracle, how barbaric seem family "catastrophes" which ruin the relationship between father and children, and the happiness of the mother, which break down and destroy the characters of the future men and women of the U.S.S.R.

In our country there must be no childhood catastrophes, no failures, no percentage, not even a hundredth per cent, of defective goods! And yet in some families things do go wrong. Rarely is it a catastrophe, sometimes it is an open conflict; far more often the conflict is secret: not only do parents fail to see it, they fail to see any of its portents.

In a letter received from a mother, I read:

We have only one son, but it would be better if we had none. . . . This awful, indescribable misfortune has made us old before our time. It is not only sad, it is painful and distressing to watch a young man going further and further downhill when he could be among the best. After all, youth nowadays means happiness and joy!

Every day he is killing us, steadily and persistently killing us by his conduct, by everything he does.

The father's appearance is not very attractive: his face is broad, unshaven, lopsided. He is slovenly. There are hen feathers or something on his sleeve; one feather has even stuck to his finger; the finger is gesticulating over my inkstand, and so is the feather.

"I am a worker . . . understand? I work . . . and I teach him. . . . Ask him if that's not so. Well, what have you got to say: Did I teach you or didn't I?"

On a chair by the wall sits a boy of about thirteen, handsome, dark-eyed, grave. He looks his father straight in the eye without flinching. In the boy's face I can read no feelings, no expression but calm, cold attention.

The father waves his fist, his distorted face going purple.

"The one and only, eh? Robbed me and left me . . . with nothing but what I stand up in!"

His fist lunges toward the wall. The boy blinks, then resumes his coldly serious examination of his father.

The father falls back tiredly into his chair, drums with his fingers on the table, and looks around, completely at a loss. An upper muscle in his cheek twitches rapidly, deformed by an old scar.

He lowers his big head and spreads his arms despairingly.

"Take him somewhere. . . . Well . . . I failed. Take him. . . ."

He says this in a defeated, pleading voice, but suddenly he gets excited again, and again brandishes his fist.

"But how can it be? I was a partisan. Look at me . . . that was a Shkuro saber . . . split my head open! For their sake, for yours!"

He turns toward his son and thrusts his hands into his pockets. Then he speaks with that extreme pathos which comes only from the lips of a dying man:

"Misha! How could you?! My only son! . . ."

Misha's eyes remain cold, but suddenly his lips move, some momentary thought shows itself for an instant and vanishes.

I see that these two are enemies and will remain enemies for a long time, perhaps for life. Their characters have clashed over some trifle or other, in some dark corner of the soul instincts have been aroused, temperaments fired. An unexpected explosion is the usual culmination of careless treatment of character—this father, of course, used the rod. And the son rose up against his father, free and proud—it was not for nothing that his father fought with the Shkuro gang! That was how it started. Now the father is driven frantic—and the son?

I looked at Misha sternly and said quietly:

"You'll go to the Dzerzhinski Commune! Today!"

The boy straightened up on his chair. Real bonfires of joy flamed in his eyes, and the room seemed to grow brighter. Misha did not say anything, but leaned back in his chair and directed his newborn smile straight at the Shkuro scar and tormented eyes of his father. And only then did I read in his smile unconcealed, implacable hatred.

The father sadly lowered his head.

When Misha left with the inspector, the father asked me, as if he were addressing an oracle:

"Why have I lost my son?"

I made no answer. Then the father asked:

"Will it be all right for him there?"

Books, books, books up to the ceiling. Well-loved names on splendid bindings. An enormous writing table. On the table—more books, a monumental sarcophagus of an inkstand, sphinxes, bears, candlesticks.

This study bubbles with life; the books do not merely stand on the shelves, they rustle in people's hands; newspapers do not merely lie about among the cushions on the sofa, they are spread out and read; here events are knowledgeably discussed and come to life. Through the tobacco smoke one has glimpses of bald pates, elaborate coiffures, shaven chins, American mustaches and amber cigarette holders; and behind horn-rimmed spectacles eyes glisten with the fine dew of wit.

In the spacious dining room tea is served, tea which is not rich old-fashioned samovar tea, not tea to be drunk, but refined tea, tea which is almost symbolic, an occasion for china, lace table napkins and the severe beauty of the ascetic biscuit. Slightly languid, a little naïve, the exquisite auburn-haired hostess conducts the tea party with her pampered, manicured hands. Tea is attended by a merry-flock of names of artistes and ballerinas, mischievous short stories and lighthearted small talk from life. Well, and if a snack is served with the tea and the smiling host makes two or three rounds with the decanter? Then after tea the company will go back into the study, light up again, squash the newspapers on the sofa, loll on the cushions and, throwing back their heads, roar with laughter over the latest funny story.

Is there anything wrong with that? Who knows? But among these people there is always a wide-eyed, twelve-year-old Volodya running to and fro, rather thin and pale, but an energetic lad. When for some reason a hitch occurs in the smooth flow of anecdotes, Daddy "serves up" Volodya—just a tiny portion of him. In theatrical parlance this is called an "entr'acte."

Daddy draws Volodya onto his knee, tickles the back of Volodya's head and says:

"Volodya, why aren't you in bed?"

Volodya replies:

"Why aren't you?"

The guests are delighted. Volodya lowers his eyes to Daddy's lap and smiles shyly—guests like it better that way.

Daddy pats Volodya on any suitable spot and asks:

"Have you finished *Hamlet* yet?"

Volodya nods.

"Did you like it?"

This time, too, Volodya is not at a loss, but now shyness is out of place.

"Pooh, not much! If he's in love with that . . . um . . . Ophelia, why don't they get married? They just dawdle along and you have to read and read!"

A fresh burst of laughter from the guests. From a corner of the sofa somebody's cozy bass adds the necessary spice: "He doesn't want to pay alimony, the rogue!"

This time Volodya laughs too, so does Daddy, but the appropriate funny story has already taken the stage: "Do you know what the priest said when he was told to pay alimony?"

"End of entr'acte." Volodya is rarely served up as part of the program—Daddy realizes that Volodya is pleasant only in small doses. Volodya does not like such a system of doses. He runs to and fro among the crowd, passes from one guest to another, tags on even to strangers and fishes intently for a chance to make a sortie, to show himself off, to raise a laugh from the guests and to exalt his parents.

At tea Volodya's ringing voice suddenly breaks into a story.

"She's his mistress, isn't she?"

Mother throws up her hands and exclaims:

"Did you hear that? Volodya, what are you saying?!"

But on Mother's face, together with a certain degree of false surprise, are written involuntary delight and pride; she takes this boyish freeness as evidence of talent. In the general list of elegant bric-a-brac Volodya's talent is also acceptable: Japanese cups, little knives for lemon, napkins and—such a wonderful son.

In the midst of their trivial and foolish vanity the parents are unable to look closely into their son's character and see there the first signs of their future family troubles. Volodya has a very complicated look in his eyes. He tries to make them into innocent childish eyes—that is "by special request," for his parents; but in those very same eyes glitter sparks of insolence and habitual falsehood—that is for himself.

What kind of a citizen will he make?

Dear parents!

You sometimes forget that in your family there is a person growing, a person for whom you are responsible.

Do not console yourselves with the idea that this is no more than a moral responsibility.

There may come a moment when you will lose heart and spread out your arms in bewilderment, and then, perhaps, you will mutter to quieten that very same sense of moral responsibility: "Volodya was such a wonderful boy! Simply everyone was delighted with him."

But will you never understand who is to blame?

However, catastrophe may not occur.

The moment comes when parents first feel there is something slightly wrong. Then this feeling deepens, that there is something really unhealthy in what they had thought was their happy family. For a time the worried parents submit to this, whisper unhappily to each other in the bedroom, but maintain their dignity in public, pretending that all is well and no tragedy has occurred, for the outward appearance of the family is wholesome enough.

The parents act just like all producers of shoddy goods: the latter are offered to society as the proper article.

When the first little "child" trouble occurs in your family, when you see in your child's eyes a little animal, as yet small and weak but already hostile, why do you not look back, why do you not set about reviewing your own conduct, why are you too weak-minded to ask yourself: Have I, in my family life, acted like a Bolshevik?

But I am sure you are looking for an excuse. . . .

A man in spectacles, with a short red beard, a rubicund, cheerful man, suddenly stirred his spoon in his glass, pushed the glass aside and snatched out a cigarette.

"You pedagogues are always reproaching people over methods. No one is quarreling about that, methods are methods. But solve the basic conflict, my friends!"

"What conflict?"

"Oho! What conflict? You don't even know what it is? None of that—you solve it!"

"All right then, I will. What are you getting excited about?"

He drew appreciatively at his cigarette, his full lips ejected a small ring of smoke, then a tired smile appeared on his face.

"You won't solve anything. The conflict is one of the insoluble variety. It's no solution to say sacrifice this or sacrifice that. That's just a pat answer! Suppose I can't sacrifice one thing or the other, what then?"

"But what's the conflict, I'd like to know?"

My companion squinted at me through tobacco smoke; twisting his cigarette between his fingers to stress the fine shades of his sorrow, he said:

"On the one hand you have your job in society, your social duty, on the other your duty to your child, to your family. Society takes all my time: morning, afternoon, and evening—the use of every moment is allotted and mapped out. And the child? It's just simple arithmetic: giving your time to your child means sitting at home, keeping out of life, becoming a philistine, in fact. You must talk to your child, you must explain a lot to him, you must bring him up, damn it all!"

He looked at me with an air of pompous impatience and stubbed out his unfinished cigarette in the ash tray.

"Have you a son?" I asked cautiously.

"Yes, in the sixth class, thirteen years old. Good fellow, learns well, but he's a young vagabond already. He treats his mother as a servant. He's rude. I never see him. And just imagine this. A friend of his came round the other day, and there they were sitting in the next room, and suddenly I hear my Kostik swearing. Not just a word or two, mind you, simply turning the air blue."

"Were you frightened?"

"What do you mean 'frightened'? At the age of thirteen there is nothing he doesn't know, no secrets exist for him. Probably knows dirty stories as well and all kinds of filth!"

"Of course he does!"

"Well, there you are! And where was I? Where was I, his father?"

"You are annoyed that other people have taught your son swearwords and dirty stories and that you had no chance to take part in it?"

"Now, you are joking!" roared my companion. "But joking does not solve the conflict!"

Agitated, he signed for the tea and left the room.

But I was not joking at all. I had asked him a question and his reply had been mere babble. He drinks tea in the club and chatters to me—he would call that social work too. And give him more time, what will he do with it? Wage a campaign against lewd stories? But how? What age was he when he himself began swearing? What is his program? What ideas has he, besides the "basic conflict"? And where did he storm off to? Perhaps to educate his son, or perhaps he was going somewhere else to discuss the "basic conflict"?

The "basic conflict"—lack of time—is the favorite excuse of unsuccessful parents. Protected from responsibility by the "basic conflict," they imagine themselves indulging in salutary talks with their children. A comforting picture: the parent talks and the child listens! But the making of speeches and sermons to one's own children is an incredibly difficult task. For such a speech to have a beneficial educative effect, a fortunate coincidence of many circumstances is required. In the first place you have to choose an interesting theme; then it is essential that you should know how to express yourself well and how to illustrate what you have to say; apart from this the child must be blessed with unusual patience.

On the other hand, suppose your speech pleases the child. At first glance it may seem that this is good, but in practice there are parents who will be furious if that happens. What kind of an edifying speech is it that aims at bringing joy to the child? Everybody knows that joyfulness can be attained by many other means; "edifying" speeches, on the contrary, aim at distressing the listener, wearing him down, reducing him to tears, to moral exhaustion.

Dear parents!

Please do not think that there is no sense at all in talking to your child. We are only warning you against expecting too much from such talks.

Precisely those parents who bring up their children badly and who are in general quite devoid of any educational ability exaggerate the value of pedagogical talks.

Educational work, they imagine, is carried on in this fashion. The educator takes his stand at point A. Three yards away is point B defended by the child. The educator brings his vocal cords into action, the child picks up the appropriate sound waves with his hearing apparatus. The waves penetrate by means of the eardrums to the child's soul and are distilled there into some special educational potion.

Sometimes the positions of subject and object vary a little, but the distance of three yards remains the same. As if attached to a lead, the child circles round the educator, all the while experiencing the action of the vocal cords or some other type of direct influence. Sometimes the child breaks away from the lead and in a short time is discovered in the dreadful cesspool of life. In such a case the educator, father or mother, protests in a trembling voice: "He's got quite out of hand! All day roaming the streets! You know what kind of boys there are in our yard? Young ruffians! Who knows what they get up to out there? Some of them are even juvenile delinquents, I bet. . . ."

Both the voice and eyes of the orator beg: catch my son, save him from the street boys, put him on the pedagogical lead again, let me carry on educating him.

Such education certainly requires much spare time and, of course, it means spare time wasted. The system of tutors and governesses, permanent overseers and constant nagging, broke down long ago without ever creating in history a single vivid personality. The best, the most lively children invariably broke loose.

A Soviet person cannot be educated by the direct influence of one personality, whatever qualities this personality may possess. Education is a social process in the broadest sense of the term. Everything contributes to education: people, things, events, but first of all and above all— people. Of these, parents and teachers hold first place. The child enters into an infinite number of relationships with the whole complex world of surrounding reality. Each one of these relationships is irresistibly developing, overlapping with other relationships, and becoming more complicated as the physical and moral growth of the child increases.

Nothing in this "chaos" seems to yield to any calculation. Nevertheless at each given moment definite changes are created in the personality of the child. And it is the task of the educator to direct and guide this development.

Senseless and hopeless is the attempt made by some parents to shield the child from the influence of life and substitute individual domestic training for social education. It is bound to end in failure: either the child breaks out of the domestic prison or you produce a freak.

Then it is life that is responsible for the child's upbringing? But where does the family come in?

No, it is the family or, if you like, the parents that are responsible for the child's upbringing. But the training provided by the family collective cannot mold the child out of nothing. A limited assortment of family impressions or pedagogical lectures from Father will not suffice as material for the future man. It is Soviet life in all its multiform variety that provides that material.

In the old days, in well-to-do families children used to be called "angelic souls." In our days it has been said that children are "flowers of life." That is good. But rash-minded, sentimental people have not taken the trouble to think over the meaning of these beautiful words. Once children are described as "flowers," it means to such people that we should do nothing but go into raptures over them, make a fuss over them, smell them, sigh over them. Perhaps they even think we should teach the flowers themselves that they are a fragile "luxury" bouquet.

This purely aesthetic and thoughtless enthusiasm contains the seeds of its own failure. The "flowers of life" should not be imagined as a "luxury" bouquet in a Chinese vase on your table. However much you enthuse over such flowers, however much fuss you make over them, these flowers are already dying, they are already doomed and they are sterile. Tomorrow you will simply have them thrown away. At best, if you are incorrigibly sentimental, you will dry them in a bulky volume, but you can expect little joy from that: give yourself up as much as you like to memories, look at them as much as you like, you will have nothing but hay, just hay.

No, our children are not flowers of that kind at all. Our children blossom on the living trunk of our life; they are not a bouquet, they are a wonderful apple orchard. And this orchard is ours. Here the right of property means something fine, believe me! It is hard, of course, not to admire such an orchard, hard not to rejoice over it, but it is even harder not to work in it. Be so kind as to take on this job: dig, water, get rid of the caterpillars, prune out the dead branches. Remember the words of the great gardener, Comrade Stalin:

"People should be reared with care and

attention as a gardener rears his chosen fruit-tree."

Note the word: fruit. Not only fragrance, not only range of colors, but fruit, that is what should interest you especially. And for this reason do not descend upon the flowers with nothing but raptures and kisses—take up your spade, your scissors and watering can, and fetch the ladder. And when the caterpillar appears in your garden, reach for the insecticide. Do not be afraid of it, shake it around a bit, let even the flowers feel a little uncomfortable. By the way, a good gardener never has trouble with caterpillars.

Yes, let us be gardeners. This excellent comparison will help us to explain a few things about the difficult problem of who educates the child—parents or life?

Who cultivates the tree in an orchard?

The soil and the air give it substance, the sun gives it the valuable power of combustion, the winds and storms bring it toughness in battle, its fellow trees save it from sterility. Both in the tree and around it extremely complex chemical processes are always at work.

What can the gardener change in this laborious work of life? Should he just wait helplessly and submissively till the fruit are ripe and he can pluck them and gorge himself on them with greedy in-difference?

That is exactly what savages do in the wilds of Tierra del Fuego. And that is what many parents do.

But a real gardener would never act like that.

Man learned long ago to approach nature cautiously and tenderly. Now he has learned to transform nature, to create new natural forms, to apply his powerful corrective to the life of nature. And we should remember that we Soviet educationalists also are no longer "servants of nature," but her masters.

Our education is a similar corrective. And only on these lines is education possible. To lead a child wisely and surely along the rich paths of life, amid its flowers and through its storms and tempests, is a task which every man can accomplish if he really wants to do so.

Nothing annoys me more than the disgusting panic-stricken howl:

"Street urchins!!"

"You see, everything was all right, but then Seryozha got friendly with a lot of urchins in our yard. . . ."

This "lot of urchins" corrupt Seryozha. Seryozha roams off no one knows where. Seryozha has taken a length of worsted from the closet and sold it. Seryozha came home past midnight, smelling of vodka. Seryozha insulted his mother.

Only the most hopeless simpleton can believe that all this was brought about by "a lot of urchins," "street urchins."

Seryozha is not unique. He is perfectly ordinary, a standard type which everybody is quite tired of, and it is not "street urchins" or the "urchins in our yard" but lazy and unscrupulous parents that have made him what he is. He is not produced in a flash; the process is a persistent and patient one, beginning from the time when Seryozha was one and a half years old. A large number of thoroughly disgraceful characteristics in the family's behavior contributed to the making of him: blank idleness, aimless daydreaming, petty tyranny and, above all, unpardonable irresponsibility and an infinitesimal sense of duty.

Seryozha is indeed a real "street ur-chin," but it was the family, and only the family, that made him one. Perhaps in your yard he does meet failures like himself; together they make up the usual gang of youngsters, all of them equally demoralized and equally "street." But in that same yard you will find dozens of children for whom the family body and the family corrective have created principles and traditions which help them to overcome the influence of the street boys without avoiding them and without barricading themselves off from life within the family walls.

The decisive factor in successful family upbringing lies in the constant, active, and conscious fulfillment by parents of their civic duty toward Soviet society. In those cases where this duty is really felt by parents, where it forms the basis of their daily lives, there it necessarily guides the family's work of upbringing too, there no failures or catastrophes are possible.

But there is, unfortunately, a category of parents, a fairly numerous category, with whom this rule does not work. These people seem to be good citizens, but they suffer either from inability to think consistently, or from a weak sense of direction, or from not being observant enough. And for this reason alone their sense of duty does not operate in the sphere of their family relationships, nor, consequently, does it operate in the sphere of their children's upbringing. And for this reason alone they meet with more or less serious failures, and produce for society human brings of dubious quality.

Others are more honest. They say sincerely: "You have to know how to bring up a child. Perhaps I am not doing it right, really. It takes knowledge to bring up children."

In other words: everybody wants to bring up their children well, but not everyone knows the secret. Some people have discovered it, some people make full use of it, but you are completely in the dark, no one has revealed the mystery to you.

This being so, the eyes of all turn toward the teachers' training colleges and institutes.

Dear parents!

Between ourselves, in their families our pedagogical brethren produce, proportionately, about the same quantity of defective goods as you do. And, on the contrary, fine children are often brought up by parents who have never seen either the front door or the back door of pedagogical science.

And pedagogical science pays little attention to family upbringing. That is why even the most learned pedagogues, although they know the why and wherefore of things very well, when bringing up their own children try to rely more on common sense and worldly wisdom. But perhaps more often than others they are guilty of a naive belief in the pedagogical "secret."

I once knew such a professor of education. He would always treat his only son as a problem to be solved with the aid of books and profound psychological analyses. Like many pedagogues he believed that there must exist somewhere in the world some kind of pedagogical trick which would bring complete and delightful satisfaction both to educator and child, satisfy all principles and bring about the reign of peace and quiet and eternal bliss! The son was rude to his mother at dinner. The professor thought for a moment and arrived at an inspired solution:

"Fedya, since you have insulted your mother, it follows that you do not appreciate our home, that you are unworthy to sit at our table. Very well, beginning tomorrow I shall give you five rubles a day—eat your dinner where you like."

The professor was pleased. In his opinion he had reacted to his son's rudeness brilliantly. Fedya was also pleased. But the trick plan did not work. There was a period of peace and quiet, but the eternal bliss was missing.

The professor expected that in three or four days' time Fedya would come and fling his arms round his father's neck, saying: "Father, I was wrong! Don't shut me out from home!"

But it did not happen like that, or rather, not quite like that. Fedya became very fond of visiting cafés and restaurants. The only thing that disconcerted him was the small allowance his father had given him. He made one or two amendments to the scheme; he rooted about the house and showed some initiative. Next morning, the professor's trousers were missing from his closet and in the evening the son came home drunk. In touching tones he proclaimed his love for his mama and papa, but did not raise the question of returning to the family table. The professor took off his belt and waved it in front of his son's face for some minutes.

After a month the professor threw in the sponge and asked for his son to be sent to a labor colony. According to him Fedya had been spoiled by various comrades of his.

"You know what children there are about!"

Some parents, if they heard of this affair, would undoubtedly say: "Very well! But all the same, how *is* one supposed to act if one's son is rude to his mother at dinner?"

Comrades! Perhaps you will ask me next how one should act if one loses a purse full of money? Think it over and you will find the answer at once: buy yourself a new purse, earn some more money and put it into the purse.

If a son insults his mother, no tricks will do any good. It means that you have brought up your son very badly and that you have been doing so for a long time. You must begin the work of bringing him up all over again, you must change a lot of things in your family, think over a lot of things, and, above all, put yourself under the microscope. And as for how you should act immediately after rudeness, that is a question to which one cannot give any general answer—it depends on each individual case. One must know what kind of a person you are and how you have acted toward your family. Perhaps you yourself were rude to your wife in the presence of your son. Incidentally, if you treated your wife badly when your son was not at home— take that into consideration too.

No, tricks in family upbringing must be firmly discarded. The care and upbringing of children is a big, a serious, and a terribly responsible task, and it is, of course, also a difficult task. No easy tricks can help you out here. Once you have a child, it means that for many years to come you must give him all your power of concentration, all your attention and all your strength of character. You must be not only father and guardian of your children, you must also be organizer of your own life, because your quality as an educator is entirely bound up with your activities as a citizen and your feelings as an individual.

CHAPTER **14**

Soviet Personality Theory: Myasishchev

Introduction

From a political point of view, the following selection by V. M. Myasishchev (1893–1973) may be the most important one in this book. Anton Makarenko, whose views about human nature were presented in Chapter 13, was a theorist who did not know he was one. He was an activist—a teacher, an administrator, a practical individual who had to deal with difficult problems without any elaborate theorizing, and possibly even without much knowledge of "foreign" theories. Myasishchev, another Russian, is quite a different type of person: highly sophisticated in "foreign" theories, he is prepared not only to show their lack of value but to present a "correct" theory based on Marxist philosophy and Pavlovian physiological findings.

In reading this selection, try to keep in mind how translations of foreign materials (i.e., English, French, and German) probably presented information to Myasishchev, as well as how translators of this theorist have presented his views to us. You will notice in this selection, as in the preceding one by Makarenko, the overriding importance given to *social usefulness* in personality theory by these Soviet writers.

V. M. MYASISHCHEV
Personality and Neuroses

In order to overcome alien theories in a positive way and to give adequate ammunition to its practical application, the Marxist teaching on personality had to be developed both in general and medical psychology and I. P. Pavlov's teachings on higher nervous activity had to be elaborated. We therefore tried a positive approach but at the same time had to present a critique of alien views and our disagreement with them.

Our critical essays concerning the various trends will be published under separate cover. Therefore in summarizing our views on personality and neuroses we shall point out the trends and views which need a particularly careful critical analysis. In the first place we shall speak of the more widespread concepts, the most reactionary ones or those which may appear to be close to ours and under the guise of this closeness lead us to an incorrect solution of the problem under discussion. The so-called personalism, neo-Freudianism, existentialism and microsociology require most attention. The importance of personalism lies in the fact that it is the opposite of impersonalism, that is of lack of individual responsibility which often makes itself felt both in theory and in practice in various fields and which should be overcome. Although a prominent psychologist, a representative of Personalism, William Stern, defines personalistic as a trend in the psychological and pedagogical sciences and personalism as a philosophy, in his writings he gives concrete proof of the impossibility of separating science from philosophy. The views of Stern coincide with those of the philosophers of the school of personalism (Breitman, Flueling and others) in recognizing that personality stands at the height of world development and in regarding the "all-embracing personality," or deity of teleologism,[1] as the extension of the theory of personality into the cult of the "strong" personality; but this latter concept is incompatible not only with the historical-materialistic conception of human attitudes but with any humanistic conceptions in general.

The neo-Freudians (Fromm, Kardiner, Horney, Sullivan and others) reject the Freudian teaching concerning the decisive role of instincts and stress the role of culture. They do not overcome Freudianism fundamentally but cover it up with different terminology or create new, not very convincing and poorly justified concepts, such as "the true ego," "existentialist dichotomy," etc.

The fact that all the neo-Freudians operate more or less widely with the concept of human relations and interpersonal relations is of importance. This concept acquires particular importance in the work of Harry Stack Sullivan (1953). However, he lacks the correct understanding of what constitutes the social nature of man, that is to say that individual relations and interrelations are determined by

Reprinted from V. M. Myasishchev, *Personality and Neuroses* (Washington, D.C.: U.S. Commerce Department, 1963), pp. 265–281.

[1] [Teleologism = Future/orientation.—R.C.]

social relations and the history of their development flowing from them. The existentialist dichotomy of Erich Fromm is an attempt to consider the inner conflict in a neurosis as an inevitability inherent in all human existence.

If we say that Freudianism and neo-Freudianism represent two different forms of psychobiologism, then contemporary existentialism, as a philosophical basis of psychology and psychiatry, can be regarded as a school of militant idealism which opposes the Marxist-Leninist teachings on being and consciousness with its own teachings on existence and essence, separating the first from the second.

Existentialism is a most reactionary and idealistic teaching which equates knowledge of essence to introspective self-cognition. It is quite understandable that this teaching, which has become fairly widespread abroad, particularly in West Germany and in France, stands in sharp contradiction to dialectical and historical materialism. Without having added anything new to the problem of the relationship of the external, apparent and the real essence of phenomena, existentialism in psychiatry (Binswanger and others) deforms reality and even today stands on the position of its founders: Kirkegaard, Heidegger and others.

The social nature of personality highlights the need to illuminate the relationship between the social and the individual. One of the fundamental errors of Freud himself as well as of the neo-Freudians lay in the fact that the social was explained through the individual and individual-psychological. This position is, as is well known, one of the fundamental defects of bourgeois sociology, of microsociology and social psychology. Marxism teaches that the objective social being moulds the individual being of man, his conscious-

ness, and his internal world. Therefore the individual is explained through the social. Meanwhile the social psychology and microsociology which are particularly widespread in the United States and in France bring forth opposing theories (Moreno, 1953; Gurwitch, 1953). Apparently no matter how much time they devote to the study of social realities and the behavior of the individual connected with it, in this question of principle they occupy positions diametrically opposed to ours. Lacking the possibility to analyze on these pages the above-mentioned teachings on personality, we have touched upon them only because the vast foreign literature on the problem of personality and character also operates with social and psychological concepts and presents vast empirical data which confirm the social nature of man and the significance of social conditions for his development. However, the empirical investigation, the explanation and the very act of collecting data confront the researcher with a dilemma: to admit the determining role of the social (in accordance with historical materialism) or to affirm the dependence of the social on the individual, i.e., of psychologism in sociology.

The profound, genetic study of man in an individual-historic and social-historic setting is based upon the positions of historical materialism, the very ones that Soviet psychology and neuropsychiatry aim to implement.

In the preceding chapters we developed our understanding of personality. We tried to overcome the one-sidedness of the process and functional types of psychology as encountered in the psychology of personality and its relations. While moulding the personality, social conditions and social relations find expression in individual attitudes. This constitutes the social nature of personality.

The key to the understanding of the physiological side of personality is Pavlov's (1954) postulate that higher nervous activity represents "a system of conditioned reflexes." If the problem of conditioned reflexes as elements of higher nervous activity has been elaborated, the problem of *their system has not been elaborated.* The principle of systems was elaborated by Pavlov toward the end of his life. Therefore the problems of the higher nervous activity as of a system remain a task for further investigation. The simple system of conditioned reflex formations has been studied under the name of the dynamic stereotype, but we would be doing a disservice to physiology of the higher nervous activity of man and to psychology if we would say that the psychic individuality of man is a dynamic stereotype.

It would be erroneous to determine the most complex formation, based on a synthesis of the inborn and the acquired, as the dynamic stereotype because it would considerably exaggerate, and divorce from real experience, the concept of stereotype, by substituting the simple for the complex. The concept of psychic individuality combines the concepts of personality and character. The interrelation between these two concepts has not as yet been satisfactorily appraised, neither in psychology nor in practice. Two trends come to the fore (Kovalev & Myasishchev, 1957). According to one of these trends the character is considered to be a part or component of personality, exerting an influence over a protracted period, like the emotional-volitional traits of man. The representatives of the other trend view character as personality reflected in individual traits or peculiarities. In essence, however, both trends attempt to define the distinctive characteristics of a man. In the first case the emotional-volitional traits are considered to be the distinctive features, in the other no separate distinguishing features are singled out. But the emotional-volitional features, in their generally accepted meaning, could be characterized differently. *The personality, the psyche and the consciousness of man at any given moment, as we tried to show earlier, represent a unity of reflection of objective reality and of man's attitude toward it.* The history of the environmental development of man is reflected in his whole personality and moulds his attitude to reality. Therefore the perceptive and cognitive activity come forward not as personality traits but as processes or properties directly connected with the reflection of objective reality. And, contrariwise, the emotional-volitional properties are the direct expression of man's attitudes.

In discussing the problem of human relations we first dwelled upon certain prevailing psychological concepts which had been considered one-sidedly, functionally and procedurally. These are the concepts of interest, needs, love, hostility, etc. We then were faced with the problem of a physiological understanding of attitudes and we fully accepted Pavlov's formula that psychic attitudes are temporary connections. Thus the experimental, acquired nature of attitudes was stressed, as well as their close relation to the concepts of association and of the conditioned reflex.

But further elaboration required a better definition and an internal delimitation of these interconnected concepts. In determining the psychic attitudes of man the following traits were included: (1) selectivity, (2) activity, (3) character of the total personality, and (4) consciousness. We repeatedly called attention to the fact established by Pavlov on the impossibility of establishing and producing a conditioned reflex without involving the corresponding center for the unconditioned reflex. This involvement of the center of the system is of primary importance as it is the essential condition for the forming of the temporary connection or of the conditioned reflex; secondly, this allows us to separate the theory of conditioned reflexes from the impersonal and mechanistic theory of associations and at the same time explains the possibility of the forming of associations; and thirdly, it constitutes that central condition through which an indifferent stimulus creates a certain new formation in the organism, i.e., a temporary connection or a conditioned reflex.

It is thanks to this that in the conditioned reflex, which reflects reality, we also find an element of the subjective and unconditioned, which represents an individual, internal and selective activity. *A temporary connection thus reveals the unity of reflection of the objective reality and of the attitudes toward it.* This unity in the elementary functions is also expressed in the complex and the highest functions—in the personality and in consciousness which comprise an integration of reality reflection and of attitude. We developed this view in a number of essays, and recently a noted psychologist, S. L. Rubinshtein (1959), has accepted our point of view.

There is no doubt that at the different stages of the transfer from the simple to the complex a number of problems still to be resolved are encountered. The need to delimit the concept of attitude as a *principle* of psychological investigation and of a psychic *category* (to differentiate it from processes, functions and states) should be pointed out in the first place. In limiting and delimiting the concept of attitude, two psychological concepts had to be taken into consideration which (one some time ago and the other quite recently)

were being applied in solving various psychological and, in part, medical problems to explain the psychogenesis of morbid states and lend validation to their psychotherapy. These are the concepts of *set* and of *significance.*

In the Soviet Union the concept of set was fully developed by academician D. N. Uznadze (1949). In numerous and interesting experiments conducted by Uznadze and his collaborators at the Institute of Psychology of the Georgian SSR, set[2] is considered to be a readiness, based on experience, to a certain type of reaction. The essential feature of this obvious fact is the integral nature of set and its link with needs, which were stressed by Uznadze and his pupils. Quite often in everyday language the terms "set" and "attitude" are being confused. Therefore the links between both concepts and the difference between them should be discussed.

There is no doubt that in Uznadze's desire to link set with personality and its needs, the attempt to establish a dynamic, integral psychology of personality was reflected. The methods used by Uznadze stress the acquired nature of set. This concept is essential and is close to the concept of conscious attitude. But along with these common features an essential difference between the two concepts should be pointed out. A formed attitude is conscious, i.e., man realizes the nature of his attitude to the object, while set is unconscious. In a conscious attitude, formed by past experience, there is an awareness of present and future. Attitude is retrospective and prospective. Set determines the action in the present on the basis of the past. Set is only retrospective. Set is justly considered as a dynamic stereotype, while attitudes becoming

---

[2] [Set = Tendency or disposition to respond differentially.—R.C.]

habitual change their nature to a considerable degree. The comparative experimental research on set and attitude done here by Van-Su (1959) clearly shows the connection as well as the difference between them.

The need for man to register the significance of the influence to which he is being subjected, of the task which he is solving, of the object which he perceives and of the person with whom he interacts is quite obvious. We have repeatedly considered this problem in connection with the problem of attitudes.

N. F. Dobrynin devoted a great deal of attention to the problem of significance and thus has contributed to the development of the psychology of meaning. The role of the significance of the object in the development of various psychological processes was shown by Dobrynin and his collaborators in a number of experiments. However, in accordance with the postulate of A. N. Leont'yev (1959) concerning the need to separate sense and significance, it is important to discern the subjective significance in accordance with the sense and the objective significance in accordance with the meaning.

Significance is the importance an object has for someone in some respect; significance stands close to the category of value relations, but significance does not exist without the personality and its attitudes. It should be pointed out here that the bringing forward of such concepts as "significance," "importance" and "value" represents a total personality attitude (see above) to psychological problems. These concepts should therefore be taken into consideration in the appraisal of a person's character as well as in the education, training and medical treatment of the person.

Having elucidated some related questions we can now return to the problem of personality and character. We attempted to define a personality as a conscious human being endowed with a definite system of attitudes which are characterized by direction, level, structure and dynamics. Individualism and collectivism represent the assessment of attitudes toward oneself and others. The social aspect of man is characterized by his attitude to *work* and to *property*. The diversified nature of these attitudes shows the level of *labor* activity as well as *diligence* and the *type of work* with respect to which man has a positive attitude. The same can be said about property.

As a social product, personality is determined both in content and direction first by the social significance of this direction. The social-historical and individual-psychological concepts of individualism and of collectivism in their various shadings come here to the fore as the basic traits of man. We viewed *direction* as the dominating attitude which subordinates all others and determines the life path of man. In characterizing the direction of the person we take into consideration what is decisive in a personality. But the mental level, the depth and breadth of the personality is characterized by the degree of the richness of its content. The *level* of a personality is characterized by the degree of its consciousness, the richness of its ideology and by the secondary role of the strictly personal (petty-bourgeois and selfish) and of the vitally personal (individual and animal).

The richness and productivity of a personality are the result of development, a most complex product of the correlation between the aptitudes of man and the environment; this correlation develops along a spiral (Kovalev & Myasishchev, 1960).

As the result of the many-sidedness of the personality, as of a system of attitudes, there emerge properties which are determined by the correlation between the various components of the system. If the dominant attitude embraces all sides of a personality, this then is an integrated personality. Some authors (Polan) consider harmony, the coordination of all parts of a personality and its integrity to represent the subordination of all properties to a single one. Contrasts bring about disharmony, internal contradictions and instability. This latter state has been known for quite some time in the clinic of borderline states and has attracted attention as a correlation between the process of excitation and inhibition since the time of the publication of Pavlov's research on typology.

In the complex psychic formation of the personality and of its behavior the correlation between the force of personal impulses corresponds to the internal idea-regulating tendencies of behavior. At a socially high level it is expressed by such personality traits as high principles, high ideals and moral fortitude. Colloquially one speaks of strong personalities and strong characters. In the essay on psychological types we pointed out that a strong type of temperament, as a physiological concept, does not coincide with moral strength as a psychological concept, but that *there is one physiological explanation for the strength of temperament and another for moral strength.* The latter most likely demonstrates the stability of temporary connections which are determined by social requirements and by their dominant role in man's behavior.

The character of man, according to the meaning of the term, is a psychological distinction, peculiar to this person only and differentiating it from others. One might think that ''personality'' is a general concept while ''character'' is a particular, individual, concept, but this is not so. One can speak of the personality and of the character in a general way, from the point of view of the type of personality and character or of a single, specific personality and specific character.

Taking into consideration the existing definitions of personality and character, the existing imprecision in the delimination of these concepts should be pointed out. We think it proper to view them as different levels of the psychological study of man. Thus in the personality we see the whole of the psychic properties of man while in the character we see the degree of the ability to express its individuality and to influence and affect the environment. In this sense the character represents a level of distinction which is expressed in the influence of the personality and its ability to transform reality.

Thus if we defined personality as mainly a system of attitudes, we define character as a system of attitudes and a method of implementing these attitudes in life.

However, the problems of personality are not limited to what we have said. On the contrary a number of questions which should be elucidated still remain. Some of these questions are: methods for an experimental study of the personality and of its attitudes; the types and the classification of personality; the moving force and the laws governing the development of personality. The most important practical, pedagogical, vocational organization together with the medical aspects connected with these questions also should be examined. The same can be said concerning a methodology for the psychology of personality, and methods of obtaining psychological data in the school, at work and in the clinic. These methods are: observation, talk, study of the products of the person's activity, and the experiment. We had already mentioned A. F. Lazurskiy's method of the natural experiment. A number of tests on experimental studies of personality exist abroad; the central point of these studies is experiments with the aid of "projective" tests (the methods of Murray, Rorschach, Jung, Rosenzweig and others).

It is a well-known fact that investigation through tests has been subjected to severe criticism in the Soviet Union. What is known as "projective tests" lack a general theory, but the interpretations, which may or may not be psychoanalytically oriented, are regarded as an expression of the basic positions and tendencies of the personality manifested in response to sensory stimulation (the Rorschach method), words (word-association methods), drawings (in the majority of projective tests) and stories. In diagnosing emotions and character some Soviet scientists have been using an assortment of drawings, pictures and post cards (P. G. Bel'skiy and V. N. Nikol'skiy, A. Ye. Petrova, P. M. Petrov). Independently of foreign investigators they recognized the demonstrability and significance of the results of these investigations. However, their work did not produce a sufficiently well substantiated theory for these experiments and did not exert wide influence.

The existence of the above-mentioned methods makes their further elaboration mandatory, but failure to investigate them properly has adversely affected the development of personality studies. The need to interpret material arises irrespective of the methods by which it has been gathered. It is essential to note certain aspects, the first of them being the need to apply the principle of a concrete historical study, i.e., of establishing a link between the properties of the personality and the conditions of its historical development.

Besides, the inadmissibility of explaining the simple through the complex and the need in the presence of complex formations to study their manifestations and their qualitative features in the simple so far has not been properly taken into consideration in concrete psychological, physiological and clinical studies. This concerns the attempts to reduce personality to impulses or to a complex of conditioned reflexes. It is as erroneous to substitute instinct for consciousness as it is to substitute a single reflex for the whole reflex system.

The principle of the dominant formulated by Ukhtomskiy also belongs here; it is considered as a certain order of prevalence of a given process or property in the various manifestations of the nervous activity. With respect to personality and character traits this concept has been used in a similar way by L. Klages (1926), whose philosophical positions are alien and even inimical to ours. Among his erroneous general views, the principle of the application of the dominant to the manifestations of character is, however, included. But the application of the principle of the dominant in a graphological analysis of character, as was done by Klages, constitutes a specific application of the general principle of dealing with the personality with the aid of a system of qualities in the order of their diminishing role.

The complexity of personality manifestations mentioned above requires the following structural analysis: personality traits will be defined in their correlation and not in accordance with separate manifestations. In the course of experimental study of the simplest elements by which human characteristics are expressed, we observed the correlation between speech, motions and vegetative reactions. A more complex study of character structure will deal with the correlation between and the respective role of the idea and of personal drives, of the personal and collective, of the personal and vital (of sex and food urges). These considerations should be kept in mind when interpreting factual material and developing methods for personality research. The classification of personality and character also presents considerable difficulties, and this is why there are few generally accepted theses and many disagreements.

Empirically the richest classification is the one established by Lazurskiy (1921). It is known that S. L. Rubinshtein, who once fully elaborated the postulates of Soviet psychology, did not attempt to establish a classification of personalities and characters. Neither do we propose a classification, but we consider that by pointing out the fundamental personality traits we are establishing the basic criteria and are laying the ground for a future classification.

The characteristic personality traits mentioned above constitute not only a differentiation of types according to dominant traits but also form the basis for the classification. In doing this we based ourselves not only upon empirical data but upon principled theoretical positions which let us view traits as genetically basic and typical determining personality attributes. The problem of neuroses constitutes one of the most important fields in the study of personality and its pathology. What has been said about the personality, its traits, direction, level, structure and tendencies is clearly manifested in neuroses. The pathogenesis of neurosis cannot be understood unless the structure of the personality and its genesis are taken into account. In the first place, human neuroses as morbid changes in brain function cannot be understood either in their mechanism or in their origin without the knowledge of the specifically human properties of the higher nervous activity. The difficulties or impairments in the relations of man with other people, with social reality and with the tasks which are presented to him by that reality constitutes, both physiologically and psychologically, the source of neuroses. Now, after Pavlov's discoveries in the field of higher nervous activity, the next task in the study of human neuroses is joint clinical-psychological and neurophysiological analysis of these disorders. We stress the clinical-psychological side because due to a persistent fear of psychology and to a poor understanding of its role many feel constrained to speak of clinical-psychopathological data, though psychopathology is pathological psychology; or they invoke clinical data, although the core of the clinical picture of neurosis is an impairment of behavior, activity and reactions which constitute the psychological picture of the ailment.

This is why the etiology and pathogenesis of the neurosis deserve particular attention. Pavlov (1954) used to say that neuroses in animals correspond to those forms of disorder which in man are known as psychogenic. In comparing the etiology and pathogenesis of human and animal neuroses we will find in both a clash of the processes of excitation and inhibition. However, as we had already pointed out in the 1930s, human neuroses will appear in various clinical forms; neuroses express a contradiction between the personality's tendencies and possibilities, the demands upon life and of life and the external and internal possibilities of man.

The collision between excitation and inhibition, which is an indisputable fact in the pathogenesis of neuroses, presents the clinician with two problems in human pathology: first to find the sometimes extremely violent and stubborn source of the ailment, and next to uncover the characteristic symptoms of the morbid collision. If in Pavlov's experiments animal neurosis was produced by the stimulation of the food reflex and the disruption of function was determined by the force of excitation, in man neurosis is generated by specifically human attitudes which are the bases for internal and external conflicts. While these attitudes do not exclude the role of instincts, although humanized, they extend beyond them in such attitudes as the sense of duty, responsibility, self-respect, affection and the maintenance of a principled position. The pathogenic understanding is faced with the problem: what personality attributes promote the overcoming of difficulties and the solution of conflicts and which predispose to the development of a morbid reaction? These personality attributes are the traits of character. Pathological characters were described in psychopathology quite a while ago and a direct connection between them and the picture of neuroses was asserted. Thus Sukhanov (1912) and Gannushkin (1924) described the hysterical and psychasthenic character. However, the connections are more complex. No doubt that in certain characters there is a predisposition, but it also occurs that people with hysterical and psychasthenic characters do not become decompensated until they are faced with an acute conflict they are unable to solve, which becomes pathogenic. The character may become one of the predisposing factors if it was formed under unfavorable conditions of earlier development (for instance a sensitive, stubborn, egocentric, or overly self-reliant character, etc.).

The factors which sharpen the sensitivity, create contradictions and "personal" conflicts are the very ones which predispose to neurotic decompensation and which present difficulties in overcoming the contradictions. The formal attitude narrowly tied to the theory of con-stitutionalism in the concepts of character still prevails. But specific clinical analysis makes it possible to define with greater precision the notion concerning the limits of the significance of one or the other attribute and of its genesis. Thus aggression and anxiety are often mentioned as neurotic characteristics. They are usually presented as opposites, but it should be stressed that anxiety can coincide with aggressiveness. There is mention of anxiety in general, but universal anxiety is encountered less often than anxiety with a specific content; thus psychasthenic shyness and timidity represent fear of people. But there are cases where no fear of people exists while there is fear of storms and animals: dogs and cattle. Even with respect to people fear can be differentiated in the following manner: some are unafraid of people generally, while they are afraid of drunks because "a sober person is more or less reasonable while one never can tell what can get into a drunk's head." It is essential to understand the content of emotions and emotional attitudes and substitute this approach to the constitutional and fatalistic approach to the attributes of human character.

The same can be said about the feeling of aggression. It can likewise be asserted with respect to sensitivity and impressionability and about stable inertia of impressions and emotions; this was already mentioned in one of our earlier chapters where the schemes of Kretchmer and Ewald were discussed, schemes essential for the understanding of the attributes of character but nevertheless formal.

The exacerbation of certain human traits can be explained by the history of human relations and of human experience. One cannot, however, forget when applying the historical approach to the understanding of personality that external toxicity in acting upon and damaging the brain and the human organism changes the general reactivity and the body's endurance (traumas, intoxications and alimentary dystrophies). As can be seen from clinical experience, because of the conditions which prevail in the Soviet Union, the purely psychogenic states become less and less frequent. And this is why under the action of factors which weaken both the organism and the personality there is an increase in the frequency of neurotic states; they occur with change in excitability as a result of various diseases. We have repeatedly stressed this important problem and have rejected the principle of a "negative" diagnosis. It is no easier to explain the mechanism of the formation of symptoms than the pathogenesis of neuroses. In a neurosis the symptoms are either put down in a clinical description without an explanation or, as the psychoanalysts do, they are selected in accordance with some fancy imaginary scheme and explained symbolically.

We have already discussed some phases of the formation of symptoms in neuroses. A symptom may be produced by overstrain and breakdown with accompanying over-excitation or excessive transmarginal inhibition. It can be caused through association or arise on the basis of a temporary connection between some external impressions, or between a pathogenic state and the fundamental decompensating conditions. Thus the link between the symptoms and the pathogenic situation and the investigation of the history of the ailment permit us to ascertain their onset and development. In other cases this link has a purely symbolical character. A simple example of this is a feeling of aversion which can produce symptoms of nausea and vomiting, or a negative impression to what has been seen or heard which can produce blindness or deafness, respectively. In a number of cases the symptoms express the relaxation of the pathogenic tension along constitu-

tional paths or along the paths of a temporarily weakened system such as the vascular, gastric, sexual, etc.

In a number of circumstances, upon which we cannot dwell now, central excitation, accompanied by an over-excitation of the organ, forms a connection between the action of the stimulus and the functional state of the given organ, due to the excited emotional state and to the reception by the cortex of afferent information from the respective organ. This connection becomes stably fixed. V. M. Bekhterev has shown the multi-level structure of the innervation of peripheral organs. This applies particularly to the internal organs. Unfavorable conditions which change the excitability of the whole system of innervation may arise at the various levels of this multi-organ system; it may start in the central cortex elements where ideas are formed and end in the peripheral contractive and secretory functions of the organ. As we pointed out in the introduction, in our latest essays we proposed to substitute the faulty term "neurosis of the organ" by the term "neurosis of the system." In the somatic sphere as well as in the neuropsychic this symptom is a manifestation of morbid excitation or of transmarginal excitation and inhibition. We cannot always bring to light the history of the origin of hysterical anesthesia, hyperesthesia, and impairments of speech, motor or vegetative and visceral functions. The pathogenic tension, which is followed by the excitation of several systems, causes a parabiotic state of "breakdown" (over-excitation or inhibition) in that system which is pathologically more labile, which gets over-excited by the situation and which has a certain specific significance in the picture of the morbid state.

The problem of the significance, essence or importance of one or another object or influence acquired objective meaning when I. P. Pavlov's work became known. For the animal it is the connection with the vitally significant unconditioned reflex after the involvement of the respective center, for man it is the connection with a vitally significant condition. The reservation should be made, however, that for man not only the associative connection, that is the temporary connection with the unconditioned stimulus is vitally significant, but also the essence, the sense, that is the basic characteristics of the object, phenomenon or situation and the object's link with the vital interests, which for man are in the first place of a social, moral or economic order. *The reason that a neurosis is essentially a personality disease is that it is produced by conditions of significance in the system of the personality's attitudes.*

But in a physiological approach to the pathogenesis of neuroses the dynamics of the morbid states with their changing symptoms should also be taken into account. This becomes particularly clear in an obsessive neurosis. Thus masturbation may produce an obsession; in this state there may be an internal struggle due to esthetic, social or moral reasons. Being ashamed of his "vice," the masturbator is afraid of being revealed and, as was pointed out by Bekhterev quite some time ago, erythrophobia[3] is often connected with masturbation. The fear of revelation in connection with masturbation produces over-anxiety, insecurity and timidity. But erythrophobia along with over-anxiety and timidity in this case are secondary reaction formations. Psychologically and logically their origin is clear. But it is more difficult to explain it physiologically. In erythrophobia a temporary connection is established between the flushing and the fear of the revelation; over-anxiety is a complex reaction of the disorder,

the fear of humiliation in the eyes of public opinion because of "the dirty vice." No doubt, here emotion plays a certain role but so does the prospect of social evaluation, i.e., a complex intellectual formation, a product of the second signal system,[4] which first should be factually and psychologically described and understood and only later given a physiological explanation in accordance with the growth of the possibilities for this explanation.

So that true facts should not be set aside and we should not delude ourselves by applying some physiological terms, we must understand that today the possibility of a scientific, physiological explanation is still limited to relatively simple events, that the manifestations of personality in neuroses are exceedingly complex and that in the presence of complex phenomena it is a mistake to explain the complex through the simple.

We have touched upon the problem of personality in neuroses because the role of personality in the disorder is particularly pronounced in this group of cases. However, in other mental diseases, the more the reactive components of the ailment come to the fore, the greater is the role played by the personality. The role of personality is felt not only in mental but in various other diseases. The basic, well known neurogenic and somatic morbid forms are hypertension and ulcer. Diabetes and hyperthyroidism should also be added. We already pointed to the erroneousness of considering hypertension and ulcer disease as neuroses, although the significant role that personality and the psyche play in their origin and development cannot be denied. By the same token we refute the term "neurosis of the organs" because neurosis strikes man as a whole, the total personality and not a single organ.

---

[3] [Erythrophobia = Fear of blushing.—R.C.]

[4] [Second signal system = Speech.—R.C.]

Without dwelling any further upon those still insufficiently elaborated questions, we want to point out the importance of developing them further as it is in these very states that the so-called influence of the personality and the psyche on the soma is manifested. In the discussion of general neuroses and in the neuroses of the various systems we shall turn to the task of overcoming the formal-dynamic approach to the study of the healthy and morbid personality and of substituting the study of content.

Neurosis also represents a personality disorder because only in neurosis the personality is revealed to the investigator so fully and clearly, and because in no other condition does the disease-inducing and the beneficial role of human relations nor the maiming and curing force of influence come so much to the fore, nor is the role of conditions created by man so fully pronounced. *This is why the field of the struggle with neuroses is a borderline field between education and medicine.* As we attempted to show, psychotherapy in its basic form is as much a method of treatment as a method of reeducating the personality. Hypnosis represents a particular form of psychotherapy which may be called experimental psychotherapy. We have hardly mentioned it here because we omitted the questions of the experimental study of personality and of the treatment of personality diseases. Hypnosis belongs to this latter group. Psychotherapy, in all its manifestations, is a method of acting upon not only the psyche but upon the human organism through the psyche. The medical, practical and theoretical significance of this problem cannot be underestimated because *the theory of medicine and the understanding of the role of the interrelation of the somatic and psychic factors in the development of disease, its prevention and cure occupy a most important place.* Unfortunately, only

a few scientists properly understand the Sechenov and Botkin theory of nervism.[5] It signifies that the highest and most complex formations, which develop from the simple and the lower in turn assume a regulating function over them. It is obvious that if a pathogenic influence of the psyche and of the personality upon disease exists, then the personality and the psyche should be taken into account in the prevention not only of the psychogenic but of various other diseases as well.

The prophylactic position of Soviet medicine is well known. A remarkable scientist and physician, V. M. Bekhterev (1912), already during the period of tsarist reaction in 1912 wrote: "Let the physician generally and the psychiatrist specifically be not only a representative of his profession but let him also be a public figure; his task should embrace in equal measure the treatment of the sick and, in the broadest meaning of the word, the protection of health of the population. Simultaneously medicine, having left the circle of special knowledge, will become a science of great social import protecting the health of the population, this being the mightiest bulwark for state development."

I. P. Pavlov said that hygiene was the medicine of the future. Here, in the USSR, the social hygiene measures have been widely applied. However, research in individual as well as in neuropsychic hygiene is still lagging sharply behind social hygiene research. Without repeating what has been said in another essay (Myasishchev, 1959), we want to stress that neuropsychic hygiene is indissolubly linked with the upbringing of a socially healthy personality, that the problem of the strength, endurance and balance of the nervous system in man is not only a physiological but also a psychological,

---

[5] [Nervism = Hypothesis that nerves control al bodily functions.—R.C.]

social and educational problem as well. The understanding of the content of these features (attributes) requires the understanding of their rapport with the whole system of the attitudes of man to reality.

The strength, balance and stability of the nervous system as an expression of the dynamic attributes of the brain are at the same time an expression of the content system of the integral attitudes of man to life. The basis of the neuropsychic health of man is the unity of physical and mental health. In this unity not only the functional and formal aspects should be taken into account but the conscious attitude of the personality toward work, the process and results of work and to those who participate in collective labor.

Much remains to be done so that the medical men understand that in the disease of an organism the patient's whole personality always participates in some measure (and sometimes in a determining measure). In this connection *the attitude toward psychiatry must be changed, and it should be understood that it is a science concerned not only with mental disease but in the first place with human health and with factors which determine it.*

The teaching on human personality and on neuropsychic health can develop only within a framework of a society which in its very foundations guarantees a healthy development of man. We think that there is no need to prove that this is a socialist society; but unfortunately we still have to struggle for the recognition of the fact that in order to assure a harmonious and healthy development of man and personality more attention should and can be devoted to the development and strengthening of the science of personality itself. Some satisfaction can be gained from the fact that some signs of growing interest can be observed and thus some prospects for future improvement can be seen.

REFERENCES

Bekhterev, V. M. The basic tasks of psychiatry as an objective science. *Russkiy vrach,* No. 6, 1912.

Gannushkin, P. B. *Klinika i dinamika psikhopatiy* [*The clinic and the dynamics of psychopathies*]. Moscow, 1924.

Gurwitch, G. *Determinismes sociaux et liberté humaine.* Paris, Presses universitate, 1953.

Klages, L. *Handschrift und charakter.* Leipsig: Barth, 1940. (Originally published, 1916).

Kovalev, A. G. & Myasishchev, V. N. *Psikhicheskiye osobennosticheloveka* [*The psychic characteristics of man.*] (Vol. 1, *Character*). Leningrad: Leningrad State University, 1957.

Kovalev, A. G., & Myasishchev, V. N. *Psikhicheskiye osobennosticheloveka* [*The psychic characteristics of man*]. (Vol. 2, *Aptitudes*). Leningrad: Leningrad State University, 1960.

Lazurskiy, A. F. *Klassifikatsiya lichnostey* [*A classification of personalities*]. Petrograd, 1921.

Leont'yev, A. N. *Problemy razvitiya psikhiki* [*The problems of the development of mind*]. Moscow: Academy of Pedagogical Sciences, RSFSR, 1959.

Moreno, J. L. *Who shall survive?* New York: Beacon Press, 1953.

Myasishchev, V. N. Certain problems of neuromental hygiene in the next seven years. *Voprosy psikhiatrii i nevropatologii,* Issue 6, Leningrad, 1959.

Myasishchev, V. N. *Personality and neuroses.* Washington, D.C.: U.S. Commerce Department, 1963.

Pavlov, I. P. *Collected works* (2nd ed.). Moscow: Academy of Sciences, USSR, 1954.

Rubinshtein, S. L. *Bytiye i soznaniye* [*Being and consciousness*]. Moscow: Academy of Sciences, 1959.

Sukhanov, S. A. *Patologicheskiy kharakter* [*The pathological character*]. St. Petersburg, 1912.

Sullivan, H. S. *The interpersonal theory of psychiatry.* New York: Norton, 1953.

Uznadze, D. N. The experimental bases of the psychology of set. *Psikhologiya* [*Psychology*], 1949.

Van-Su. The problem of the connection between set and human attitude. *Uchennyye zapiski LGU,* No. 265, 1959.

CHAPTER 15

Asian Personality Theory: Pande

Introduction

In the Occident one wears black to symbolize bereavement; in the Orient, white is the symbol of mourning. In China it is said one turns a screw counterclockwise to tighten it; in the West screws tighten in a clockwise direction. What seems right and natural to us, the "proper" way to do things, is unnatural and incorrect elsewhere. From the point of view of each culture, there is a "right" and a "natural" and a "proper" way.

In reading anything relative to personality theory in Asia, as in this selection by Shashi Pande (1968), the reader must be alert to the strong possibilities of apparently incongruous attitudes or positions. Things that seem evident to us may be completely disregarded by others.

In this selection psychotherapy is viewed from a completely different position from that accepted in the West—and a culture shock may well result for those who profess to "know" what psychotherapy is all about. It presents an Eastern interpretation of what psychotherapy really is. If you can put yourself in Pande's frame of reference, certainly a widening of your horizons will result.

SHASHI K. PANDE
The Mystique of "Western" Psychotherapy:
An Eastern Interpretation

Psychotherapy, conceived in a broad, generic framework, is conterminous with the history of man. And yet, psychotherapy as we conceive and recognize it today is a phenomenon of Western society and the 20th century. More than a phenomenon, it is a cultural institution of this society, deriving its roots from it and, in turn, affecting and transforming the soil and era in which it thrives.

It appears reasonable, therefore, to cast a searching glance, if possible from outside the gestalt of the Western mind, to see in which salient areas of life psychotherapy offers special satisfactions to the Western man and to ascertain which deeper needs of our times it serves. Deciphering the meaning of religious and ritualistic healing in the so-called primitive tribes has been repeatedly attempted. Reversing the telescopic sight to examine the quasiscientific rituals employed in the healing of the mind, closer at home, is perhaps overdue.

The thesis of this paper is that the intimate nature of psychotherapeutic contact, the medical aura which surrounds it, and the seemingly noninter-

Shashi K. Pande, "The Mystique of 'Western' Psychotherapy: An Eastern Interpretation," *The Journal of Nervous and Mental Disease,* 146 (June 1968): 425–432.

Note: The preparation of this paper was facilitated, in part, by support from Research Grant MH 13212 of the National Institute of Mental Health, U. S. Public Health Service, whose aid is gratefully acknowledged.

ventional and nonjudgmental activities of the therapist all make room for a transaction between two persons in which the avowed concern is for health and objectivity, but where the hidden agenda is perhaps of quite a different order. The agenda is hidden not because of any (conscious) duplicity or deliberate design but because strong forces of cultural conditioning have obfuscated a proper perception and recognition of some of the items on this agenda.

Let us examine these alternate items. If at times some appear overdrawn to the point of caricature, let it be understood that this is for the purpose of exposition only.

PSYCHOTHERAPY AS LOVE

It is increasingly accepted that insight has received a disproportionately high emphasis in our conceptual models of psychotherapy. Nevertheless, considerable effort in psychotherapy as it is largely practiced today is geared toward retrieving glimpses of the patient's unconscious. Theoretical formulation of the "dynamics" of the particular patient is the bedrock along which the stream of psychotherapy runs. "Correct" interpretations, supposedly well phrased, well timed and "well depthed," are the prized landmarks of this odyssey of the unconscious.

It is suggested here that the emphasis on insight and on uncovering the dynamics is a culturally appropriate[1] and indeed a magnificent ruse for fostering a long term and intimate relationship. Under the unconscious disguise of a layer-by-layer unfolding of the patient's onion-bound neurosis, considerable time, energy and involvement between two persons become possible, and a strongly affective relationship develops. In this setting it is possible, in the words of Truax (1964, p. 9), "to express openly our deep warmth and caring for the *person* who comes to us for help." This experience is difficult to have and to accept in an Anglo-Saxon setting, with its characteristic high ideals of self-sufficiency and responsibility for one's fate, except under the guise of "sickness" and with the lofty Greek purpose of "understanding oneself."

Not only the patient but also the therapist needs reassurance that he is engaged at a task that amounts to more than the relating of one human being to another. Terms like "work" and "productivity" appear again and again in "sessions." After all, one spends so much time and money with the stated purpose of understanding oneself and not just to hold hands. For an Easterner, it is indeed somewhat strange to observe that in this culture the father "does things together" with his son in order to strengthen the relationship with him; he plays ball, goes hunting or visits the art gallery with him. Apparently there exists a need to find a shared task in order to offer intimacy and love. In a relationship-oriented society, no *agenda* as such is necessary for the cultivation of a relationship; however, absence of a proper agenda in a work- and activity-oriented society would indeed be disconcerting. Perhaps, in some measure,

a similar stratagem is employed in the psychotherapeutic relationship to dissolve the uneasiness in relating *directly* to another human being. Both parties unwittingly set a task of nibbling away the iceberg of the "unconscious," but in a real sense they perhaps are only breaking the ice between themselves. The language is of understanding and insight, but the metalanguage is of love and human involvement. The Western preoccupation with contents in psychotherapy is understandable, since Western cognition is traditionally interested in objects of consciousness while Eastern cognition is interested in consciousness or awareness itself (Haas, 1956).

PSYCHOTHERAPY AS A DECISION-MAKING PROCESS

It is a commentary on deeper human needs that a society which above all prizes self-direction and independence in life, and which is quite sensitive to the intrusion of personal belief systems of one individual upon another, has had to invent the institution of psychotherapy. Among other things, psychotherapy copes with needs that are perhaps more forthrightly met with by other societies that are oriented toward interdependence rather than toward independence. The needs referred to are the needs for guidance, for counsel and for a mentor in life's difficult task.

Since these needs seriously conflict with other more highly regarded values in this culture, they are awkwardly expressed and just as awkwardly and indirectly responded to. Psychotherapists, whose task to an extent is to influence or persuade others in the conduct of their lives, must disguise the real intent of their activities from themselves and their patients and balance nimbly on the tightrope between persuasion and freedom. Psychotherapy, in this sense, encroaches

---

[1] Reason, essentially, is the magical master key to the West's obsessional concept of nature and man.

on the most sacrosanct area in the Western way of life. Here, the medical model of health and illness comes in handy indeed.

Moreover, the momentum of change in Western society in its recent history has prodded these needs and battered the citadel of self-direction and individual choice. The individual's greater affluence and freedom, introducing new and more and different choices, have gone hand in hand with the dissolution of old and familiar pathways. It may be accurate to say that never before was a man faced with more choices yet fewer guideposts. To an Easterner, this crossroad situation may be an invitation to thought and contemplation. But not so to the Westerner who is progress-bound and, therefore, a man in haste. It is imperative that he *commit* himself to *some* direction and give *meaning* to his life, somehow. Since the need for "engagement" with life is greater in a life-affirmative society, the individual cannot afford to stand still; he must come to grips with his problems and conflicts. It is understandable, therefore, that at times he needs help and counsel in making up his mind; yet this need runs counter to the cultural belief that an individual must decide for himself.

While involvement in psychotherapy does not specifically make decisions for the individual, it certainly creates a climate wherein this becomes possible. Psychotherapy effects this by "clarification" of crucial issues and by a better definition of the edges of the patient's responsibility. In actual practice, far more nagging goes on in psychotherapy than psychotherapists are willing to admit. To the extent that decisions are reached during the course of psychotherapy, the patient experiences satisfaction in an important, stressful area that modern living imposes.

The culturally nourished partial illusion, mutually shared by the patient and his therapist, that decisions reached in treatment are the patient's, paradoxically contributes even more to his well-being and autonomy. Indeed, in the Western cultural context, the expertise of the therapist lies in "evoking" right decisions from the patient with an apparent minimum of his own influence. Krasner (1963), commenting on the general tendency to play down the influencing aspects of therapists' role in psychotherapy and to attribute changes to the patient's desire to grow and self-actualize himself, has called this attempt to deny control and consequent responsibility the "look no hands" phenomenon.

A thematically related but commonplace incidence was revealing to the author. In his first month after arrival in North America, a nurse on the ward asked him "Do *you want* to close the door?" to which, having interpreted the question literally, he almost replied: "No, I don't want to close the door." It required some cultural acclimatization to understand that telling, instructing or, worse still, ordering someone to do something even as trivial as closing a door requires camouflaging, in this case to make it appear, out of courtesy to be sure, as if *motivation* originated in the recipient of the request rather than in the requester. It is easy to see how infinitely more subtle and disguised an undertaking like psychotherapy needs to be where the focus is on altering deep-seated attitudes and at times a whole way of life. Instead of "telling" a patient or directly tendering advice, far more effective and culturally acceptable is a solemnly phrased "interpretation" where in a haystack of cause-and-effect pseudorationality lies embedded the grain of the therapist's own point of view and is (also to an extent society's) subtle imperative to the patient in the conduct of his life. Although genuinely committed to the patient's autonomy and independence, even from his own influence, the therapist paradoxically acts as a social agent; in fact, he directs the patient to his and Western society's much prized value of freedom. Gradually, interpretation by interpretation, the therapist's influence and value systems make inroads upon the major life themes of the patient (Pande & Gart, 1968).

PSYCHOTHERAPY AS AN INTEGRATING EXPERIENCE

The dichotomy between mind and body has received much attention, and rightly so. Perhaps it is not equally apparent that a considerable gap exists between the Western concept of mind and its concept of being. Acquisition of knowledge, in the West, is primarily an intellectual undertaking; knowledge by identity, which implies an intense and close communion between the knower and the known (Radhakrishnan, 1952), is relatively ignored. Philosophical systems of the West, intricate and subtle in their logical constructions, remain nevertheless largely intellectual in scope. Even the religious tradition in the West is scholastic and intellectual rather than devotional or spiritual. In education the view that a "student needs not the logic of reason so much as a cleansing and deepening discipline of the soul" (Haas, 1956, p. 547), though by no means unknown in the Occident, is certainly not emphasized here.

Futhermore, in its overriding emphasis on efficiency and in its quest for "ever-increasing rational organization of human life" (Barrett, 1962, p. 30), Western civilization has let its day-to-day life become deeply compartmentalized. Work and play are neatly categorized (at least a serious effort is made); political and religious views are separately labeled and handled; personal life is kept distinct and isolated from professional or working life; affairs of the heart are not permitted to mix with affairs of state and business. The list is extensive; it merely represents externalization of an intricately organized, uncluttered mind which is disciplined to focus narrowly in the service of order and efficiency. Perhaps life in the 20th century, as interpreted by the West,[2] is too complex to admit of a simpler response. This may be a more *intelligent* response, but it serves to separate the *intelligence* from the rest of the being.

Psychoanalysis, the beginning of modern psychotherapy, did a singular service to Western society, inadvertently in a historical sense, by attempting to close this gap. The method lent itself extremely well to integration of *all* the experiences of a human being and toward his experiencing himself as a total being. A basic assumption of psychotherapy is that our actions express our basic motivations and tendencies more eloquently than our words; it thus becomes the task of the therapist to confront the patient with the *meaning* of his actions. For the patient, psychotherapy poses the ineluctable logic of "to know is to be." Thus, in a very real sense, psychotherapy attempts to bridge the gap between the many selves of the modern man and between the many cells of modern living. It endeavors to weave together his isolated experiences, sensations, fantasies and thoughts into an "integrated concept of his universe which will correlate and give meaning to his life

---

[2] The dominant style and temper of the 20th century itself may be seen as an epiphenomenon of *Western* civilization.

and that of others" (Williamson, 1965, p. 373). Insofar as the rules of the game do not require the therapist's personal life to be consonant with his pronouncements in therapy, his participation remains incomplete and, in an authentic sense, incongruent.

It goes without saying that in the task of integration psychotherapy only rudimentarily tackles a problem of which the real dimensions in this culture are much deeper and wider.

PSYCHOTHERAPY AS AN EXPERIENCE IN THE INTEGRATION OF THE CHILD IN MAN

It is necessary to discuss this topic separately from the previous general consideration because psychoanalytically oriented psychotherapy has given such importance to childhood experiences. Although the recent trend in psychotherapy has veered away from emphasis on the past and toward emphasis on intercurrent events in the life of the patient, the intriguing question for a non-Western observer of Western psychiatry still remains: How is it that childhood assumes such a great importance in psychotherapy?

Cultural anthropologists and historiographers have commented upon the difference that exists between the Eastern and Western concepts of time. For the East, relatively speaking, past, present and future merge into one another; for the West they are discrete entities. For the East, experience in time is like water collected in a pool (stagnant perhaps); for the West, time is more like water flowing in a stream, and one is acutely aware that what flows away, flows away forever. The arrow of time, for the West, points forward, and, with a passionate belief in progress, the Western man works in feverish anxiety to race toward the millennium. The past is pointless and the need to dissociate from it great. The view of time is reflected, of course, in the view of history and in the course of personal lives.

Comparatively speaking, in the psychological and physical growth of the child into adulthood in the Eastern setting less of an issue is made of *growth;* a relatively smaller premium is placed on becoming an adult. Consequently, the continuum is smoother, and, instead of an either-or "here is the caterpillar and here is the butterfly" dichotomy, a looser, both-and-neither "child in man and man in child" view exists. The child in the adult consequently is not altogether repressed and excluded from consciousness. Western visitors have commented upon the childlike qualities and the very peculiar blending of childish traits with very mature attributes in the Easterner.

In the West, growing from infancy to adulthood is impatiently sought after and much prized. Adulthood also symbolizes to the Western man attainment of those values[3] that the culture overwhelmingly supports: self-reliance, power, achievement (personal contribution to the millennium), responsibility, work and sexual fulfillment. Childishness in adults is unreservedly frowned upon; crying, dependence on others, excessive emotionality are considered weak. A whole hierarchy of responsibilities and privileges has been carefully worked out, especially in North American family and communal life, to lure the growing child into the world of adulthood, thus rather early making inroads on the pleasures of

---

[3] It would indeed appear that, on the whole, attainment of Eastern values (love, filial affection and obedience, simplicity, contentment, etc.) is less dependent on biological maturation.

childhood. Legally becoming an adult is duly solemnized at 21. Those who do not complete or who delay the race to adulthood are more likely to manifest their discontent by acting-out behavior, which quite often seems a caricature of the adult role in its sexual or aggressive (violent) aspects, rather than by displaying such childish traits as excessive emotionality or playfulness (more likely to be manifested by immature women).

The rush toward adulthood may be compelling, but this leaves much unfinished business behind which at times needs to be dealt with in psychotherapy, not only because integration and rehabilitation of childhood experiences are indicated, but also because on the whole the "finished" adult in the West is expected to be so different from his childhood counterpart.

It is not surprising, in the light of the unnatural partitioning between child and man, that quite often the "working through" of childhood experiences in psychotherapy is something in the nature of a revelation to the average Westerner and, therefore, is a meaningful and worthwhile experience for him.

PSYCHOTHERAPY AS A CRITIQUE AND OVERVIEW OF A LIFE STYLE

The accepting, understanding, noncritical aspects of the therapist's behavior in psychotherapy have thus far received much attention. Of equal importance, the popular concept of the psychotherapist's role closely parallels this view.

It is suggested here, however, that perhaps the more notable aspect of the therapist's functioning, as he meets his patients session after session over a length of time and at an emotionally charged phase of their lives, is that he acts as a *critique* of their lives, as a judge but

without appearing judgmental. One might say that perhaps for the first time in the patient's life his assumptive world (Frank, 1961) is *critically* reviewed by both his adult self and the therapist.

Recognition of the evaluative and critical aspects of the therapist's activity is not easy within the general context of Western culture, and it has sound reasons for being buried in the collective unconscious, so to speak, of the West. It may be useful here to consider some of these reasons.

The Biblical edict "Judge not that ye be not judged" perhaps delineates an important theme in the Western way of life. One can judge an individual's status by outward symbols; one can screen his work record to evaluate him for a job; one can judge his credit-worthiness; however, one must not judge his *conduct* and his personal life. The privacy of the life of the individual, whose home is supposedly his castle, is sacrosanct, and the conduct of his life is by and large his own business. Even when judgments are made in this sphere, they are, instead of moral judgments, usually respectability-oriented ones and concern themselves with the discretion or lack of it that the individual displayed in his "misdeed." The situation is quite different in more socially oriented cultures where the individual is held more directly responsible to his group and is available to meddling, beneficent and otherwise, by friends, relatives and neighbors.

Furthermore, the razor-edged severity of the Judeo-Christian (particularly the Anglo-Protestant) conscience, with its parsimony in tolerance, forgiveness and love,[4] renders the individual especially sensitive to personal criticism. His guilt and sense of personal responsibility are

---

[4] Paul Tillich (1957) has called this "puritanism without love."

more easily aroused. In the Western setting, therefore, one tries very hard to stay away from any connotaton of *assigning blame.*

In the action-oriented West, even words or emotions imply (latent) action. Negative criticism carries with it the possibility of active rejection and the breaking of a relationship. In contrast, consider the bitter and often crude war of words between China and Russia which, in an Eastern context, does not necessarily mean termination of the relationship; its ambivalence is taken for granted and tolerated. This relationship might break anyway, but that is not the point; a fraction of this open ambivalence in the West would mean the end. And besides, a person in the West as a rule first makes up his mind and then puts his decision to action in word or deed.

Sensitivity toward being criticized may be great, but this does not diminish the need for judgment. Nor does it eradicate the need to see oneself as he might appear to others, especially in intimate and personal spheres of life. The psychotherapeutic relationship is one medium available to those whose life conflicts have led them to seek this kind of help. It is suggested here that the dilemma of needing a critique yet being culturally sensitive or defensive about having one is characteristically resolved in the psychotherapeutic situation by nourishing a neutral, nonjudgmental and accepting image of the psychotherapist; by throwing a smoke screen of a medical setting (Szasz, 1961);[5] and by fostering the notion that the therapist does not intrude

his life, his moral and philosophical point of view into his interaction with the patient (Freud, 1957; Greenacre, 1954).

The critique of the patient's life, understandably disguised, therefore becomes another item on the hidden agenda of psychotherapy.

PSYCHOTHERAPY AS A REDRESS FROM EGO ALIENATION AND ISOLATION

Ego alienation is widely described as endemic to the modern man. Endeavors are made, with justification, to relate it to various aspects of modern living, but such endeavors generally fall short of a more basic consideration which seems to be rooted in the Western metaphysical concepts of the nature of man and his relationship with the universe. The West posits a separation, if not a frank opposition, between an individual and his environment, and it espouses a "direct relationship to the world of external reality, which, by *activity*[6] it seeks to understand, or to master, or to come to honorable terms with" (Trilling, 1956, p. 19). In Alan Watts' words, "Western culture as a whole rests on the feeling that man, as ego, is the independent observer and potential controller of a world which he experiences as profoundly *other* than himself" (Watts, 1958, p. 760).

Radically different is the Indian experience where "a constant intuition of the unity of all life" (Coomaraswamy, 1957, p. 4) is the central preoccupation and the recognition "here and now of All Things in the Self and the Self in All" (p. 9) the highest ideal. Thus, in Indian tradition, annihilation of individual consciousness and self-transcendence rather than self-assertion become the goals of human life. The Chinese,

---

[5] It is of interest to note that this society, with grooves (recently somewhat faded) for original sin indoctrination, has shown an almost enthusiastic readiness for transforming its theological paradigm, "You are a sinner," to its modern, more comfortable and curable counterpart, "You are sick."

---

[6] Italics are mine.

although not so preoccupied with transcendental realization as the Indians, nevertheless sought to model social life on the rhythm of nature; harmonious relationship with nature and the individual's integration into the Totality, into the Tao, assumed central importance for them (Reincourt, 1965).

Thus, in contrast to the Western split between ego and environment, Eastern cognition yields a sense of relatedness with the creation, an intuitive, esthetic partnership with the universe. Instead of seeking a unique place in the universe, an Easterner traditionally seeks to fit in it as a "cog in the wheel."[7]

The modern Western man's alienated feeling is the negative psychological counterpart of his emancipated, self-sufficient stature which, aided by the industrial and scientific revolutions, Protestantism, and capitalism (each particularly compatible with the Western view of man and nature), has finally become a reality. Although he has gained an independent, affluent existence, he has suffered a loss in his relatedness, and his anguish is to an extent the anguish of a fragmented, fractured consciousness.

Psychotherapeutic transaction provides the setting, albeit unnatural to an extent, in which deep and thoroughgoing communication becomes possible and the drawbridge of a "we-relationship" is gently lowered between two "skin-encapsulated"[8] solitudes. Psychotherapy, particularly analytically oriented psychotherapy, not only increases the range of consciousness but, more important by far, strives to school the participants experientially in the art of

greater awareness. To one who is truly alienated, this "purchase of friendship" (Schofield, 1964) may be greatly rewarding. Erik Erikson has termed psychoanalysis "the first systematic and active 'consciousness-expansion'" (Evans, 1967, p. 96), and according to him it is "the principal modern form of systematic introspection and meditation" (p. 95). Psychedelic therapy underlines the redress of ego alienation as one of the target-aims in psychiatric treatment. In group psychotherapy, therapeutic communities and the community psychiatry movement, one also sees a myriad of mechanical endeavors (as against a modification, in some measure, of the basic world view)[9] to bridge the "isolated islands of consciousness" (Watts, 1963, p. 18) forged by the individual-centered Western society.

SUMMARY

Tribal healing, overlaid with magic and ritual, and ideologically motivated "brain-washing" in Chinese prison camps have been explored in psychological literature. In contrast, Western psychotherapy is by and large conducted under the respectable auspices of "scientific medicine." Examining it, nevertheless, from outside the Western perspective may be revealing.

Cultural sensitivities and the structure of Western consciousness obscure the recognition of some of the basic needs

---

[7] Mencius, the Chinese philosopher, spoke laudably of the merchant who for 30 years sold the same wares at the same prices at the same location.

[8] Alan Watts (1963, p. 18) has used the term "skin encapsulated ego" to describe alienation in the modern man.

[9] World views of societies, in both the East and the West, are expressions of interest in certain directions and the development thereof. Levi-Strauss has said: "Progress . . . never represents anything more than the maximum progress in a given direction, predetermined by the interest of the observer" (1952, p. 40). Indeed, it is not possible to establish a hierarchy of cultures. Therefore, the real challenge of our times lies within a genuine encounter of the respective world views, with an openness to mutual influence; it is beset with difficulties, but so is reaching the moon!

which psychotherapy as a cultural institution serves and which lie veiled behind the quest for health and self-understanding. An analysis of these needs is here undertaken against the background of themes and premises that are distinctive to Western life. Implicit in the discussion is the view that these themes and premises create, in the East-West context, profoundly different psychological needs for the Western man and, therefore, require characteristically different solutions, psychotherapy being one such solution. Some of these themes are: emphasis on work rather than on relationships and love; self-direction and independence in life rather than interdependence and acceptance of guidance from others; a directional and linear attitude toward time rather than an ahistorical view of time; "encapsulated" individual consciousness rather than social, if not cosmic, consciousness; and a problem-solving, cerebral approach to life's conflicts rather than one emphasizing absorption and integration of experience.

The institution of psychotherapy, indeed the movement for mental health itself, may be viewed as both a symbolic and a substantive cultural undertaking to meet the deficits in the Western way of life and to cope with the negative psychological implications of its premises.

REFERENCES

Barrett, W. *Irrational man.* New York: Doubleday Anchor, 1962.

Coomaraswamy, A. K. *The dance of Shiva.* New York: Noonday Press, 1957.

Durant, W. *Our Oriental heritage.* New York: Simon & Schuster, 1954.

Evans, R. I. *Dialogue with Erik Erikson.* New York: Harper & Row, 1967.

Frank, J. D. *Persuasion and healing.* Baltimore: Johns Hopkins Press, 1961.

Freud, S. *The future of an illusion* (W. D. Robson-Scott, trans.). New York: Doubleday, 1957.

Greenacre, P. Practical considerations in relation to psychoanalytic therapy (transference). *Journal of the American Psychoanalytic Association,* 1954, *2,* 671–684.

Haas, W. S. *The destiny of the mind.* London: Faber & Faber, 1956.

Krasner, L. The behavioral scientist and social responsibility: No place to hide. Paper presented at American Psychological Association Annual Meeting. Philadelphia, 1963.

Levi-Strauss, C. *Race and history.* Paris: UNESCO, 1952.

Pande, S. K., & Gart, J. J. A method to quantify reciprocal influence between therapist and patient in psychotherapy. In J. Shlien, H. F. Hunt, J. D. Matarazzo, & C. Savage (Eds.), *Research in psychotherapy* (Vol. 3, pp. 395–415). Washington, D.C.: American Psychological Association, 1968.

Radhakrishnan, S. The religion of the spirit and the world's need: Fragments of a confession. In R. A. Schilpp (Ed.), *The philosophy of Sarvepalli Radhakrishnan.* New York: Tudor, 1952.

Reincourt, A. de. *The soul of China.* New York: Harper Colophon, 1965.

Schofield, W. *Psychotherapy: The purchase of friendship.* Englewood Cliffs, N.J.: Prentice-Hall, 1964.

Szasz, T. S. *The myth of mental illness.* New York: Hoeber-Harper, 1961.

Tillich, P. *The Protestant era.* Chicago: University of Chicago Press, 1957.

Trilling, L. *The selected letters of John Keats.* New York: Doubleday Anchor, 1956.

Truax, C. B. Current research in psychotherapy. *Canada's Mental Health,* 1964, *12,* 5–9.

Watts, A. W. Asian psychology and modern psychiatry. In C. F. Reed, I. E. Alexander, & S. S. Tomkins (Eds.), *Psychopathology.* New York: Wiley, 1958.

Watts, A. W. *Psychotherapy East and West.* New York: Mentor Books, 1963.

Williamson, E. G. Value orientation in counseling. In F. T. Sererin (Ed.), *Humanistic viewpoints in psychology.* New York: McGraw-Hill, 1965.

CHAPTER **16**

Asian Personality Theory: Doi

Introduction

When Rudyard Kipling said "East is East and West is West and never the twain shall meet," he was reflecting a common stereotype about cultural differences, implying that people from Occidental and Oriental cultures could never really understand one another. The problems *are* diverse and complicated. One factor, discussed in the following paper by L. Takeo Doi (1962), a psychiatrist with training both in the East and the West, has to do with the different concepts two cultures may have.

Some terms in one language cannot be translated too well into another. The German word *Gemeinshaftsgefühl*, used by Adlerians and by Abraham Maslow, is one example, as are the the Italian word *antipatico* and the Yiddish word *chutzpah*. But there are also concepts for which there are words in one language, but the concept itself is hardly known elsewhere. An example is the Japanese term *amae*. *Gemeinshaftsgefühl* means "feeling for community," *antipatico* means thoroughly dislikable, and *chutzpah* means colossal nerve—but what does *amae* mean in English? How could this term be translated?

Doi's thesis is that in both the United States and Japan there are fundamental, basic notions that underlie personality in one culture but that do not exist in the other culture. *Amae* is an example. This paper should present some brand new concepts for the Western reader and may help you understand a bit more about Japanese thinking.

212

L. TAKEO DOI
Amae: A key concept for understanding Japanese personality stucture

I am particularly interested in the problem of personality and culture in modern Japan for two reasons. First, even though I was born and raised in Japan and had my basic medical training there, I have had further training in psychiatry and psychoanalysis in the United States, thus exposing myself for some time to a different culture from that of Japan. Second, I have had many opportunities of treating both Japanese and non-Japanese (mostly American) patients with psychotherapy. These experiences have led me to inquire into differences between Japanese and non-Japanese patients and also into the question of what is basic in Japanese character structure. In this paper I shall describe what I have found to be most characteristic in Japanese patients and then discuss its meaning in the context of Japanese culture.

The essence of what I am going to talk about is contained in one common Japanese word, *amae*. Let me therefore, first of all, explain the meaning of this word. *Amae* is the noun form of *amaeru*, an intransitive verb that means "to depend and presume upon another's benevolence" (Doi, 1956). This word has the same root as *amai*, an adjective that means "sweet." Thus *amaeru* has a

distinct feeling of sweetness and is generally used to describe a child's attitude or behavior toward his parents, particularly his mother. But it can also be used to describe the relationship between two adults, such as the relationship between a husband and a wife or a master and a subordinate. I believe that there is no single word in English equivalent to *amaeru*, though this does not mean that the psychology of *amae* is totally alien to the people of English speaking countries. I shall come back to this problem after describing some of the clinical material through which I came to recognize the importance of what *amae* signifies.

It was in my attempt to understand what goes on between the therapist and patient that I first came across the all-powerful drive of the patient's *amae*. There is a diagnostic term in Japanese psychiatry, *shinkeishitsu*, which includes neurasthenia, anxiety neurosis, and obsessive neurosis. Morita, who first used *shinkeishitsu* as a diagnostic term, thought that these three types of neuroses had a basic symptom in common: *toraware*, which means "to be bound or caught," as by some intense preoccupation. He considered *toraware* to be closely related to hypochondriacal fear and thought that this fear sets in motion a reciprocal intensification of attention and sensation. In psychoanalytic work with neurotic patients of the *shinkeishitsu* type I have also found *toraware* to be a basic symptom, but I have evolved a different formulation of its significance (see Doi,

L. Takeo Doi, "Amae: A Key Concept for Understanding Japanese Personality Structure." Reprinted from R. J. Smith and R. K. Beardsley (eds.), *Japanese Culture: Its Development and Characteristics* (Chicago: Aldine Publishing Company, 1962); copyright © 1962 by Wenner-Gren Foundation of Anthropological Research, Inc.

1958). I have observed that during the course of psychotherapy the patient's *toraware* can easily turn into hypersensitivity in his relationship with the therapist. This hypersensitivity is best described by the Japanese word *kodawari*. *Kodawari* is the noun form of *kodawaru,* an intransitive verb meaning "to be sensitive to minor things," "to be inwardly disturbed over one's personal relationships." In the state of *kodawari* one feels that he is not accepted by others, which suggests that *kodawari* results from the unsatisfied desire to *amaeru*. Thus *toraware* can be traced back through *kodawari* to *amae*. In my observations the patient's *toraware* usually receded when he became aware of his *amae* toward the therapist, which he had been warding off consciously and unconsciously up to then.

At first I felt that if the patient became fully aware of his *amae,* he would thereupon be able to get rid of his neurosis. But I was wrong in this assumption and came to observe another set of clinical phenomena following the patient's recognition of his *amae* (see Doi, 1960). Many patients confessed that they were then awakened to the fact that they had not "possessed their self," had not previously appreciated the importance of their existence, and had been really nothing apart from their all-important desire to *amaeru*. I took this as a step toward the emergence of a new consciousness of self, inasmuch as the patient could then at least realize his previous state of "no self."

There is another observation that I should like to mention here. It is about the nature of guilt feelings of Japanese patients (see Doi, 1961). The word *sumanai* is generally used to express guilt feelings, and this word is the negative form of *sumu,* which means "to end." *Sumanai* literally means that one has not

done as he was supposed to do, thereby causing the other person trouble or harm. Thus, it expresses more a sense of unfulfilled obligation than a confession of guilt, though it is generally taken as an indication that one feels guilty. When neurotic patients say *sumanai,* I have observed that there lies, behind their use of the word, much hidden aggression engendered by frustration of their wish to *amaeru*. So it seems that in saying *sumanai* they are in fact expressing their hidden concern lest they fall from the grace of *amae* because of their aggression. I think that this analysis of *sumanai* would also apply in essence to the use of this word by the ordinary Japanese in everyday life, but in the case of the neurotic patient *sumanai* is said with greater ambivalence. In other words, more than showing his feeling or being obligated, he tends to create a sense of obligation in the person to whom he makes his apology, thus "forcing" that person eventually to cater to his wish.

I have explained three clinical observations, all of which point to the importance of *amae* as a basic desire. As I said before, the state of *amae* originally refers to what a small child feels toward his mother. It is therefore not surprising that the desire to *amaeru* still influences one's adult years and that it becomes manifest in the therapeutic situation. Here we have a perfect example of transference in the psychoanalytic sense. But then is it not strange that *amaeru* is a unique Japanese word? Indeed, the Japanese find it hard to believe that there is no word for *amaeru* in European languages; a colleague once told me that he could not believe that the equivalent for such a seemingly universal phenomenon as *amae* did not exist in English or German, since, as he put it, "Even puppies do it, you know." Let me therefore illustrate the "Japaneseness" of the concept of *amaeru* by one striking incident. The mother of a Eurasian patient, a British woman who had been a long-term resident of Japan, was discussing her daughter with me. She spoke to me in English, but she suddenly switched to Japanese, in order to tell me that her daughter did not *amaeru* much as a child. I asked her why she had suddenly switched to Japanese. She replied, after a pause, that there was no way to say *amaeru* in English.

I have mentioned two Japanese words that are closely related to the psychology of *amae: kodawaru,* which means "to be inwardly disturbed over one's personal relationships," and *sumanai,* which means "to feel guilty or obligated." Now I should like to mention a few more words that are also related to the psychology of *amae.* First, *amai,* which originally means "sweet," can be used figuratively to describe a person who is overly soft and benevolent toward others or, conversely, one who always expects to *amaeru* in his relationships with others. Second, *amanzuru,* which is derived from *amaeru,* describes the state of mind in which one acquiesces to whatever circumstances one happens to be in. Third, *tori-iru,* which means "to take in," describes the behavior of a person who skillfully maneuvers another into permitting him to *amaeru.* Fourth, *suneru* describes the behavior of a child or an adult who pouts and sulks because he feels he is not allowed to *amaeru* as much as he wants to, thus harboring in himself mental pain of a masochistic nature. Fifth, *higamu* describes the behavior of a child or an adult who feels himself unfairly treated compared to others who are more favored, often suggesting the presence of a paranoid feeling. Sixth, *tereru* describes the behavior of a child or an adult who is

ashamed of showing his intimate wish to *amaeru.* Seventh, *hinekureru* describes the behavior of a child or an adult who takes devious ways in his efforts to deny the wish to *amaeru.*

One could readily say that the behaviors or emotions described by all these Japanese words are not unknown to Westerners and that they appear quite frequently in the therapeutic situation with Western patients. But there remains the question I raised before: Why is there no word in English or in other European languages that is equivalent to *amaeru,* the most central element in all these emotions? To this, one might answer that the absence of a word like *amaeru* is no inconvenience, since it can be represented by a combination of words such as the "wish to be loved" or "dependency needs." That may be so, but does not this linguistic difference point to something deeper? Perhaps it reflects a basic psychological difference between Japan and the Western World. Before discussing this problem further, however, I would like to mention a theory of Michael Balint, a British psychoanalyst, which has much bearing on what I am talking about now.

In his psychoanalytic practice Balint observed that "in the final phase of the treatment patients begin to give expression to long-forgotten, infantile, instinctual wishes, and to demand their gratification from their environment" (Balint, 1952). He called this infantile desire passive object love, since its primal aim is to be loved; he also called it primary love, since it is the foundation upon which later forms of love are built. I imagine that he must have wondered why such an important desire is not represented by one common word, for he points out the fact that "all European languages are so poor that they cannot distinguish between the two kinds of object-love, active and passive'' (Balint, 1952).

By now it must be clear that the primary love or passive object-love described by Balint is none other than the desire to *amaeru*. But then we have to draw the curious conclusion that the emotion of primary love is readily accessible to Japanese patients by way of the word *amaeru*, while to Western patients, according to Balint, it can become accessible only after a painstaking analysis. In my observations I have also noticed that the recognition of *amae* by Japanese patients does not signify the final phase of treatment, as it did in Balint's patients. I think that we have to try to solve this apparent contradiction very carefully, because therein lies, in my opinion, an important key to understanding the psychological differences between Japan and Western countries.

The reasoning behind Balint's observation that primary love appears in its pure form only in the final phase of treatment is as follows. The primary love of an infant is bound to be frustrated, leading to the formation of narcissism, as though he said to himself, "If the world does not love me enough, I have to love and gratify myself." Since such narcissism is part of the earliest and most primitive layer of the mind, it can be modified only in the last stage of treatment, at which time the long repressed urge to be loved can re-emerge in its pure state. Then what shall we say about the Japanese, to whom this primary desire to be loved is always accessible? Does it mean that the Japanese have less narcissism? I think not. Rather I would say that the Japanese somehow continue to cherish the wish to be loved even after the formation of narcissism. It is as though the Japanese did not want to see the reality of their basic frustration. In other words, the Japanese, as does everybody else, do experience frustration of their primary love, as is well attested to by the existence of the rich vocabulary we have already encountered relating to the frustration of *amae*. But it seems that the Japanese never give up their basic desire to *amaeru*, thus mitigating the extent of violent emotions caused by its frustration.

In this connection I want to mention an interesting feature of the word *amaeru*. We do not say that an infant does *amaeru* until he is about one year old, thereby indicating that he is then conscious of his wish to *amaeru*, which in turn suggests the presence of a budding realization that his wish cannot always be gratified. Thus, from its inception, the wish to *amaeru* is accompanied by a secret fear that it may be frustrated.

If what I have been saying is true, then it must indicate that there is a social sanction in Japanese society for expressing the wish to *amaeru*. And it must be this social sanction that has encouraged in the Japanese language the development of the large vocabulary relating to *amaeru*. In other words, in Japanese society parental dependency is fostered, and this behavior pattern is even institutionalized into its social structure, whereas perhaps the opposite tendency prevails in Western societies. This seems to be confirmed by recent anthropological studies of Japanese society, notably that of Ruth Benedict, who said: "The arc of life in Japan is plotted in opposite fashion to that in the United States. It is a great U-curve with maximum freedom and indulgence allowed to babies and to the old. Restrictions are slowly increased after babyhood till having one's own way reaches a low just before and after marriage" (Benedict, 1961). It is true that the restrictions Benedict spoke of do exist for adults in Japanese society, but it should be understood that these restrictions are never meant to be drastic so far as the basic desire to *amaeru* is concerned. Rather, these restrictions are but channels through which that desire is to be duly gratified. That is why we can speak of parental dependency as being institutionalized in Japanese society. For instance, in marriage a husband does *amaeru* toward his wife, and vice versa. It is strongly present in all formal relationships, including those between teacher and student and between doctor and patient. Thus William Caudill (1961), in his observations on Japanese psychiatric hospitals, spoke of the mutual dependency he encountered in all relationships.

In this connection I cannot resist mentioning an episode that happened when I gave a talk on some characteristic Japanese words to a professional group in the United States. *Amaeru* was one of those words. After my talk one distinguished scholar asked me whether or not the feeling of *amaeru* is something like what Catholics feel toward their Holy Mother. Apparently he could not recognize the existence of such a feeling in the ordinary mother-child relationship. And if his response is representative of Americans, it would mean that in American society the feeling of *amaeru* can be indulged in perhaps only in the religious life, but here also very sparingly.

I would now like to mention a study by a Japanese scholar, Hajime Nakamura, professor of Indian philosophy at the University of Tokyo and an authority on comparative philosophy. In his major work, *Ways of Thinking of Eastern Peoples* (1960), he presents a penetrating analysis of thought patterns of Indians, Chinese, Japanese, and Tibetans on the basis of linguistic studies and observations on variations in Buddhist doctrine and practice in these four countries. What he says about the Japanese pattern of thought is parallel to what I have been saying here, though he reaches his conclusions from an entirely different source. He says that the Japanese way of thinking is greatly influenced by an emphasis on immediate personal relations and also that the Japanese have always been eager to adopt foreign cultural influences, but always within the framework of this emphasis on personal relations. To state this in psychoanalytic terms, the Japanese are always prepared to identify themselves with, or introject, an outside force, to the exclusion of other ways of coping with it. This character trait of the Japanese was touched upon by Benedict, too, when she said that "the Japanese have an ethic of alternatives" and "Japan's motivations are situational," referring particularly to the sudden complete turnabout of Japan following the defeat of the last war.

This leads, however, to the very interesting and important question of whether or not Japanese character structure has changed at all since the war. I think that Benedict was quite right in assuming that Japan as a whole willingly submitted to unconditional surrender because it was the Emperor's order, that Japan wanted only to please the Emperor, even in her defeat. But it cannot be denied that things have been changing since then. For instance, the Emperor had to declare that he no longer wished to be considered sacred. Also the Japanese have been disillusioned to find that the paramount virtue of *chu,* that is, loyalty to the emperor, was taken advantage of by the ultranationalists, who completely failed them. With the decline of *chu* there was also a decline of *ko,* that is, of filial piety. In other words, the tradition of repaying one's *on,* that is, one's spiritual debts to an emperor and to one's parents, was greatly undermined. Thus there developed the moral chaos of present day Japan.

I think, however, that the nature of this chaos has a distinctly Japanese character and can best be understood by taking into account the psychology of *amae*. It seems that heretofore the stress upon the duty of repaying one's *on* to the emperor and to one's parents served the purpose of regulating the all too powerful desire of *amae*. Since the Japanese were deprived of this regulating force after the war, it was inevitable that their desire to *amaeru* was let loose, with its narcissistic element becoming more manifest. That perhaps explains why we now find in Japan so many examples of lack of social restraint. I wonder whether this recent tendency has also helped to increase the number of neurotics. I think it has, though we have no reliable statistics to confirm it. But I am quite certain that an analysis of the psychology of *amae* such as I am attempting here would not have been possible in prewar days, because *amae* was concealed behind the duty of repaying one's *on*. It certainly was not visible to the outside observer, even to one as acute as Ruth Benedict. I would like to give you one clinical example to illustrate this point.

One of my recent patients, who was a student of law, revealed to me one day his secret thoughts, saying, "I wish I had some person who would take the responsibility of assisting me." The remarkable thing about this confession was that the Japanese word that he used for "assist" was a special legal term, *hohitsu*, which was formerly used only for the act of assisting the emperor with his task of governing the nation. In saying this, as the patient himself explained, he wanted, like the emperor, to appear to be responsible for his acts but to depend completely on his assistant, who would really carry the burden. He said this, not jokingly but, rather, with complete

seriousness. It is obvious that this confession revealed his secret desire to *amaeru*, about which he spoke more clearly on another occasion. But what I would like to point out here is that in prewar days the patient could hardly have made such a confession, using a special term reserved only for the emperor. Of course, this is a special case, and the fact that the patient was a law student accounted for his use of such a technical term. Yet I think that this case illustrates the point that I want to make, that is, the more emphasis placed upon repaying one's *on*, the less clearly seen is one's desire to *amaeru*.

In this connection, let me say a few words about the nature of so-called "emperor worship," which served as the Japanese state religion in prewar days. It is true that the emperor was held sacred, but the element of taboo was greater than that of divinity. It is really tempting to apply what Freud said about taboo to the Japanese emperor worship. As a matter of fact, he did mention the Japanese emperor in his book on *Totem and Taboo*, but not from the viewpoint of what is being discussed here. I will not go into this subject any further now, except to add one more comment concerning the effect of elimination of the emperor taboo and its related system, apart from the already discussed release of the desire to *amaeru*. Some Japanese critics voiced the opinion that the tight thought control deriving from the emperor and the family system in prewar days stifled development of healthy selfhood, that one could assert himself in those days only by way of *suneru* and *higamu*, which are interestingly enough the very same Japanese words that I have described before as indicating frustration of *amae* (Maruyama, 1960; Isono, 1960). I agree that this opinion is generally true, but I do not believe that elimination of the emperor and family system alone can lead to development of healthy selfhood or personality. This is shown by many patients, who confess that they are awakened to the fact that they have "not had self" apart from the all powerful desire to *amaeru*. Then what or who can help them to obtain their "self"? This touches upon a very important problem of identity, which I will not attempt to discuss in detail. I can say only that the Japanese as a whole are still searching for something, something with which they can safely identify themselves, so that they can become whole, independent beings.

In closing I should like to make two additional remarks. First, it may seem that I am possibly idealizing the West in a way, since I have looked at the problem of personality and culture in modern Japan from the Western point of view. I do not deny that I have. In fact I could not help doing so, because Japanese culture did not produce any yardstick to judge itself critically. I really think that it is a fine thing for the West to have developed such a yardstick for critical analysis. And it seems inevitable that it involves a kind of idealization when the non-Westerners attempt to apply such a yardstick to themselves. I know, however, that in the psychoanalytic circles of Western countries idealization has a special meaning and is not something commendable. So they would certainly not call their use of the analytical method idealization. But I wonder whether they are entirely right in assuming that their use of the analytical method stands on its own without involving any idealization on their part.

Second, though I have stated that there is no exact equivalent to the word *amaeru*

in all European languages, I do not say that *amaeru* is unique to the Japanese language. I have some information that the language of Korea and that of Ainu have a word of the same meaning. There seems to be some question about whether or not the Chinese language has such a word. I am now most curious to know whether or not the Polynesian languages have a similar word. I have a feeling that they may have. If they do, how would their psychology compare with that of the Japanese? It is my earnest hope that these questions will be answered by anthropological and psychological studies in the not too distant future.

REFERENCES

Balint, Michael. *Primary love and psychoanalytic technique.* London: Hogarth Press, 1952.

Benedict, Ruth. *The chrysanthemum and the sword.* Boston: Houghton Mifflin, 1961.

Caudill, William. Around the clock patient care in Japanese psychiatric hospitals: The role of the *tsukisoi. American Sociological Review,* 1961, *26,* 204–214.

Doi, L. Takeo. Japanese language as an expression of Japanese psychology. *Western Speech,* 1956, *20,* 90–96.

Doi, L. Takeo. Psychopathology of *shinkeishitsu. Psychiatria et Neurologica Japonica,* 1959, *60,* 733–744.

Doi, L. Takeo. Psychopathology of *jibun* and *amae. Psychiatria et Neurologica Japonica,* 1960, *61,* 149–162.

Doi, L. Takeo. Some thoughts on super-ego. *Japanese Journal of Psychoanalysis,* 1961, *8,* 4–7.

Isono, Fujiko. Family and self-consciousness. In *History of thought in modern Japan* (Vol. 6). Tokyo: Chikuma Shobo, 1960.

Maruyama, Masao. Loyalty and rebellion. In *History of thought in modern Japan* (Vol. 6). Tokyo: Chikuma Shobo, 1960.

Nakamura, Hajime. *Ways of thinking of Eastern peoples.* Tokyo: Japanese Government Printing Bureau, 1960.

CHAPTER 17

Psychosocial Theory

Introduction

Karen Horney (1885–1952), the major woman theorist in the field of personality, was essentially a Freudian revisionist. After coming to the United States from Europe during the depression in the 1930s, she noted that problems in this country were not essentially based on sexual repression, as she had been taught. A person who thought for herself, she developed an entire system of personality concepts which embodies a sympathetic view of the struggling human being.

Her style was simple, as is reflected in this selection. In contrast to Freud and others of her contemporaries, she did not adopt any special jargon, and she achieved crystal-clear communication. Both the title and the contents of this selection reflect Horney's deep love for people and her understanding of the struggle of individuals for identity.

KAREN HORNEY
The Poignancy of Neurotic Conflicts

Let me say to begin with: It is not neurotic to have conflicts. At one time or another our wishes, our interests, our convictions are bound to collide with those of others around us. And just as such clashes between ourselves and our environment are a commonplace, so, too, conflicts within ourselves are an integral part of human life.

An animal's actions are largely determined by instinct. Its mating, its care for its young, its search for food, its defenses against danger are more or less prescribed and beyond individual decision. In contrast, it is the prerogative as well as the burden of human beings to be able to exert choice, to have to make decisions. We may have to decide between desires that lead in opposite directions. We may, for instance, want to be alone but also want to be with a friend; we may want to study medicine but also to study music. Or there may be a conflict between wishes and obligations: we may wish to be with a lover when someone in trouble needs our care. We may be divided between a desire to be in accord with others and a conviction that would entail expressing an opinion antagonistic to them. We may be in conflict, finally, between two sets of values, as occurs when we believe in taking on a hazardous job in wartime but believe also in our duty to our family.

The kind, scope, and intensity of such conflicts are largely determined by the civilization in which we live. If the civilization is stable and tradition bound, the variety of choices presenting themselves are limited and the range of possible individual conflicts narrow. Even then they are not lacking. One loyalty may interfere with another; personal desires may stand against obligations to the group. But if the civilization is in a stage of rapid transition, where highly contradictory values and divergent ways of living exist side by side, the choices the individual has to make are manifold and difficult. He can conform to the expectations of the community or be a dissenting individualist, be gregarious or live as a recluse, worship success or despise it, have faith in strict discipline for children or allow them to grow up without much interference; he can believe in a different moral standard for men and women or hold that the same should apply for both, regard sexual relations as an expression of human intimacy or divorce them from ties of affection; he can foster racial discrimination or take the stand that human values are independent of the color of skin or the shape of noses—and so on and so forth.

There is no doubt that choices like these have to be made very often by people living in our civilization, and one would therefore expect conflicts along these lines to be quite common. But the striking fact is that most people are not aware of them, and consequently do not resolve them by any clear decision. More often than not they drift and let themselves be swayed by accident. They do not know where they stand; they make compromises without being aware of doing so; they are involved in contradictions without knowing it. I am referring here to normal persons, meaning neither average nor ideal but merely non-neurotic.

There must, then, be preconditions for recognizing contradictory issues and for making decisions on that basis. These preconditions are fourfold. We must be aware of what our wishes are, or even more, of what our feelings are. Do we really like a person or do we only think we like him because we are supposed to? Are we really sad if a parent dies or do we only go through the motions? Do we really wish to become a lawyer or a doctor or does it merely strike us as a respectable and profitable career? Do we really want our children to be happy and independent or do we only give lip service to the idea? Most of us would find it difficult to answer such simple questions; that is, we do not know what we really feel or want.

Since conflicts often have to do with convictions, beliefs, or moral values, their recognition would presuppose that we have developed our own set of values. Beliefs that are merely taken over and are not a part of us hardly have sufficient strength to lead to conflicts or to serve as a guiding principle in making decisions. When subjected to new influences, such beliefs will easily be abandoned for others. If we simply have adopted values cherished in our environment, conflicts which in our best interest should arise do not arise. If, for instance, a son has never questioned the wisdom of a narrow-minded father, there will be little conflict when the father wants him to enter a

profession other than the one he himself prefers. A married man who falls in love with another woman is actually engaged in a conflict; but when he has failed to establish his own convictions about the meaning of marriage he will simply drift along the path of least resistance instead of facing the conflict and making a decision one way or the other.

Even if we recognize a conflict as such, we must be willing and able to renounce one of the two contradictory issues. But the capacity for clear and conscious renunciation is rare, because our feelings and beliefs are muddled, and perhaps because in the last analysis most people are not secure and happy enough to renounce anything.

Finally, to make a decision presupposes the willingness and capacity to assume responsibility for it. This would include the risk of making a wrong decision and the willingness to bear the consequences without blaming others for them. It would involve feeling, "This is my choice, my doing," and presupposes more inner strength and independence than most people apparently have nowadays.

Caught as so many of us are in the strangling grip of conflicts—however unacknowledged—our inclination is to look with envy and admiration on people whose lives seem to flow along smoothly without being disturbed by any of this turbulence. The admiration may be warranted. These may be the strong ones who have established their own hierarchy of values, or who have acquired a measure of serenity because in the course of years conflicts and the need for decision have lost their uprooting power. But the outward appearance may be deceptive. More often, due to apathy, conformity, or opportunism, the people we envy are incapable of truly facing a conflict or of truly trying to resolve it on the basis of their own convictions, and consequently have merely drifted or been swayed by immediate advantage.

To experience conflicts knowingly, though it may be distressing, can be an invaluable asset. The more we face our own conflicts and seek out our own solutions, the more inner freedom and strength we will gain. Only when we are willing to bear the brunt can we approximate the ideal of being the captain of our ship. A spurious tranquility rooted in inner dullness is anything but enviable. It is bound to make us weak and an easy prey to any kind of influence.

When conflicts center about the primary issues of life, it is all the more difficult to face them and resolve them. But provided we are sufficiently alive, there is no reason why in principle we should not be able to do so. Education could do much to help us to live with greater awareness of ourselves and to develop our own convictions. A realization of the significance of the factors involved in choice would give us ideals to strive for, and in that a direction for our lives.[1]

The difficulties always inherent in recognizing and resolving a conflict are immeasurably increased when a person is neurotic. Neurosis, it must be said, is always a matter of degree—and when I speak of "a neurotic" I invariably mean "a person to the extent that he is neurotic." For him awareness of feelings and desires is at a low ebb. Often the only feelings experienced consciously and clearly are reactions of fear and anger to blows dealt to vulnerable spots. And even these may be repressed. Such authentic

ideals as do exist are so pervaded by compulsive standards that they are deprived of their power to give direction. Under the sway of these compulsive tendencies the faculty to renounce is rendered impotent, and the capacity to assume responsibility for oneself all but lost.[2]

Neurotic conflicts may be concerned with the same general problems as perplex the normal person. But they are so different in kind that the question has been raised whether it is permissible to use the same term for both. I believe it is, but we must be aware of the differences. What, then, are the characteristics of neurotic conflicts?

A somewhat simplified example by way of illustration: An engineer working in collaboration with others at mechanical research was frequently afflicted by spells of fatigue and irritability. One of these spells was brought about by the following incident. In a discussion of certain technical matters his opinions were less well received than those of his colleagues. Shortly afterward a decision was made in his absence, and no opportunity was given him subsequently to present his suggestions. Under these circumstances, he could have regarded the procedure as unjust and put up a fight, or he could have accepted the majority decision with good grace. Either reaction would have been consistent. But he did neither. Though he felt deeply slighted, he did not fight. Consciously he was merely aware of being irritated. The murderous rage within him appeared only in his dreams. This repressed rage—a composite of his fury against the others and of his fury against himself for his own meekness— was mainly responsible for his fatigue.

---

[1] To normal persons merely dulled by environmental pressures, a book like Harry Emerson Fosdick's *On Being a Real Person* would be of considerable profit.

[2] Cf. Chapter 10, Impoverishment of Personality [in Horney's *Our Inner Conflicts*].

His failure to react consistently was determined by number of factors. He had built up a grandiose image of himself that required deference from others to support it. This was unconscious at the time: he simply acted on the premise that there was nobody as intelligent and competent in his field as he was. Any slight could jeopardize this premise and provoke rage. Furthermore, he had unconscious sadistic impulses to berate and humiliate others—an attitude so objectionable to him that he covered it up by overfriendliness. To this was added an unconscious drive to exploit people, making it imperative for him to keep in their good graces. The dependence on others was aggravated by a compulsive need for approval and affection, combined as it usually is with attitudes of compliance, appeasement, and avoidance of fight. There was thus a conflict between destructive aggressions—reactive rage and sadistic impulses—on the one hand, and on the other the need for affection and approval, with a desire to appear fair and rational in his own eyes. The result was inner upheaval that went unnoticed, while the fatigue that was its external manifestation paralyzed all action.

Looking at the factors involved in the conflict, we are struck first by their absolute incompatibility. It would be difficult indeed to imagine more extreme opposites than lordly demands for deference and ingratiating submissiveness. Second, the whole conflict remains unconscious. The contradictory tendencies operating in it are not recognized but are deeply repressed. Only slight bubbles of the battle raging within reach the surface. The emotional factors are rationalized: it is an injustice; it is a slight; my ideas were better. Third, the tendencies in both directions are compulsive. Even if he had some intellectual perception of his excessive demands, or of the existence and the nature of his dependence, he could not change these factors voluntarily. To be able to change them would require considerable analytical work. He was driven on either hand by compelling forces over which he had no control: he could not possibly renounce any of the needs acquired by stringent inner necessity. But none of them represented what he himself really wanted or sought. He would want neither to exploit nor to be submissive; as a matter of fact he despised these tendencies. Such a state of affairs, however, has a far-reaching significance for the understanding of neurotic conflicts. It means that no decision is feasible.

A further illustration presents a similar picture. A free-lance designer was stealing small sums of money from a good friend. The theft was not warranted by the external situation; he needed the money, but the friend would gladly have given it to him as he had on occasion in the past. That he should resort to stealing was particularly striking in that he was a decent fellow who set great store by friendship.

The following conflict was at the bottom of it. The man had a pronounced neurotic need for affection, especially a longing to be taken care of in all practical matters. Alloyed as this was with an unconscious drive to exploit others, his technique was to attempt both to endear and intimidate. These tendencies by themselves would have made him willing and eager to receive help and support. But he had also developed an extreme unconscious arrogance which involved a correspondingly vulnerable pride. Others should feel honored to be of service to him: it was humiliating for him to ask for help. His aversion to having to make a request was reinforced by a strong craving for independence and self-sufficiency that made it intolerable for him to admit he needed anything or to place himself under obligation. So he could take, but not receive.

The content of this conflict differs from that of the first example but the essential characteristics are the same. And any other example of neurotic conflict would show a like incompatibility of conflicting drives and their unconscious and compulsive nature, leading always to the impossibility of deciding between the contradictory issues involved.

Allowing for an indistinct line of demarcation, the difference, then, between normal and neurotic conflicts lies fundamentally in the fact that the disparity between the conflicting issues is much less great for the normal person than for the neurotic. The choices the former has to make are between two modes of action, either of which is feasible within the frame of a fairly integrated personality. Graphically speaking, the conflicting directions diverge only 90 degrees or less, as against the possible 180 degrees confronting the neurotic.

In awareness, too, the difference is one of degree. As Kierkegaard[3] has pointed out: "Real life is far too multifarious to be portrayed by merely exhibiting such abstract contrasts as that between a despair which is completely unconscious, and one which is completely conscious." We can say this much, however: a normal conflict can be entirely conscious; a neurotic conflict in all its essential elements is always unconscious. Even though a normal person may be unaware of his conflict, he can recognize it with comparatively little help, while the essential tendencies producing a neurotic conflict are deeply repressed and can be unearthed only against great resistance.

The normal conflict is concerned with an actual choice between two possibilities, both of which the person finds really desirable, or between convictions, both of which he really values. It is therefore possible for him to arrive at a feasible decision even though it may be hard on him and require a renunciation of some kind. The neurotic person engulfed in a conflict is not free to choose. He is driven by equally compelling forces in opposite directions, neither of which he wants to follow. Hence a decision in the usual sense is impossible. He is stranded, with no way out. The conflict can only be resolved by working at the neurotic trends involved, and by so changing his relations with others and with himself that he can dispense with the trends altogether.

These characteristics account for the poignancy of neurotic conflicts. Not only are they difficult to recognize, not only do they render a person helpless, but they have as well a disruptive force of which he has good reason to be afraid. Unless we know these characteristics and keep them in mind, we shall not understand the desperate attempts at solution[4] which the neurotic enters upon, and which constitute the major part of a neurosis.

---

[3] Sören Kierkegaard, *The Sickness unto Death* (Princeton, N.J.: Princeton University Press, 1941).

[4] Throughout the text I shall use the term "solve" in connection with the neurotic's attempts to do away with his conflicts. Since he unconsciously denies their existence he does not, strictly speaking, try to "resolve" them. His unconscious efforts are directed toward "solving" his problems.

CHAPTER 18

Sociometric Theory

Introduction

Jacob L. Moreno (1892–1974) is representative of those personality theorists who apparently start out on their own without prior reference to other theorists. Like Abraham Maslow, Moreno was primarily a social reformer. Indeed, in his early years he attempted, among other things, to form a prostitutes' union, to classify refugees into sociometric groups, and to form a new religion. Fascinated by drama, he constructed a theatre of spontaneity in Vienna where actors could make up their parts as they went along; eventually this became the psychodrama stage from which he conducted thousands of demonstrations of on-the-spot treatments.

Moreno has not received the attention he deserves for a variety of reasons. One may be his rather unique and apparently somewhat disorganized way of communication. He had a private logic of his own and a private vision of how the world would operate if it accorded to his logic. A most fascinating individual, he deserves a full-length biography.

While his best known effort is psychodrama, his most enduring concern was personality and social theory, which in this selection is fairly lucidly presented. Moreno should be read very carefully, to follow his thought patterns. His grand vision is intriguing indeed.

J. L. MORENO
Spontaneity-creativity and energy systems

Spontaneity-creativity is *the* problem of psychology; indeed, it is *the* problem of the universe. I have often been criticized for moving without stopping and signaling from one dimension of conceptualization to another. But it is difficult to convey the full meaning of undeveloped concepts like spontaneity and creativity which are in transition from a pre-scientific to a scientific formulation without using all available objective and subjective resources. I am moving, therefore, from a discussion of spontaneity and creativity in human relations, searching for empirical evidence, to a cosmic outlook.

The time-space-energy frame of reference has become universally accepted in the physical sciences. The concept of spontaneity-creativity has found wide approval in the cultural sciences. The question is whether they can be adapted to one another. Let us first examine, therefore, the physical idea of the conservation of energy. Max Planck, the physicist, gives a vivid account of his first encounter with this principle. "My mind absorbed avidly, like a revelation, the first law I knew to possess absolute, universal validity, independently from all human agency: The principle of the conservation of energy. I shall never forget the graphic story Müller told us, at his *raconteur's* best, of the bricklayer lifting with great effort a heavy block of stone to the roof of a house. The work he thus performs does not get lost; it

J. L. Moreno, "Spontaneity-Creativity and Energy Systems." Reprinted from *Sociometry*, 1955, *18*, 360–374, with permission of Beacon House, Inc.

remains stored up, perhaps for many years, undiminished and latent in the block of stone, until one day the block is perhaps loosened and drops on the head of some passerby" (Planck, 1949).

The law of conservation of energy has become an axiom in the physical sciences and a model for some of the best known psychological and social systems. Take, for instance, the concept of libido in psychoanalytic theory. In accordance with this theory Freud thought that if the sexual impulse does not find satisfaction in its direct aim, it must displace its unapplied energy elsewhere. It must, he thought, attach itself to a pathological locus or find a way out in sublimation. He could not even for a moment conceive of this unapplied affect "vanishing" because he was, like most scientists of his generation, biased by the physical idea of the conservation of energy. If we, too, were to follow this percept of the energy-pattern when we consider spontaneity, we should have to believe that a person has a certain amount of spontaneity stored up to which he adds as he goes on living—but in smaller and smaller quantities the more he is dominated by cultural conserves. As he performs actions, he draws from this reservoir; if he is not careful he may use it all up—or even overdraw! But the following alternative principle, the principle of spontaneity-creativity, seemed to us to be just as plausible as the foregoing and for theoretical ends more productive. As long as this person is trained to rely habitually upon conserves he will try to build up a reservoir of spontaneity, and the greater

FIGURE 18.1. Field of rotating operations between spontaneity–creativity–cultural conserve (S–C–CC).

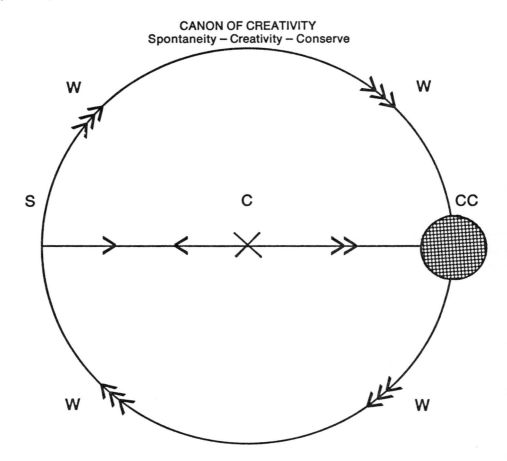

CANON OF CREATIVITY
Spontaneity – Creativity – Conserve

S = Spontaneity.
C = Creativity.
CC = Cultural (or any) Conserve (for instance, a biological conserve, that is, an animal organism; or a cultural conserve, that is, a book, a motion picture; or a robot, that is, a calculating machine).
W = Warming up, the "operational" expression of spontaneity.
The circle represents the field of operations between S, C, and CC.

Operation I: Spontanity arouses Creativity, C. S→C.
Operation II: Creativity is receptive to Spontaneity. S←C.
Operation III: From their interaction, Cultural Conserves, CC, result. S→C→ > >CC.
Operation IV: Conserves (CC) would accumulate indefinitely and remain "in cold storage." They need to be reborn; the catalyzer Spontaneity revitalizes them. CC→ > > >S→ > > >CC.

S does not operate in a vacuum; it moves either toward Creativity or toward Conserves.
Total Operation

Spontaneity–Creativity–Warming up act $-\frac{\text{Actor}}{\text{Conserve}}$

From J. L. Moreno, *Who Shall Survive?*, 2nd ed. (New York: Beacon House, 1953), p. 46.

his savings are, the less frequency will he need to produce new spontaneity; he can live from his savings. But if this person is conditioned not to produce any reservoir of spontaneity and therefore not to rely upon a "bank account," he has no alternative but to produce in any novel situation the amount of emotion, thought and action demanded from him. At times he may have to use more of this, say spontaneity, and at other times less—in accord with what the situation or task requires. If he is well trained, he will not produce less than the exact amount of spontaneity needed, for if this were to happen he would need a reservoir from which to draw, and he will likewise not produce more than the situation calls for because the surplus might tempt him to store it, thus completing a vicious circle which ends in a cultural conserve (Moreno, 1940). [See Figure 18.1]

Definitions

The mystic aura which has in the past surrounded such concepts as spontaneity, creativity, love, goodness, catharsis, affinity, attraction, repulsion, choice, etc., hindered their accurate observation and analysis. But I postulated that spontaneity and creativity are observable facts and can be subjected to experiments, laboratory studies and systematic analysis. We may not be able to reproduce in an experimental setting high range creativity or high range spontaneity. They are rare in life itself and hard to observe. They may occur as rarely in an experimental setting but it is able to provoke middle range or low range spontaneity in a controllable environment.

The experimental setting was a theater of spontaneity. Its productions portrayed interpersonal relations and social situations. The quality of performance seemed to depend primarily upon the spontaneity

and creativity of the performer in the course of interaction. They, however, appeared intangible and mysterious to the onlooker. Because the spontaneity, creativity and motivations of the participants were left unconscious, the interactional processes taking place before us looked mechanical. The actors looked like puppets manipulated by strings, without spelling out the deeper meaning. "Many hundreds of spontaneity tests were made in this laboratory and many hundreds of productions were presented. Day by day the results of these tests were interpreted and analyzed. This led to a mass of systematic knowledge in preparation for a theory of spontaneity and creativity which could be based upon actual achievements" (Moreno, 1940). Every actor was evaluated as to his readiness to act, as sudden or insidious onset, being overheated or at ease and free of anxiety, showing an adequate or inadequate response to a situation. Every production was evaluated as the creativity of its content and as to the competency of the interactors towards each other. I gradually arrived at a few hypothetical definitions which I expected to be tested, rejected or confirmed in the course of experimentation. The methods of measurement were raw in the beginning, if one looks at them from the present day of sophistication; but the door was left open for the gradual application of every suitable type of measurement.

A. Spontaneity

Spontaneity is the variable degree of adequate response to a situation of a variable degree of novelty. Novelty of behavior by itself is not the measure of spontaneity. Novelty has to be qualified against its adequacy in situ. Adequacy of behavior by itself is also not the measure of spontaneity. Adequacy has to be qualified against its novelty. The novelty, for instance, of extreme psychotic behavior may be to such a degree incoherent that the actor is unable to solve any concrete problem, to plan an act of suicide, to cut a piece of bread or to solve a thought problem. We speak then of pathological spontaneity. The adequacy of behavior may be unnovel to a degree which results in strict, rigid or automatic conformity to a cultural conserve. Such adherence may gradually obliterate the ability of the organism and the talent of the actor to change. Spontaneity operates in the here and now. The novelty of a moment demands a past which does not contain this particular novelty. Spontaneity research has enabled us to recognize the various phases and degrees of spontaneity as one continuous process, the reduction and loss of spontaneity, impulsive abreactions and the pathological excesses as well as adequate and disciplined spontaneity, productive and creative spontaneity. It recognized also that spontaneity does not operate in a vacuum but in relation to already structured phenomena, cultural and social conserves.

The questions are: What value has a novel response and when is a response adequate? A novel response like two plus two is seven or a horse has 15 eyes and 25 legs may have, within certain contexts of artistic creation, more creativity than the stereotype response two and two is four or a horse has two eyes and four legs; in other words a logically correct response is not always the indication of creative behavior, and, of course, inadequate responses are not necessarily indications of non-creativity. There are all kinds of mixtures possible of near-adequacy and near-novelty which may pass as comparatively creative. Each performance has to be evaluated within its own context. We should not give a higher creativity rating to an individual who says automatically

"Two and two is four" although it may be more adequate and useful than a mental patient who says in a manic state at one moment "Two and two is seven," and at another moment "Two and two are five billion," etc. The freedom in association of words and gestures may have at times the merit of preparing the ground for a creativity state, whereas the one who insists that "two and two is four" may be the hopeless case of an individual who is always right.

An "adequate" response is *appropriateness, competency* and *skill* in dealing with a situation, however small or great the challenge of its novelty. A man can be creative, original, dramatic, but not always have spontaneously an appropriate response in new situations. On the other hand, if he would have only stereotype responses available, however much dramatized and alarming, he would fall within the domain of inadequacy of response. For instance, if a woman is married to a man whose rate of creativity is superior to hers, his competency and skill in social relations, a larger number of significant roles for the setting in which he functions, she is threatened with falling out of the relationship unless she is able to approximate his range and depth of creativity towards herself and others. Another illustration (Moreno, 1953) is the creation of new organisms, at the time when animal life was confined to the sea. A new animal organism would arise when it would undergo, through the evolutional process, anatomical and physical changes. These changes would be a novel response to the old situation of the sea.

It appeared, therefore, useful to differentiate three types of spontaneity:

1. Whenever a *novel* response occurs without adequacy, that is, undisciplined or pathological spontaneity.

2. Whenever an *adequate* response oc-

curs without significant characteristics of novelty and creativity.

3. Whenever an adequate response occurs *with* characteristics of novelty and creativity.

B. Creativity

Creativity manifests itself in any series of creativity states or creative acts. Spontaneity and creativity are not identical or similar processes. They are different categories, although strategically linked. In the case of Man, his spontaneity may be diametrically opposite to his creativity; an individual may have a high degree of spontaneity but be entirely uncreative, a spontaneous idiot. Creativity belongs to the categories of the substance—the arch substance. It is the elementary X without any specialized connotation, the X which may be recognized by its acts. In order to become effective, it (the sleeping beauty) needs a catalyzer. The catalyzer of creativity is spontaneity.

Creativity is related to the "act" itself; spontaneity is related to the "readiness" of the act. The finished product of a creative process, the cultural conserve, has its roots in a spontaneous creative matrix, the original manifestation of creativity. The difference between a cultural conserve and the spontaneous creative matrix of this conserve at the moment when it is springing into existence is fundamental. Let us imagine the music of the Ninth Symphony at the moment it was being created by Beethoven, and let us also imagine the same music as a work of art—a finished product—separated from the composer himself. On the surface, it may appear as if the creative units which went into the Ninth Symphony—its musical themes, its climaxes, its harmonies, etc.—must also have been in its original matrix, and that no difference exists between the one in its state in Beethoven's

mind and the other in its conserved state—except only that of locus. It might seem as if it were merely a transposition of the same material—the same sum total of creative units—from one locus in time (the mind of Beethoven) to another (the musical score). Closer inspection, however, will show that this is not true. As Beethoven was walking through his garden trying intensively to warm up to his musical ideas, his whole personality was in an uproar. He made use of every possible physical and mental starter he could muster in order to get going in the right direction. These visions, images, thoughts and action-patterns—both musical and non-musical inspirations—were the indispensable background out of which the music of the Ninth Symphony grew. But all this background (which cannot truthfully be divorced from the state in which Beethoven was when he was truly being a creator) is not to be found in the finished product—the musical score or its performance by a noted orchestra. Only the result is there. The fact that this background has been deleted from our present-day idea of Beethoven is the result of an intellectual trick which is played upon us by millenia of being indoctrinated by cultural conserves. If we look upon the initial spontaneous-creative phase in Beethoven's composition of the Ninth Symphony as a positive phase and not as a transition in the direction of an end-product, we can see in Beethoven's musical compositions, his concepts of God, the universe and the destiny of humanity, in the loves, joys and griefs of his private life and—especially—in the gestures and movements of his body a united pattern from which a *surface* layer (the cultural conserve) can be lifted to satisfy certain pragmatic demands. At the moment of composition, Beethoven's mind experienced these concepts, visions and images in conjunction with the developing symphony. They were integral parts of a creative act—of a series of creative acts. He made a cross-section through them in such a way that only the material which could be fitted into the prospective conserve was included; the direction of the cross-section was determined by its frame. In this particular instance, the frame was that of musical notation; in another case it might have been the frame of language notation; at still another, it might have been a mechanical invention; at still another, it might have been a human relationship, a matrimonial relationship or a working crew.

We should guard ourselves to diagnose a state of creativity from the signs of easy overt warm-up. We should not depreciate a state of creativity because it has a slow and difficult onset. We should not over-rate overt and overheated activity and under-rate inflexibility and passivity. We should not over-rate unconserved response and under-rate conserved response. We should not be biased in favor of novelty and originality and in disfavor of "traditional" but adequate response. On the other hand, we should not be biased in favor of slow and difficult onset, inflexibility or traditional response; only careful analysis of the objective facts should decide whether it is high, average or low creativity. We usually over-rate the finished product of the cultural conserve, the finished poem, the great music, the balanced interpersonal relation, and the organized behavior of a group as to their actual, present dynamic creativity. We are deceived by the comparative perfection and smoothness of a cultural conserve and evaluate it as if it would be the immediate delivery of a creative act. We underestimate the "spontaneous creative matrix" of a poem, of a symphony, of a love relation, of an initial group forma-

tion because of their frequent inferiority as to perfection and smoothness. The sermon on the mount was first a "burning" spontaneous creative matrix long before it became a cultural conserve which every minister can repeat fervently ad infinitum. We are to such an extent enraptured with the high grade conserves of a culture that we forget their origin from poorly structured but spontaneous-creative matrices. It is that spontaneous creative state which we try to bring to a test and all the stages leading up to the cultural conserve, not only the finished product.

C. The warming-up process

The warming up process, the operational manifestation of spontaneity, is a general condition existing before and in the course of any creative act—before and during an act of sleeping, eating, sexual intercourse, walking, artistic creation or any act of self realization. Spontaneity is generated in action whenever an organism is found in the process of warming-up. Whether spontaneity generates warming-up or warming-up generates spontaneity is similar to the question: "Which is first—the chicken or the egg?"

It is useful to differentiate several types of warming-up:

1. *Undirected warming-up,* individual or group—vague, chaotic, confused, moving towards several goals on several tracks simultaneously.

2. *Directed warming-up,* individual or group—moving without any deviation clearly and powerfully towards a creative act, its exclusive, specific goal. Midway between undirected and directed warming-up, there are many perceptual cues emerging. In the course of getting ready to make a response, the individual may

try to get oriented—to get out of the fog when driving a car or to find the melody which fits into his musical composition or to find a mathematical formula for a hypothetical question or to find an ending for a poem or an answer to his wife's quarrels. As soon as he is sure what to do, he has sudden flashes of perception, then he acts quickly—registers the ending of the poem in his mind, rushes to the piano and tries the melody, writes a letter resigning from his job or talks to his wife, etc. Often perceptual spontaneity, however, is indistinguishable from readiness to act.

3. *A general state of warming-up*—The individual is aware that a novel response will be required from him in the situation in which he is, for instance: A girl who is taken out on a blind date for the first time, or a doctor who makes his first call in medical practice or a pastor who renders his first sermon. The individual is excited in various degrees of intensity, the organism gets ready for an unexpected event—his heart rate may be increased, pulse may be more rapid, his respiration rate increased, etc.

4. *Immediate warming-up* in an emergency situation.

5. *Chain warm-up*—an idea or feeling being augmented by traveling from one actor to another and returning to the initiating actor.

D. Cultural conserves

Cultural conserves are products of creativity; they are antipodal to the spontaneous creative matrices which emerge every time a creative process is in the making, in the intensive heat of status nascendi. They aim at being the finished products of a creative process and, as such, have assumed an almost sacred quality. The cultural conserve renders to the individual a service similar to that which it renders as a historical category to culture at large—continuity of heritage—securing for him the preservation and the continuity of his creative ego. But spontaneity and creativity never cease entirely to affect cultural conserves, some "amount" of them enters into every one of its renderings, in a greater or lesser degree. By "amount" of spontaneity, we do not mean amounts which are stored up or conserved. Even the greatest possible amount of stored-up spontaneity and creativity could not make a butterfly anything more than a butterfly. Yet even the smallest amount of "free" spontaneity, summoned and created by a being on the spur of the moment—a product, in other words, of the moment—is of greater value than all the treasures of the past, of past "moments." Spontaneous creativity—however supreme it may be in itself—once conserved is, by definition, no longer spontaneity; it has lost its actuality in the universe. What "conserved" creativity truly represents, at best, is power, a means of expressing superiority when actual superiority has ceased to be available.

HYPOTHESES

1. Everything that is *negative* presupposes something that is *positive*. Anxiety, fear and defense are negative categories; they presuppose a positive category, spontaneity. Frustration, projection, substitution and sublimation are negative categories; they presuppose a positive category, creativity. Energy, matter, sexuality, tele are sub-forms of creativity.

2. All men are endowed with spontaneity and creativity, although there may be considerable differences in degree of endowment.

3. They exist sui generis.

4. They are not identical with intelligence or memory and not derivative of conditional reflexes or sexual automatic responses.

In order to make experiments feasible, we must be ready to "compromise" and try to simulate a nearly lifelike setting. If the investigator is not willing to compromise but limits himself to the study of spontaneity and creativity on very high levels, he may never be able to get creativity into his test tube and measure and observe it there from close distance. It is the small, average and minute types of creativity which are important in the daily life of human beings, in their work relations, family relations, business relations, etc., and not the great creativity of exceptional individuals. If the concepts of spontaneity and creativity are central to human behavior, they must be traceable in every human act and co-act, on all levels of human performance from the most trivial to the highest. In the application of the scientific method to such high level concepts as spontaneity and creativity, we must make heartbreaking compromises in order to get an experimental contact with them. But we will not compromise to the other extreme, diluting and pushing spontaneity and creativity out of the experiment; they must be continuously considered before an experiment is set up and during its ongoing. We should not sell them "down the river" out of fear that they may complicate the experiment.

If spontaneity and creativity are of central importance in human behavior then there must be some *constancy,* frequency and regularity of appearance. If there is constancy, then there should be also predictability. We have been inclined in the past to relate spontaneity and crea-

tivity only to artistic productions. Sociometrists have tried to point out, and I believe successfully, the great amount of spontaneity and creativity operating in interpersonal relations. They were among the first to bring them from the philosophical heaven down to earth.

SPONTANEITY AND CREATIVITY TESTS

Optimal conditions created by the actors and for the actors in order to make "tests" feasible are (1) total extemporaneity of production to (2) extreme realism of the production (not pretending or as if fictitious), complete carrying out of episodes as they are felt and experienced by the subjects. If they have experiences beyond realization, in situ, in ordinary life, they are given on the stage laboratory opportunity to be realized, "surplus" realization and "surplus" reality.

Optimal conditions created by the experiments for the actor: (1) minimally structured situations alien to the private roles of the actor, and (2) various stages of structured situations up to entirely planned.

The tests, as far as they have been used in our psychodramatic institutes, have tried to probe spontaneity and creativity (1) in interpersonal situations, (2) in person-object relations. It was found that some people have more spontaneity and creativity towards people than towards objects; that some people have more spontaneity and creativity towards objects than towards people; and that some people have low or high spontaneity and creativity towards both. The question whether a life situation can be approximated on the stage so as significantly to correlate an individual's behavior in a stage situation to his behavior in the real world can be answered in the positive; but regardless of success in approximating outside behavior, the crucial material of the psychodramatic laboratory is *the production emerging in the Here and Now.* If total spontaneity and creativity is permitted to the actor as far as they are available to him, his past, present and future will enter the production anyway. It is the immediate frame of reference for evaluation.

SYSTEM OF SPONTANEITY-CREATIVITY AND EINSTEIN'S UNIVERSE

The experimental findings of spontaneity-creativity research contradict the principle of conservation of energy, at least in the realm of the psycho-social-cultural world of man; but that is how far my authority goes. In the following, I will try to give a picture of the universe, drawing evidence from other sciences. No science is an island by itself. All sciences must borrow from each other in a movement towards unity.

Let us see how spontaneity-creativity could be fitted into a system of universal energy. In the spontaneity-creativity theory, energy as an organized system of physical forces is not entirely given up. It reappears in the form of the cultural conserve. But instead of being the fountainhead, at the beginning of every process, such as libido, it is at the end of a process, an end product. It is a counterpart to the bricklayer's work of lifting a heavy stone (in Planck's story) which remained stored up and latent, until one day it is loosened and drops on the head of some passerby. Such a counterpart may be, for instance, Beethoven's work stored up in a musical conserve, latent on a gramophone record,

until it is let loose years later upon an audience. Beethoven's musical energy did not get lost. Cultural conserves can be explained, therefore, as operating in accord with the principle of the conservation of energy. E (energy) $= M$ (mass) analogous to C (conserve) (Formula I).

But "up to a point" creativity itself may be explainable in energy terms, energy as conceived by Einstein and as long as we leave an area free for the yet unknown processes of creativity (X). Being the ultimate source of all conserves, it may be considered as the most precious, the highest grade of energy in the universe, analogous to some substances in the physical world—tiny particles of metals like uranium store enormous amounts of energy. Einstein's energy is not only conservable and convertible into matter, but also de-conservable. The concept of physical energy has reached such an unprecedented degree of latitude and flexibility that one can postulate that C (creativity) includes E (energy) $= M$ (matter). Energy and matter would be then subforms of creativity, X standing for the yet unknown process of creativity in the universe, $C = X + E$ (or M) (Formula II).

The fitting of the spontaneity-creativity principle into the system of conservation of energy may have appeared to be indispensable as long as the principle of conservation of energy was held to possess absolute universal validity independently from all human agencies. I have raised my voice against the absoluteness of this principle (Moreno, 1940), driven to doubt by observations of spontaneity and creativity on the level of human productivity. As long as the doubt was raised from the side of the social sciences only, it may have been pushed aside as fantastic by the "exact" sciences. But my critique has received in recent years support from leaders in physics themselves. Says Planck: "The principle of the conservation of energy, after all, is an experimental law. Accordingly, although today it is considered to be universal and all-embracing, its validity may one day have to be restricted—and *in fact, such a curtailment of its universal applicability has been sometimes suspected in nuclear physics*" (Planck, 1949). (Italics mine.) The development of nuclear physics has brought at last a revolutionary change in the concept of physical energy. It was brought about by the growing influence of Einstein's relativity theory upon the entire field. It started with Becquerel's discovery that uranium is radioactive but it was Einstein's mass-energy equation which crystallized into a universal law of physics. Gradually the notion began to spread that matter is not indestructible. It began to dawn that matter can be created and that matter can be converted into energy by splitting of the nucleus of certain elements or by fusion of certain elements. This does not mean that the principle of the conservation of energy has been given up; it is valid rule but its universal applicability has been curtailed.

The rigid, narcissistic picture of the universe of classical physics received another blow when Heisenberg formulated the so-called uncertainty principle which has shaken the validity of another "absolute" law, the law of causality.

The question remaining is the place of spontaneity in this formula. No one has ever seen spontaneity. Spontaneity is a hypothesis. It is supposed to manifest itself in the warming-up process of a creative act. Spontaneity itself has been hypothecated as "unconservable" energy (Moreno, 1953), a type of energy which is spent as it emerges, a type of catalyzer

which may have its "fellow travelers" in all departments of the universe. If we stretch our imagination, we can compare it with ferments or enzymes, the living catalyzers of chemical processes, or with radioactive elements, the physical catalyzers of energy. Radioactive matter would then correspond to the spontaneous-creative matrices of cultural conserves. Just as radioactive matter ceases to give off rays spontaneously but is stored in the crust of the earth as conserved and stable elements, spontaneous-creative matrices lose their "heat" when transformed into cultural conserves. "There are some forces which produce a perceptual effect without any expenditure whatever of energy. These are what we may call 'guiding forces' such as, for instance, the resistance due to the rigidity of railroad rails which forces the wheels of a train forward at a predetermined curve without a predetermined expenditure of energy" (Moreno, 1953, p. 62). There are apparently forms of energy in the physical universe which, like spontaneity, do not leave any residua. The formula of creativity-energy can then be extended to include spontaneity. It is then S (spontaneity) $+ C$ (creativity) $+ c$ (conserve) $= X + E$ (or M) (Formula III).

At last the deepest and rarest forms of creativity, as the two great trinities—Silence, Goodness, and Anonymity; and Truth, Beauty, and Love—can be well understood as forms of "surplus" energy which are, similar to spontaneity, not conservable. With them it is like "existence standing still." There may exist spontaneous-creative states without accompanying warming-up processes. Love, beauty and truth go hand in hand because they are offsprings of the same parentage; what is good is also beautiful and truthful; what is true is also beautiful and good; and what is beautiful is also good and truthful. One cannot imagine love without spontaneity, beauty without creativity and truth without both; it is a spontaneous-creative matrix in locus nascendi which unites them.

Atomic nuclear research seems to confirm in principle, or at least does not contradict, the picture of the universe which the theory of spontaneity-creativity has envisaged. Its structure is not permanently set but when novel situations emerge, the responses to the surrounding field take the form of creative acts. As long as the universe was visualized as dominated by eternal, rigid laws, there was no place for "uniqueness" and for "explosive" changes and with it no place for creativity as the ultimate principle, at least not for the on-going, here-and-

nowness of it. But a revolution has taken place on the highest level of conceptualization. We can say with greater certainty than ever that the supreme power ruling the world is Spontaneity-Creativity. It has created a rational cosmos which coexists interdependently with man's perception of it but amenable to his intervention as long as he knows and abides by its rules.

REFERENCES

Moreno, J. L. Mental catharsis and the psychodrama. *Sociometry,* 1940, *4,* 209–243.

Moreno, J. L. *Who shall survive?* New York: Beacon House, 1953.

Planck, Max. *Scientific autobiography.* New York: Philosophical Library, 1949.

CHAPTER 19

Self-Actualization Theory

Introduction

Abraham H. Maslow (1908–1970) was basically a scientist who attempted to give due credit to both biology and sociology in his explanations about the formation and maintenance of the human personality. Nonetheless he was a paradigm of the humanist. In this selection, all three of these elements are clearly seen. His scholarship, his sense of balanced fairness, and his humanity are well exemplified in this attempt to put into proper perspective the age-old issue of heredity and environment.

Personality theorists are frequently on one side or the other of the issue of the biological vs. the cultural aspects of the personality. Maslow makes it quite clear here that both must be considered, in interaction. In recent years, there appears to be a tendency away from the notion that personality is primarily based on environmental contingencies reacting on a basically neutral body, to greater consideration of the importance of biological needs.

A. H. MASLOW
The instinctoid nature of basic needs

INSTINCT THEORY RE-EXAMINED

Why re-examine instinct theory?

The theories of basic needs sketched out in previous papers (Maslow, 1943a, 1943b, 1948a, 1948b, 1949, 1950) suggest and even call for a reconsideration of the instinct theory, if only because of the necessity for differentiating between the more and less "basic," more and less "healthy," and more and less "natural." Furthermore, we ought not to postpone indefinitely an examination of certain related questions brought to our unavoidable attention by this and other theories of basic needs (Angyal, 1941; Cattell, 1950; Fromm, 1947; Goldstein, 1939; Murray, 1938), e.g., the implied discarding of cultural relativity, the implied theory of constitutionally given values, the unmistakable narrowing of the jurisdiction assigned to associative learning, etc.

There are, in any case, many other theoretical, clinical, and experimental considerations pointing in this same direction, i.e., the desirability of re-evaluating instinct theory and perhaps even of resurrecting it in some form or other. All these support a certain skepticism with regard to the current stress by psychologists, sociologists, and anthropologists on the plasticity, flexibility, and adaptability of

Abraham H. Maslow, "The Instinctoid Nature of Human Needs." Reprinted from the *Journal of Personality*, 1954, *22*, 326–347. Copyright © 1954 by Duke University Press.

Note: The author acknowledges with thanks the help of Bertha Maslow and Zipporah Varon in preparing this article.

the human being and his ability to learn. Human beings seem to be far more autonomous and self-governed than modern psychological theory makes allowance for.

This is implicit in the following theoretical and experimental contributions:

1. The homeostasis concept of Cannon (1932), the death-instinct theory of Freud (Fenichel, 1945; Freud, 1949), the complacency theory of Raup (1926), etc.

2. The appetite or "free choice" or "cafeteria" experiments (Young, 1948, 1949).

3. The "instinct-satiation" experiments of Levy (1928, 1934, 1937, 1938, 1942, 1944), as well as his work on maternal overprotection (1943).

4. The various psychoanalytic discoveries about the deleterious effects of overdemanding toilet training and hasty weaning in children (Ribble, 1943).

5. The host of observations which have led progressive educators, nursery-school workers, and practical child psychologists to lean toward a more permissive regime in all their dealings with children (Murphy, 1947).

6. The system of concepts explicitly underlying Rogers' nondirective therapy (Scheinfeld, 1943).

7. The many neurological and biological data are reported by the vitalists (Dreisch, 1938), by emergent evolutionists (Bergson, 1944), by the modern experimental embryologists (Spemann, 1938; Weiss, 1939), and by such holists as Goldstein (1939) on spontaneous organismic readjustment after damage.

These and other researches which will be mentioned combine to suggest strongly that the organism is more trustworthy, more self-protecting, self-directing, and self-governing than it is usually given credit for. In addition, we may add that various recent developments have shown the theoretical necessity for the postulation of some sort of positive growth or self-actualization tendency within the organism which is different from its conserving, equilibrating, or homeostatic tendency, as well as from the tendency to respond to impulses from the outside world. This kind of tendency to growth or self-actualization, in one vague form or another, has been postulated by thinkers as diverse as Aristotle and Bergson, and by many other philosophers. Among psychiatrists, psychoanalysts, and psychologists it has been found necessary by Goldstein, Rank, Jung, Horney, Fromm, Rogers, May, and Maslow.

Perhaps, however, the most important influence in favor of re-examining the instinct theory is the experience of the psychotherapists, especially the psychoanalysts. In this area the logic of facts, however unclearly seen, has been unmistakable; inexorably, the therapist has been forced to differentiate more basic from less basic wishes (or needs, or impulses). It is just as simple as this; the frustration of some needs produces pathology, the frustration of other needs does not. These troublemaking needs are inconceivably stubborn and recalcitrant. As Freud pointed out, they resist all blandishments, substitutions, bribes, and alternatives; nothing will do for them but their proper gratifications. They behave always like stubborn, irreducible, final, unanalyzable facts which must be taken as "givens" or as starting points not to be questioned. It should be an overwhelm-ingly impressive point that almost every school of psychiatry, psychoanalysis, clinical psychology, social work, or child therapy has *had* to postulate some doctrine of instincts or instinctlike needs no matter how much they disagree on other points.

Inevitably, such experiences remind us of species characteristics, of constitution, and of heredity rather than of superficial and easily manipulated associations. Wherever a choice has had to be made between the horns of this dilemma, the therapist has almost always chosen the instinct rather than the conditioned response or the habit as his basic building block. This is, of course, unfortunate, for as we shall see there are other intermediate and more valid alternatives from among which we may now make a more satisfying choice, i.e., there are more than two horns to the dilemma.

But it does seem clear that, from the point of view of the demands of general-dynamic theory, the instinct theory, as presented especially by James, MacDougall, and Freud, had certain virtues which were not sufficiently appreciated at the time, perhaps because its mistakes were so much more evident. Instinct theory accepted the fact that man was a self-mover; that his own nature as well as his environment helped to decide his behavior; that his own nature supplied him with a ready-made framework of ends, goals, or values; that most often, under good conditions, what he wants is what he needs (what is good for him) in order to avoid sickness; that all men form a single biological species; that behavior is senseless unless one understands its motivations and its goals; and that on the whole, organisms left to their own resources often display a kind of biological efficiency or "wisdom" that needs explaining.

Mistakes of instinct theory

It will be our contention in this paper that many of the mistakes of the instinct theorists, while profound and deserving of rejection, were by no means intrinsic or inevitable, and that, furthermore, a fair number of these mistakes were shared by both the instinctivists and their critics.

1. The semantic and logical errors were most flagrant. The instinctivists were accused deservedly of *ad hoc* creation of instincts to explain behavior they could not understand, or whose origins they could not determine. But of course, being properly forewarned, *we* need not hypostatize, confuse labels with facts, or propound invalid syllogisms. We know much more about semantics today.

2. We now know so much more about ethnology, sociology, and genetics that we can avoid both the simple ethnocentrism and class-centrism and the simple social Darwinism that brought the early instinctivists to grief. This is in contrast, for instance, to the state of affairs in neurology. Here we have little more evidence than the instinctivists did. We do not yet know, e.g., if the need for love is governed by subcortical centers. (But see Beach, 1937; Lashley, 1938.)

We must now also recognize that the recoil from the ethnological naïveté of the instinctivists was so extreme and sweeping as to constitute in itself a mistake, i.e., cultural relativity. This doctrine, so influential and so widely accepted during the last two decades, is now being very widely criticized (R. Benedict, unpublished lectures on synergy in society; Gardner, 1950; Goldstein, 1939; Maslow, 1949, 1950; Niebuhr, 1947; Schooland, 1942). Certainly it is now again respectable to seek for cross-cultural species characteristics as the instinctivists did.

Apparently we must (and can) avoid both ethnocentrism and an overstated cultural relativism. For instance, it seems quite clear that instrumental behaviors (means) are far more relative to local cultural determinants than are the basic needs (ends) (Maslow, 1943a, 1949, 1950).

3. Most anti-instinctivists, e.g., Bernard (1924), Watson (1930), Kuo (1924), etc., in the twenties and thirties criticized instinct theory on the ground that instincts could not be described in specific stimulus-response terms. What this boils down to is the accusation that instincts do not conform to simple behavioristic theory. This is true; they do not indeed. Such a criticism however is not taken seriously today by dynamic psychologists who uniformly consider that it is impossible to define *any* important human whole-quality or whole-activity in *SR* terms alone. Such an attempt can breed little more than confusion. We can take as a single typical instance the confounding of reflex with the classical lower-animal instinct. The former is a pure motor act; the latter is this and a great deal more, i.e., predetermined impulse, expressive behavior, coping behavior, goal object, and affect.

4. Even on logical grounds alone there is no reason why we should be forced to choose between the full instinct, complete in all its parts, and the noninstinct. Why may there not be instinct-remnants, instinctlike aspects of impulse alone or of behavior alone, differences of degree, partial instincts?

Too many lesser writers used the word "instinct" indiscriminately to cover need, aim, ability, behavior, perception, expression, value, and emotional concomitants, singly or in combination. The result was a hodgepodge of loose usage in which almost every known human reaction was characterized as instinctive by one or another writer, as Marmor (1942) and Bernard (1924) have pointed out.

Our main hypothesis is that human *urges* or *basic needs* alone may be innately "given" to at least some appreciable degree. The pertinent behavior or ability, cognition or affection need not also be innate, but may be (by our hypothesis) learned, canalized, or expressive. (Of course, many of man's *abilities* or *capacities* are strongly determined or made possible by heredity, e.g., color vision, ability to articulate, etc., but they are of no concern to us at this point.) This is to say that the hereditary component of basic needs may be seen as simple conative lack, tied to no intrinsic goal-achieving behavior, as blind, directionless demands, like Freud's id-impulses. (We shall see that the satisfiers of these basic needs seem also to be "intrinsic" in a definable way.) What has to be learned is goal-bent (coping) behavior.

It was a severe mistake of both the instinctivists and their opponents to think in black-and-white, dichotomous terms instead of in terms of degree. How could it be said that a complex set of reactions was either *all* determined by heredity or *not at all* determined by heredity? There is no structure, however simple, let alone whole-reaction, that has genic determinants alone. Even Mendel's sweet peas needed air and water and food. For that matter even the genes themselves have an environment, i.e., neighboring genes.

At the other extreme it is also obvious that nothing is completely free of the influence of heredity, for man is a biological species. This fact, determined by heredity, is a precondition of every human action, ability, cognition, etc.; i.e., everything that a human being can do is made possible by the fact that he is a member of the human species. This membership is a genic matter.

One confusing consequence of this invalid dichotomy is the tendency to define any activity as noninstinctive if *any* learning can be demonstrated; or contrariwise, to define an activity as instinctive if *any* hereditary influence at all can be demonstrated. Since for most, perhaps all, urges, abilities, or emotions it is easy to demonstrate both kinds of determination, such arguments must be forever insoluble.

The instinctivists and anti-instinctivists both were all-or-nothing; we of course need not be. This is an avoidable mistake.

5. The paradigm for the instinct theorists was the animal instinct. This led to various mistakes, e.g., failing to look for instincts unique to the human species. The one most misleading "lesson," however, that was learned from the lower animals was the "axiom" that instincts were powerful, strong, unmodifiable, uncontrollable, unsuppressible. However this may be for salmon, frogs, or lemmings, it need not therefore be true for humans.

If, as we feel, basic needs have an appreciable hereditary base, then we may very well have blundered when we looked for instincts with only the naked eye and considered an entity instinctive only when it was obviously and unmistakably independent of all environmental forces. On this point, see Howells (1933, 1945, 1947; Howells & Vine, 1940). Why should there not be needs which, though instinctoid, yet are easily repressed, suppressed, or otherwise controlled, and which are easily masked, modified, or even suppressed by habits, suggestions, cultural pressures, guilt, and so on (as for instance, seems to be true for the love need)? That is to say, why not *weak* instincts?

It may be that the motive power behind the culturalists' attack on instinct theory comes largely from this mistaken identification of instinct with overpowering strength. The experience of every ethnologist contradicts such an assumption and attack is therefore understandable. But if we were properly respectful of both the cultural and the biological (as the writer is) and if further we consider culture to be a stronger force than instinctoid need (as the writer does), then it would seem not a paradox but an obvious matter of course that it should be maintained (as the writer maintains), that we ought to *protect* the weak, subtle, and tender instinctoid needs if they are not to be overwhelmed by the tougher, more powerful culture, rather than the other way about. This could be so even though these same instinctoid needs are in another sense "strong," i.e., they persist, they demand gratification, their frustration produces highly pathological consequences, etc.

6. Still another possibility must be kept in mind with regard to the assumption of unchangeability and unmodifiability of hereditary traits. It is this: Even if a trait be primarily determined by genic heredity, it may yet be modifiable—even perhaps *easily* modifiable or controllable if we are fortunate enough in our discoveries. If we assume cancer to have a strong hereditary component, this need not stop anyone from hunting for a means to control it. If only on a priori grounds, we must also admit the possibility that IQ may turn out to be measurably hereditary and at the same time improvable by education.

7. We must make room for far more variability in the realm of instincts than was allowed by the instinct theorists. The needs to know and to understand seem to be obviously potent only in intelligent in-dividuals. They seem to be practically absent in the feebleminded. Levy (1942) has shown that the maternal impulse varies so widely in women as to be not detectable in some. The special talents, which very likely have genic determinants, e.g., as in music, mathematics, art (Scheinfeld, 1943), are absent in most people.

The instinctoid impulses can disappear altogether, as apparently animal instincts cannot. For example, in the psychopathic personality the needs for loving and being loved have disappeared and, so far as we know today, this is a permanent loss, i.e., the (adult) psychopathic personality is incurable by any known psychotherapeutic technique. Such destroyed needs may not return in some even when environmental conditions improve. Similar material has been obtained from the Nazi concentration camps. Bateson's and Mead's (1942) observations on the Balinese may also be pertinent. The adult Balinese is not a loving person in our Western sense and need not be. Since the motion pictures from Bali show that the infants and children cry and bitterly resent the lack of affection, we can only conclude that this loss of affectionate impulse is an acquired loss.

8. We have seen that instincts and flexible, cognitive adaptation to the novel tend to be mutually exclusive in the phyletic scale. The more of one we find, the less of the other we may expect. Because of this the vital and even tragic mistake (in view of the historical consequences) has been made from time immemorial of dichotomizing instinctive impulses and rationality in the human being. It has rarely occurred to anyone that they might *both* be instinctoid in the human being, and more important, that their results or implied goals might be identical rather than antagonistic.

It is our contention that the impulse to

know and to understand may be exactly as conative as the needs to belong or to love.

In the ordinary instinct-reason dichotomy, it is a badly defined instinct and a badly defined reason which are opposed to each other. If they were correctly defined in accordance with modern knowledge, they would be seen as not contrasting or opposing or even as strongly different from each other. "Healthy" reason, as definable today, and "healthy" instinctoid impulses point in the same direction and are *not* in contrast with each other. As a single example, all the scientific data now available indicate that it is psychiatrically desirable for children to be protected, accepted, loved, and respected. But this is precisely what children ("instinctively") desire. It is in this very tangible and scientifically testable sense that we assert instinctoid needs and rationality to be very probably synergic and not antagonistic. If this turns out to be true, we shall thereby have resolved the age-old problem of which should be master, instinct or reason, a question now as obsolete as, e.g., "Which should be the boss in a good marriage, the husband or the wife?"

9. From instinct theory, as understood at the time of its heyday, flowed many social, economic, and political consequences of the most conservative and even antidemocratic nature, as is conclusively demonstrated by Pastore (1938), especially in his analysis of McDougall and Thorndike (the writer would add Jung and perhaps Freud). These arose from the (mistaken) identification of heredity with fate, inexorable, irresistible, and unmodifiable.

This conclusion was erroneous, as we shall see. *Weak* instinctoid needs need a beneficent culture for their appearance, expression, and gratification, and are easily blasted by bad cultural conditions. Our society, for instance, must be con-

siderably improved before weak hereditary needs may expect gratification.

In any case Pastore's (1938) correlation is shown to be not an intrinsic one by the recently revealed necessity to use two continua and not just one. The continuum liberal-conservative has given way to the two continua of socialist-capitalist *and* democratic-authoritarian, even in scientific questions. There may now be counted environmentalist-authoritarian-socialist, or environmentalist-democratic-socialist, or environmentalist-democratic-capitalist, etc., etc.

In any case, to accept as intrinsic an antagonism between instincts and society, between individual interests and social interests, was a terrific begging of the question. Possibly its main excuse was that in the sick society it actually tends to be true. But, as Benedict has proved, it *need* not be true. And in the good society, or at least in the kind she describes, it *cannot* be true. Individual and social interests under healthy social conditions are synergic and *not* antagonistic (Maslow, 1950). The false dichotomy persists only because erroneous conceptions of both individual and social interests are the natural ones under bad individual and social conditions.

10. One lack in instinct theory, as in most other theories of motivation, was the failure to realize that impulses are dynamically related to each other in a hierarchy of differential strength. If impulses are treated independently of each other, various problems must remain unsolved, and many pseudoproblems are created. For instance, the essentially holistic or unitary quality of the motivational life is obscured and the insoluble problem of making "lists" of motives is created. In addition, the value- or choice-principle is lost which permits us to say one need is higher than another, more important than another, or even more

"basic" than another. By far the most important single consequence of this atomizing of the motivational life is to open the door to instincts toward Nirvana, death, quiescence, homeostasis, complacency, equilibrium. This is so because the *only* thing that a need taken discretely can do is to press for gratification, which is to say, its own obliteration.

This neglects the obvious fact that the gratification of any need, while putting that need to rest, allows other weaker needs which have been pushed aside to come into the foreground to press their claims. Needing never ceases. The gratification of one need "creates" another (Maslow, 1943b, 1948a, 1948b).

11. Co-ordinate with the "bad-animal" interpretation of instincts (Maslow, 1949) was the expectation that they would be seen most clearly in the insane, the neurotic, the criminal, the feebleminded, or the desperate. This follows naturally from the doctrine that conscience, rationality, and ethics are no more than acquired veneer, completely different in character from what lies beneath, and are related to that underneath as manacles to prisoner. From this misconception follows the phrasing of civilization and all its institutions, school, church, court, legislation, as bad-animality-restraining forces.

This mistake is so crucial, so tragedy laden, that it may be likened in historical importance to such mistakes as the belief in divine right of kings, in the exclusive validity of any one religion, in the denial of evolution, or in the belief that the earth is flat. Any belief that makes men mistrust themselves and each other unnecessarily and causes them to be unrealistically pessimistic about human possibilities must be held partly responsible for every war that has ever been waged, for every racial antagonism, and for every religious crusade.

This false theory of human nature, curiously enough, has been upheld by both instinctivists and anti-instinctivists to this day. Those who hope for a better future for the human species, the optimists, the Humanists, the Unitarians, the liberals, the radicals, and environmentalists in general all reject the instinct theory with horror because, so misinterpreted, it seems to condemn all human beings to irrationality, to war, and to divisiveness and antagonism in a jungle world.

The instinctivists, similarly misinterpreting, but refusing to struggle against unavoidable fate, have generally given up optimism with no more than a shrug of the shoulders. Some people of course have renounced it eagerly.

We are reminded here of the alcoholism into which some people go so eagerly, and some reluctantly; the ultimate effects are often similar. This explains why Freud can be found in the same camp with Hitler on many issues and why such wonderful individuals as Thorndike and McDougall could be forced to Hamiltonian and anti-democratic conclusions by the sheer logic of "bad-animal" instinctivism (Pastore, 1938).

Recognize instinctoid needs not to be "bad," but neutral or "good" and a thousand pseudoproblems solve themselves and fade out of existence.[1] As a

---

[1] Destructiveness, hostility, cruelty, masochism, greed, the tendency to dominate and exploit, all these have been considered "animal," innate, instinctive. It is only recently that we have been taught by the revisionist psychoanalysts that this "bad" side of human nature is a reactive *product* (rather than a cause) of frustration, unhappiness, warping, neurosis. The truly basic needs—the suggested substitute for the old instincts—as listed in another paper (Maslow, 1943b) are, after the physiological needs, for safety, belongingness, love, respect, self-esteem, autonomy, self-actualization (Maslow, 1950), knowledge, understanding, and beauty. There is certainly nothing bad, evil, or sinful about such desires; indeed most of them are considered by our culture to be "good."

single instance, the training of children would be revolutionized even to the point of not using a word with so many ugly implications as "training." The shift to acceptance of legitimate animal demands would push us toward their gratification and towards greater permissiveness.

In our culture, the average deprived child, not yet completely acculturated, i.e., not yet deprived of all his healthy animality, keeps on pressing for admiration, for safety, autonomy, for love, etc., in whatever childish ways he can invent. The ordinary reaction of the sophisticated adult is to say "Oh! he's just showing off," or "He's only trying to get your attention," and thereupon to banish him from the adult company. That is to say, this diagnosis is customarily interpreted as an injunction *not* to give the child what he is seeking, *not* to notice, *not* to admire, *not* to applaud.

If, however, we should come to consider such pleas for acceptance, love, or admiration as legitimate demands, of the same order as complaint of hunger, thirst, cold, or pain, we should automatically become gratifiers rather than frustrators. A single consequence of such a regime would be that both children and parents would have more fun, would enjoy each other more, and would surely, therefore, love each other more.

This ought not be misinterpreted as implying complete and indiscriminate permissiveness. Some minimum of acculturation, i.e., "training," acquisition of culturally demanded habits, would still be necessary, although in an atmosphere of basic-need gratification such peripheral and artificial acquisitions should make no particular trouble.

No permissiveness is implied, furthermore, with respect to neurotic needs, addiction needs, habit needs, familiariza-

tion needs, fixations, or any other non-instinctoid needs.

In any case there has been too easy an identification of animal instincts with "bad" animals like the wolf, tiger, or pig, rather than with better or at least milder animals like the deer, elephant, or dog. This projection or expression of an already existent world-view, though in itself amusing, has had many evil consequences throughout history, e.g., Darwin's relative neglect of co-operation in the animal world (Kropotkin, 1924). It is bad enough when zoological data are misapplied so as to exhort the human being to take some other species as a model for his own; it is even more damaging when the "worst" species are chosen as models. Why the wolf rather than the chimpanzee?

BASIC NEEDS AS INSTINCTOID

All the foregoing considerations encourage us to the hypothesis that basic needs are in some sense, and to some appreciable degree, constitutional or hereditary in their determination. Such a hypothesis cannot be directly proved today, since the direct genetic or neurological techniques which are needed do not yet exist. Other forms of analysis, e.g., behavioral, familial, social, ethnological, are generally of more service in disproving rather than in proving the hereditary hypothesis save in unequivocal cases, and our hypothesis is by no means unequivocal.

In the following pages are presented such available data and theoretical considerations as can be marshaled in support of the instinctoid hypothesis.

1. The chief argument in favor of offering new hypotheses is the failure of the old explanation. The instinct theory was

drummed out by a complex of environmentalistic and behavioristic theories which rested almost entirely on associative learning as a basic, almost an all-sufficient, tool of explanation.

On the whole it may fairly be said that this approach to psychology has failed to solve the problems of dynamics, e.g., of motives, their gratification, and frustration, and the consequences thereof, e.g., health, psychopathology, psychotherapy.

It is not necessary to go into a detailed argument to substantiate this conclusion. It is sufficient to note that clinical psychologists, psychiatrists, psychoanalysts, social workers, and all other clinicians use behavioristic theory almost not at all. They proceed stubbornly in an *ad hoc* way to build an extensive practical structure on very inadequate theoretical foundations. They tend to be practical men rather than theorists. Be it noted that to the extent that theory *is* used by the clinicians it is a crude and unorganized dynamic theory in which "instincts" play a fundamental role, i.e., modified Freudian theory.

In general all association theorists, and most other nonclinical psychologists as well, agree in admitting as "instinctoid" only such psychological impulses as hunger, thirst, etc. On this basis, and with the aid of the conditioning process alone, it is assumed that all higher needs are derived or learned. That is to say, we learn to love our parents because they feed us and in other ways reward us. Love, for this theory, is the by-product of a satisfactory business or barter arrangement, or, as the advertising people might say, it is synonymous with customer satisfaction.

No single experiment known to the writer has ever been performed that shows this to be true for the needs for love, safety, belongingness, respect, understanding, etc. Certainly the data of conditioning do not support such a hypothesis; on the contrary, such needs behave far more like the unconditioned responses upon which conditioning is originally based than like conditioned responses.

As a matter of fact, the theory runs into many difficulties even at the common-observation level. Why is the mother so eager to give out "rewards?" What are *her* rewards? How rewarding are the nuisances of pregnancy and the pains of parturition? If, indeed, the relationship is at bottom a *quid pro quo* arrangement, why should she enter into such a poor business deal? Furthermore, why do clinicians (Goldfarb, 1945; Levy, 1937; Ribble, 1943; Spitz, 1945) unanimously affirm that a baby needs not only food, warmth, good handling, and other such rewards, but also love, as if this were something over and above the rewards? Can this be no more than redundancy? Is the efficient and unloving mother more loved than the inefficient (or poverty stricken) and loving mother?

Many other disquieting questions suggest themselves. What exactly is a "reward"—even a physiological reward? We must assume that it is a physiological pleasure since the theory in question purports to prove that all other pleasures are derived from physiological ones. But are safety gratifications physiological, e.g., being held gently, not roughly handled, not dropped sharply, not frightened, etc.? Why does cooing to the infant, smiling at him, holding him in one's arms, paying attention to the young child, kissing him, embracing him, etc., *seem* to please him? In what sense is *giving*, rewarding, feeding the child, sacrificing for it, rewarding to the giver?

Evidence is accumulating that indicates the *manner* of rewarding to be as effective (or as rewarding) as the reward itself. What does this mean for the concept of reward? Does regularity and dependability of feeding reward the hunger need? Or some other? Which need is rewarded by permissiveness? By respect for the child's needs? By weaning or toilet training the child when *he* wishes? Why do institutionalized children develop psychopathologically so often, no matter how well cared for they may be, i.e., physiologically rewarded (Goldfarb, 1945; Spitz, 1945, 1946)? If love hunger is ultimately a request for food, why can it not be stilled by food? Can a sign or symbol for a satisfier be more satisfying than the satisfier itself?

Murphy's (1947) highly useful concept of "canalization" supplies us with relevant data. Murphy points out that arbitrary associations may be made between an unconditioned stimulus and any other stimulus because this latter arbitrary stimulus is only a signal and not itself a satisfier. When one deals with physiological needs, like hunger, *signals will not do—only satisfiers will do.* Only food will allay hunger. In a fairly stable world, such signal learning will take place and be useful, e.g., the dinner bell. But a far more important kind of learning which is *not* merely associative in nature is canalization, i.e., learning which objects are proper satisfiers and which not, and which of the satisfiers are *most* satisfying or most to be preferred for other reasons.

The relevance to our argument lies in the writer's observation that healthy gratification of love needs, respect needs, understanding needs, and the like is by canalization, i.e., by some intrinsically proper gratification and not by arbitrary associations. Where the latter do occur, we speak of neurosis and of neurotic needs, e.g., fetishism.

2. The ordinary biological criteria of instinct do not help us very much, partly because we lack data, but also because we must now permit ourselves considerable doubt about these criteria themselves. See, however, Howells' challenging experiment (Howells & Vine, 1940) and the theoretical papers following (Howells, 1945, 1947), as well as Schooland's experiment (1942), which indicate a new possibility of bypassing the difficulty.

As we have seen above, a serious mistake of the early instinct theorist was to overstress man's continuity with the animal world, without at the same time stressing the profound differences between the human species and all others. We can now see clearly in their writings the unquestioned tendency to define and list instincts in a universal animal way, i.e., so as to cover any instinct in any animal. Because of this, any impulse found in men and *not* in other animals was often thought, *ipso facto,* to be noninstinctive. Of course it is true that any impulse or need found in man *and* all other animals is thereby proved to be instinctive beyond the need for any further evidence. This does not however disprove the possibility that some instinctoid impulses may be found only in the human species, or as appears to be the case with the love impulse, in common with chimpanzees alone of all the animal world. Homing pigeons, salmon, cats, etc., each have instincts peculiar to the species. Why could not the human species also have characteristics peculiar to it?

The commonly accepted theory has been that instincts steadily drop out as we go higher in the phyletic scale, to be replaced by an adaptability based on a vastly improved ability to learn, to think, and to communicate. If we define an instinct, in lower animal style, as a complex of innately predetermined urge, readiness to perceive, instrumental behavior and skill, and goal object (and possibly even affective accompaniment if we could ever find a way of observing it), then this theory seems to be true. Among the white rats we find by this definition a sexual instinct, a maternal instinct, and a feeding instinct (among others). In monkeys the maternal instinct remains, the feeding instinct is modified and modifiable, and the sexual instinct is gone, leaving behind only an instinctlike urge. The monkey has to learn to choose his sexual mate and has to learn to perform the sexual act efficiently (Maslow, 1936). The human being has *none* of these (or any other) instincts left. The sexual and feeding urges remain, and perhaps even the maternal urge (Levy, 1942), although very faintly, but instrumental behavior, skills, selective perception, and goal objects must be learned, mostly in the sense of canalization. He has no instincts, only instinct-remnants and instinct-anlagen.

Side by side with this evolutionary development there *may* be found another one, namely for the gradual appearance as we ascend the phyletic scale of new and "higher" urges, instinctoid in nature, i.e., predetermined in greater or lesser degree by the structure and functioning of the organism. We say "may" because, although we present our hypotheses confidently for human beings, practically nothing is known about "higher" urges in subhuman animals. It remains a task for the future to decide to what degree, and in what sense, rats, dogs, cats, and monkeys show urges to safety, belongingness, love, respect, autonomy, self-confidence, curiosity, understanding, or beauty. (Be it noted again that we speak here of instinctoid *impulses* or *urges* and *not* of predetermined instrumental behaviors, abilities or mode of gratification, i.e., *not* of instincts.)

One group of experiments shows that this is a testable hypothesis. It has been shown by Crawford (1937) and Maslow (1940) that the young chimpanzee is an "altruistic," undominating, friendly, and fostering animal. This too is the impression of all who have worked with them. Wolfle and Wolfle (1939), repeating Crawford's experiments with rhesus macaques, found this *not* to be true for them. We may for the moment say then that humans may share with chimpanzees *alone* of all the species in the animal kingdom behavior that is altruistic, friendly, loving, etc., in a nonreflex sense (perhaps dogs should be included on the basis of common observation).

Other needs of this same sort, i.e., *stronger* in the human being than in other animals, are those for information, for understanding, and for beauty (or symmetry, order, perfection, etc.). Certainly no one will deny that these urges come to climax rather than to obsolescence in the human being. Men are the most scientific, the most philosophical, the most theological, and the most artistic of all animals. Furthermore, there can be little doubt that, at least for some people, these are needs in the same sense that safety, love, etc., are needs, but that they are instinct-anlagen rather than instinct-remnants.

Unfortunately, we have practically no experimental, or even clinical information about these needs, important though they obviously are.

It may be supposed on a priori grounds that extrinsic, acquired determinants of these urges, though undoubtedly present, are just as undoubtedly minimal. Most theorists hold or assume that the love need is created or constructed by conditioning upon physiological need satisfaction, e.g., that we *learn* to love because in the past the loved one has been a food-warmth-protection giver. This doctrine of derived needs would have to maintain then that the needs for knowledge, understanding, and beauty were acquired through conditioning upon physiological satisfaction, i.e., that they were and are signals for food, etc. Common experience supports such a contention almost not at all. It is, on the face of it, even less likely than the similar theory of acquisition of the love need.

3. One reason for considering basic needs to be instinctoid in nature has already been mentioned. Frustration of these needs is psychopathogenic, all clinicians agree. This is not true for neurotic needs, for habits, for addictions, for the preferences of familiarization, for instrumental needs, and it is true only in a special sense for the act-completion needs and for the talent-capacity-expression needs. (It will be the writer's contention in a forthcoming publication that at least this variety of needs *can* be differentiated on operational or on pragmatic grounds and *should* be differentiated for various theoretical and practical reasons. By basic needs in this context are meant specifically and only those described in Maslow, 1943b.)

Clearly, therefore, the basic needs stand in a special psychological and biological status. There is something different about them. The burden of proof that they are not appreciably instinctoid rests upon anyone who denies this.

4. The gratification of basic needs leads to consequences that may be called variously "desirable," "good," "healthy," self-actualizing. The words "desirable" and "good" are used here in a biological rather than in an a priori sense and are susceptible to operational definition. These consequences are those that the

healthy organism itself tends to choose, and strives toward under permissive conditions (Maslow, 1948a).

These psychological and somatic consequences have already been sketched out in a paper on basic need gratification (Maslow, 1948b) and need not be examined further here except to point out that there is nothing esoteric or nonscientific about this criterion. It can easily be put on an experimental basis, or even on an engineering basis, if we remember only that the problem is not very different, e.g., from choosing the right oil for a car. One oil is better than another if, with it, the car works better. It is the general clinical finding that the organism, when fed safety, love, and respect, "works" better, i.e., perceives more efficiently, uses intelligence more fully, thinks to correct conclusions more often, digests food more efficiently, is less subject to various diseases, etc.

5. The requiredness of basic need gratifiers differentiates them from all other need gratifiers. The organism itself, out of its own nature, points to an intrinsic range of satisfiers for which no substitute is possible as is the case, for instance, with habitual needs, or even with many neurotic needs. This requiredness is also responsible for the fact that the need is finally tied to its satisfiers by canalization rather than by arbitrary associations.

6. The effects of psychotherapy are of considerable interest for our purpose. It seems to the writer to be true for all major types of psychotherapy that, to the degree that they consider themselves successful, they foster, encourage, and strengthen what we have called basic, instinctoid needs, while they weaken, or expunge altogether the so-called "neurotic" needs. Especially for those therapies which explicitly claim only to leave the person what he essentially and deep-down *is*,

e.g., the therapies of Rogers, Fromm, Horney, etc., is this an important fact, for it implies that the personality has some intrinsic nature of its own, and is not created *de novo* by the therapist but is only *released* by him to grow and develop in its own style.

There is here in principle a gold mine of data for the theories of motivation, self-actualization, values, learning, cognition in general, interpersonal relations, acculturation and de-acculturation, etc. Unfortunately these data on the implications of therapeutic change have not yet been accumulated.

7. The clinical and theoretical study of the self-actualizing man, as far as it has gone, indicates unequivocally the special status of our basic needs. By those needs, and by no other, is the healthy life ruled (Maslow, 1950). Furthermore, these individuals are readily seen to be impulse-indulgent as the instinctoid hypothesis would demand rather than impulse-controlling. On the whole, however, we must say for this kind of research that, like the research on therapeutic effects, it is yet to be done.

8. Within anthropology, the first rumbles of dissatisfaction with cultural relativism came from field workers who felt that it implied more profound and irreconcilable difference between peoples than actually existed. The first and most important lesson that the writer learned from a field trip was that Indians are first of all people, individuals, human beings, and only secondarily Blackfoot Indians. By comparison with similarities, the differences, though undoubtedly there, seemed superficial. Not only they but all other peoples reported in the literature seemed to have pride, to prefer to be liked, to seek respect and status, to avoid anxiety. Furthermore, the constitutional differences observable in our own culture are observable all over the world, e.g., differences in intelligence, in forcefulness, in activity or lethargy, in calmness or emotionality, etc.

Even where differences have been seen they may confirm the feeling of universality since they are very often immediately understandable as reactions of the sort that *any* human being would be prone to in similar circumstances, e.g., reactions to frustration, to anxiety, to bereavement, to triumph, to approaching death.

It is granted that such feelings are vague, unquantifiable, and hardly scientific. Yet, taken together with other hypotheses presented above, and in other publications, the weak voice of instinctoid basic needs, the unexpected detachment and autonomy of self-actualizing people and their resistance to enculturation (Maslow, 1950), the separability of the concepts of health and of adjustment (Fromm, 1947), it seems fruitful to reconsider the culture-personality relationship so as to give a greater importance to determination by intraorganismic forces, at any rate in the healthier person.

If he is shaped without regard to this structuring, it is true that no bones are broken and no obvious or immediate pathology results. It is, however, completely accepted that the pathology *will come,* if not obviously then subtly, and if not sooner, then later. It is not too inaccurate to cite the adult neurosis as an example of such early violence to the intrinsic (though weak) demands of the organism.

The resistance of the person to acculturation in the interests of his own integrity and of his own intrinsic nature is then, or should be, a respectable area of study in the psychological and social sciences. The person who gives in eagerly to the distorting forces of his culture, i.e., the "well adjusted man," may be less healthy than the delinquent, the criminal, or the neurotic, who may be demonstrating by his reactions that he has spunk enough left to resist the breaking of his psychological bones.

From this same consideration, furthermore, arises what seems at first to be a topsy-turvy, hind-end-to paradox. Education, civilization, rationality, religion, law, government, all have been interpreted by most writers as being primarily instinct-restraining and suppressing forces. But if our contention is correct that instincts have more to fear from civilization than civilization from instincts, then perhaps it ought to be the other way about (if we still wish to produce better men and better societies); perhaps it should be at least one function of education, law, religion, etc., to safeguard, foster, and encourage, even to *teach* the recognition, expression and gratification of the instinctoid needs.

REFERENCES

Angyal, A. *Foundations for a science of personality.* New York: Commonwealth Fund, 1941.

Bateson, G., & Mead, M. *Balinese character.* New York: New York Academy of Sciences, 1942.

Beach, F. A. The neural basis of innate behavior, I. Effects of cortical lesion upon the maternal behavior in the rat. *Journal of Comparative and Physiological Psychology,* 1937, *24,* 393–440.

Bergson, H. *Creative evolution.* New York: Modern Library, 1944.

Bernard, L. L. *Instinct: A study in social psychology.* New York: Holt, 1924.

Cannon, W. *Wisdom of the body.* New York: Norton, 1932.

Cattell, R. *Personality.* New York: McGraw-Hill, 1950.

Crawford, M. P. The cooperative solving of problems by young chimpanzees. *Comparative Psychological Monographs,* 1937, *68,* 14.

Driesch, H. *Embryonic development and induction.* London: Oxford University Press, 1938.

Fenichel, O. *The psychoanalytic theory of neurosis.* New York: Norton, 1945.

Fromm, E. *Man for himself.* New York: Rinehart, 1947.

Gardner, M. Beyond cultural relativism. *Ethics,* 1950, *61,* 38–45.

Goldfarb, W. Psychological privation in infancy and subsequent adjustment. *American Journal of Orthopsychiatry,* 1945, *15,* 247–255.

Howells, T. H. Heredity as a differential element in behavior. *University of Colorado Studies,* 1933, *20,* 173–193.

Howells, T. H. The obsolete dogmas of heredity. *Psychological Review,* 1945, *52,* 23–34.

Howells, T. H. Lamarckian-Darwinian reorientation. *Psychological Review,* 1947, *54,* 24–40.

Howells, T. H., & Vine, D. O. The innate differential in social learning. *Journal of Abnormal and Social Psychology,* 1940, *35,* 537–548.

Kropotkin, P. *Ethics.* New York: Dial Press, 1924.

Kuo, Z. Y. A psychology without heredity. *Psychological Review,* 1924, *31,* 427–448.

Lashley, K. S. Experimental analysis of instinctive behavior. *Psychological Review,* 1938, *45,* 445–472.

Levy, D. M. Fingersucking and accessory movements in early infancy. *American Journal of Psychiatry,* 1928, *6,* 88–118.

Levy, D. M. Experiments on the sucking reflex and social behavior of dogs. *American Journal of Orthopsychiatry,* 1934, *4,* 203–224.

Levy, D. M. Primary affect hunger. *American Journal of Psychiatry,* 1937, *94,* 643–652.

Levy, D. M. On instinct-satiation: an experiment on the pecking behavior of chickens. *Journal of General Psychology,* 1938, *18,* 327–348.

Levy, D. M. Psychosomatic studies of some aspects of maternal behavior. *Psychosomatic Medicine,* 1942, *4,* 223–227.

Levy, D. M. *Maternal overprotection.* New York: Columbia University Press, 1943.

Levy, D. M. On the problem of movement restraint. *American Journal of Orthopsychiatry,* 1944, *14,* 644–671.

Marmor, J. The role of instinct in human behavior. *Psychiatry,* 1942, *5,* 509–516.

Maslow, A. H. A theory of sexual behavior in infra-human primates. *Journal of Genetic Psychology,* 1936, *48,* 310–338.

Maslow, A. H. Dominance-quality and social behavior in infra-human primates. *Journal of Social Psychology,* 1940, *11,* 313–324.

Maslow, A. H. A comparative approach to the problem of destructiveness. *Psychiatry,* 1942, *5,* 517–522.

Maslow, A. H. Conflict, frustration, and the theory of threat. *Journal of Abnormal and Social Psychology,* 1943, *38,* 81–86 (a)

Maslow, A. H. Dynamic theory of human motivation. *Psychological Review,* 1943, *50,* 370–396. (b)

Maslow, A. H. A preface to motivation theory. *Psychosomatic Medicine,* 1943, *5,* 85–92. (c)

Maslow, A. H. "Higher" and "lower" needs. *Journal of Psychology,* 1948, *25,* 433–436. (a)

Maslow, A. H. Some consequences of basic need gratification. *Journal of Personality,* 1948, *16,* 402–416 (b)

Maslow, A. H. Our maligned animal nature. *Journal of Psychology,* 1949, *28,* 273–278.

Maslow, A. H. Self-actualizing people: a study of psychological health. *Personality Symposium No. 2,* 1950, *1,* 11–34.

McDougall, W. *The energies of men.* London: Methuen, 1932.

McDougall, W. *Frontiers of psychology.* New York: Appleton-Century, 1935.

Murphy, G. *Personality.* New York: Harper & Brothers, 1947.

Murray, H. *Explorations in personality.* New York: Oxford University Press, 1938.

Niebuhr, R. *The nature and destiny of man* (Vol. 1). New York: Scribners, 1947.

Pastore, N. *The nature-nurture controversy.* New York: King's Crown Press, 1938.

Raup, R. *Complacency.* New York: Macmillan, 1926.

Ribble, M. *The rights of infants.* New York: Columbia University Press, 1943.

Scheinfeld, A. *You and heredity.* New York: Lippincott (Stokes), 1939.

Scheinfeld, A. *Women and men.* New York: Harcourt, Brace, 1943.

Schooland, J. B. Are there any innate behavior tendencies? *Genetic Psychology Monographs,* 1942, *25,* 219–287.

Spemann, H. *Embryonic development and induction.* London: Oxford University Press, 1938.

Spitz, R. Hospitalism. *Psychoanalytic Study of the Child,* 1945, *1,* 53–74.

Spitz, R. Anaclitic depression. *Psychoanalytic Study of the Child,* 1946, *2,* 313–342.

Watson, J. *Behaviorism.* New York: Norton, 1930.

Weiss, P. *Principles of development.* New York: Holt, 1939.

Wolfle, D., & Wolfle, H. M. The development of cooperative behavior in monkeys and young children. *Journal of Genetic Psychology,* 1939, *55,* 137–175.

Young, P. T. Appetite, palatability, and feeding habit: a critical review. *Psychological Bulletin,* 1948, *45,* 289–320.

Young, P. T. Food-seeking drive, affective process, and learning. *Psychological Review,* 1949, *56,* 98–121.

CHAPTER **20**

Needs-Press Theory

Introduction

Henry A. Murray (1893–   ) is the grand old man of personality theory. In addition to establishing his own needs-press theory, he has made contributions in a number of related areas, most notably the development of the well-known projective *Thematic Apperception Test* (TAT), employed by practically every clinical psychologist who does any kind of diagnostics.

The selection on this test included here illustrates Murray's sane and sensible views on diagnosis, as well as his general personality theory. He sees an individual as being pushed by internal needs and pulled by external press. (This word, *press,* is both singular and plural.) In employing the TAT, the sensitive interpreter can make shrewd guesses about what is bothering or motivating the individual, how he sees life, his general attitude toward himself and people. In short, in a miniature situation, the diagnostician can get a fairly complete portrait of the subject.

While the TAT instrument and its theory may seem obvious, Murray quite correctly points out its complexities and subtleties. Essentially, this instrument (as is true of all projective tests) is only as good as the examiner. Murray also explains that the TAT can be used in a formal, structured manner with various counts of diagnostic signs, or it can be employed in an informal, artistic manner. In any case, it represents an ingenious attempt to X-ray a person's mind.

HENRY A. MURRAY
Thematic Apperception Test

PURPOSE

The Thematic Apperception test, familiarly known as the T.A.T., is a method of revealing to the trained interpreter some of the dominant drives, emotions, sentiments, complexes, and conflicts of a personality. Special value resides in its power to expose the underlying inhibited tendencies which the subject or patient is not willing to admit or cannot admit because he is unconscious of them (Morgan & Murray, 1935).

DESCRIPTION

The material consists of nineteen pictures printed on white Bristol board and one blank card, calling for a total of twenty stories. Although it is, of course, possible to get along without any pictures by simply directing the subject to "make up a story," it has been found (1) that pictures are effective in stirring the imagination, (2) that they serve to force the subject to deal in his own way with certain classical human situations, and finally (3) that the advantages of using standard stimuli are here, as in other tests, considerable (Balken, 1945; Christenson, 1943; Murray et al., 1938; Rapaport, 1943).

Experience has shown that in the long run the stories obtained are more reveal-

ing and the validity of the interpretations is increased if *most* of the pictures include a person who is of the same sex as the subject. This does not mean that it is necessary to have two completely different sets of pictures, since some pictures of proved value contain no human figures; others portray an individual of each sex, and in others the sex of the one figure shown is questionable. In fact, eleven of the pictures (including the blank card) have been found suitable for both sexes.

There are four sets of the pictures (B for young boys; G for young girls; M for males over fourteen years; and F for females over fourteen years). A number that is not followed by any letter (B, G, M, or F) designates a picture which is suitable for both sexes and all ages. BM means that the picture is suitable for boys and older males; GF, that it is suitable for girls and older females. B means that the picture is for young boys only; G for young girls only; BG for boys and girls; M for males over fourteen only; F for females over fourteen only; and MF for males and females over fourteen. Each set is divided into two series of ten pictures each, the pictures of the second series being purposely more unusual, dramatic, and bizarre than those of the first. One full hour is devoted to a series, the two sessions being separated by a day or more. (The serial number is printed on the back of each picture.)

RATIONALE

The procedure is merely that of presenting a series of pictures to a subject and en-

Henry A. Murray, "Thematic Apperception Test." Reprinted from "Tests of Personality: Picture and Drawing Techniques," in *Contributions toward Medical Psychology,* edited by Arthur Weider. Copyright 1953, the Ronald Press Company, New York.

couraging him to tell stories about them, invented on the spur of the moment. The fact that stories collected in this way often reveal significant components of personality is dependent on the prevalence of two psychological tendencies: (1) the tendency of people to interpret an ambiguous human situation in conformity with their past experiences and present wants, and (2) the tendency of those who write stories to do likewise, i.e., draw on the fund of their experiences and express their sentiments and needs, whether conscious or unconscious.

If the pictures are presented as a test of imagination, the subject's interest, together with his need for approval, can be so involved in the task that he forgets his sensitive self and the necessity of defending it against the probings of the examiner, and, before he knows it, he has said things about an invented character that apply to himself, things he would have been reluctant to confess in response to a direct question. As a rule, the subject leaves the test happily unaware that he has presented the psychologist with what amounts to an X-ray picture of his inner self. Recent attempts to "standardize" the procedure of administration, scoring, and interpretation have yielded promising results (Aron, 1948; Piatrowski, 1949; Rosenzweig, 1949; Rosenzweig & Fleming, 1949; Rotter, 1946; Wyatt, 1947).

ANALYSIS AND INTERPRETATION OF THE STORIES

Training of the interpreter

A layman with refined intraceptive intuitions and beginner's luck can often, without any experience in testing, make valid and important inferences by feeling his way into the mental environment of the author of a set of T.A.T. stories; and even an old hand at the game must rely on the same process—empathic intuition, disentangled as far as possible from personal elements. No true scientist will scorn the use of a function which when properly disciplined is capable of yielding precise and pertinent information. Of course, intuition alone is highly unreliable; what is required is a rigorously trained critical intuition.

Besides a certain flair for the task, an interpreter of the T.A.T. should have a background of clinical experience and, if he is to get much below the surface, knowledge of psychoanalysis and some practice in translating the imagery of dreams and ordinary speech into elementary psychological components. In addition, he should have had months of training in the use of this specific test and much practice in analyzing stories when it is possible to check each conclusion against the known facts of thoroughly studied personalities. Interpretations *in vacuo* often do more harm than good, since the apparent plausibility of clever interpretations creates convictions which merely serve to confirm the interpreter in the error of his ways. T.A.T. stories offer boundless opportunities for the projection of one's own complexes or one's pet theories, and the amateur psychoanalyst who is disrespectful of solid facts is only too apt to make a fool of himself if, in interpreting the T.A.T., he gives free rein to his imagination. The future of the T.A.T. hangs on the possibility of perfecting the interpreter (psychology's forgotten instrument) more than it does on perfecting the material.

Necessary basic data

Before starting to interpret a set of stories the psychologist should know the following basic facts: the sex and age of the subject, whether his parents are dead or separated, the ages and sexes of his siblings, his vocation, and his marital status. Without these easily obtained public facts (which the T.A.T. was not designed to reveal) the interpreter may have difficulty orienting himself as he reads. A blind analysis is a stunt which may or may not be successful; it has no place in clinical practice.

MODES OF CONTENT ANALYSIS

In dealing with the content of stories, the method which we recommend is that of analyzing each successive event into (1) the force or forces emanating from the hero and (2) the force or forces emanating from the environment. An environmental force is called a "press."

The hero

The first step in analyzing a story is to distinguish the character with whom the subject has identified himself. This is (1) the character in whom the story-teller was apparently most interested, whose point of view was adopted, whose feelings and motives have been most intimately portrayed. He (or she) is usually (2) the one who most resembles the subject, an individual of the same sex, of about the same age, status or role, who shares some of the subject's sentiments and aims. This character, called "hero" (whether it be male or female) is usually (3) the person (or one of the persons) depicted in the picture, and (4) the person who plays the leading role in the drama (hero in the literary sense), who appears at the beginning and is most vitally involved in the outcome.

Although most stories have but one hero (readily distinguishable by these criteria), the interpreter should be prepared to deal with certain common complications. (1) The identification of the storyteller with the character sometimes shifts during the course of the story: there is a sequence of heroes (first, second, third, etc.). (2) Two forces of the subject's personality may be represented by two different characters, for example, an antisocial drive by a criminal, and conscience by a law-enforcing agent. Here we would speak of an "endopsychic thema" (internal dramatic situation) with two "component heroes." (3) The subject may tell a story that contains a story, such as one in which the hero observes or hears about events in which another character (for whom he feels some sympathy) is leadingly involved. Here we would speak of a "primary" and a "secondary" hero. Then (4) the subject may identify with a character of the opposite sex and express a part of his personality just as well in this fashion. (In a man this is commonly a sign of a high feminine component and in a woman of a high masculine component.) Finally, there may be no discernible single hero; either (5) heroship is divided among a number of equally significant, equally differentiated partial heroes (e.g., a group of people); or (6) the chief character ("hero" in the literary sense) obviously belongs to the object side of the subject-object situation; he is not a component of the story-teller's personality but an element of his environment. The subject, in other words, has not identified with the principal character to the slightest extent but has observed him as he would a stranger or disliked person with whom he had to deal. The subject himself is not represented or is represented by a minor character ("hero" in our sense).

Characterization of the heroes by the interpreter should include the following: superiority (power, ability), inferiority, criminality, mental abnormality, solitariness, belongingness, leadership, and quarrelsomeness (the degree to which he becomes involved in interpersonal conflicts).

Motives, trends, and feelings of the heroes. The interpreter's next task is to observe in great detail everything that each of the twenty or more heroes feels, thinks, or does, noting evidences of type of personality or of mental illness as well as everything that is unusual: either uncommon (or unique) or common but unusually high or low in intensity or frequency. (To be able to discriminate what is unusual, the interpreter must have had a good deal of experience with this test, beside knowing Rosenzweig's (Rosenzweig & Fleming, 1949) norms for the T.A.T.)

In describing or formulating the reactions of the heroes, the interpreter is free to use any set of variables he chooses. He may analyze the behavior in accordance with a comprehensive conceptual scheme which gives every psychologically significant variable its due place, or he may confine himself to the observation of a few traits. It all depends on what he wants to know about his subject. He may be interested in evidences of extraversion-introversion, of masculinity-femininity, of ascendance-submission; or he may be looking for signs of anxiety, guilt, or inferiority; or he may want to trace certain deep-rooted sentiments to their source.

Our practice is to use a comprehensive list of twenty-eight needs (or drives) classified according to the direction, or immediate personal goal (motive), of the activity. A need may express itself subjectively as an impulse, a wish, or an intention, or objectively as a trend of overt behavior. Needs may be fused so that one action satisfies two or more at once; or one need may function merely as an instrumental force, subsidiary to the satisfaction of another dominating need. Be-

side the needs, our list of variables belonging to the hero includes a few inner states and emotions.

The strength of each variety of need and of each variety of emotion manifested by the hero is rated on a 1 (one) to 5 (five) scale, 5 being the highest possible mark for any variable on a single story. The criteria of strength are intensity, duration, frequency and importance in the plot. The slightest suggestion of a variable (e.g., a flash of irritability) is given a mark of 1, whereas an intense form (e.g., violent anger) or the continued or repeated occurrence of a milder form (e.g., constant quarreling) is scored 5. Marks of 2, 3, and 4 are given for intermediate intensities of expression. After the twenty stories have been scored in this way, the total for each variable is compared to the standard score (if there is one available) for subjects of the given age and sex, and the variables which are either well above or well below the standard are listed and scrutinized in relation to each other.

Forces of the hero's environment

The interpreter should observe the details as well as the general nature of the situations, especially the human situations, which confront the heroes. Here again he should be set to underscore uniqueness, intensity, and frequency, and to record the significant absence of certain common elements. Special note should be taken of physical objects and human objects (other characters) which are not shown in the pictures but invented by the imagination of the story-teller. Mark the traits which recur among the people with whom the hero deals. Are they, for the most part, friendly or unfriendly? Are the women more friendly or less friendly than the men? What are the characteristic traits of the older women (mother figures) in the stories? of the older men (father figures)?

Our practice is to use a comprehensive list of press (kinds of environmental forces or situations) classified according to the effect that they have (or that they promise or threaten to have) upon the hero. In our list more than half the press directed toward the hero are trends of activity originating in other characters; that is to say, they are needs of the persons with whom the hero deals. This being understood, it is not hard to see that the concept of press can be extended to include the absence of required beneficial press (lack, deprivation, loss, dispossession) and also to include bodily disturbances to which the personality must adjust (physical pain, injury, disfigurement, disease). Here again, the strength of each press that occurs in the story is rated on a 1 to 5 scale, 5 being the highest possible mark for any press on a single story. As usual, the criteria of strength are intensity, duration, frequency and general significance in the plot. After rating the twenty stories, the total score for each press is compared to the standard score for subjects of given age and sex, and the press which are conspicuously high or low are recorded and examined in relation to each other.

Outcomes

The next important matter to which the interpreter should attend is the comparative strength of the forces emanating from the hero and the forces emanating from the environment. How much force (energy, determination, enduring effort, competence) does the hero manifest? What is the strength of the facilitating or beneficial forces of the environment as compared to the opposing or harmful forces? Is the hero's path of achievement difficult or easy? In the face of opposition

does he strive with renewed vigor (counteraction), or does he collapse? Does the hero make things happen, or do things happen to him? To what extent does he manipulate or overcome the opposing forces, and to what extent is he manipulated or overcome by them? Is he coercing or coerced? mostly active or mostly passive? Under what conditions does he succeed: when others help him? or when he strives alone? Under what conditions does he fail?

After committing an offense or crime, does the hero get properly punished? does he feel guilty, confess, atone and reform? or is the misdemeanor treated as a matter of no moral significance and the hero allowed to "get away with it" without punishment or fateful consequence? How much energy does the hero direct against himself?

Viewing each event, each interaction of press and need, from the point of view of the hero, the interpreter must estimate the amount of hardship and frustration experienced, the relative degree of success and failure. What is the ratio of happy and unhappy endings?

Themas

The interaction of a hero's need (or fusion of needs) and an environmental press (or fusion of press) together with the outcome (success or failure of the hero) constitutes a "simple thema." Combinations of simple themas, interlocked or forming a sequence, are called "complex themas." When used precisely, the term designates the abstract dynamical structure of an episode; when used loosely it means plot, motif, theme, principal dramatic feature of the story.

To take up the hero and the environment separately, as we have just outlined, involves the dislocation of the two fundamental elements of each concrete event. This is useful, since it is enlightening to know that a given subject's heroes manifest, let us say, an unusual amount of anxiety, passivity, and abasement or that their environments are peopled with many threatening domineering figures. But now the interpreter has reached the point where it is necessary to put reality together again; and he does this by taking each unusually high need in turn and noting the press with which it is most commonly combined in the stories; after which he observes with which needs and emotions the unusually high press most often interact. In this way the interpreter will obtain a list of the most prevalent themes (need-press combinations), to which he will add any other themes which, though not frequent enough to result in a high total score for the need or press involved, seem significant for one reason or another—uniqueness, vividness, intensity, explanatory value.

It is also possible to make an over-all thematic analysis without scoring the separate variables. Here it is a matter of viewing each story as a whole and picking out the major and minor themes, the plot and subplots. The question is: What issues, conflicts, or dilemmas are of the greatest concern to the author? There are common themes, for example, centering round problems of achievement, rivalry, love, deprivation, coercion and restraint, offense and punishment, conflict of desires, exploration, war, and so forth.

Interests and sentiments

These are treated separately since the author displays his own interests and sentiments not only by attributing them to his heroes but in his choice of topics and in his manner of dealing with these. Of par-

ticular importance is the positive or negative cathexis (value, appeal) of older women (mother figures), older men (father figures), same-sex women, and same-sex men (some of whom may be sibling figures).

INTERPRETATION OF SCORES

A set of stories is analyzed and scored at first regardless of the probable personal significance of their content. The result is a list of unusually high and unusually low variables (needs, emotions, and press) and a list of prevalent themes and outcomes, together with a host of observations too specific to be caught in the net of any conveniently brief-conceptual scheme. Then two tentative assumptions are made, to be corrected later if necessary. The first is that the attributes of the heroes (needs, emotional states, and sentiments) represent tendencies in the subject's personality. These tendencies belong to his past or to his anticipated future and hence stand presumably for potential forces which are temporarily dormant; or they are active in the present. (Of these past, present, or expected tendencies, the subject may be more or less unconscious.) They represent (not literally in most cases but symbolically) (1) things the subject has done or (2) things he has wanted to do or been tempted to do or (3) elementary forces in his personality of which he has never been entirely conscious, although they may have given rise to fantasies and dreams in childhood or later; and/or they represent (4) feelings and desires he is experiencing at the moment and/or (5) anticipations of his future behavior, something he would like to do or will perhaps be forced to do, or something he does not want to do but feels he might do because of some half-recognized weakness in himself.

The second assumption is that the press variables represent forces in the subject's apperceived environment, past, present, or future. They refer, literally or symbolically, to (1) situations he has actually encountered or (2) situations which in reveries or dreams he has imagined encountering, out of hope or fear, or (3) the momentary situation (press of the examiner and the task), as he apperceives it, and/or (4) situations he expects to encounter, would like to encounter, or dreads encountering. Roughly the press may be interpreted as the subject's view of his world, the impressions he is likely to project into his interpretations of an existing situation and into his anticipations of future situations.

Some knowledge of the subject's past history and present circumstances plus a little intuition is required to decide whether a given element belongs to the subject's past, present, or anticipated future. As it happens, the discrimination of the temporal reference is not a matter of critical importance.

To guide the intuitions of the interpreter from this point, all that can be offered in this short discussion are a few guiding principles coming out of several years of practical experience. The testing of these and other suggestions constitutes a program for the future. In any event the conclusions that are reached by an analysis of T.A.T. stories must be regarded as good "leads" or working hypotheses to be verified by other methods, rather than as definite diagnoses.

In arriving at his final conclusions the interpreter should take account of the following points:

1. If the test has been unskillfully administered, if the subject has not been involved in the task, if the stories are short and sketchy, the content may be psychologically irrelevant, composed for the most part of impersonal elements: (*a*) elements given in the picture, (*b*) parts of events witnessed by the subject, (*c*) fragments from books he has read or movies he has seen, or (*d*) inventions of the moment—none of these being representative of a determining tendency in his personality.

2. Under average conditions about 30 per cent of the stories (six out of twenty) will fall in the impersonal category, although even from these a few items of significance can usually be extracted.

3. One must not lean too heavily on the subject's judgment in deciding whether a given item is personal or impersonal. According to our findings, more than half of the content which subjects trace to newspapers, magazines, books, and movies are objective equivalents of unconscious memories or complexes in their own personalities. Some internal selective factor has operated to determine each subject's attention to, registration of and eventual recall of just these, rather than countless other, elements of his experience.

4. The T.A.T. draws forth no more than twenty small samples of the subject's thought. To suppose that these will invariably provide a skeleton of the total personality is unduly optimistic. Just as in a series of interviews or in a psychoanalysis there are some totally unproductive hours, so there are sets of T.A.T. stories composed of impersonal or superficially personal elements from which it is impossible to infer the underlying determinants of character.

5. It is convenient to distinguish two levels of functioning: first-level functioning—physical and verbal behavior (actual overt deeds); and second-level functioning—ideas, plans, fantasies, and dreams about behavior. The conduct of the sub-

ject in relation to the examiner and to the task belongs to the first level, but the content of his *stories* belongs to the second level. Since individuals vary greatly in ideomotor conductance (extent to which ideas and fantasies become objectified in action), the interpreter must be prepared to find subjects with low conductance whose stories are indicative of their mental preoccupations but not of their overt behavior, actual or potential.

6. It is also convenient to distinguish three, if not more, layers in normal socialized personalities: the inner layer is composed of repressed unconscious tendencies which in their crude form are never, or very rarely, expressed in thought (second level) and never, or very rarely, objectified in action (first level). The middle layer is composed of tendencies which appear in thought (second level) in undisguised form, may perhaps be confessed to one or more suitable individuals, and may also perhaps be objectified in action (first level) privately and secretly. The outer layer is composed of tendencies which are publicly asserted or acknowledged (second level) and/or openly manifested in behavior (first level). It is for the interpreter to determine, if he can, to which of these three layers each conspicuous variable noted in the T.A.T. stories belongs.

7. It may be stated, as a rough generalization, that the content of a set of T.A.T. stories represents second-level, covert (i.e., inner- and middle-layer) personality, not first-level, overt or public (i.e., outer-layer personality. There are plenty of ways of discovering the most typical overt trends; the T.A.T. is one of the few methods available today for the disclosure of covert tendencies. The best understanding of the total structure of personality is obtained when the psy-

chologist considers the characteristics of manifest behavior *in conjunction with* the T.A.T. findings.

8. Half-unmindful of the fact that they are dealing with imaginal productions, rather than records of actual behavior, some interpreters are inclined to assume that variables which are unusually strong and variables which are unusually weak in the T.A.T. stories will be unusually strong and unusually weak respectively in the subject's manifest personality. There is some pragmatic basis, to be sure, for this expectation, inasmuch as statistical studies have shown that with most variables there is a positive correlation between the strength of their imaginal (T.A.T.) expressions and the strength of their behavioral expressions. We cannot lean very heavily on this over-all finding, however, since not only do we find numerous individual exceptions, but in the case of certain other important drives and emotions, especially those which are customarily repressed, the exact opposite is generally true. Here one is reminded of the principle that currents of thought are more rigidly influenced by strong needs which have been inhibited or rested for a long time than by needs which have recently been fully satisfied or fatigued by overt action. What is revealed by the T.A.T. is often the very opposite of what the subject consciously and voluntarily does and says in his daily life. Thus the picture that emerges from this test may be unrecognizable by the individual's casual, or even intimate, acquaintances.

9. Although the T.A.T. was not designed to reveal first-level, outer-layer personality (public behavior), the interpreter can often guess some of its characteristic features by taking note of the following points:

a. The stories composed in the first session (in response to the first ten pictures) are more closely related to the outer layer of personality, as a rule, than those composed in the second session, many of which express inner-layer tendencies and complexes symbolically.

b. Tendencies which are not restricted by cultural sanctions are likely to be as strong in their overt as in their covert manifestations.

c. Knowing a few facts about the subject, the interpreter, feeling his way into the atmosphere of the stories and noting repetitions and elements congruent with these, can usually without much difficulty distinguish the portions (about 15 per cent of the stories) which are almost literally and consciously personal. Out of this nucleus of impressions a portrait of the middle- and outer-layer personality will usually emerge. Portions requiring depth interpretation are usually derived from the inner layer.

10. Experiments have shown that the sex of the examiner must be taken into account. This is especially true when analyzing the stories of a subject who entertains an unusual amount of hostility toward members of the sex to which the examiner belongs. The prestige and attitude of the examiner can also affect to some extent the course of some of the stories. One might predict that standard scores will not be exactly the same for all examiners, that some, for example, will, in the long run, instigate more affiliation and less aggression than will others.

11. Still more important as determinants are the life situation and the momentary emotional state of the subject. The average college man about to enter the armed forces will introduce the theme of war into at least two of his twenty stories. Marital conflicts will be prominent in the stories of a woman con-

templating divorce. A young man who has just been refused by his girl will receive an uncommonly high mark on the variable dejection, and so forth.

DEPTH INTERPRETATION

To summarize in a few paragraphs the theories and practices of psychoanalysis, a knowledge of which is necessary for depth interpretation, would be both presumptuous and misleading, since a little information might influence some amateurs to believe that they were Magi of the unconscious. Depth interpretation requires the examiner to orient himself so that he views each story and parts of each story as if the teller were a child trying with imagery to objectify his own body or certain functions or organs of his body (cf. a psychosomatic symptom) or to represent the body of another person or as if the teller were trying to depict in a disguised form a certain encounter with one of his parents or siblings or to suggest some traumatic event experienced in childhood. Inferences of this sort can be validated only by data derived from some kind of psychoanalysis, and it would be better if expert workers submitted their depth interpretations only to those analysts and others who have the ability and the opportunity to verify them.

FORMAL ANALYSIS

Under this heading we include the discrimination of a variety of attributes descriptive of the topic, structure, style, mood, degree of realism, and power of the plot and of the language of the stories. It is among these attributes that we look for evidences of temperament, emotional maturity, observational ability, intellectuality, aesthetic imagination, literary ability, verbal facility, psychological insight, reality sense, intraception-extraception, integrity (normality) of cognition, and so forth. Obsessional, manic and depressive trends are not difficult to recognize. Disjunctivity of theme and language and the occurrence in the narrative of incongruities of feeling and action and of bizarre elements—these bespeak mental disorientation. The first valuable contribution in this area of research was made by Masserman and Balken (1938).

Various manuals for treating T.A.T. data are available (Aron, 1949; Bellack, 1947; Clark, 1941; Stein, 1948; Thompson, 1949; Tomkins, 1947).

RELIABILITY

Seeing that the T.A.T. responses reflect the fleeting mood as well as the present life situation of the subject, we should not expect the repeat reliability of the test to be high, even though the bulk of the content objectifies tendencies and traits that are relatively constant. Studies on this point have been undertaken (Combs, 1946; Harrison & Rotter, 1945; Mayman & Kutner, 1947).

USES

The T.A.T. will be found useful in any comprehensive study of personality and in the interpretation of behavior disorders, psychosomatic illnesses, neuroses, and psychoses. As now constituted, it is not suitable for children under four years of age (Balken & Vander Veer, 1944). The technique is especially recommended as a preface to a series of psychotherapeutic interviews or to a short psychoanalysis (Bellak, Pasquarelli, & Braverman, 1949; Deabler, 1947; Freed & Eccker, 1946;

Rosenzweig, 1949). Since the T.A.T. and the Rorschach yield complementary information, the combination of these two tests is peculiarly effective.

REFERENCES

Aron, B. *A manual for analysis of the Thematic Apperception Test.* Berkeley, Calif.: Willis E. Berg, 1949.

Balken, E. R. Thematic apperception. *Journal of Psychology,* 1945, *20,* 189–197.

Balken, E. R. & Vander Veer, A. H. Clinical application of the Thematic Apperception Test to neurotic children. *American Journal of Orthopsychiatry,* 1944, *14,* 421–440.

Bellak, L. *Bellak T. A. T. blank: For recording and analyzing Thematic Apperception Test stories.* New York: Psychological Corp., 1947.

Bellak, L., Pasquarelli, B. A., & Braverman, S. The use of the Thematic Apperception Test in psychotherapy. *Journal of Nervous & Mental Disease,* 1949, *110,* 51–65.

Christenson, J. A. Jr. Clinical application of the Thematic Apperception Test. *Journal of Abnormal and Social Psychology,* 1943, *38,* 104–106.

Clark, R. M. A method of administering and evaluating the Thematic Apperception Test in group situations. *Genetic Psychology Monographs,* 1941, *31,* 3–55.

Combs, A. W. The validity and reliability of interpretation from autobiography and the Thematic Apperception Test. *Journal of Clinical Psychology,* 1946, *2,* 240–247.

Deabler, H. L. The psychotherapeutic use of the Thematic Apperception Test. *Journal of Clinical Psychology,* 1947, *3,* 246–252.

Eron, L. D. Frequencies of themes and identifications in the stories of schizophrenic patients and nonhospitalized college students. *Journal of Consulting Psychology,* 1948, *12,* 387–395.

Freed, H., & Eccker, W. F. The Thematic Apperception Test: Its value in routine psychiatric practice, *Disorders of the Nervous System,* 1946, *7,* 146–151.

Harrison, R., & Rotter, J. B. A note on the reliability of the Thematic Apperception Test. *Journal of Abnormal and Social Psychology,* 1945, *40,* 97–99.

Masserman, J. H., & Balken, E. R. The clinical application of fantasy studies. *Journal of Psychology,* 1938, *6,* 81–88.

Mayman, M., & Kutner, B. Reliability in analyzing Thematic Apperception Test stories. *Journal of Abnormal and Social Psychology,* 1947, *42,* 365–368.

Morgan, C. D., & Murray, H. A. A method for investigating fantasies: The Thematic Apperception Test. *Archives of Neurology and Psychiatry,* 1935, *34,* 289–306.

Murray, H. A., et al. *Explorations in personality.* New York: Oxford University Press, 1938.

Piatrowski, Z. A new evaluation of the Thematic Apperception Test. In W. Wolff (Ed.), *Personality: Symposia on topical issues, No. 2.* New York: Grune & Stratton, 1949.

Rapaport, D. The clinical application of the Thematic Apperception Test. *Bulletin of the Menninger Clinic,* 1943, *7,* 106–113.

Rosenzweig, S. Apperceptive norms for the Thematic Apperception Test: The problem of norms in projective methods. *Journal of Personality,* 1949, *17,* 475–482.

Rosenzweig, S. & Fleming, E. E. Apperception norms for the Thematic Apperception Test: An empirical investigation. *Journal of Personality,* 1949, *17,* 483–503.

Rotter, J. B. Thematic Apperception Tests: Suggestions for administration and interpretation. *Journal of Personality,* 1946, *15,* 70–92.

Stein, M. I. *The Thematic Apperception Test: An introductory manual for its clinical use with adult males.* Cambridge, Mass.: Addison-Wesley, 1948.

Thompson, C. E. The Thompson modification of the Thematic Apperception Test. *Rorschach Research Exchange,* 1949, *13,* 469–78.

Tomkins, S. S., with the collaboration of Tomkins, E. J. *The Thematic Apperception Test: The theory and technique of interpretation.* New York: Grune & Stratton, Inc., 1947.

Wyatt, F. The scoring and analysis of the Thematic Apperception Test. *Journal of Psychology,* 1947, *24,* 319–30.

CHAPTER **21**

Transactional Analysis

Introduction

Eric Berne (1910–1970), the developer of transactional analysis, was trained as a psychoanalyst, but, like a great many others who started in this modality, he became dissatisfied with what he had been taught and went on to develop his own theory. Essentially, transactional analysis is a here-and-now type of theory of human relationships which is the basis for a system of psychotherapy intended to improve these relationships, or transactions.

Berne has been compared to Sigmund Freud, especially in terms of his tripartite division of a person's "ego" state into Parent/ Child/Adult, which superficially appears similar to Freud's Ego/Id/ Superego. A more apt comparison, however, might be to Alfred Adler in terms of the dynamics of the interactions, with each party in a transaction having certain goals and adopting certain lifestyles in the attainment of these goals. For example, "script analysis," a technique discussed in this selection, is essentially similar to Adler's "lifestyle analysis."

The extremely rapid acceptance of this sytem of psychotherapy is most likely explained by the last paragraph in this selection, which points out the small technical vocabulary needed to handle a transactional analysis group.

ERIC BERNE
The formal aspects of transactional analysis

The formal exposition of the principles of transactional analysis has been set down in three previous volumes (Berne, 1961, 1963, 1964), and will be given here only in the barest outline. Those principles were first derived from actual clinical material in treatment groups and only later stated formally and supported by documentation. This process will be reversed here; the principles will be given first and the clinical aspects clarified later.

STRUCTURAL ANALYSIS

Ego states

Every human being has at his disposal a limited repertoire of ego states, which fall into three types. Parental ego states are borrowed from parental figures and reproduce the feelings, attitudes, behavior, and responses of those figures. Adult ego states are concerned with the autonomous collecting and processing of data and the estimating of probabilities as a basis for action. Child ego states are relics from the individual's childhood and reproduce his behavior and state of mind at a particular moment or epoch of his development, using, however, the increased facilities at his disposal as a grown-up. It is assumed that there are three organs which mediate the organization and implementation of these three types of ego states. The extero-

psyche is concerned with Parental ego states, the neopsyche with Adult ego states, and the archaeopsyche with Child ego states.

The superego, ego, and id as defined by Freud are regarded as determinants of special characteristics of each type of ego state, but neither the ego states themselves nor the organs that "give rise" to them correspond to the Freudian "agencies." Superego, ego, and id are inferential concepts, while ego states are experiential and social realities. The descriptive study of ego states takes precedence over the study of the influences that determine them. In doctrinal terms, structural analysis precedes psychoanalysis. In structural language, psychoanalysis is essentially a process of deconfusing the Child ego state, but that ego state must first be isolated and described, and the Adult ego state must simultaneously be decontaminated and recathected so that it is free to assist with the subsequent analytic work.

The term "transactional analysis" is used to describe the system as a whole, which is divided into a logical and clinically useful sequence of phases: structural analysis, transactional analysis proper, game analysis, and script analysis. The diagnosis of ego states has been described elsewhere (Berne, 1961), and is a special art to be cultivated by the therapist. A Parental ego state exhibited by a patient is referred to colloquially as his "Parent," an Adult ego state is called his "Adult," and an archaic ego state is called his "Child." Gratifying therapeutic results

Eric Berne, "The Formal Aspects of Transactional Analysis." From *Principles of Group Treatment* by Eric Berne. Copyright © 1966 by Eric Berne. Reprinted by permission of Oxford University Press, Inc.

may be obtained from structural analysis alone, hence it is worth-while for its own sake; the fact that it builds a solid foundation for further progress is an additional advantage.

The "weak ego"

Two special features of structural analysis should be mentioned. First, there is nothing in this approach which corresponds exactly to the "weak ego" of conventional terminology. Every human being (except perhaps some with the most severe types of organic brain injuries) is regarded as possessing the complete neurological apparatus for neopsychic functioning. In certain cases the Adult ego state may be spoken of as "weakly cathected," but it is never dealt with as though there were some inherent defect in its structure. In clinical practice it can be verified that even mentally retarded people and "deteriorated" schizophrenics possess the complete apparatus for Adult ego functioning, and the therapeutic problem is to cathect this apparatus in order that it may take its normal place in the patient's psychic organization. As an analogy: if no radio is heard in someone's house that does not mean he lacks one; he may have a good one, but it needs to be turned on and warmed up before it can be heard clearly.

In this respect, then, structural analysis is more optimistic than other therapeutic systems, and this optimism is warranted by the results. If a patient is treated as though he had a "weak ego," he is likely to respond accordingly; if he is treated as though he had a perfectly good ego which only needs to be activated, experience shows that there is a good chance that his Adult ego state will become more and more active in his life: that is, he will become more rational and objective toward the outside world and toward himself.

"Mature" and "immature"

The second distinguishing feature is that the words "mature" and "immature" are never used in transactional analysis. Some of the reasons for this have already been implied in the previous paragraph. In general those are rather fatuous conceptions based on an essentially patronizing attitude. It is not that one person is "mature" and another "immature"; it is merely that one person chooses to exhibit his Child ego state more often than another. To take two rather clear-cut examples: an alcoholic may have a high capacity for processing certain kinds of data during his working hours, but when he relaxes his Adult ego state after work, he may behave in a child-like way. On the other hand one who is thought of as "mature" by his associates—a steady, "co-operative" community leader—may one day turn out to be an embezzler or a murderer, taking almost everyone by surprise. The question raised by these commonplace cases is as follows: is the responsible man who commits indiscretions when he is intoxicated to be called "immature," and the man who lives compliantly until he commits a crime to be thought of as "mature?"

Special distinctions

The structural analyst must be familiar with certain functional distinctions in the Parent and Child. What is loosely spoken of as "the Parent" may signify either the Parental ego state—that is, a reproduction of nurturing, angry, or critical behavior on the part of one or both parents—or the Parental influence—that is, behavior historically determined by borrowed parameters. In the Parental ego state, a woman is behaving as mother behaved; under the Parental influence, she is behaving as mother would have liked; and this includes specific maternal permissions or instigations as well as the specific maternal prohibitions generally included under the concept of superego. Hence this purely transactional, behavioral approach avoids the complications and limitations imposed by words like "identification" and "superego," impositions which are largely irrelevant to therapeutic progress, at least in group treatment. The Child similarly is exhibited in two phases: the adapted Child, who is acting under the Parental influence, as evidenced by such adaptations as compliance or withdrawal; and the expressive Child, who acts autonomously in expressing creative, angry, or affectionate tendencies.

Second-order structural analysis

At a late stage in treatment, second-order structural analysis may be indicated. This will reveal that the Parent has its own internal structure, such as that shown in Figure 21.1, where that aspect of the patient's personality structure is divided into "mother" and "father" segments, each of these in turn having Parent, Adult, and Child components, since the actual mother and father, being human beings, also have the usual repertoires of ego states. For patients in an advanced stage of structural analysis, each subdivision of Figure 21.1 may have clinical and historical significance. Correspondingly, the Child ego state, at the time it was originally fixated, already had

Parent, Adult, and Child components, so that second order structural analysis may reveal an even more archaic ego state embedded in the Child ego state as currently exhibited by the patient. Thus a woman who ordinarily talks and acts like a ten-year-old girl may under stress feel and respond like a confused ("schizophrenic") two-year-old.

TRANSACTIONAL ANALYSIS

Complementary transactions

Transactional analysis consists of determining which ego state is active at a given moment in the exhibition of a transactional stimulus by the agent, and which ego state is active in the response given by the respondent. Complementary transactions are those in which the vectors are parallel; that is, the response complements the stimulus. A Parental husband speaking to a Child-like wife will ex-

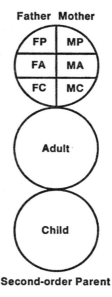

Father Mother

FP	MP
FA	MA
FC	MC

Adult

Child

Second-order Parent

FIGURE 21.1. Structural diagram of a personality

pect a Child-like response from her, as shown in Figure 21.2A. An Adult stimulus anticipates an Adult response, as shown in Figure 21.2B. This principle gives the first rule of communication: As long as the vectors are parallel, communication can proceed indefinitely. This is a necessary but not the sole condition for a "good" relationship; if the transactions become unpalatable enough, the relationship may deteriorate even though the vectors remain parallel.

Crossed transactions

If an Adult stimulus, such as an interpretation or comment, elicits a Child-to-Parent reaction, the vectors are crossed, as shown in Figure 21.3. This type of crossing is the commonest source of difficulty in social, occupational, and domestic life, and is known as Crossed Transaction Type I. In therapy it con-

stitutes the typical transference reaction. An Adult-to-Adult stimulus eliciting a Parent-to-Child response forms Crossed Transaction Type II (Figure 21.4). This is the classical counter-transference reaction. It will be apparent that there are seventy-two varieties of crossed transactions, but I and II are the commonest types found in clinical work. The study of crossed transactions gives rise to the second rule of communication: If the vectors are crossed, communication is broken off, and the relationship is "bad"; or in its clinical converse, if communication is broken off, there has usually (or always?) been a crossed transaction.

Ulterior transactions

Both complementary and crossed transactions are simple transactions. Ulterior transactions are of two types. The angular transaction (Figure 21.5) is most com-

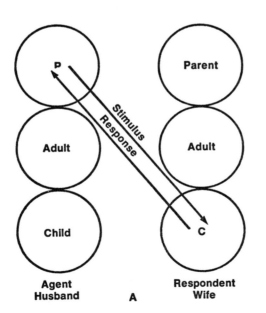 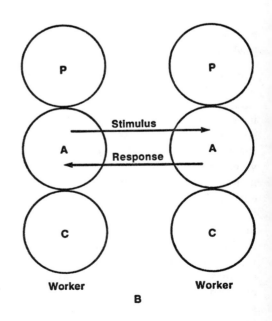

FIGURE 21.2. Complementary transactions

monly used by professionals who deal with people in their daily work. Here an ostensible Adult-to-Adult stimulus conceals another stimulus directed at the Child (or sometimes the Parent) of the respondent. The desired response comes from the respondent's Child, while the agent is in the clear because his stimulus was factually Adult. In the classical example a professional salesman who knew exactly what he was doing was showing some stoves to a housewife. She asked: "How much is that one over there?" The salesman replied: "You can't afford that one." The housewife declared defiantly: "That's the one I'll take." Here the salesman's answer to her question (his transactional stimulus) was factual, since his estimate of her financial standing was correct. As a professional salesman, however, he knew that her Child would be listening to his Adult judgment and would respond on the basis of some child-like

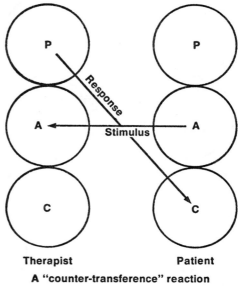

Therapist   **Patient**
A "counter-transference" reaction

FIGURE 21.4. A transactional diagram: Crossed Transaction Type II

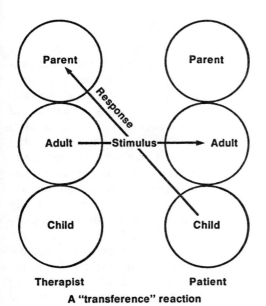

Therapist   **Patient**
A "transference" reaction

FIGURE 21.3. A transactional diagram: Crossed Transaction Type I

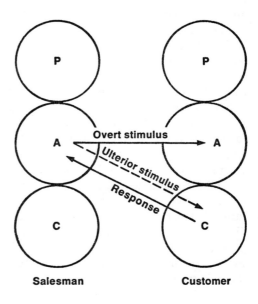

Salesman   **Customer**

FIGURE 21.5. An angular transaction

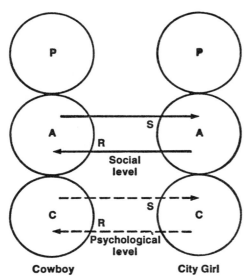

FIGURE 21.6.   A duplex transaction

feeling (although he used other terminology). She disregarded his accurate factual statement of what she could afford and responded the way he wanted her to.

The second type of ulterior transaction is the duplex transaction (Figure 21.6) in which at the social or overt level—the level found on the tape recording or the transcript—the stimuli and responses are Adult-to-Adult; but it is evident to a sophisticated observer that below the surface there is another and more meaningful level, the psychological or covert level, where there is Child-to-Child or Parent-to-Child communication. This duplicity gives rise to the third rule of communication: The behavioral outcome of an ulterior transaction is determined at the psychological and not at the social level. In its pragmatic (e.g. research) inverse, this rule reads: No kind or amount of processing of the social level can predict the behavioral outcome of an ulterior transaction; prediction is universally contingent on a knowledge of the psychological level.

GAME ANALYSIS

A game is a series of ulterior transactions with a gimmick, leading to a usually well-concealed but well-defined pay-off. For a detailed discussion the reader is referred to the writer's volume *Games People Play* (Berne, 1964). The most important thing to remember is that the definition of a game is quite precise, and unless a series of transactions is ulterior and has a definite pay-off it does not constitute a game. On the other hand, transactional games should not be confused with the types of games dealt with in mathematical game theory (Luce & Raiff, 1957), although there are certain similarities (Winkelman, 1964).

SCRIPT ANALYSIS

The script, or unconscious life plan of the individual, may not come to light except in very advanced groups. It will then be found that the patient is actually spending his whole life in a predetermined way based on decisions he made in early childhood, when he was much too young to make such serious commitments. These decisions remain unconscious, and choices of partners and action are rationalized on grounds which are actually irrelevant since the chief function of partners is to play roles in the protagonist's script, and the ultimate goal of human behavior (under ordinary civil conditions offering the possibility of choice) is to bring about the desired culmination of the script, which may be either tragic or constructive.

In clinical work the tragic scripts are the ones most often found, since people with constructive scripts do not usually feel the need for psychotherapy. In general a script is based on a childhood theory that somewhere there is a kind of Santa Claus who will bring the individual a magic gift to crown his life. People wait varying lengths of time before they fall into despair about the appearance of this Santa Claus, and it is this despair which, other things being equal, determines when they seek treatment—some at 20, some at 40, and some at 60. Failing "Santa Claus," there are four alternatives from which the individual can choose. The most decisive is suicide in one form or another. The second choice is sequestration from society, along with other people in despair, in a state hospital or a prison (or sometimes in isolated areas or in certain types of rooming houses found in big cities). The third alternative is to get rid of the people who are held to be responsible for the failure—by divorce, homicide, sending the children to boarding school, etc. The fourth alternative is getting better, which means to give up the hope of Santa Claus, to abandon previous destructive games, and to start anew living in the world as it is. It will be apparent that script analysis by its very nature has an existential quality.

TIME STRUCTURING

In order to analyse most profitably the proceedings of groups, there are two approaches. The first is descriptive, dividing the proceedings into discussion, description, and expression. Discussion is concerned with events that are removed from the current group meeting in time or place, including discussions of what happened at the last meeting. In some new groups a definite geographical and temporal progression can be noted. The members begin by talking about things that happened far away and years ago, in Philadelphia or in Alaska, and gradually approach the place and time of the current group meeting. When they arrive there, the discussion takes on a more personal nature, typically beginning with shoes and working upward. Discussion is usually an evasive maneuver. Description is an intellectual way of handling feelings. In structural language the Adult tells the group what the Child is feeling, but the Child himself does not show in such a description. Expression means the direct expression of affect concerning the here and now at the time the affect is felt. Discussion and description are essentially pastimes, and expression may be part of a game or it may signify progress toward genuine game-free intimacy. The last distinction is crucial for therapeutic progress.

Time structuring in groups is based on particular needs.

1. The least differentiated is stimulus hunger, which drives the individual to social action in order to avoid sensory deprivation.

2. More specific is recognition hunger, an Adult's version of the infant's need to be touched, in which "verbal touching" replaces physical touching. The unit of recognition is called a "stroke," by analogy to physical caressing in infancy, where the units more literally take the form of strokes.

3. Structure hunger expresses the antipathy to monotony, stereotypy, and boredom. People are willing to pay almost any price to have their time structured for them, since few are capable of structuring their own time autonomously

for very long. Hence the large salaries paid to entertainers.

4. A derivative of structure hunger is leadership hunger. One of the most important functions of a leader is to supply purposeful programs on the basis of which the members can structure their time. A psychotherapist satisfies this hunger, for example, by structuring the group in such a way as to promote the most economical, stable, and speedy recoveries.

The options open to a member for structuring his time at any kind of gathering (roughly in order of safeness) are as follows:

1. Withdrawal. There are three kinds of withdrawal:

a. Extraneous fantasies, in which the individual mentally leaves the gathering to indulge in fantasies of what he would do elsewhere.

b. Autistic transactions. These may be either *unadapted* or *adapted.* Unadapted autistic transactions are those which are impractical under the circumstances, such as fantasies of rape and killing involving members of the gathering. Adapted autistic transactions are found in inhibited individuals who may have something to say which is quite appropriate to the situation, but who are too shy to say it.

2. Rituals. These are stereotyped, predictable exchanges such as greeting and farewell rituals. The unit of ritualistic exchanges is the stroke.

3. Pastimes. Pastimes are similar to rituals except that the transactions are less stereotyped and take the less ceremonial form of multiple-choice sentence-completion transactions as in the pastime called "General Motors": "I like a (Chevrolet, Ford, Plymouth) better than a (Chevrolet, Ford, Plymouth) because (complete in 25 words or less)." The respondent then

says: "Yes, very true, but might I just add one item: *I* like a (Chevrolet, Ford, Plymouth) better than a (Chevrolet, Ford, Plymouth) because (complete in 25 words or less)."

4. Activity. An activity is what is commonly called work. Since the kind of therapy group we are interested in here does not engage in such activities, they do not present a problem to the therapist. Briefly, activities are programed by the external material of the activity itself so that the transactions are based on the needs of the moment; e.g. "Pass me the hammer" is said when the external material demands that a hammer be used.

5. Games. Since the experienced transactional therapist will quickly break up rituals and pastimes to move on to games, and since, on the other hand, real intimacy rarely occurs in groups, most of the proceedings of transactional groups will consist of games and game analysis. These will be amply illustrated below.

6. Intimacy. Intimacy is a game-free exchange of internally programed affective expressions, and must be sharply distinguished from pseudo-intimacy, which is common in institutionalized forms of group therapy where affective expression is encouraged without careful assessment of its authenticity. In the latter case the affective expression is largely socially (externally) rather than internally programed, and is usually part of a game in which the patient compliantly participates. It is different from the poignant experience which ensues when real intimacy, on the rarest of occasions, occurs in a group.

One advantage of transactional analysis, as previously noted, is that the technical vocabulary needed to handle the proceedings of a treatment group is relatively small. A clear understanding of four words—Parent, Adult, Child, and game—is the primary requirement for a short-term group or for the first phase of a long-term group, and selections from the secondary vocabulary (such as "script") can be added as need arises.

REFERENCES

Berne, E. *Transactional analysis in psychotherapy.* New York: Grove, 1961.

Berne, E. *The structure and dynamics of organizations and groups.* Philadelphia: Lippincott, 1963(a).

Berne, E. *Games people play.* New York: Grove, 1964.

Luce, R. D., & Raiff, H. *Games and decisions.* New York: John Wiley & Sons, 1957.

Winkelman, N. W. A clinical and sociocultural study of 200 psychiatric patients started on chlorpromazine ten and one-half years ago. *American Journal of Psychiatry,* 1964, *120,* 861–869.

CHAPTER **22**

Developmental Theory

Introduction

Erik Homberger Erikson (1902–   ), an original thinker who allies himself with psychoanalysis even though his ideas are far from Freud's, is chiefly known for his conception of the necessary psychological stages of growth people go through. The individual must pass these various stages but can succeed or fail in any of them. One who fails may proceed to further stages and appear to be an adult, but nonetheless that person will be incapacitated.

Erikson identifies eight developmental stages, in comparison to Freud's three stages of oral, anal, and phallic development. The stages identified by Erikson—trust vs. mistrust, autonomy vs. shame or doubt, initiative vs. guilt, industry vs. inferiority, identity vs. role confusion, intimacy vs. isolation, generativity vs. stagnation and integrity vs. despair—occur from the first year of life (trust vs. mistrust) to late adulthood (integrity vs. despair).

Each stage of life presents a crisis kind of decision concerning where to go. The baby must, on the continuum of trust/mistrust, make some sort of decision which will color its whole life. The importance of these ideas is that they make it possible to view individuals as in a constant process of growth and development and to identify crisis stages. Of all the stages, the one Erikson has mainly concerned himself with is that of adolescence (stage 5, identity vs. role confusion). In this selection you will find Erikson's sensitive and sympathetic views about the problems of adolescence.

ERIK H. ERIKSON
Memorandum on youth

I

In responding to the inquiry of the Commission on the Year 2000, I will take the liberty of quoting the statements put to me in order to reflect on some of the stereotyped thinking about youth that has become representative of us, the older generation. This, it seems to me, is prognostically as important as the behavior of the young people themselves; for youth is, after all, a *generational phenomenon,* even though its problems are now treated as those of an outlandish tribe descended on us from Mars. The actions of young people are always in part and by necessity reactions to the stereotypes held up to them by their elders. To understand this becomes especially important in our time when the so-called communications media, far from merely mediating, interpose themselves between the generations as manufacturers of stereotypes, often forcing youth to live out the caricatures of the images that at first they had only "projected" in experimental fashion. Much will depend on what we do about this. In spite of our pretensions of being able to study the youth of today with the eyes of detached naturalists, we are helping to make youth in the year 2000 what it will be by the kinds of questions we now ask. So I will point out the ideological beams in our eyes as I attempt to put into words what I see ahead. I will begin with questions that are diagnostic and then proceed to those that are more prognostic in character.

I would assume that adolescents today and tomorrow are struggling to define new modes of conduct which are relevant to their lives.

Young people of a questioning bent have always done this. But more than any young generation before and with less reliance on a meaningful choice of traditional world images, the youth of today is forced to ask what is *universally relevant* in human life in this technological age at this junction of history. Even some of the most faddish, neurotic, delinquent preoccupation with "their" lives is a symptom of this fact.

Yet, this is within the context of two culture factors which seem to be extraordinary in the history of moral temper. One is the scepticism of all authority, the refusal to define natural authority (perhaps even that of paternal authority) and a cast of mind which is essentially anti-institutional and even antinomian.

I do not believe that even in the minority of youths to whom this statement is at all applicable there is a scepticism of *all* authority. There is an abiding mistrust of people who act authoritatively without authentic authority or refuse to assume the authority that is theirs by right and necessity. Paternal authority? Oh, yes—

Erik H. Erikson, "Memorandum on Youth." Reprinted by permission of *Daedalus,* Journal of the American Academy of Arts and Sciences, Boston, Massachusetts. Summer 1967, *Toward the Year 2000: Work in Progress.*

pompous fathers have been exposed everywhere by the world wars and the revolutions. It is interesting, though, that the word *paternal* is used rather than *parental,* for authority, while less paternal, may not slip altogether from the parent generation, insofar as a better balance of maternal and paternal authority may evolve from a changing position of women. As a teacher, I am more impressed with our varying incapacity to own up to the almost oppressive authority we really do have in the minds of the young than in the alleged scepticism of *all* authority in the young. Their scepticism, even in its most cynical and violent forms, often seems to express a good sense for what true authority is, or should be, or yet could be. If they "refuse to define natural authority"—are they not right if they indicate by all the overt, mocking, and challenging kinds of "alienation" that it is up to *us* to help them define it, or rather redefine it, since we have undermined it—and feel mighty guilty?

As to the essentially anti-institutional cast of mind, one must ask what alternative is here rejected. It appears that the majority of young people are, in fact, all too needy for, trusting in, and conforming to present institutions, organizations, parties, industrial complexes, supermachineries—and this because true personal authority is waning. Even the anti-institutional minority (whom we know better and who are apt to know our writings) seem to me to plead with existing institutions for permission to rebel—just as in private they often seem to plead with their parents to love them doubly for rejecting them. And are they not remarkably eager for old and new uniforms (a kind of uniformity of nonconformity), for public rituals, and for a collective style of individual isolation? Within this minority, however, as well as in the majority, there are great numbers who are deeply interested in and responsive to a more concerted critique of institutions from a newer and more adequate ethical point of view than we can offer them.

The second factor is an extraordinary hedonism—using the word in the broadest sense—in that there is a desacralization of life and an attitude that all experience is permissible and even desirable.

Again, the word *hedonism* illustrates the way in which we use outdated terms for entirely new phenomena. Although many young people entertain a greater variety of sensual and sexual experiences than their parents did, I see in their pleasure seeking relatively little relaxed joy and often compulsive and addictive search for *relevant* experience. And here we should admit that our generation and our heritage made "all" experience relative by opening it to ruthless inquiry and by assuming that one could pursue radical enlightenment without changing radically or, indeed, changing the coming generations radically. The young have no choice but to experiment with what is left of the "enlightened," "analyzed," and standardized world that we have bequeathed to them. Yet their search is not for all-permissibility, but for new logical and ethical boundaries. Now only direct experience can offer correctives that our traditional mixture of radical enlightenment and middle-class moralism has failed to provide. I suspect that "hedonistic" perversity will soon lose much of its attractiveness in deed and in print when the available inventory has been experimented with and found only moderately satisfying, once it is permitted. New boundaries will then emerge from new ways of finding out what really counts, for there is much latent affirmation and much overt solidarity in all this search. All you have to do is to see some of these nihilists with babies, and you are less sure of what one of the statements as yet to be quoted terms the "Hegelian certainty" that the next generation will be even more alienated.

As for the desacralization of life by the young, it must be obvious that our generation desacralized their lives by (to mention only the intellectual side) naïve scientism, thoughtless scepticism, dilettante political opposition, and irresponsible technical expansion. I find, in fact, more of a search for resacralization in the younger than in the older generation.

At the same time society imposes new forms of specialization, of extended training, of new hierarchies and organizations. Thus, one finds an unprecedented divorce between the culture and the society. And, from all indications, such a separation will increase.

Here, much depends on what one means by the word *imposes*. As I have already indicated, in much of youth new hierarchies and organizations are accepted and welcome. We are apt to forget that young people (if not burdened with their parents' conflicts) have no reason to feel that radical change as such is an imposition. The unprecedented divorce we perceive is between *our* traditional culture (or shall I spell it *Kultur?*) and the tasks of *their* society. A new generation growing up with technological and scientific progress may well experience technology and its new modes of thought as the link between a new culture and new forms of society.

In this respect, assuming this hypothesis is true, the greatest strains will be on the youth. This particular generation, like its

predecessors, *may come back to some form of accommodation with the society as it grows older and accepts positions within the society. But the experiences also leave a "cultural deposit" which is cumulative consciousness and—to this extent I am a Hegelian—is irreversible, and the next generation therefore starts from a more advanced position of alienation and detachment.*

Does it make sense that a generation involved in such unprecedented change should "come back to some form of accommodation with the society"? This was the fate of certain rebels and romantics in the past; but there may soon be no predictable society to "come back to," even if coming back were a viable term or image in the minds of youth. Rather, I would expect the majority to be only too willing to overaccommodate to the exploiters of change, and the minority we speak of to feel cast off until their function becomes clearer—with whatever help we can give.

II

Having somewhat summarily disavowed the statements formulated by others, I would now like to ask a question more in line with my own thinking, and thereby not necessarily more free from stereotypy: Where *are* some of the principal contemporary sources of identity strength? This question leads us from diagnosis to prognosis, for to me a sense of identity (and here the widest connotation of the term will do) includes a sense of anticipated future. The traditional sources of identity strength—economic, racial, national, religious, occupational—are all in the process of allying themselves with a new world-image in which the vision of an anticipated future and, in fact, of a future in a permanent state of planning will take over much of the power of tradition. If I call such sources of identity strength *ideological,* I am using the word again most generally to denote a system of ideas providing a convincing world-image. Such a system each new generation needs —so much so that it cannot wait for it to be tested in advance. I will call the two principal ideological orientations basic to future identities the *technological* and the *humanist* orientations, and I will assume that even the great politico-economic alternatives will be subordinated to them.

I will assume, then, that especially in this country, but increasingly also abroad, masses of young people feel attuned, both by giftedness and by opportunity, to the technological and scientific promises of indefinite progress; and that these promises, if sustained by schooling, imply a new ideological world-image and a new kind of identity for many. As in every past technology and each historical period, there are vast numbers of individuals who can combine the dominant techniques of mastery and domination with their identity development, and *become* what they *do.* They can settle on that *cultural consolidation* that follows shifts in technology and secures what mutual verification and what transitory familiarity lie in doing things together and in doing them right—a rightness proved by the bountiful response of "nature," whether in the form of the prey bagged, the food harvested, the goods produced, the money made, the ideas substantiated, or the technological problems solved.

Each such consolidation, of course, also makes for new kinds of entrenched privileges, enforced sacrifices, institutionalized inequalities, and built-in contradictions that become glaringly obvious to outsiders—those who lack the appropriate gifts and opportunities or have a surplus of not quite appropriate talents. Yet it would be intellectual vindictiveness to overlook the sense of embeddedness and natural flux that each age provides in the midst of the artifacts of organization; how it helps to bring to ascendance some particular type of man and style of perfection; how it permits those thus consolidated to limit their horizon effectively so as *not* to see what might destroy their newly won unity with time and space or expose them to the fear of death—and of killing. Such a consolidation along technological and scientific lines is, I submit, now taking place. Those young people who feel at home in it can, in fact, go along with their parents and teachers— not too respectfully, to be sure—in a kind of *fraternal identification,* because parents and children can jointly leave it to technology and science to provide a self-perpetuating and self-accelerating way of life. No need is felt to limit expansionist ideals so long as certain old-fashioned rationalizations continue to provide the hope (a hope that has long been an intrinsic part of an American ideology) that in regard to any possible built-in evil in the very nature of super-organizations, appropriate brakes, corrections, and amendments will be invented in the nick of time and without any undue investment of strenuously new principles. While they "work," these super-machineries, organizations, and associations provide a sufficiently adjustable identity for all those who feel actively engaged in and by them.

All of us sense the danger of overaccommodation in this, as in any other consolidation of a new world-image, and maybe the danger *is* greater today. It is the danger that a willful and playful testing of the now limitless range of the technically possible will replace the search for the criteria for the optimal and the ethically permissible, which includes what can be given on from generation to generation. This can only cause subliminal panic, especially where the old decencies will prove glaringly inadequate, and where the threat or the mere possibility of overkill can be denied only with increasing mental strain—a strain, incidentally, which will match the sexual repression of the passing era in unconscious pathogenic power.

It is against this danger, I think, that the nonaccommodators put their very existence "on the line," often in a thoroughly confounding way because the manifestations of alienation and commitment are sometimes indistinguishable. The insistence on the question "to be or not to be" always looks gratuitously strange to the consolidated. If the question of being oneself and of dying one's own death in a world of overkill seems to appear in a more confused and confusing form, it is the ruthless heritage of radical enlightenment that forces some intelligent young people into a seemingly cynical pride, demanding that they be human without illusion, naked without narcissism, loving without idealization, ethical without moral passion, restless without being classifiably neurotic, and political without lying: truly a utopia to end all utopias. What should we call this youth? *Humanist* would seem right if by this we mean a recovery, with new implications, of man as the measure, a man far grimmer and with much less temptation to congratulate himself on his exalted position in the universe, a self-congratulation that has in the past always encouraged more cruel and more thoughtless consolidations. The new humanism ranges from an *existential* insistence that every man *is* an island unto himself to a new kind of humaneness that is more than compassion for stray animals and savages, and a decidedly *humanitarian* ac-

tivism ready to meet concrete dangers and hardships in the service of assisting the underprivileged anywhere. Maybe *universalist* would cover all this better, if we mean by it an insistence on the widest range of human possibilities—beyond the technological.

But whatever you call it, the universalist orientation, no less than the technological one, is a *cluster* of ideas, images, and aspirations, of hopes, fears, and hates; otherwise, neither could lay claim to the identity development of the young. *Somewhat* like the "hawks" and the "doves," the technologists and the universalists seem almost to belong to different species, living in separate ecologies. "Technological" youth, for example, expects the dominant forces in foreign as well as in domestic matters to work themselves out into some new form of balance of power (or is it an old-fashioned balance of entirely new powers?). It is willing, for the sake of such an expectation, to do a reasonable amount of killing—and of dying. "Humanist" youth, on the other hand, not only opposes unlimited mechanization and regimentation, but also cultivates a sensitive awareness of the humanness of any individual in gunsight range. The two orientations must obviously oppose and repel each other totally; the acceptance of even a part of one could cause an ideological slide in the whole configuration of images and, it follows, in the kind of courage to be—and to die. These two views, therefore, face each other as if the other were *the* enemy, although he may be brother or friend—and, indeed, oneself at a different stage of one's own life, or even in a different mood of the same stage.

Each side, of course, is overly aware of the dangers inherent in the other. In fact, it makes out of the other, in my jargon, a negative identity. I have sketched the danger felt to exist in the technological orientation. On the "humanist" side, there is the danger of a starry-eyed faith in the certainty that if you "mean it," you can move quite monolithic mountains, and of a subsequent total inertia when the mountain moves only a bit at a time or slides right back. This segment of youth lacks as yet the leadership that would replace the loss of revolutionary tradition, or any other tradition of discipline. Then there is the danger of a retreat into all kinds of Beat snobbishness or into parallel private worlds, each with its own artificially expanded consciousness.

III

As one is apt to do in arguing over diagnosis, I have now overdrawn two "ideal" syndromes so as to consider the prognosis suggested in a further question presented to me:

Is it possible that the fabric of traditional authority has been torn so severely in the last decades that the re-establishment of certain earlier forms of convention is all but unlikely?

I have already indicated that I would answer this question in the affirmative; I would not expect a future accommodation to be characterized by a "coming back" either to conventions or to old-fashioned movements. Has not every major era in history been characterized by a division into a new class of *power-specialists* (who "know what they are doing") and an intense new group of *universalists* (who "mean what they are saying")? And do not these two poles determine an era's character? The specialists ruthlessly test the limits of power, while the universalists always in remembering man's soul also remember the "poor"—

those cut off from the resources of power. What is as yet dormant in that third group, the truly under-privileged, is hard to say, especially if an all-colored anticolonial solidarity that would include our Negro youth should emerge. But it would seem probable that all new revolutionary identities will be drawn into the struggle of the two ideological orientations sketched here, and that nothing could preclude a fruitful polarity between these two orientations—provided we survive.

But is not the fact that we are still here already a result of the polarization I have spoken of? If our super-technicians had not been able to put warning signals and brakes into the very machinery of armament, certainly our universalists would not have known how to save or how to govern the world. It also seems reasonable to assume that without the apocalyptic warnings of the universalists, the new technocrats might not have been shocked into restraining the power they wield.

What speaks for a fruitful polarization is the probability that a new generation growing up with and in technological and scientific progress as a matter of course will be forced by the daily confrontation with unheard-of practical and theoretical possibilities to entertain radically new modes of thought that may suggest daring innovations in both culture and society. "Humanist" youth, in turn, will find some accommodation with the machine age in which they, of course, already participate in their daily needs and habits. Thus, each group may reach in the other what imagination, sensitivity, or commitment may be ready for activation. I do not mean, however, even to wish that the clarity of opposition of the technological and the humanist identity be blurred, for dynamic interplay needs clear poles.

What, finally, is apt to bring youth of

different persuasions together is a change in the generational process itself—an awareness that they share a common fate. Already today the mere division into an older—parent—generation and a younger —adolescing—one is becoming super-annuated. Technological change makes it impossible for any traditional way of being older (an age difference suggested by the questions quoted) ever to become again so institutionalized that the younger generation could "accommodate" to it or, indeed, resist it in good-old revolutionary fashion. Aging, it is already widely noted, will be (or already is) a quite different experience for those who find themselves rather early occupationally outdated and for those who may have something more lasting to offer. By the same token, young adulthood will be divided into older and younger young adults. The not-too-young and not-too-old specialist will probably move into the position of principal arbiter, that is, for the limited period of the ascendance of his speciality. His power, in many ways, will replace the sanction of tradition or, indeed, of parents. But the "younger generation," too, will be (or already is) divided more clearly into the older- and the younger-young generation, where the older young will have to take over (and are eager to take over) much of the direction of the conduct of the younger young. Thus, the relative waning of the parents and the emergence of the young adult specialist as the permanent and permanently changing authority are bringing about a shift by which older youth will have to take increasing responsibility for the conduct of younger youth—and older people for the orientation of the specialists and of older youth. By the same token, future religious ethics would be grounded less in the emotions and the imagery of infantile guilt, than in that of mutual responsibility in the fleeting present.

In such change we on our part can orient ourselves and offer orientation only by recognizing and cultivating an age-specific *ethical* capacity in *older* youth, for there are age-specific factors that speak for a differentiation between morality and ethics. The child's conscience tends to be impressed with a moralism which says "no" without giving reasons; in this sense, the infantile super-ego has become a danger to human survival, for suppression in childhood leads to the exploitation of others in adulthood, and moralistic self-denial ends up in the wish to annihilate others. There is also an age-specific ethical capacity in older youth that we should learn to foster. That we, instead, consistently neglect this ethical potential and, in fact, deny it with the moralistic reaction that we traditionally employ toward and against youth (*anti-institutional, hedonistic, desacralizing*) is probably resented much more by young people than our dutiful attempts to keep them in order by prohibition. At any rate, the ethical questions of the future will be less determined by the influence of the older generation on the younger one than by the interplay of subdivisions in a life scheme in which the whole life-span is extended; in which the life stages will be further subdivided; in which new roles for both sexes will emerge in all life stages; and in which a certain margin of free choice and individualized identity will come to be considered the reward for technical inventiveness. In the next decade, youth will force us to help them to develop ethical, affirmative, resacralizing rules of conduct that remain flexibly adjustable to the promises and the dangers of world-wide technology and communication. These developments, of course, include two "things"—one gigantic, one tiny—the irreversible presence of which will have to find acknowledgment in daily life: the Bomb and the Loop. They together will call for everyday decisions involving the sanctity of life and death. Once man has decided not to kill needlessly and not to give birth carelessly, he must try to establish what capacity for living, and for letting live, each generation owes to every child planned to be born—anywhere.

One can, I guess, undertake to predict only on the basis of one of two premises: Either one expects that things will be as bad as they always have been, only worse; or one visualizes what one is willing to take a chance on at the risk of being irrelevant. As I implied at the beginning, a committee that wants to foretell the future may have to take a chance with itself by asking what its combined wisdom and talent would wish might be done with what seems to be given.

CHAPTER **23**

Gestalt Theory

Introduction

Frederick (Fritz) Perls (1893–1970), was a true original. I think of him as a latter-day Diogenes, with his lantern held high searching for truth in the most unlikely places. He is perhaps more like J. L. Moreno than any of the other authors represented in this book, a brilliant therapist with a poetic attitude toward life who saw it in a most unique way. If you start by reading the last paragraph of this selection, you can get an idea of the kind of original thinker he was.

Perls was obsessed with the moment and was very clearly a here-and-now theorist: He believed that the essence of therapy was to have a self-encounter right here and right now! His favorite technique, the "hot seat" in therapy, illustrates this philosophy well. He insistently probed what the person he was dealing with was feeling at the immediate moment, and he dug in deeply.

Perls was not at all interested in the past or in the future—and in this selection he criticizes those who do favor these points of view.

This short extract should generate some hunger in readers to try to understand Perls's message. Even though his writing is somewhat idiosyncratic, he makes a clear case for his various views.

FREDERICK S. PERLS
Time: Past and future, past and present

TIME

Everything has extension and duration. We measure extension in length, height and width; duration in time. All these four dimensions are measures applied by man. This chair opposite me *is* not forty inches high, but *I* can so measure it and, if I throw the chair over, its height is only twenty inches, the previous height becoming the width. Time is measured in one dimension—length. We say a long and a short time ago, but we never speak of broad or narrow time. The expression "it is high time" has its origin probably from high tide or from the water-clock. Whilst for objective measuring, we take fixed points (B.C. and A.D., a.m. and p.m.), the psychological zero-point is the ever present, reaching, according to our organization, forward and backward like the maggot that eats its way through cheese, leaving traces of its existence behind.

Omitting the dimensions of time leads to fallacies in logic, to cheating in arguments: Logic maintains that $a = a$, that, e.g., an apple can replace itself in another context. This is correct so long as the extension only of the fruit is considered, as is mostly done. But it is incorrect as soon as its duration is taken into account. The unripe apple, the tasty fruit and the rotting one are three different phenomena of the time-space event "apple." But being utilitarians we take of course the edible fruit as referent when we use the word "apple."

As soon as we forget that we are time-space events, ideas and reality clash. Demands for lasting emotions (eternal love, loyalty) might lead to disappointment, vanishing beauty to depression. People who have lost the rhythm of time will soon be out of date.

And what is this rhythm of time?

Apparently our organization has an optimum in the experience of the sense of time—of duration. In language this is expressed as passing—pastime—the past; (in French, *le pas—passer—passe;* in German, *ver-"gehen"—Ver-"gang" enheit*). The zero-point is thus, for us, the walking speed. Time marches on! Time which is flying, or crawling, or even standing still denotes the plus and minus deviation. Such a judgment contains its psychological opposite; we would like the flying time to slow down, and to hurry it up when it is crawling.

Concentration on things as time-space events is experienced as patience, a tension between a wish and its fulfillment, as impatience. Apparently, in this case, the image exists merely in extension, the time component being split off as impatience. In this way time awareness, or the sense of time, enters the human life and psychology.

Einstein is of the opinion that the time sense is a matter of experience. The small child has not yet developed it. The awakening of a suckling occurs when the hunger tension has become so high as to inter-

---

Frederick S. Perls, "Time: Past and Future, Past and Present." Reprinted from F. S. Perls, *Ego, Hunger and Aggression* (New York: Random House, 1969).

rupt sleep. This is not due to any sense of time: on the contrary, the hunger helps to create such a sense. Although we do not know of any organic equivalents of the time sense, its existence has to be assumed, if not by anything else than by the accuracy with which some people can tell the correct time.

The longer the delay of wish gratification, the greater the impatience, when the concentration remains on the object of gratification. The impatient person wants the immediate, *timeless* joining of his vision with reality. If you wait for a tram, the idea "tram" might slide into the background and you might entertain yourself by thinking, observing, reading or whatever pastime is at hand until the tram arrives. If, however, the tram remains a figure in your mind, then ¶ appears as impatience, you feel like running to meet the tram.[1] "If the mountain does not come to Mohammed, Mohammed must go to the mountain." If you suppress the tendency to run towards the tram (and this self-control has become, with most of us, automatic and unconscious) you become restless, annoyed; if you are too inhibited to let off steam by swearing and becoming "nervous," and if you repress this impatience, you will probably transform it into anxiety, headache or some other symptom.

Someone was asked to explain Einstein's theory of relativity. He answered: "When you spend an hour with your girl, the time flies; an hour seems like a minute; but when you happen to sit on a hot stove, time crawls, seconds seem like hours." This does not conform to the psychological reality. In an hour of love,

if the contact is perfect, the time factor does not enter the picture at all. Should the girl, however, become a nuisance, should contact with her be lost and boredom set in, then you might start counting the minutes until you can get rid of her. The time factor will also be experienced, if time is limited, when you want to cram as much as possible into the minutes at your disposal.

There are, however, exceptions to the rule. The repressed memories in our Unconscious are, according to Freud, timeless. This means that they are not subject to change as long as they remain in a system isolated from the rest of the personality. They are like sardines in a tin which apparently remain forever six weeks old or whatever their age was, when they were caught. As long as they are isolated from the rest of the world very little change takes place until (by being eaten up or oxydized) they return to the world metabolism.

The time centre of ourselves as conscious human time-space events is the present. *There is no other reality than the present.* Our desire to retain more of the past or to anticipate the future might completely overgrow this sense of reality. Although we can isolate the present from the past (causes) and from the future (purpose), any giving up of the present as the centre of balance—as the lever of our life—must lead to an unbalanced personality. It does not matter if you sway over to the right (over-conscientiousness) or to the left (impulsiveness), if you overbalance forward (future) or backwards (past), you can lose your balance in any direction.

This applies to everything, and, of course, to the psycho-analytical treatment as well. Here the only existing reality is the analytical interview. Whatever we experience there, we experience in the pres-

---

[1] The symbol ¶ as used by Perls (see F. S. Perls, *Ego, Hunger and Aggression,* New York: Random House, 1969, p. 23) means "joining function or energy." The symbol ‡ (see p. 296) means a "disjoining" process. (R.C.)

ent. This must be the basis for every attempt at "organismic reorganization." When we remember, we remember at that very second and to certain purposes; when we think of the future we anticipate things to come, but we do so at the present moment and from various causes. Predilection for either historical or futuristic thinking always destroys contact with reality.

Lack of contact with the present, lack of the actual "feel" of ourselves, leads to flight either into the past (historical thinking) or into the future (anticipatory thinking). Both "Epimetheus" Freud and "Prometheus" Adler, co-operating with the neurotic's desire to dig into the past or to safeguard the future, have missed the Archimedic point of readjustment. By giving up the present as a permanent referent the advantage of going back to the past in order to profit from our experiences and mistakes, changes into its opposite: it becomes detrimental to development. We become sentimental or acquire the habit of blaming parents or circumstances (resentment); often the past becomes a "consummation devoutly to be wished for." In short, we develop a retrospective character. The prospective character, in contrast, loses himself in the future. His impatience leads him to phantastic anticipations which—in contrast to planning—are eating up his interest in the present, his contact with reality.

Freud has the correct intuition in his belief that contact with the present is essential. He demands free-floating attention, which means awareness of all experiences; but what happens is that slowly but surely patient and analyst become conditioned to two things: firstly, to the technique of free associations, of the flight of ideas and, secondly, to a state in which analyst and patient form, as it were, a company fishing for memories, the free-floating attention floating away. Open-mindedness is in practice narrowed down to the almost exclusive interest in the past and the libido.

Freud is not exact about time. When he says the dream stands with one leg in the present, with the other in the past, he includes the past few days into the present. But what happened even only a minute ago is past, not present. The difference between Freud's conception and mine may seem irrelevant, yet actually it is not merely a matter of pedantry, but a principle involving practical applications. A fraction of a second might mean the difference between life and death. . . .

The disregard of the present necessitated the introduction of "transference." If we do not leave room for the spontaneous and creative attitude of the patient, then we have either to search for explanations in the past (to assume that he transfers every bit of his behaviour from remote times to the analytical situation) or, following up Adler's teleological thinking, we have to restrict ourselves to finding out what purposes, what arrangements the patient has in mind, what plans he has up his sleeve.

By no means do I deny that everything has its origin in the past and tends to further development, but what I want to bring home is, that past and future take their bearings continuously from the present and have to be related to it. Without the reference to the present they become meaningless. Consider such a concrete thing as a house built years ago, originating in the past and having a purpose, namely to be lived in. What happens to the house if one is satisfied with the historical fact alone of its having been built? Without being cared for, the house would fall into ruin, subjected, as it would be, to the influence of wind and weather, to dry and wet rot, and other decaying influences which, though small and sometimes invisible, have an accumulative effect.

* * * *

Freud has shaken up our concepts of causality, morality and responsibility; but he stopped half-way: he has not driven the analysis to its ultimate conclusions. He said we are not as good or bad as we believe we are, but we are unconsciously mostly worse, sometimes better. Accordingly, he transferred responsibility from the Ego to the Id. Furthermore, he unmasked intellectual causes as rationalizations and decided that the Unconscious provides the causes for our actions.

How can we replace causal thinking? How do we overcome the difficulties of taking our bearings from the present and achieving a scientific understanding without asking for reasons? I have mentioned before the advantages that accrue from functional thinking. If we have the pluck to attempt to follow modern science in its decision that there are no ultimate answers to the "Why?" we come across a very comforting discovery: all relevant questions can be answered by asking: "How?" "Where?" and "When?" Detailed description is identical with concentration and increased knowledge. Research requires detailed descriptions, without neglecting the context. The rest is a matter of opinion or theory, faith or interpretation.

By applying our ideas of the present we can improve our memory and powers of observation. We speak of memories coming into our mind: our Ego is more or less passive towards them. But if we go back into a situation, imagining that we are really on the spot, and then describe in detail what we see or do, using the present tense, we shall greatly improve our capacity for remembering. . . .

The futuristic thinking, which in Adler's psychology stands in the foreground, is in Freud's conception relegated to secondary importance (e.g. secondary gain from illness). He stuck to causes, although in the *Psycho-Pathology of Everyday Life* (Freud, 1901) he has brought many examples to show that forgetting and memories have tendencies and not only causes. On the one hand the memories determine the neurotic's life, and on the other he remembers or forgets for certain purposes. An old soldier might remember deeds he can boast about—he might even invent memories *for the purpose of boasting.*

Our manner of thinking is determined by our biological organization. The mouth is in front of us and the anus at the back. These facts have something to do with what we are going to eat or to meet, and also of what we are leaving behind or what we pass. Hunger certainly has some connection with the future, and the passing of the stool with the past.

PAST AND FUTURE

Although we do not know much more about time than that it is one of the four dimensions of our existence, we are able to define the present. The present is the ever-moving zero-point of the opposites past and future. A properly balanced personality takes into account past and future without abandoning the zero-point of the present, without seeing past or future as realities. All of us look both backward and forward, but a person who is unable to face an unpleasant present and lives mainly in the past or future, wrapped up in historic or futuristic thinking, is not adapted to reality. Thus reality , . . gets a new aspect provided by the sense of actuality.

Day-dreaming is one of the few occupations which are generally recognized as flight from the zero-point of the present into the future, and in such a case it is customary to refer to this as escape from reality. On the other hand, there are people who come to the analyst, only too willing to comply with the popular idea of psycho-analysis—namely to unearth all possible infantile memories or traumata. With a retrospective character the analyst can waste years in following up this wild-goose chase. Being convinced that digging up the past is a panacea for neurosis, he merely collaborates with the patient's resistance of facing the present.

The constant delving into the past has a further disadvantage, in that it neglects to take into account the opposite, the future, thereby missing the point in a whole group of neuroses. Let us consider a typical case of anticipatory neurosis: A man, on going to bed, worries about how he will sleep; in the morning he is full of resolutions as to the work he is going to do in his office. On his arrival there he will not carry out his resolutions, but will prepare all the material he intends conveying to the analyst, although he will not bring forward this material in the analysis. When the time comes for him to use the facts he has prepared, his mind occupies itself instead with his expectation of having supper with his girl friend, but during the meal he will tell the girl all about the work he has to attend to before going to bed, and so on and on. This example is not an exaggeration, for there are quite a number of people always a few steps or miles ahead of the present. They never collect the fruits of their efforts, as their plans never make contact with the present—with reality.

What is the use of making a man, haunted by unconscious fear of starvation, realize that his fear originated in the poverty experienced in his childhood? It is much more important to demonstrate that by staring into the future and striving for security he spoils his *present* life; that his ideal of accumulating superfluous wealth is isolated and separated from the sense of life. It is essential that such a man should learn the "feel of himself," should restore all the urges and needs, all the pleasures and pains, all the emotions and sensations that make life worth living, and which have become background or have been repressed for the sake of his golden ideal. He must learn to make other contacts in life besides his business connections. He must learn to work *and* play.

Such people develop an open neurosis once they have lost their only contact with the world—the business contact. This is known as the neurosis of the retired business-man. Of what use is an historical analysis to him, except for providing a pastime to fill a few hours of his empty life? Sometimes a game of cards might serve the same purpose. At the seaside one often finds this type of man (having no contact with nature), who would refuse to leave the stuffy cardroom, to have a look at the beauty of a sunset. He would rather stick to his senseless occupation of exchanging cards, of holding on to his "dummy" than to face contact with nature.

Other types that look into the future are the worriers, the astrologists, the safety-first-never-take-a-chance fellows.

Historians, archaeologists, explanation seekers and complainers look in the other direction, and most attached to the past is the person who is unhappy in life, "because" his parents have not given him a proper education, or who is sexually impotent, "because" he acquired a castration complex, when his mother had threatened to cut off his penis as a punishment for masturbation.

Seldom is the discovery of such a "cause" in the past a decisive factor in the cure. The majority of people in our society have not had an "ideal" education, and most people have experienced castration threats in their childhood without becoming impotent. I know of a case in which all the possible details of such a castration complex came to the surface without essentially influencing the impotency. The analyst had interpreted the patient's disgust towards the female sex. The patient had accepted the interpretation, but never managed to feel, to experience nausea. So he could not change disgust into its opposite, appetite.

The retrospective person avoids taking the responsibility for his life and actions; he prefers placing the blame on something that happened in the past instead of taking steps to remedy the present situation. For manageable tasks one does not need scapegoats or explanations.

In the analysis of the restrospective character one always finds a distinct symptom: the suppression of *crying*. Mourning is a part of the resignation-process, necessary if one is to overcome the clinging to the past. This process called "mourning labor" is one of the most ingenious discoveries of Freud. The fact that resignation requires the work of the whole organism demonstrates how important the "feel of oneself" is, how the experience and expression of the deepest emotions is needed to adjust oneself after the loss of a valuable contact. In order to regain the possibility of making contact anew, the task of mourning must be finished. Though the sad event is past, the dead is not dead—it is still present. The mourning labour is done in the present: it is not what the dead person meant to the mourner that is decisive, but what he still *means* to him. The loss of a crutch is of no importance if one was injured about five years ago and has since been cured; it matters only if one is still lame and needs the crutch.

Although I have tried to deprecate futuristic and historical thinking, I do not wish to give a wrong impression. We must not entirely neglect the future (e.g. planning) or the past (unfinished situations), but we must realize that the past has gone, leaving us with a number of unfinished situations and that *planning must be a guide to, not a sublimation of, or a substitute for, action.*

People often make "historical mistakes." By this expression I do not mean the confounding of historical data but the mistaking of past for actual situations. In the legal sphere laws are still valid which have long since lost their *raison d'être.* Religious people, too, dogmatically hold on to rites which once made sense but which are out of place in a different civilization. When the ancient Jew was not allowed to drive a vehicle on the Sabbath, it made sense, for the beast of burden should have a day's rest, but the pious Jew of our time submits to unnecessary inconvenience by refusing to use a tram which runs in any case. He changes sense into nonsense—at least so it appears to us. He looks at it from a different angle. Dogma could not retain its dynamic, could not even exist, if it were not supported by futuristic thinking. The believer holds up the religious law *in order to* be in "God's good books," to gain prestige as a religious man or to avoid unpleasant pricks of conscience. He must not feel the historical mistake he makes, otherwise his life-gestalt, the sense of his existence, would fall to pieces, and he would be thrown into utter confusion by the loss of his bearings.

Similar to the historical are the futuristic mistakes. We expect something, we hope for something, and we are disappointed, maybe very unhappy, if our hopes are not fulfilled. We are then very much inclined to blame either fate, other people, or our own inabilities, but we are not prepared to see the fundamental mistake of expecting that reality should coincide with our wishes. We avoid seeing that we are responsible for the disappointment which arises from our expectation, from our futuristic thinking, especially if we neglect the actuality of our limitations. Psycho-analysis has overlooked this essential factor, although it has dealt abundantly with disappointment "reactions."

The most important "historical mistake" of classical psycho-analysis is the indiscriminate application of the term "regression." The patient evinces a helplessness, a reliance on his mother, unbefitting an adult, becoming to a child of three. There is nothing to be said against an analysis of his childhood (if the patient's historical mistake is sufficiently emphasized), but in order to realize a mistake we must contrast it with its opposite, the correct behaviour. If you have spelt a word wrongly you cannot eliminate the mistake unless you know the correct spelling. The same applies to historical or futuristic mistakes.

The patient in question has perhaps never reached the maturity of an adult and does not know what it feels like to be independent of his mother, how to make contact with other people; and unless he is made to feel this independence, he cannot realize his historical mistake. We take it for granted that he has this "feel," and we are only too ready to assume that he has reached the adult position and has regressed to childhood only temporarily. We are inclined to overlook the question of situations. As his behaviour is normal in situations representing no difficulties or in matters requiring reactions similar to those expected of a child, we take it for

granted that he is essentially grown-up. When more difficult situations arise, however, he proves that he has not developed a mature attitude. How can we expect him to know how to change if he does not realize the difference between infantile and mature behaviour? He would not have "regressed" if his "self" was already mature, if he had assimilated and not only copied (introjected) adult behaviour.

We may conclude then that the immediate future is contained in the present, especially in its unfinished situations (completion of the instinct cycle). Large parts of our organism are built for "purposes." Purposeless, e.g. senseless, movements can range from slight peculiarities to the inexplicable behaviour of the insane.

Conceiving the present as the result of the past we find as many schools of thought ,as we find causes. Most people believe in a "primary cause" like a creator, others fatalistically stick to the inherited constitution as the only recognizable and deciding factor, whilst for others, again, the environmental influence is the only cause of our behaviour. Some people have found economics to be the cause of all evil, others the repressed childhood. The present, in my opinion, is the coincidence of many "causes" leading to the ever changing, kaleidoscopic picture of situations which are never identical.

PAST AND PRESENT

Whilst it is not possible as yet to give a full account of the relations between past and present, enough material is available to attempt an incomplete classification as follows:

1. The influence of the constitution (inheritance).

2. The training of the individual (conditioning through environmental influence).

3. Futuristic memories.

4. The compulsion of repetition (the incompleteness of situations).

5. Accumulation of undigested experiences (traumata and other neurotic memories).

1. In regard to *constitution* the relationship between past and present is rather obvious. Let us take the functioning of the thyroid gland as an example. Cretinism (myxoedema) is due to something that happened in the past. Will delving into the past have any value except to gratify our scientific curiosity or to teach us about the illness' origin, so that this knowledge may help us to cure it to-day? We continually add thyroid hormones to comply with the *present* thyroxin deficiency.

2. The *training of the individual* can be compared with the building of roads; the aim is to direct the traffic in the most economical way. If, however, the conditioning is not a very deep one, it is liable to deteriorate just as badly built roads are likely to break up. Deterioration tends towards annihilation. Old roads will disappear; our minds will forget. Some roads, however, are built like the old Roman highways. Once we have learned to read, many years of not reading may still leave the reading capacity intact.

If, however, a reconditioning takes place, if the traffic is directed on to new roads, the situation will be different: if we are compelled to speak a foreign language and make little use of our native tongue, we experience a deterioration of the latter, and after some years we may often find it difficult to remember words which were formerly automatically at hand. The reconditioning, on the other hand, the

switching back to the native tongue, would take less time than it originally took to learn it in childhood.

When we attempt to stop the progress of a neurosis we try to recondition the patient to the biological, usually called normal or natural, functions. At the same time we must not forget the training, the conditioning of undeveloped attitudes. We can appreciate F. M. Alexander's methods[2] from the point of view of reconditioning, if we don't forget the need to dissolve at the same time the dynamic influence of the wrong *gestalt*. If we merely superimpose one *gestalt* on to another, we encage, repress, but nevertheless keep alive, the wrong gestalt; by dissolving the latter we set free energies for the functioning of the whole personality.

3. The expression *teleological, futuristic memories* sound paradoxical, but we often remember past experiences for future purposes. From the psycho-analytical point of view the most interesting category of this kind is the danger signal. If several motor-car accidents have occurred at the same place on a highway the authorities may put up a danger signal. These danger signals are erected not in memory of those killed; they are created for the "purpose" of safeguarding against future accidents.

The danger signal for the neurotic is not, as Freud says, the anxiety attack. The nervous person puts his *memories* as stop signals all over the place, wherever he scents the possibility of danger. To him this procedure seems reasonable; he appears to act according to the proverb: "Once bitten, twice shy." He may, for instance, have fallen in love and been disappointed. He therefore takes great care

---

[2] See Alexander, F. M. *Resurrection of the body.* Ed. by E. Maisel. New York: University Books, 1969 (R.C.)

that such a "disaster" should not happen again. As soon as he feels the slightest sign of affection he produces (consciously or unconsciously) the memory of his unpleasant experience as a red stop light. He completely disregards the fact that he makes an historical mistake, that the present situation might differ considerably from the previous one.

Unearthing traumatic situations from the past might provide even more material for danger signals, might restrict even more the neurotic's activities and spheres of life, as long as he has not learned to differentiate between previous and present situations.

4. A very delicate matter to deal with is the *compulsion of repetition,* in itself an amazing discovery of Freud's which he unfortunately carried to absurd conclusions. He saw in the monotony of the repetitions a tendency towards mental ossification. These repetitions, Freud contends, become rigid and lifeless, like inorganic matter. His speculations about this life-denying tendency led him to the conjecture that there is a definite urge working behind the scene: a death or nirvana instinct. He concluded further that just as the organismic libido is turned outwards as love, so the death instinct turns outwards as a tendency to destroy. He even went so far as to explain life as a permanent struggle between the death instinct and the disturbing libido. This antireligious man re-enthrones Eros and Thanatos, the scientist and atheist regresses to the gods which he had fought a lifetime to destroy.

In my opinion Freud's construction contains several mistakes. I do not agree with him that the gestalt of "compulsion of repetition" has the character of rigidity, although a distinct tendency towards ossification exists in *habits.* We know that the older a person grows or the less elastic his outlook on life is, the more impossible

any change of habits becomes. When we condemn certain habits and call them vices we imply that a change is desirable. In most cases, however, they have become part of the personality to such a degree that all conscious efforts fail to change them and that all efforts are confined to ridiculous resolutions which bribe the conscience for the moment without influencing the issue.

Principles are no less obstinate. They are substitutes for an independent outlook. The owner would be lost in the ocean of events if he were not able to orientate himself by these fixed bearings. Usually he is even proud of them and does not regard them as weaknesses, but as a source of strength. He hangs on to them because of the insufficiency of his own independent judgment.

The dynamic of habits is not homogeneous. Some are dictated by economy of energy and are "conditioned" reflexes. Habits are often fixations or have originally been fixations. They are kept alive by fear but might be changed into "conditioned" reflexes. This insight involves that a mere analysis of habits is as insufficient for "breaking" them as are resolutions.

The structure of the "compulsion of repetition" proper is quite different from that of habits and principles. We have previously chosen the example of a man who becomes disappointed again and again in his friends. We would hardly call this a habit or a principle. But what then is this compulsory repetition? To answer this question we have to make a detour.

Kurt Lewin carried out the following memory experiments: A number of people were given some problems to solve. They were not told that it was a memory test but were under the impression that an intelligence test was being carried out. The next day they were asked to write down the problems they remembered, and, strangely enough, the *unsolved* problems were far better remembered than those which had been solved. The libido-theory would lead us to expect the opposite, namely that narcissistic gratification would make people remember their successes. Or did they all have Adler's inferiority complexes and did they only remember the unsolved tasks as a warning to do better next time? Both explanations are unsatisfactory.

The word "solution" indicates that a puzzling situation disappears, is dissolved. With regard to the actions of the obsessional neurotic it has been realized that the obsessions have to be repeated until their task is finished. When a death wish is dissolved, psycho-analytically or otherwise, interest in the performing of the obsessional rites (the "undoing" of the death wish) will recede into the background and later disappear from the mind.

If a kitten tries to climb a tree and fails, it repeats its attempts over and over again until it succeeds. If a teacher finds mistakes in the pupil's work he makes him re-do it, not for the sake of repeating mistakes, but to train him in the proper solution. Then the situation is completed. Teacher and pupil lose all interest in it, just as we do after having solved a crossword puzzle.

Repeating an action to the point of mastery is the essence of development. A mechanical repetition without perfection as its aim is contrary to organic life, contrary to "creative holism" (Smuts). The interest is held only as long as the task in hand is unfinished. Once it is completed the interest disappears till a new task creates interest again. There is no savings bank from which the organism (as the libido theory suggests) can draw the required amount of interest.

Compulsory repetitions, too, are by no means automatic. On the contrary, they are vigorous attempts at solving relevant problems of life. The need for a friend is, in itself, a very healthy expression of the desire for human contact. The permanently disappointed man is wrong only in so far as he looks for this *ideal* friend over and over again. He might deny the unpleasant reality in day-dreams or even in hallucinations; he might try to become this ideal himself or to mould his friends to it, but he cannot come to a fulfilment of his desires. He does not see that he makes a fundamental mistake: he looks for the cause of his failure in the wrong direction—outside instead of inside himself. He looks upon his friends as the causes of his disappointment, not realizing that his own expectations are responsible. The more idealistic his expectations are, the less they conform to reality, the more difficult the contact problem will become. This problem will not be solved and the compulsion of repetition will not cease before he has adjusted his expectations of the impossible to the possibilities of reality.

The compulsion of repetition is thus nothing mechanical, nothing dead, but is very much alive. I fail to see how one can deduce from this a mystical death instinct. This is the one instance where Freud left the solid ground of science and wandered off into regions of mysticism, as did Jung with his special development of the libido theory and his conception of the Collective Unconscious.

It is not for me to find out what made Freud invent this death instinct. Perhaps illness or approaching old age made him wish for the existence of such a death instinct which could be discharged in the form of aggression. If this theory were correct, anyone sufficiently aggressive would have the secret of prolonging life. Dictators would live *ad infinitum.*

Freud alternatively uses the terms "nirvana" and "death instinct." While nothing could justify the conception of the death instinct, the nirvana instinct might find some justification. One must protest against the word instinct and apply rather the word tendency. Every need disturbs the equilibrium of the organism. The instinct indicates the direction in which the balance is upset—as Freud has realized with regard to the sex instinct.

Goethe had a theory similar to Freud's, but to him not libido, but destruction, symbolized by Mephistopheles, appeared as the disturber of man's "love for unconditional peace." But this peace is neither unconditional nor lasting. Gratification will restore the organismic peace and balance until—soon enough—another instinct will make its demands.

To mistake the "instinct" for the tendency towards equilibrium is like mistaking the goods which are being weighed on a pair of scales for the scales themselves. We might call this inherent urge to come to rest through gratification of an instinct, "striving for nirvana."

The postulation of the nirvana "instinct" may also have been the outcome of wishful thinking. Those short periods in which the scales of our organism have regained their balance are the moments of peace and happiness, only too soon to be disturbed by new demands and urges. Often we would like to isolate this restful feeling from its place in the instinct-gratification cycle and make it last longer. I understand that Hindus in their disapproval of the body and its sufferings, in their attempts to kill all desires, declared the state of nirvana to be the ultimate aim of our existence. If the striving for nirvana is an instinct, I am at a loss to see why they have put such an amount of energy and training into achieving their aim, since an instinct takes care of itself and does not require any conscious effort.

A great deal more could be said about the so-called death instinct.[3] The insight into its true nature could have been gained long ago, had not Freud's pupils, fascinated by his greatness, swallowed everything he said as a religion—much as I myself did in former years.

5. This swallowing of mental material brings us to another form of the past-present relations: the large class of *traumatic and introjected memories.*

A simple example is the stupid pupil with the excellent memory, who learns whole passages by heart and can repeat them easily on the examination papers, but is at a loss to explain the meaning of what he has written. He has taken in the material without assimilating it. Common to this class of memories which more than anything else has attracted the interest of Freud is the fact that they all lie in a kind of mental stomach. Three things can happen: either one vomits this material up (like a reporter), or defaecates it undigested (projection), or suffers from mental indigestion, a state which is covered by Freud's remark, "the neurotic suffers from memories."

To understand this mental indigestion fully and to provide a cure for it, we have to consider the details of hunger instinct and organismic assimilation. Disturbances in assimilation will—on the psychological side—promote the development of paranoia and paranoic character. . . .

---

[3] In my opinion ¶ as well as ‡ forces are responsible for death, but death is not responsible for aggression. In the case of the hardening of the arteries a certain amount of calcium joins in the tissues of the arteries and makes them rigid, thus disturbing the proper nourishment of the tissues. A simple example of the ‡ energy is the ulcer of the stomach, where the stomach juices destroy the walls of the organ. For explanation of the meaning of these symbols see page 287.

CHAPTER 24

Rational-Emotive Theory

Introduction

One of the most prodigiously productive individuals in the history of psychology must be Albert Ellis (1913–   ), whose normal working schedule as a clinical psychologist involves seeing patients from 9:30 in the morning to 11:00 at night. Despite this killing schedule, he has had published no fewer than 450 papers and 38 books.

Ellis's theory of psychotherapy can be almost completely described by Shakespeare's dictum: "There's nothing good or bad but thinking makes it so." His A–B–C theory is similar to R. S. Woodworth's S–O–R concept in that it centers on the organism (O), not the stimulus (S) nor the response (R). For Ellis, it is not the activating event (A) nor the consequence (C) that is important, but rather the belief system (B) that explains variable human behavior.

Ellis has never made explicit his own personality theory, and in this selection he explains not only why he has not yet developed a theory but why he does not think much of other theories. Now, at my urging, Ellis has finally made a first attempt at a comprehensive theory. This original contribution to the book is remarkable for its attack on other theories and as an initial gathering of Ellis's notions regarding notions to attempt his own complete system of personality theory. It also has some special interest in that it suggests how difficult it is to develop a personality theory.

ALBERT ELLIS
Toward a theory of personality

During the past several years, I have begun to develop a theory of personality that significantly disagrees with the views of other personality theorists who have also originated schools of psychotherapy—such as Adler, Freud, Jung, Reich, and Rogers. In this paper I shall first state why virtually all existent personality theorists make wrong conclusions about how humans function; then I shall outline and defend my own theory, which is developing out of the practice of rational-emotive therapy (Ellis, 1962, 1973a, 1973b, 1977; Ellis & Grieger, 1977; Morris & Kanitz, 1975).

WHY PERSONALITY THEORISTS OFTEN GO WRONG

Personality theorists almost invariably go wrong because, like most humans, they think crookedly. Their tendency to cognize irrationally leads them astray in various respects. They consequently come up with highly brilliant views of "human nature" which often include almost incredible errors of logic and antiempiricism. Examples of crooked thinking in personality theories include the following.

1. *Attribution of special reasons to events and behaviors.* Humans tend to attribute special (transpersonal) reasons to various nonhuman events. Because they then feel comfortable (in the Gestalt

Note: I wrote this paper specifically for this book because the editor, while recognizing that rational-emotive therapy includes a theory of personality, did not think that any of my writings truly covered this theory.

psychology sense of effecting "closure") with these "explanations," they then wrongly believe they have "proved" the validity of their assertions. Thus, primitives pray for rain; it eventually does rain; and they see their prayers as an explanation for the downpour. Sailors observe a certain kind of cloud formation before it rains; and they loosely see this formation "causing" a storm. The primitives clearly believe in magic, for their prayers have no connection whatever with the rain. But sailors also think crookedly: for cloud formations only constitute part of a worldwide pressure system of events, ranging from conditions at the North Pole to those at the Equator, all of which contribute to the downpour. Meteorologists know about these causes but often fail to explain them to lay people when they talk about the "causation" of rain; and we lay people buy the simple explanation of the rain clouds causing storms and do not bother with other complications that go with these causal connections.

And so with personality theories. If I murder someone and you want to "explain" the "cause" of my act, you will likely focus upon some outstanding "influences"—for example, my mother taught me that hostility pays off, or my early religious teachings led me to embrace an eye-for-an-eye philosophy. Certainly, these influences *may* have affected me. But of a hundred children whose mothers or whose early religious teachings favored hostility, very few, if any, would murder someone later in life! Literally hundreds of influences may have contributed to my act, such as (*a*) my tendency to demand that things go my way, (*b*) my rebellion against social teachings, (*c*) my low frustration tolerance, (*d*) my vulnerability to feeling hurt, (*e*) my happening to have a gun when I experienced extreme hostility, and so on. Considering all these possible "causes," your simplistic, unitary "explanation" of my murderous act hardly seems accurate; even though it may show some mild degree of causality.

Rational-emotive therapy (RET) holds that any special, exclusive reason for a behavioral act or personality pattern rarely, if ever, exists. If I murder regularly (and thus have the "trait" of a murderer), I may do so for many reasons, none of which probably has exclusive importance. If I regularly kill people, probably simultaneously: (*a*) I have a strong innate predisposition toward feeling hostile at "injustices," (*b*) I think murder is justified under certain conditions, (*c*) I believe I can get away with homicide, (*d*) I have somehow developed a low frustration tolerance, (*e*) I have problems, perhaps connected with my early interpersonal experiences, in relating to others, (*f*) I think in absolutistic, *mus*turbatory ways, and so on. Any one of these tendencies or conditions could make me a confirmed murderer; and a combination of several of them would increase the probability of my turning into one. Your selecting one primary "cause" of my homicidal character merely shows that almost all humans frequently attribute "special," determining causes to the origin or development of personality traits, when the "real" causes probably arise out of multifaceted, often obscure, partly accidental conditions.

2. *Illogical thinking about special reasons for personality behaviors.* Once we attribute special causative reasons for personality behaviors, we usually tend to

feel so convinced of their truth that we ignore evidence that contradicts our hypotheses. Such reasons seem to "fit" the observed facts of human functioning; and in perceiving this good fit we convince ourselves of their indubitable "truth." Even when we finally surrender these "explanations" for another set, we may do so because they jibe better with our preconceived aesthetic notions of good fit. They have greater "elegance." They "feel" better than the old ones. So we decide that (for now and for all time to come) they *are* better.

We can easily, then, convince ourselves of the validity of an elegant theory—by (*a*) ignoring data that do not fit, (*b*) falsifying data that fit poorly, or (*c*) failing to seek better theories that fit the data more accurately. When the "true" explanations for a given behavior remain truly multifaceted and complex, we have more temptation than usual to settle for special reasons for this behavior—simply because a simple explanation fits better and feels better.

3. *Environmentalist prejudices.* The great majority of psychologists remain do-gooders, hoping not merely to understand but also to help change dysfunctional behaviors. They believe that the basic way to do this consists of relearning, or behavior modification. They also know that some behaviors (e.g., obsessions and phobias) have such strong instinctive or overlearned factors that people have great difficulty in changing them.

Because of their essential altruism and hopefulness, some personality theorists who begin with the assumption, "We must help people change their disordered traits," go on to the empirical observation, "Humans find it very difficult to change solidly rooted inherited predispositions," and wind up with the illogical conclusion, "Therefore, such traits must have arisen from learning rather than hereditary tendencies.''

Other forms of illogical thinking about environmental influences on personality include:

a. Because people have great difficulty in making certain personality changes, they find it impossible to change.

b. Because a behavior has learned elements, it has virtually no innate component, and one can fairly easily unlearn it.

c. If a personality trait involves a hereditary predisposition, one cannot change it.

d. Because one has learned to behave badly, one has no responsibility for continuing this behavior, or environmental conditions have to change before one can modify this behavior.

e. Because others have conditioned one to behave in a defeating manner, helpers must recondition one to behave differently.

f. Because the environment significantly contributes to dysfunctioning, only through someone's significantly changing the environment will one have the ability to act less dysfunctionally.

g. Because virtually all human behavior includes learning, learning constitutes the main element in this behavior, and one must use external forces to modify it.

Due to do-goodism and cognitive slippage, the importance of environmental factors in the formation and changing of personality tends to get enormously exaggerated; almost all systematic views of psychotherapy fall victim to this kind of exaggeration.

4. *Overemphasis on dramatic incidents from the past.* We humans tend to dramatize so-called traumatic incidents and to remember them vividly. Thus, you may vividly recall how you wet yourself at age four and made a fool of yourself in class at age six. Because these remembrances leave dramatic effects, people make erroneous conclusions such as:

a. The original occurrence *caused* negative self-ratings.

b. Having no memory or bad feelings about them results from the mechanism of repression.

c. Recalling such "traumatic" memories and the accompanying feelings has curative effects.

d. That particular happening and one's original reaction to it invariably "caused" one's present lifestyle and tells the therapist a great deal about one's personality.

e. If one reacted dysfunctionally to an early remembered incident, one must react the same way in similar circumstances today and for the rest of one's life.

Dramatic early events in people's lives may well tell us something about them personalitywise. But theorists tend to overemphasize this phenomena and to make all-encompassing, and often false, conclusions about it. Just as people make false "observations" and conclusions about contemporary dramatic events (e.g., accidents), so too do they and their psychological observers easily make misleading "observations" and conclusions about past dramatic events. Such events probably had *some* importance, but we tend to make them *all*-important. Since most people experience satisfaction in reviewing their past histories, they foolishly expend much time and energy talking to therapists about their past when they would do themselves more good by thinking about their present and future. For this reason, woefully inefficient psychotherapies, such as psychoanalysis, continue to have immense popularity (Ellis, 1962; Ellis & Harper, 1975).

5. *Overgeneralization.* People have an exceptionally strong tendency to

overgeneralization, as Aaron Beck (1976), Albert Ellis (1962, 1977), George Kelly (1955), and Alfred Korzybski (1933) have pointed out. Because of this tendency, personality theorists seem to make certain valid observations about human personality and then go on to make certain overgeneralized, hence partly false, conclusions about these observations. Here are some examples:

a. Because humans desire certain things—such as approval and success—they *must* have them to achieve any significant degree of happiness.

b. Because dreams to some degree show people's underlying wishes and anxieties, virtually all dreams consist of wish fulfillments or indicate deep-seated fears.

c. Because dreams and free associations sometimes reveal material of which the individual has little awareness, they constitute the royal road to the unconscious and give highly accurate information.

d. Because people sometimes symbolize sex organs in their dreams by objects such as guns or keyholes, every time they dream about such objects they really mean sex organs.

e. Because some individuals feel inferior due to physical or other deficiencies, such deficiencies always lead to feelings of inferiority.

f. Because feelings of love frequently enhance happiness, everyone requires a fine one-to-one relationship to exist in a "normal" or "healthy" manner.

Hundreds of such overgeneralizations contribute to false views of personality. The human tendency to jump from "Some people do this some of the time," to "Virtually everyone does this all of the time," and from "A minority of individuals under certain conditions act this way," to "The majority of people always act this way," leads to misleading, and virtually pandemic, views of personality.

6. *Hereditarian biases.* Many psychologists have hereditarian biases and consequently overemphasize the importance of innate influences on personality (Pastore, 1949). Cyril Burt, for example, for many years seems to have faked data to support his theories about the importance of genetic factors in intelligence (Evans, 1976). Typical hereditarian mistakes include such conclusions as:

a. Because heredity represents a strong element in virtually all behavior, it almost exclusively determines that behavior.

b. If certain individuals have an innate tendency to act in a certain way, virtually all the members of their groups act that way because of their genetic differences from other groups.

c. If a personality trait has strong hereditarian influences, people with that trait find it virtually impossible to change it significantly.

d. If one personality trait has strong heredity determinants, other traits must have equally strong innate determinants.

Hereditarian overgeneralizations lead to many false conclusions about personality. Proenvironmentalist theorists overemphasize the significance of learned factors, while prohereditarians overemphasize innate factors. Environmentalists tend to forget that social learning rests on an inherited tendency to learn or to adopt social "conditioning" (Ellis, 1976). Hereditarians tend to forget that no matter what their genetic background, humans start learning immediately after birth. Both sets of theorists, failing to look at the other side of the fence, overlook the fact that all behaviors include a combination of learned and innate factors, and both tend to present a one-sided view of personality.

7. *Human autism and grandiosity.* Humans often take an autistic, grandiose cosmological view. They conceptualize that the universe revolves around them and runs in accordance with their wishes and goals. They will not accept that the world seems to have no intrinsic purpose, and that it has no interest, concern, or love for them. They exist and it exists; and their existence, of course, depends on an outside world in which they live. But individuals and the world have no necessary connection. The universe existed without humans probably for billions of years and may well do so for billions of future years. We have no evidence that it exists *just* for us.

People seem loath to accept the great influence of accident, purposelessness, and unintentionality in cosmology. They consequently tend to invent special reasons for personality behaviors, and they frequently come up with semimystical, transpersonal, religiously oriented views that have nothing to do with reality.

8. *Self-rating influences.* Humans value life and happiness and, reasonably enough, rate their performances with how well these permit them to enjoy life. But then they jump to rating their total selves, and this has no sensible basis (Ellis, 1962, 1972, 1975; Ellis & Harper, 1975). That doesn't stop humans from continuing to rate their essences as well as their deeds!

Personality theorists tend to make the same error. They talk in favor of self-esteem, self-confidence, and self-regard, not realizing that even if we do achieve self-esteem we harm ourselves thereby if we remain preoccupied with our own ratings rather than simply changing our dysfunctional behaviors. If we rate ourselves as "good," we imply that we can also be rated as "bad"—and as a consequence we live on the verge of anxiety,

due to these self-determined "report cards."

Personality theory includes an enormous "self-worth" literature—most of it quite misleading! For humans, as such, do not actually have differential worth. They merely have aliveness. Intrinsic worth or value differs little from other mythical entities, such as "spirit" and "soul" (Ellis, 1972).

9. *Absolutistic and musturbatory thinking.* People tend to take proper probabilistic views (e.g., "I like others' approval") and then escalate them into absolutes and musts (e.g., "I must have others' approval"). This kind of thinking also leads personality theorists astray, who promulgate *musts by* the dozen instead of more realistic it-would-seem-better-ifs (Ellis, 1973a, 1973b, 1977; Ellis & Grieger, 1977). Some of the *musts* that theorists uphold include:

a. You must have a happy, secure childhood to achieve a happy adult life.

b. If you have an emotional problem, you must have prolonged intensive therapy.

c. To change your behavior, you must have specific reinforcers, such as money or love.

d. Self-defeating behavior must result from irrational ideas.

e. You must feel terribly anxious about the possibility of eventually dying.

f. When people treat you unfairly, you must feel real hostility toward them.

10. *Defensiveness and resistance to change.* Personality theorists generally tend to resist change in their thinking, and they construct defenses against acknowledging defects in their theories. They consequently ignore evidence that contradicts their views. They claim their theories explain practically all aspects of personality. They give specious answers to the objec-

tions of critics. They avoid probing new areas that might uncover evidence that confutes their hypotheses. They neglect to even read other personality theorists. They come to conclusions that do not jibe with the evidence they themselves turn up. They cling to views that have long outlived their usefulness. They see flaws in their own theories but refuse to acknowledge these flaws publicly.

Possibly for ego-bolstering and grandiose reasons, personality scientists hold to and promulgate views that never had, or at least no longer have, a high degree of validity. Let me see, therefore, if I can do at least a little better!

TOWARD A NEW THEORY OF PERSONALITY

Assuming, as claimed above, that many contemporary theories of personality have woeful inadequacies and little likelihood of verification, can a more valid theory arise out of clinical data?

The A-B-C theory of personality

Rational-emotive therapy has implied from its very beginning a theory of personality, stemming from its theory of personality change. Scores of clinical reports have given evidence for the validity of this A-B-C theory by citing case histories of people who came for RET in a state of near despair and, after consultation, usually soon thereafter emerged as significantly improved—with their symptoms gone, with new understanding of how they created their problems, and with a readiness to face the world and make for themselves a better, more joyous existence (Ellis, in press; Murphy & Ellis, 1977). In addition to clinical evidence, the A-B-C theory has considerable experimental

backing. DiGiuseppe, Miller, and Trexler (in press) and Murphy (Murphy & Ellis, 1977) have comprehensively reviewed clinical outcome studies in which some subjects experienced RET and others experienced no therapy or other forms of psychotherapy. When the researchers made statistical comparisons between experimental (RET) and control groups, in almost all these studies subjects given RET changed their behavior significantly better than did non-RET subjects (Ellis, in press).

We can state the essence of RET theory in this way: When people feel upset at point C (emotional Consequence), after they have undergone some unpleasant Activating Event (at point A), they almost always conclude that A caused C. They say, "No wonder I feel depressed; my mate has just left me," or "Of course I feel anxious in view of this exam that I may fail." For most people—including clients and personality theorists—the connection between A (Activating Experience) and C (emotional Consequence) seems evident and obvious.

RET rejects this "evident" explanation, and RET therapists have taught thousands of clients to reject it over the past two decades. The stimulus does not explain the reaction; S-R theorizing does not work. RET conceptualization, following Woodworth (Woodworth & Schlosberg, 1954) constitutes an S-O-R theory. RET makes B, the individual's Belief System, the crucial issue. A does not determine C—B does! Consequently, if two people get labeled "stupid," and one laughs at the statement and the other feels depressed, we cannot explain these radically different Consequences by A (the Activating Event) but rather by B (the Belief System) *about* A.

The salient points of RET have appeared in much detail elsewhere (Ellis, 1962, 1971, 1973a, 1973b, 1977; Ellis & Grieger, 1977; Ellis & Harper, 1975; Maultsby, 1975). Now, the crucial issue arises: How do people obtain their Belief Systems—rational Beliefs (rBs) and irrational Beliefs (iBs)? Why does Johanna have such a healthy attitude and behave so sanely while her brother, John, has such an unhealthy view of life and acts so unsuccessfully?

Hereditarian influences on personality

Although almost all formal views of modern personality formation say otherwise, it seems probable that the main influence on human personality comes from heredity. It seems almost impossible to deny this, since if we humans do exhibit different personality traits as we react to environmental conditions, we obviously inherit this kind of teachability or conditionability. Thus, we seem unusually teachable compared to "lower" animals. Our teachability, mediated through our unusually large and specially wired cerebral cortex, comprises one of the main essences of our humanity. Sub-human animals remain much more driven by instincts, while humans largely have what Maslow (1954) called "instinctoid" tendencies—strong predispositions to act in certain ways that nonetheless can get radically modified by environmental and educational influences.

RET-oriented personality theory hypothesizes that probably 80 percent of the variance of human behavior rests on biological bases and about 20 percent on environmental training (Ellis, 1976). We find a good example of this in the iB's (irrational Beliefs) which spark people's disturbances. At first blush, these beliefs seem to stem primarily from cultural learning: from absorbing the standards that parents, schools, churches, and other institutions teach. Almost all of us largely subscribe to these standards, in spite of the fact that many of them appear insane and inane. Do not our personalities, then, get mainly set by culture?

Yes—and no! Our "normal" standards do seem to follow cultural prescriptions and proscriptions—so that most of us wear considerable clothing even when temperatures soar, permit ourselves to love intensely only one member of the other sex at a time, and try to win the approval of many people whom we hate or in whom we have little interest. We do these silly things to follow cultural conventions. But in addition, because we innately tend to elevate *preferences* into *musts,* we frequently convince ourselves that we *have to* do these preferable things; that we must find it awful and horrible (rather than merely damned annoying) if we do not; and that we rate as thoroughly *rotten persons* if we fall below cultural standards.

Just as we often take stupid cultural norms and make them into absolutistic *shoulds,* we do much the same thing with sensible rules. Thus, our culture teaches us that we had better wear warm clothes in winter—but we tend to add that we *must* wear the most fashionable clothes, no matter how uncomfortable or expensive we personally find them. Our culture tells us the advantages of falling in love; so we often insist that we *have to* love and gain the love of the most special person in the world, who will madly love us forever! Our culture informs us that we will benefit by having others approve of us (so that they will give us jobs, act companionably, do us favors, and so on). And then we demand that virtually everyone we meet, including perfect strangers we will rarely encounter again, *must* like us!

This kind of *mast*urbation—admittedly

encouraged but not demanded by our society—seems largely innate. Just about all humans in all cultures frequently *must*urbate—even though they soon note its pernicious results. We demand guarantees; we insist that we have to do well, others must treat us considerately, and world conditions have to arrange themselves so that we get almost everything we want immediately, easily. Just about all children frequently think this way, and virtually no adults fully surrender this kind of crazy thinking.

Personality consists not merely of our silly demandingness but perhaps even more of our wishing, wanting, and desiring. Wants give purpose to life. If we had no desires (as extreme Zen Buddhism strives for, in a state called Nirvana), we would hardly survive; and if we did, who would really want to? Desiring, seeking, striving, yearning seem the main essence of living.

But where do most of our desires originally come from? Almost certainly, from biological predispositions. We naturally enjoy eating. We innately enjoy and prefer certain odors, sights, and sounds. We fundamentally like to play, to build, to create. In all these pursuits, we learn cultural standards and generally follow them. In our society, for example, we eat beef but not grasshoppers; we copulate in private rather than in public; and we play tennis and golf more than we perform archery. But just about all our culturally taught pursuits rest on a pronounced biological basis; as Karl Buehler (1965) stated, we inherently have a "function pleasure."

The RET emphasis on the importance of the biological bases of human behavior attempts to balance the environmentalist position, which has predominated personality and therapy theory for the last half century. Freud (1965) had strong biological leanings, but virtually all his main followers, including Fromm (1941, 1975), Horney (1965), Sullivan (1953), and Berne (1964) have overemphasized so-called cultural and early childhood conditioning. Many good reasons exist for suspecting that self-defeating behavior basically has innate (as well as acquired) causes. Since I have elsewhere (Ellis, 1976) reviewed these reasons in detail, I shall not repeat them here.

Multiplicity of origins and maintainers of personality

The RET theory of personality posits a multiplicity of origins and maintainers of personality, often environmental as well as biologically based, such as: (1) Interpersonal relations with other humans; (2) specific teachings by others; (3) teachings through impersonal communications, such as books and other forms of mass media; (4) group influences; (5) reinforcers or rewards, such as money, social approval, honors, medals, or compliments; (6) penalizers, such as disapproval, failures, fines, imprisonment, or threats; (7) self-ratings—evaluations of the self as "good" or "bad"; (8) self-observation—noting how one behaves and comprehending the usual consequences of such behavior; (9) modeling after others, particularly after outstanding individuals; (10) identifying with certain people or groups and going along with their behavior; (11) formulating goals, purposes, and ideals and striving to achieve them; (12) magical and mystical notions, such as belief in perfection, in utopia, or in rewarding or punishing deities; (13) gullibility and suggestibility to the teachings and persuasions of others; (14) urges favoring freedom and individuality; (15) innate tendencies to seek love, pleasure, and self-actualization; (16) emotional consequences of behavior considered "beneficial" by the individual: feeling "good" about operating according to the "correct" norms of self or others, achieving success, and so on; feeling "bad" about violations of laws, ethics, customs, traditions, or mores, and specifically feeling anxious, guilty, and depressed about such violations.

Because people have so many internal and external influences and because these significantly conflict with each other in many ways, human behavior displays both consistencies and inconsistencies. Consistencies ("personality traits") probably arise out of the strength and statistical prevalence of one influence over another. But no matter how much "evidence" we find for our "explanations" of personality, we never have all the facts; we can always think of an alternative "reason" that also connects with the known data; we can easily find five or more "answers" for the existence of the same trait; and we have no sure way of knowing which one, two, or all of these answers truly account for the personality factors we seek to explain. In view of this, a truly dynamic psychology had better include not only "vertical" factors—relate to past and future—but also "horizontal" considerations—and concern itself with the organism's selection calculus relative to a decision for action considering the importance of all these and other influences of past and present, of near and far, of inner and outer factors.

Does theorizing about personality, then, seem a rather hopeless pursuit? To some extent, yes. For the present, and perhaps never, we probably will not arrive at precise, certain hypotheses that cover all or most of the observed data. Nonetheless, if we watch the kinds of errors outlined in the first part of this article, we can at least come up with some tentative (and I hope highly tentative!) conclusions.

RET's stand on ten major dimensions of personality

Many personality analysts have come up with major dimensions of personality on which various theorists can take a stand. Coan (1968) outlined six dimensions, and Corsini (1977) has added four more. On these factors (as described in Corsini, 1977), RET makes the following choices:

1. *Objective-subjective.* Objective theories of personality feature explicit, observable, unequivocal behavior that one can count and number; subjective theories concern themselves with the inner personal life of an individual. In this respect, RET favors observing and counting behavior for research purposes. But it largely deals with inner personal life, with the ineffable individual, and sees the person as having *some* degree of choice or "free will" and a significant ability to change his or her traits (behavior patterns). Thus RET mainly remains in the subjective camp.

2. *Elementaristic-holistic.* Elementaristic theory sees the person as composed of parts: organs, units, elements put together to make a whole. Holistic theories see the person as having a central unity and the parts as aspects of the total entity. While RET sees people as having units or elements (e.g., high sexuality or low energy) that influence their whole lives, it also sees them as having interacting parts (including cognitions, emotions, and behaviors) that cannot really be separated, and it primarily sees them as having a holistic or central "consciousness" or "will" that tends to direct these various parts.

3. *Apersonal-personal.* Apersonal theories have impersonal, statistically based outlooks and consider generalities rather than individualities. Largely based on group norms, they differ from personal theories, which deal with the single individual in an idiographic manner. RET distinctly uses general laws of behavior, statistically based—e.g., the probability law that behind virtually every "emotional" disturbance lies an irrational idea, and this idea takes the form of some *should* or *must*. It claims unusual efficiency as a theory of personality and of personality change precisely because it has inducted these general laws from observations of many people and has clinically and experimentally tested them often. It therefore claims a scientific, partly nomothetic basis. But it also deals, especially in therapy, with individuals in their own right, emphasizes their uniqueness and their changeability, accords them personal responsibility for their own disturbance and change, and sees them idiographically. We can label RET as largely being a personal theory of personality.

4. *Quantitative-qualitative.* A quantitative theory makes it possible to measure units of behavior. A qualitative theory does not see behavior as exactly measurable, viewing it as too complex for such dealings. RET stresses quality rather than quantity, since (as noted in this article) personality seems infinitely complex in its origins and development, so that we can only partially and inaccurately quantify it. RET hypothesizes, however, that quantity frequently metamorphizes into quality in behavioral change. Forcing oneself *many times* to think and act differently finally helps one to "naturally" enjoy something one previously disliked—or vice versa.

5. *Static-dynamic.* Static theory sees the individual as a reactor, not a learner; filled with instincts, and based on generalizations presented by heredity. Dynamic theory concerns itself with the individual as a learner, with interactions between behavior and consciousness and between consciousness and unconsciousness. RET sees people as having instinctoid tendencies rather than fixed instincts—and as having, for example, the tendency to see their own behaviors (including their own disturbances) and to change these. In this sense, in spite of its strong emphasis on heredity, RET has an unusually powerful dynamic quality.

6. *Endogenistic-exogenistic.* Endogenous theories view the person as biologically based. Exogenistic theories consist of social learning theories. RET supports both endogenistic *and* exogenistic views. It sees the person as biologically based, but it also strongly holds that people have the innate capacity to make themselves less conditionable, less suggestible, and more self-directing. RET also sees humans as inheriting strong tendencies toward gregariousness and social learning, so that they always remain highly affectable by both their heredity and their social environment.

7. *Deterministic-indeterministic.* Deterministic theories see individuals as not responsible for their behavior, as the pawns of society, heredity, or both. Indeterministic theories put emphasis on self-direction and place control within the person. RET stands mainly in the indeterministic camp. But it sees choice as *limited*. It hypothesizes that the more rationally people think and behave, the less deterministic they act. But rationality itself has its limits and hardly leads to completely free, healthy, or utopian existences!

Knowability

8. *Past-future.* Some theories see the individual in terms of past influences, biological or social, and others see the person as explained by his or her anticipation of future goals. RET takes a two-headed-arrow stand in this respect, for it definitely sees people in terms of what they have inherited and learned in the past, but it also strongly sees them as able to think for themselves, make some free choices, and, by hard work and effort, carry out their goals. RET therapy techniques emphasize the present and future and waste little time with the past.

Rational Irrational

9. *Cognitive-affective.* Cognitive theories include the so-called ego theories, which see people as essentially rational, with the emotions subserving the intellect. Conversely, affective theories of personality see them as operating on an emotional basis, with the intellect at the service of the emotions. Although RET has a reputation for cognitive therapy, its personality theory contains strong affective elements as well. It says that humans inextricably intertwine and cannot really separate their emotions and cognitions, and that what we call "emotion" largely consists of and results from powerful evaluations or cognitions. Secondly, RET places cognition or "intellect" squarely in the service of "affect" or emotion. It hypothesizes that people get born with a tendency to "value" or "feel" or "desire" in order to survive and to survive reasonably happily; and that the term "rational," as used in RET, only applies to thoughts, emotions, and acts that abet these basic affective goals. Although RET uses cognitive, emotive, and behavioral methods of treatment, and uses them on theoretical grounds and not merely because they work, its aim and philosophy remain exceptionally hedonistic.

10. *Unconsciousness-consciousness.*

Proactive Reactive

Theories that stress the unconscious see the person as having considerable investment below the level of awareness. Consciousness refers to awareness, and consciousness theories see the individual as basically rational. In this personality dimension RET leans toward the consciousness side, but it heavily emphasizes the role of "unconscious" automaticity and habituation in the formation of disturbance. It therefore advocates a great deal of behavior therapy, forced practice, throwing oneself into doing "risky" things whether one likes to do so or not, and *in vivo* homework assignments designed to bring about "nonthinking" habituation or dehabituation.

Other RET hypotheses about personality

RET posits many concepts about personality, some of them unique and some held by other systems, especially by other cognitive-behavior therapeutic formulations. Some of the main RET personality hypotheses that now have a large amount of clinical and experimental research data behind them (Ellis, in press) include:

1. Human thinking and emotion do not constitute two disparate or different processes, but significantly overlap. Cognition represents a mediating operation between stimuli and responses. Emotions and behaviors stem not merely from people's reactions to their environment but also from their thoughts, beliefs, and attitudes about that environment.

2. People self-reflexively "talk" to themselves, and the kinds of things they say, as well as the form in which they say them, significantly affect their emotions and behaviors and sometimes lead to emotional disturbance.

3. Humans have the ability not only to think (and generalize) but to think about

their thinking and to think about thinking about their thinking. When disturbed, they often tend to think about their disturbances and thereby create additional anxiety or depression.

4. People cognize, emote, and behave interrelatedly. Cognition contributes to emotion and to action; emotion to cognition and to action; and action to cognition and to emotion. When people change one of these three modalities they concomitantly tend to change the other two.

5. When people expect something to happen they act significantly differently than when they have no such expectancies. Their cognitive expectancy influences both their emotions and their behaviors.

6. Humans have powerful innate and/ or acquired tendencies to construct basic values and to think and act rationally (to abet) and irrationally (to sabotage) such values. They frequently have irrational or absolutistic ideas that interfere with healthy thoughts, emotions, and behaviors.

7. People have strong tendencies not only to rate their acts, behaviors, performances, and traits as "good" or "bad" but to rate their *selves* or *essences* similarly, and these self-ratings constitute one of the main sources of their disturbances.

8. People have a strong tendency to do things that seem easier in the short run even though they may bring poor future results.

SUMMARY AND CONCLUSION

While a full theory of human personality would go beyond the here and now and would look backwards into history to seek out biological and environmental causes and forward into the anticipated future, a multiplicity of factors makes all theories partly fanciful. These factors include poor reporting, the crucial element of how theorists construe and misconstrue the facts of biology and social influence, and the existence of so many elements in personality that no theory can put them all together properly. This explains why we have so many competing theories, all plausible, none satisfactory. While theory making seems an interesting but harmless occupation, it would appear more useful if theorists and experimenters concentrated on (1) the here-and-now aspects of behavior rather than its "origins" or "development," and (2) effective methods of modifying dysfunctional behaviors more than the "whys" of how they arose.

With such a practical emphasis, social scientists would not only come to better conclusions about how people change, they would also tend to discover which elements of therapy prove most effective and elegant, would hasten their discarding of the many useless and iatrogenic therapies now prevalent, and would help more people live increasingly satisfying lives. As a model, RET has helped researchers, in their efforts to discover efficient ways of helping humans overcome intractable pain, to discover some basic facts of the nervous system which have led theories about the biological and sociological origins and development of pain (Cherry, 1977).

In psychotherapy, research on therapy procedures by Bandura (1971), Beck (1976), Goldfried (Goldfried & Davison, 1976), Kanfer (1970), Mahoney (1974), Meichenbaum (1977), Mischel (1976), and many other experimenters has led to significant advances in personality theory. If this kind of research continues, we have a good prospect of looking more closely at the origins of human personality and disentangling (if possible) hereditarian from environmental influences. Without such research and the basic solid knowledge of behavior which it tends to give, the present confusing situation in which almost 100 separate theories of personality and personality change keep competing for attention (and the situation grows worse annually) will continue, and we may never come to any definitive conclusions.

As a basic issue, there is the question of whether personality theory shall be viewed as religion or science. If religion, then anyone can have a revelation and state that boys universally crave sexual intercourse with their mothers—or similar garbage. Given a beard and a doctoral degree, one can make any assertion without any proof, and obtain many devout listeners. If we read the 100 or so personality theories in existence, from the completely biological theory of William Sheldon (1942) to the almost completely psychological theories of George Kelly (1955), we can find literally tens of thousands of assertions made in good faith by honest people, few of which have any proven validity and, worse, many of which seem completely unprovable. Thus we can have evidence that the moon does not consist of green cheese, but we seem to have no way of proving the existence or nonexistence of archetypes.

Personality theorists might do well to take some of the hypotheses in this article as the beginning of a truly scientific inquiry into personality. In this way we might finally determine the nature of people in the here and now, in their interactions in life, and in therapy, and do so under controlled clinical and experimental conditions. Wouldn't this seem preferable to the continual creation of fanciful and intellectually *mustur-batory* conceptionalizations that lead nowhere—as a reading of the latest issues of many journals devoted to personality theory will show?

REFERENCES

Bandura, A. *Psychological modeling: Conflicting theories.* Chicago: Aldine, 1971.

Beck, A. T. *Cognitive therapy and the emotional disorders.* New York: International Universities Press, 1976.

Berne, E. *Games people play.* New York: Grove Press, 1964.

Buehler, K. *Die krise der psychologie.* Stuttgart: Gustave Fisher, 1965.

Cherry, L. Solving the mysteries of pain. *New York Times Magazine,* January 30, 1977, pp. 12–13, 50–53.

Coan, R. W. *The optimal personality.* New York: Wiley, 1968.

Corsini, R. *Current personality theories.* Itasca, Ill.: F. E. Peacock, Publishers, 1977.

DiGiuseppe, R., Miller, N., & Trexler, L. Outcome studies of rational-emotive therapy. *Counseling Psychologist,* in press.

Ellis, A. *Reason and emotion in psychotherapy.* New York: Lyle Stuart, 1962.

Ellis, A. *Growth through reason.* Palo Alto: Science and Behavior Books, and Hollywood: Wilshire Books, 1971.

Ellis, A. Psychotherapy and the value of a human being. In J. W. Davis (Ed.), *Value and valuation.* Knoxville: University of Tennessee Press, 1972, 117–139. (Reprinted; New York: Institute for Rational Living, 1972.)

Ellis, A. *Humanistic psychotherapy: The rational-emotive approach.* New York: Julian Press and McGraw-Hill Paperbacks, 1973. (a)

Ellis, A. Rational-emotive therapy. In R. J. Corsini (Ed.), *Current psychotherapies.* Itasca, Ill.: F. E. Peacock, Publishers, 1973. (b)

Ellis, A. *How to live with a "neurotic"* (Rev. ed.). New York: Crown Publishers, 1975.

Ellis, A. The biological basis of human irrationality. *Journal of Individual Psychology,* 1976, *32,* 145–168.

Ellis, A. *How to live with—and without—anger.* New York: Reader's Digest Prss, 1977.

Ellis, A. Rational-emotive therapy: Research data that supports the clinical and personality hyotheses of RET and other modes of cognitive behavior therapy. *Counseling Psychologist,* in press.

Ellis, A., & Grieger, R. *Rational-emotive therapy: A handbook of theory and practice.* New York: Springer, 1977.

Ellis, A., & Harper, R. A. *A new guide to rational living.* Englewood Cliffs, N.J.: Prentice-Hall, and Hollywood: Wilshire Books, 1975.

Evans, P. The Burt Affair . . . sleuthing in science. *APA Monitor,* December 1976, *1,* 4.

Freud, S. *Standard edition of the works of Sigmund Freud.* London: Hogarth Press, 1965.

Fromm, E. *Escape from freedom.* New York: Rinehart, 1941.

Fromm, E. *The anatomy of human destructiveness.* Greenwich, Conn.: Fawcett, 1975.

Goldfried, M. R., & Davison, G. C. *Clinical behavior therapy.* New York: Holt, Rinehart & Winston, 1976.

Horney, K. *Collected writings.* New York: Norton, 1965.

Kanfer, F. Self-regulation: Research, issues and speculations. In C. Neuringer & J. L. Michael (Eds.), *Behavior modification in clinical psychology.* New York: Appleton-Century-Crofts, 1970.

Kelly, G. *The psychology of personal constructs.* New York: Norton, 1955.

Korzybski, A. *Science and sanity.* Lancaster, Pa.: Lancaster Press, 1933.

Mahoney, M. *Cognition and behavior modification.* Cambridge, Mass.: Ballinger, 1974.

Maslow, A. H. The instinctoid nature of basic needs. *Journal of Personality,* 1954, *22,* 326–347.

Maultsby, M. C., Jr. *Help yourself to happiness.* New York: Institute for Rational Living, 1975.

Meichenbaum, D. H. *Cognitive behavior therapy.* New York: Plenum, 1977.

Mischel, W. The self as the person. In A. Wandersman (Ed.), *Behavioristic and humanistic approaches to personality change.* New York: Pergamon, 1976.

Morris, K. T., & Kanitz, J. M. *Rational-emotive therapy.* Boston: Houghton Mifflin, 1975.

Murphy, R., & Ellis, A. *A comprehensive bibliography of rational-emotive therapy and cognitive-behavior therapy.* New York: Institute for Rational Living, 1977.

Pastore, N. *The nature-nurture controversy.* New York: King's Crown Press, 1949.

Sheldon, W. *Varieties of human temperament.* New York: Harper, 1942.

Sullivan, H. S. *Conceptions of modern psychiatry.* New York: Norton, 1953.

Woodworth, R. S., & Schlosberg, H. *Experimental psychology.* New York: Holt, 1954.

CHAPTER **25**

Reality Therapy Theory

Introduction

William Glasser (1925–   ) developed a systematic way of dealing with individuals on the basis of pure common sense, stating in effect that life is a game, and to win in this game, one has to play within the rules and according to winning principles. This is more or less his definition of reality. Thus, for example, if a patient in a mental hospital wants to be released, it would not be proper to say he should be released because he believes he is God, but it would be proper to operate in conformity to the concepts of those who hold the keys.

This selection is from a summary article by Glasser with Leonard Zunin which appeared in another companion volume I edited, *Current Psychotherapies* (Itasca, Ill.: F. E. Peacock Publishers, 1973). It demonstrates the uniqueness of this point of view, as well as comparing it with other systems. Reality Therapy essentially stresses the importance that humans place on their identity, their acknowledgment of their unique individuality. Thus it is essentially a here-and-now theory, as is true of a number of others presented in this book: Kelly's personal constructs theory, Perls's Gestalt therapy, Moreno's sociometric theory, and Ellis's rational-emotive theory, for example. In such theories, the time perspective is relatively limited to the present moment; where the person came from, how he developed his personality, and where he is headed are considered either unimportant or unnecessary. The essential thing to consider is the present moment: the *now*.

You will find in this selection that although this theory is of a surface rather than a depth type, and despite its being a here-and-now theory, it is nonetheless fairly well developed and carefully thought out.

WILLIAM GLASSER and LEONARD ZUNIN
Basic concepts in reality therapy

Reality Therapy is based upon the premise that there is a single basic psychological need that all people in all cultures possess from birth to death; that is the need for an identity: the need to feel that we are somehow separate and distinct from every other living being on the face of this earth, that no matter where we go we will not find another person who thinks, looks, acts, and talks exactly as we do. This need is universal and transcends all cultures. Its significance is evidenced, for example, in religious teachings of both primitive and civilized societies. Every organized religion appears to deal with the basic question of what happens to a person's identity after death.

Identity has been defined as "a stream with many fibers that runs through all the days of your life and ties them together in a unique strand called 'I'." Further, it is not sufficient to realize that one is a distinct entity, but in addition one must have meaning associated with his identity. That is, one must see himself as having either a success identity or a failure identity, based upon his involvement with others.

Reality Therapy differs from other therapeutic endeavors, such as psychoanalysis, the strict behavioral therapies like operant conditioning, and from some of the newer therapeutic fads, in that Reality Therapy is applied not only to the problems of people who are extremely irresponsible and incompetent, but also because it can be applied equally well to daily living. It is not a therapy exclusively for the "mentally ill," incompetent, disturbed, or emotionally upset; it is a system of ideas which can help anyone learn to gain a successful identity and to help others do so. Reality Therapy is readily understandable and it may be applied by anyone who understands these principles without prolonged, specific training other than the application of effort, sensitivity, and common sense.

That the principles of Reality Therapy are easily understood, that they may be applied by anyone, parents with children, ministers with their congregations, husbands and wives with each other, employers with their employees, salesmen with their prospects, in no way makes this therapy less professional. The value of the therapy is not diminished simply because a system of ideas is understandable and usable by the majority of individuals. The reality therapist brings, to problem situations, a special ability, rather a wider variety of abilities, to become involved, a basic ingredient of Reality Therapy. He has more experience in how to make successful plans and perhaps more experience to guide people to examine their plans and their own behavior. He may confront them with the irresponsibility of their behavior and lead them toward commitments, while not accepting excuses which they may attempt to make. Of significance: what the therapist is attempting to do should be clearly understandable to the patient and to everyone involved.

William Glasser and Leonard Zunin, "Basic Concepts in Reality Therapy." Reprinted from R. J. Corsini (ed.), *Current Psychotherapies* (Itasca, Ill.: F. E. Peacock Publishers, 1973), pp. 292–298.

Once the ability for successful involvement has been established, the principles of Reality Therapy then evolve into a system or a way of life which helps a person to become successful in almost all of his endeavors. If he isn't successful, we try at least to understand where he lacks success and try, even if success seems impossible, to search in one direction after another to understand that the options are never really closed. There are innumerable options in society to find success one way or another. We believe that transference, as previously described in other therapeutic approaches, not only occurs in the therapeutic experience but also occurs in the experiences, on a regular basis, of everyday life. All of us make certain assumptions and have certain distorted impressions about other individuals. These distorted impressions are based upon our experiences from other sources and with other people. For example, when we meet someone for the first time, we may like or dislike him for reasons that are unknown or unclear to us. It may be that he reminds us of a past friend or acquaintance or relative or loved one, but always it's because each new person triggers old associations. In contrast, rather than to attempt to enhance this phenomenon and then analyse it, the reality therapist attempts to decrease the distortion. The reality therapist presents himself as himself; and in fact, as therapy progresses, will shatter distortions that the patient may have. He may question them but never reinforce them. If the patient relates to the reality therapist as saying, "You remind me of my father," the reality therapist may say, "I am not your father, but I would be interested in knowing what you see as similar in us." Rather than reinforcing the development of transference phenomenon and then analyzing the so-called transference, the reality therapist attempts in every way possible to present himself as a genuine, concerned, real person, helping the patient face reality, understand reality and accept reality.

OTHER SYSTEMS

Reality Therapy differs from conventional therapy in at least six major aspects:

1. Reality Therapy rejects the orthodox concept of mental illness in the various categories by which it is described—paranoic, schizophrenic, manic, and so forth. We believe most forms of mental disturbance are best described as irresponsibility; and, regardless of behavior symptoms, the proper solution is to show the patient the unreality and self-defeating nature of his behavior. The reality therapist helps the patient to discover behavior which will satisfy and/or help him to fulfill his basic psychological needs without hurting himself or other people. Reality Therapy, of course, acknowledges that a tiny fraction of so-called mental disturbances are caused by known biochemical disorders or brain damage.

2. Conventional theory places great emphasis on examining the patient's past experience. It is believed that once the patient understands the root causes of his behavior he will change. Reality Therapy disagrees with that point of view and is, therefore, not particularly interested in the patient's past behavior. If it had been acceptable, the person would not be in therapy. The entire focus is on the present and the future.

3. Conventional psychiatry places great emphasis on the theory of transference which states that the patient can be induced to transfer to his therapist attitudes, feelings, and ideas that he held or still holds toward important and significant people in his past. The therapist then attempts to make the patient aware of his

transference and, through this insight, enable him to change his behavior. The reality therapist feels that significantly constructive benefit is achieved by relating to the person as himself and not as a transference figure. Most patients live with enough misconceptions and distortions of reality and do not need to have these misconceptions enhanced in a therapeutic situation.

4. Conventional psychotherapy believes that if a patient is to change he must gain insight into his unconscious mind. Unconscious conflict is considered more important in many cases than conscious problems. Thus the conventional emphasis is on dreams, transference, and free association. The reality therapist does not permit patients to use unconscious motivations as an excuse for misbehavior. The emphasis is upon what the patient is doing, particularly his present attempts to succeed or what he intends to do. It is our contention that insight does not produce change although it may be intellectually interesting.

5. Orthodox psychiatry generally avoids specific value judgments. It also avoids dealing with the issue of right and wrong. Deviant behavior is considered a product of mental illness, and the patient is often felt not morally responsible because he is considered helpless to do anything about it. The basic premise of Reality Therapy is almost the exact opposite, that the patient's problem is the result of his inability to comprehend and apply values and moral principles in his daily life. The patient is confronted with the fact that he is responsible for his own behavior. In fact, the reality therapist believes that no basic change can occur in therapy unless and until an individual acknowledges that he is responsible for his behavior.

6. Conventional therapy does not generally include teaching people to behave in a better manner by setting up specific plans and helping people to make commitments to follow through with their plans. Conventional therapy generally assumes that once patients understand themselves and the unconscious sources and roots of their problems, they will spontaneously learn better behavior themselves. Reality Therapy on the other hand seeks to teach patients better ways of behaving that will enable them to fulfill their basic psychological needs.

An increasing number of individuals have been expressing ideas, aspects of which are identical to or closely aligned with Glasser's ideas.

Dr. O. Hobart Mowrer broke with theories of behavior that pictured man as a helpless victim of heredity or environment. He has developed a new method known as Integrity Therapy for treating emotional problems. His philosophy is almost the opposite of Freudian theory. Mowrer states that instead of mental problems resulting from the individual's attempts to live up to a naturally high moral code, rather they occur when man does not live up to his own moral convictions. Mowrer has stated "the problem presented by psychopathology is one that is best conceptualized, not as illness, but rather as a kind of ignorance and moral failure and the strategy of choice of preventing and correcting these conditions is manifestly educational and ethical." (Mowrer, 1961)

Dr. Willard H. Mainord seems to agree with Reality Therapy concepts in many important respects. First, he is dissatisfied with orthodox therapy, especially psychoanalysis. Second, he believes that the mentally disturbed are not sick in the medical sense, but are irresponsible. Third, he believes the therapist must help the patient to discover that irresponsibility does not pay and responsibility does. Fourth, he thinks that a good society is one where virtue is rewarded. "If the patient to discover that irresponsibility does not pay and responsibility curate communication, the 'crazy' behavior will have no payoff value and will disappear sometimes dramatically." (Mainord, forthcoming)

"The Third Force" psychology of Abraham Maslow (1954), the late distinguished psychologist, is closely aligned to Reality Therapy. Maslow believed that most individuals have a capacity for creativeness, spontaneity, caring for others, curiosity, continual growth, the ability to love and be loved, and of all other characteristics found in self-actualized people. A person who is behaving badly is reacting to the deprivation of his basic needs. If his behavior improves he begins to develop his true potential and move toward greater health and normalcy as a human. Maslow felt that one of the great errors of the behavioral scientist, the psychiatrist, and the psychologist is the belief that right and wrong behavior have no scientific basis. Maslow, like Glasser, felt that in the final analysis irresponsibility was just as damaging to the individual as to his society.

The psychiatrist Alan Wheelis, in his book *The Desert* (1970), states "much of our suffering is just so obscure . . . frigidity, social anxiety, isolation, boredom, dissatisfaction with life—in all such states we may see no correlation between the inner feeling and the way we live, yet no such feeling can be independent of behavior; and if only we find connections we may begin to see how a change in the way we live will make for a change in the way we feel."

THEORY OF PERSONALITY

. . . Reality Therapy views identity as a single, basic requirement of all mankind, which transcends all cultures and exists from birth to death. Although identity can be viewed through several different ports, it is most useful to regard identity from a therapeutic vantage point, as success identity versus failure identity. Each individual develops an identity image. He feels that he is relatively successful or unsuccessful. We are not referring to success as measured in titles or labels or finances, but rather in terms of the individual's own self-image. This may or may not conform to the image that others have of him. It is indeed possible for an individual to regard himself as basically a failure in life when others around him regard him as an outstanding success.

Formation of a failure identity seems to occur most often at age four or five, coincidental with the age at which the child enters school. Prior to that time most children view themselves as successful. It is at about this age that we find the individual developing the social skills, verbal skills, intellect, and thinking ability which enable him to begin to define himself in terms of being a successful or unsuccessful person. As the months and the years progress, the individual who regards himself as successful appears to associate with other successful people, and the individual who sees himself as a failure associates with others who have failure identity. The two groups become increasingly detached and divergent. For example, it is indeed rare for a person with a success identity to have, as a close and personal friend, someone who is a known criminal, felon, heroin addict, and so forth. Gradually the incongruity and the disparity between the two groups is widened as a result of a commonality of individuals with a failure identity. The commonality is the one of loneliness. In our Western culture these individuals all appear to experience an extreme degree of loneliness, and lonely people clearly have difficulties in helping other lonely people, except to provide transient solace. At the same time, those individuals with a success identity continue to compete, usually in a constructive manner, and reinforce one another's successes. Failures have difficulty, on a regular basis, facing the real world and find it uncomfortable, anxiety-evoking, disparaging, and depressing.

In reviewing those individuals who seem to have a success identity, it appears they have two traits that are consistent and ever-present. First, they know that somewhere out there in the world, there is at least one other person who loves them for what they are. And also they love at least one other person in the world around them. Secondly, individuals with a success identity have the knowledge and understanding that most of the time they are worthwhile human beings and, at least one, and hopefully more than one other individual also feels they are worthwhile. In Reality Therapy we see worth and love as two very different elements. Consider, for example, the extreme case of the "spoiled" child. One may fantasize that a child, if showered with "pure love," whose parents' "goal" was never to frustrate or stress or strain this child in any way, and when he was faced with a task or difficulty always has his parents to perform this task for him, this child always relieved of responsibility, would develop into an individual who would feel loved but would not experience worth. Worth comes through accomplishing tasks and achieving success in the accomplishment of those tasks. On the other hand, not infrequent is the depression of a man of seemingly broad business success who knows he is worthwhile to others. He is aware that not one but many, many people feel he is a successful, worthwhile human being. This man, however, may be experiencing an absence of love in his life, because he cannot point to one person and say "there is at least that one in-dividual that I truly love and who truly loves me," and his depression is understandable.

The identity that we develop comes from our involvement with others as well as our involvement with ourselves. Our identity develops from recalling objects of one's love and gratification because that which we love and have loved tends to be associated with and psychologically incorporated into ourselves; what we admire, we tend to exemplify, what we dislike, we tend to reject. We also discover our identity by observing those causes or concerns with which we are involved. That to which we devote our energy and our time is a reflection of what and who we are. We discover an identity of ourselves during crises. In a moment of panic or threat of self-exposure or embarrassment, we behave often in ways impossible for us to predict. By reflecting back on our behavior during these moments we further clarify and understand who we are.

Others also play an important role in helping us to clarify and understand our identity. What others reflect back to us, if we are willing to give our eyes and ears the freedom to see and hear, is a most meaningful mirror of one's identity. This is what occurs in psychotherapy and in friendships. Our beliefs and value systems, our religion or lack of religion, and philosophy further clarify our identity. We also see ourselves in relation to the living conditions, the climate and economic and social status of others.

Lastly, our physical image in relation to others, including our physical structure, our grooming and our clothes, help us to see ourselves in relation to others and to clarify our own identity.

Those individuals who appear to develop a failure identity and have difficulty and feel a sense of discomfort in a real world handle this sense of discomfort in two general ways. They may either deny reality or ignore it. What we consider mental illness is really the various ways in which an individual denies reality. Mental illness may manifest itself in a wide variety of ways. In Reality Therapy, we do not feel that specific diagnostic terms are helpful or useful in providing an effective method of change for the mentally ill. The person who is mentally ill has changed the real world in his own fantasy to make himself feel more comfortable. He denies reality to protect himself from facing the feeling of being meaningless and insignificant in the world around him. For example, both the grandiose delusion and the persecutory delusion of the so-called schizophrenic provide the same support or solace for him. Is there any difference between the individual who feels that the FBI, the CIA, the President, and all of the political leaders are following him, and the person who feels he is Jesus or Napoleon or God or the Governor or the President? Both individuals are changing the world in their own mind and in their own fantasy to assist them in feeling important, meaningful and significant in the world.

Those individuals who ignore reality are people that we feel are aware of the real world and choose, rather than to deny and change reality in their own mind, to simply ignore it. These individuals are referred to as delinquents, criminals, "sociopaths," "personality disorders," and so on. They are basically the antisocial individuals who choose to break the rules and regulations of society on a regular basis, thereby ignoring reality.

VARIETY OF CONCEPTS

In contrast to other theoretical psychotherapeutic frameworks, which discuss a variety of instincts and drives, we in Reality Therapy believe that each human being has a single most important basic social need for identity. This need is intrinsic and inherited within each individual and transmitted from generation to generation. It is a need for an individual identity interrelated with one's social identity. A person's identity defines him in relation to his involvement with others. This need for involvement, we feel, is an integral part of the organism and is the primary intrinsic driving force governing all behavior. Although early parental influence is exceedingly important and crucial, we believe that other areas such as peer relationships and, specifically, involvement in school potentially wield a tremendously unrecognized magnitude of influence on the evolving identity of the child. Ordinarily, one thinks that the need for love will be fulfilled in the home rather than in the school or outside institutions as a result of peer relationships. However, teachers are overwhelmed with children who need affection, and who are struggling with their own identity and self-concept. Glasser believes that helping to fulfill the needs for love and worth is unequivocally one of the functions of school, and unless this is recognized, individual failure identity can unknowingly be reinforced. In his book *Schools Without Failure* (1969) he discussed how the school can and should get involved to help children fulfill their need for love and worth. In the context of school, love can best be thought of as social responsibility. When children do not learn to be responsible for each other, to care for each other and to help each other, not only for the sake of others but for their own sake, love becomes a weak and limited concept. Glasser believes that the schools have not adequately faced the problem of failure caused by loneliness. Cultural and environmental influences have a profound effect upon shaping the identity of the child which begins to formulate in each individual as a success or a failure identity by the age of five or six.

Individual autonomy, we believe, is directly related to maturity. This is the ability to let go and relinquish environmental supports and substitute individual internal psychological support, the ability of an individual to psychologically stand on his own two feet. This, of course, does not mean not to be involved, not to give, not to love, and so forth. It means for the individual to take responsibility for who he is and what he wants in life and to develop responsible plans to fulfill his needs and his goals.

We believe that all individuals have goals and that these goals can be developed in a hierarchy of levels of aspiration. In a rather philosophical sense, it is literally impossible not to have a goal in life, even if the goal is not to have a goal.

In Reality Therapy, individuals are assisted in understanding, defining and clarifying their own life goals both immediate and long-term. In fact, this is one of the first steps in psychotherapy. Secondly, the individual is assisted in clarifying the ways in which he hampers his own progress toward his goals and he is assisted in understanding alternatives. With the phase of compromise, planning, and modification of behavior, resultant change in behavior begins to occur.

The concept of alternatives is dealt with directly in therapy. Often people with emotional problems see very few, if any, alternative avenues of approach, and part of the function of the therapist is to assist the patient in understanding that alternatives are usually unending. Even a man facing a firing squad has some limited alternatives. He might pray, curse, collapse, spit, hold his breath, scream, try to escape to the best of his ability, face the firing squad with equanimity, bite his lip,

stick out his tongue, and so on. These alternatives are limited since the apparently inevitable fact is the person will be shot. However, they are not as limiting as they might seem even in this restricted example because by various subtle shifts in behavior, in rare instances individuals have been known to have executions stayed. The alternatives, of course, in life's situations go far beyond the alternatives of a man facing a firing squad. In Reality Therapy, a person may first be asked to list all of the possible alternatives to a situation without any initial judgment of these alternatives. When one eliminates judgment of alternatives he can have an open mind in listing them. Interestingly, when alternatives become apparent in a nonjudgmental way, the individual is often amused by how ridiculous are some of the alternatives he might choose. Nonetheless, it helps each person to understand that alternatives are unlimited. After this concept is integrated into the thinking of a person facing a difficult situation, then the therapist can assist the person in placing various value judgments on the most reasonable possible alternatives and ferreting out the most likely and effective alternatives. From this more limited list of alternatives the individual then can begin to weigh and select his eventual choice.

The unconscious, as has been defined by other systems, for example, by the psychoanalytic approach, we believe has little evidence to support its validity. The evidence of the existence of an unconscious is shaky; it includes hypnosis, dreams, and the psychopathology of everyday life—slips of the tongue, and so forth. We believe that this is less than adequate evidence for the existence of a well-defined unconsciousness. Certainly it is apparent that each individual has various levels of memory recollection and we feel that however scientifically significant it may be to understand these various levels of memory, they are not germane to the psychotherapeutic process and not helpful in helping people to change current behavior. Not that an accurate concept of the unconscious is irrelevant or unimportant but just that it is, in our opinion, not related to doing clinical therapy. Furthermore, it is our opinion that individuals forget not only traumatic and unfortunate incidents that happen to them in the past but also forget positive meaningful and character-building experiences. Far too little attention has been placed on understanding this latter notion.

The concept of individual uniqueness has been discussed earlier in this chapter and is essential to motivation. To understand that each individual believes and knows that he is unique in the world, is directly related to his success versus failure identity.

We believe that each individual has a health or growth force. Basically people want to be content and enjoy a success identity, to show responsible behavior and to have meaningful interpersonal relationships. Suffering does not disappear without a change in identity, which amounts to a change in what one is and how one lives, feels and behaves. Identity change follows change in behavior. To a great extent we are what we do, and if we want to change what we are we must begin by changing what we do and undertake new ways of behaving. We do believe that certain homeostatic mechanisms cause the individual to protest and resist change in behavior as existing behavior for better or for worse represents, to some limited extent, security as well as in some cases entrenched and conditioned modes of behaving. The effort to change, which may be considerable, only comes from motivation through involvement with meaningful others. Thus the importance of the therapeutic involvement in Reality Therapy. Further, fixed change usually occurs only if action is maintained over a significant period of time.

Learning is an integral concept of Reality Therapy. Learning occurs in all activities of life and is one of the mainstays of the psychotherapeutic process. A wide variety of learning concepts and basic learning theory is incorporated into the general framework of the theoretical as well as the clinical base of Reality Therapy. A special kind of learning occurs through the involvement in the psychotherapeutic situation. We are what we do and to a great extent we are what we learn to do and identity becomes the integration of all learned and unlearned behavior.

A variety of previously established concepts in use by other psychotherapeutic systems are felt not to be relevant to Reality Therapy. These concepts among others include the Oedipus complex, racial unconsciousness, organ inferiority, libido, fictive goals, private logic, and collective unconsciousness. Again, it is not our intent to state that these concepts are in error although they may very well be; or that they are not important, but only that they are not necessary in the practice of psychotherapy.

REFERENCES

Glasser, William. *Schools without failure.* New York: Harper & Row, 1969.

Mainord, Willard A. *Therapy #52—The Truth* (in press).

Maslow, A. H. The instinctoid nature of basic needs. *Journal of Personality,* 1954, *22,* 326–347.

Mowrer, O. H. *The crisis in psychiatry and religion.* New York: Van Nostrand, 1961.

Wheelis, Alan, *The desert.* New York: Basic Books, 1970.

CHAPTER 26

Social Learning Theory

Introduction

Albert Bandura (1925–   ) an ex-president of the American Psychological Association, has spent most of his professional career obtaining evidence relative to observational learning, which holds that people learn their ways of behaving from watching others. This commonsense conclusion would be readily accepted as a valid notion by anyone who works with children, but nevertheless it must be experimentally proven. From the point of view of scientific knowledge, it is necessary to know about such elements as sex differences in modeling, the effects of various kinds of models, and whether people will actually put into practice what they have learned. In dozens of fundamental experiments, Bandura and his associates and colleagues have found the answers with some precision.

This selection differs from the others in this book in that it is essentially a series of hypotheses about behavior and a summary of research studies that give evidence of the validity of the hypotheses. It shows how a nomothetic research worker conceptualizes problems, how results are obtained and conclusions are formed.

Perhaps most importantly, this summary can provide a stimulus for other theoretical notions to be studied as exhaustively, so that unequivocal evidence can be obtained for other concepts of how humans develop and maintain their individuality.

ALBERT BANDURA
Behavior therapy and identificatory learning

Most current research on social learning is focused on the shaping of new patterns of behavior through rewarding and punishing consequences. Despite the widespread acceptance and application of differential reinforcement principles to human learning, it is doubtful that many social responses would ever be acquired if social training proceeded solely by these methods. This is particularly true of behavior for which there is no reliable eliciting stimulus apart from the cues provided by others as they exhibit the behavior. If a child had no occasion to hear speech, for example, or, in the case of a deaf-blind person, no opportunity to watch the mouth and laryngeal responses of a verbalizing model (Keller, 1927), it would probably be impossible to teach him the kind of verbal responses that constitute a language.

Even in cases where some stimulus is known to be capable of eliciting an approximation to the desired behavior, the process of learning can be considerably shortened and accelerated by the provision of social models. Indeed, informal observation of the process of social learning as it occurs in naturalistic situations reveals that the behavior of models in one form or another is utilized to some degree in facilitating learning, regardless of whether the person is being taught the responses necessary for playing golf, swimming, performing surgical operations, flying an airplane or conducting psychotherapeutic interviews. In fact, in many cultures "the word for 'teach' is the same as the word for 'show,' and the synonymity is literal" (Riechard, 1948). In one Guatemalan subculture, for example, the acquisition of complex vocational skills proceeds entirely on the basis of imitation (Nash, 1958). In learning to operate a cotton textile machine, the young Cantelense apprentice stands beside the machine and observes the operator perform the set of responses necessary for running the loom. During the training period the learner asks no questions and is given no verbal instructions or practice in operating the textile machine. As soon as the apprentice feels that she has mastered the necessary sequence of responses through observation, the machine is turned over to her. Typically, on the first trial she performs almost as skillfully as did the model operator.

Adult-role behavior is transmitted to young children in a similar manner. The young Cantelense girl is provided with a miniature water jar, a small broom and a tiny grinding stone modeled after her mother's domestic utensils. The child constantly observes and imitates her mother's behavior, with little or no direct tuition. Although parents in our culture generally do not provide their young daughters with miniature stainless steel kitchens, they do supply them with a varied array of play materials—toy kitchen ensembles, dolls with complete nursery equipment and wardrobes, cooking utensils and other junior-sized homemaker kits—that serve

Albert Bandura, "Behavior Theory and Identificatory Learning." Reprinted from *American Journal of Orthopsychiatry*, 1963, *33*, 591–601.

much the same purpose. In games utilizing such stimulus material, children frequently reproduce the entire parental-role behavior—including the appropriate mannerisms, voice inflections, and attitudes—which the parents have never directly attempted to teach. These examples illustrate the efficacy of imitative learning, since children acquire complex patterns of social behavior *in toto,* without proceeding through a slow, laborious response-acquisition process involving differential reinforcement and extinction.

This type of learning is generally labeled "imitation" in social learning theory, and "identification" in most theories of personality. These concepts are treated in the present paper as synonymous, because both encompass the same behavioral phenomenon, that is, the tendency for a person to match the behavior or attitudes as exhibited by actual or symbolized models. Numerous distinctions have been proposed, of course, at one time or another. Some writers, for example, reserve the term "identification" for matching behavior falling within a class of responses defined as meanings, and "imitation" for highly specific acts (Mowrer, 1950). Similarly, Parsons (Parsons & Shils, 1951) contrasts imitation to identification in terms of specificity and diffuseness of learning, with the additional qualification that a "generalized cathetic attachment" is an essential antecedent of identification but unnecessary or absent in the case of imitation. Others define imitation as matching behavior occurring in the presence of the model, and regard identification as involving the performance of the model's behavior in the latter's absence (Mowrer, 1950).

Distinctions can be drawn between these and other related terms (for example, introjection and incorporation) based on certain stimulus, mediating or response variables. However, one might question whether it is meaningful to do so, since essentially the same learning process is involved regardless of the content of what is learned, the object from whom it is learned, or the situation in which the relevant behavior is emitted. Therefore, in the interests of clarity, precision and parsimony, I shall employ a single concept, imitation, to refer to the occurrence of matching behavior.

The findings of a series of experiments I have recently conducted on imitation throw some light on this process of learning.

EFFECTS OF NURTURANCE ON IMITATION

First, consider an experiment that was designed to test the influence of nurturance on imitation (Bandura & Huston, 1961). If the behavioral attributes of a model are repeatedly paired with positive reinforcement, the model's characteristics take on secondary reinforcement value for the child and, consequently, should be imitated to a greater extent than if the model's behavior had not been positively conditioned. To test this prediction, nursery school children were subdivided into a nurturant and nonnurturant experimental condition.

In the *nonnurturant* condition a female in the role of the model brought the child to the experimental room and, after instructing him to play with toys that were spread on the floor, she busied herself with paper work at a desk, totally ignoring the child.

With children in the *nurturant* condition, in contrast, the model sat on the floor close to the child. She responded readily to the child's bids for help, approval and attention, and in general was positively demonstrative and rewarding to the child.

Immediately following the second social interaction session, the experimenter entered the room and instructed the model and the child that they were going to play a game in which they would take turns in guessing which of two boxes contained a picture sticker. In executing each trial, the model exhibited relatively novel verbal, motor and aggressive responses that were totally irrelevant to the discrimination task to which the child's attention was directed. At the starting point, for example, the model made a verbal response and then marched slowly toward the appropriate box repeating, "March, march, march." On the lid of each box was a rubber doll, which the model knocked off aggressively. She emitted additional verbal responses as she raised the lid of the container and removed a sticker. The child then took his turn and the number of the model's responses he reproduced was recorded.

The expected facilitating effect of nurturance on imitation was clearly confirmed. Children who experienced the

prior nurturant relationship with the model marched and verbalized imitatively, and reproduced other responses resembling that of the model to a substantially greater extent than did children who were in the nonnurturant group (Table 26.1). Aggression, however, was readily imitated by the children, regardless of the quality of the model-child relationship.

Some additional evidence that the model's behavior may have taken on positive valence and was reproduced by the children for its intrinsically rewarding value is provided by the fact that, while waiting for the next trial, children in the nurturant group, unlike those in the nonnurturant condition, not only marched to the boxes but also marched about the experimental room repeating, "March, march, march."

The finding that children in the nurturant group, as compared with those in the nonnurturant condition, displayed considerably more verbal behavior apart from their imitative verbalizations indicates that exposure to a model possessing rewarding qualities not only facilitates imitation of the specific characteristics exhibited by the model, but also increases the occurrence of behavior of a whole response class (for example, verbal behavior).

TABLE 26.1. Significance of differences in imitative behavior exhibited by children in the nurturant and nonnurturant experimental conditions

| Response category | Number of children imitating | | |
	Nurturant (N = 20)	Nonnurturant (N = 20)	p
Nonaggressive behavior...	15	7	.04
Marching............	13	5	.05
Verbal behavior.......	9	2	.05
Other imitative responses	6	1	.06
Aggressive behavior......	20	16	ns
Partially imitative verbal responses.......	12	5	.04

GENERALIZATION OF IMITATIVE AGGRESSION IN THE ABSENCE OF THE MODEL

In the preceding study, imitative responses were elicited in the presence of the model. A more decisive test of imitative learning is the demonstration of the generalization of imitative responses to a setting from which the model is absent. Therefore, a second experiment was conducted (Bandura, Ross & Ross, 1963b) in which one group of nursery school children observed aggressive adult models, and a second group viewed models who were subdued and nonaggressive in their behavior. Half the children in the aggressive and nonaggressive conditions observed same-sex models, while the remaining children in each group viewed models of the opposite sex. A control group of children who had no exposure to the models was also included.

Children in the *aggressive model condition* observed the model perform a number of fairly unique aggressive responses toward a large, inflated plastic doll. These were to be scored as imitative aggressive acts when reproduced later by the child. For example, the model sat on the doll and punched it repeatedly in the nose, pommelled it on the head with the mallet, tossed the doll in the air aggressively, and kicked it about the room. This sequence of physically aggressive acts was interspersed with distinctive verbally aggressive responses.

With children in the *nonaggressive model* condition, in contrast, the model assembled the tinker toys in a subdued manner, totally ignoring the doll.

Following the exposure session, all children were mildly frustrated before being tested for delayed imitation of the behavior of the model. They then spent 20 minutes in an experimental room containing a variety of toys including some that could be employed in imitative or nonimitative aggression. The children's behavior was rated in five-second intervals by observers who witnessed the sessions through a one-way mirror.

Before discussing the findings, I would like to describe two additional experimental treatments conducted as part of a subsequent study (Bandura, 1963), which replicated the design of the present experiment in every detail except that the aggressive models were presented on film.

IMITATION OF FILM-MEDIATED AGGRESSIVE MODELS

Most of the research on the possible effects of film-mediated stimulation upon subsequent aggressive behavior has focused primarily on the need-reducing function of fantasy. While the experimental evidence for the catharsis theory is equivocal, the modeling influence of pictorial stimuli has received little research attention. In view of the fact that children are exposed to televised stimulation for approximately one-sixth of their waking hours (Schramm & Parker, 1961), it is of considerable interest to determine the extent to which film-mediated human and cartoon models may serve as an important source of imitative behavior, and to compare their effects to that of real-life models.

Children in the *human film-aggression condition* were simply shown films of the same adult male and female who performed in the real-life condition in the previous experiment. Similarly, the aggressive behavior they displayed in the film was identical with their real-life performances.

For children in the *cartoon film-aggression condition,* a film projected on a lenscreen of a television console showed the female model costumed as a black cat, pommelling the plastic doll with the mallet, sitting on it and punching it in the nose, tossing the doll in the air and kicking it about the room.

In both film conditions, at the conclusion of the film, the children were subjected to the frustration experience, and then observed in the test situation.

While children who observed the real-life and the film-mediated models did not differ from each other, all three groups performed approximately twice as much aggression as did the children in either the control group or the nonaggressive model condition. The corresponding mean total aggression scores for children in the real-life, human-film, cartoon-film, control and nonaggressive model groups were 83, 92, 99, 54 and 42, respectively.

Exposure of children to models displaying aggression not only increased their aggressiveness, it was also highly effective in shaping the form of the children's aggressive behavior. Illustration of the extent to which some of the children became virtually "carbon copies" of their models in aggressive behavior is presented in Figure 26.1 [not shown here]. The top frame shows the female model performing the four novel aggressive responses; the lower frames depict a boy and a girl reproducing the behavior of the female model they had observed earlier on film.

Children who observed real-life aggressive models displayed more imitative aggression than children who had viewed the cartoon model. The real-life and human-film aggressive groups, however, did not differ in this respect. Overall findings based on a variety of measures of non-imitative aggression revealed that exposure to human models portraying aggression on film was the most influential method of eliciting aggressive behavior. A similar heightening of aggressive tendencies in adults following exposure to aggressive excerpts from a commercial movie has been demonstrated recently by Walters, Llewellyn-Thomas and Acker (1962).

In general, the aggressive male model was more influential than the female model in eliciting aggressive behavior. It was evident from the children's spontaneous comments that, even at this early age, aggression was clearly sex-typed as appropriate masculine behavior. This probably also accounts for the fact that girls displayed significantly less imitative and nonimitative aggression than boys did, but displayed more partially imitative behavior in which the aggressive component of the model's responses was omitted.

The results yielded by these studies also provide some evidence that the behavior exhibited by adult models may be highly influential in shaping children's frustration-reactions. For example, children who observed the aggressive models displayed significantly more aggression (both imitative and nonimitative) when subsequently frustrated, than children who were equally frustrated but had no prior exposure to models exhibiting aggression. Moreover, children who viewed nonaggressive models displayed more nonaggressive behavior to frustration in comparison to the aggressive model groups, and less aggression than the control subjects.

Identification with the aggressor (Freud, 1939), whereby a person presumably transforms himself from an object to an agent of aggression by adopting the attributes of an aggressive, threatening model in order to allay anxiety, is widely accepted as an explanation of the imitative learning of aggression.

There is considerable evidence that children of aggressively punitive parents frequently exhibit aggressive patterns of behavior. It does not necessarily follow, however, that the presence of aggression in parent and child is an outcome of a process of defensive identification. In fact, the findings yielded by studies of child-training antecedents of aggressively antisocial adolescents (Bandura & Walters, 1959) and of young, hyperaggressive boys (Bandura, 1960) provide some evidence that the similarity is, in part, a function of direct training in discrimination. Typically the parents of hyperaggressive boys punish aggression directed toward themselves, but encourage and reward a son's aggressive behavior directed toward persons outside the home.

The necessity of invoking a defensive mechanism can be further questioned by the fact that, in the experimental studies, children readily imitated aggressive adult models who were more or less neutral figures and constituted no threat whatsoever. Apparently, the mere observation of aggression was a sufficient condition for the imitative learning of aggressive behavior. Whether or not the children would have exhibited a greater amount of imitative aggression had they been treated by the models in a threatening manner is, of course, unknown.

INFLUENCE OF REINFORCEMENT AND SOCIAL MODELS ON MORAL JUDGMENTS

Most of the theorizing in the area of personality development has been guided by various forms of stage theories. According to Freudian theory (Freud, 1933), for example, personality changes are programmed in an oral-anal-phallic sequence; Erikson (Erikson, 1950) characterizes personality development in terms of an eight-stage sequence; Gesell (Gesell & Ilg, 1943) describes marked, predictable cyclical changes in behavior over yearly or even shorter temporal intervals; and Piaget (Piaget, 1948) delineates numerous different stages for different segments of behavior.

Although there appears to be relatively little consensus among these theories concerning the number and content of stages considered to be crucial, all share the assumption that social behavior can be categorized in terms of a relatively prefixed sequence of stages with varying degrees of continuity or discontinuity between successive developmental periods. Typically, the emergence of these presumedly age-specific modes of behavior is attributed to ontogenetic factors, rather than to experiential events, which are likely to be favored in a social learning theory of the developmental process.

Recently McDonald and I completed an experiment in which a social learning theory combining both the principles of operant conditioning and imitation was applied to a developmental problem that has been approached from a stage point of view (Bandura & McDonald, 1963).

According to Piaget (Piaget, 1948), one can distinguish two clear-cut stages of moral judgments demarcated from each other at approximately seven years of age. At the first stage, defined as *objective responsibility,* children judge the gravity of a deviant act in terms of the amount of material damages, and disregard the intentionality of the action. In contrast, at the second or *subjective responsibility* stage, children judge conduct in terms of its intent rather than its material consequences. While these stages are prefixed (for example, Piaget reports that young children are relatively incapable of adopting a subjective orientation, and he was unable to find a single case of objective morality in older children), the factors responsible for the transition from one stage to the other are not entirely clear.

The purpose of this experiment was to demonstrate that moral orientations are less age-specific than implied by Piaget, and that children's moral judgments can be altered and even reversed by the manipulation of reinforcement contingencies, and by the provision of appropriate social models.

In the first phase of the experiment (the base test), following the procedure employed by Piaget, children were administered pairs of story items each of which described a well-intentioned act that resulted in considerable damage, contrasted with a selfishly or maliciously motivated act producing minor consequences. The children were asked to select which of the two story characters performed the "naughtier" act.

On the basis of their initial performances, children who were decidedly subjective in their moral orientation and those who gave predominantly objective responses were assigned to one of the three following experimental conditions.

One group of children observed adult models who expressed moral judgments running counter to the children's orientation, and the children were reinforced with approval for adopting the models' evaluative responses. A second group observed the models but received no rein-

forcement for matching the models' behavior. The third group had no exposure to the models but were reinforced whenever they expressed moral judgments that ran counter to their dominant evaluative tendencies. Thus the experimental design permitted a test of the relative influence of direct social reinforcement, of the behavior of models, and of these two factors combined in shaping children's moral judgments.

Following the experimental treatments, the children were administered additional pairs of stories by a different experimenter, to obtain further information about the generality and the stability of the changes in judgmental responses in the absence of any models or social reinforcement. This constituted the post-test.

It was predicted that the combined use of models and social reinforcement would be the most powerful condition for altering the children's behavior, and that the provision of models alone would be of in-

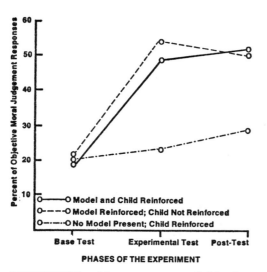

FIGURE 26.2. Mean percentage of objective moral judgment responses produced by subjective children on each of three test periods for each of three experimental conditions. (From Bandura, 1962.)

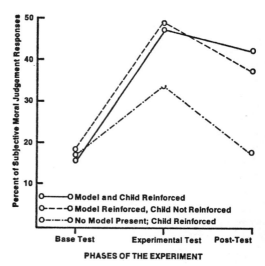

FIGURE 26.3. Mean percentage of subjective moral judgment responses produced by objective children on each of three test periods for each of three experimental conditions. (From Bandura, 1962.)

termediate effectiveness. Since the presence of a strong, dominant response limits the opportunity for reinforcement of an alternative response that is clearly subordinate, it was expected that social reinforcement alone would be the least effective of the three treatment methods.

Figure 26.2 presents the curves for the acquisition and maintenance of objective moral-judgment responses by subjective children for each of the three experimental treatments.

Statistical analyses of these data reveal that children who simply observed objective models and those who were reinforced for matching their model's moral judgments significantly altered their moral orientation in the direction of objectivity. Of even greater interest is the finding that children in these two conditions remained objectively oriented in their post-experimental judgmental behavior.

Contrary to prediction, the provision of models alone was as effective in modifying children's moral judgments as was the experimental treatment combining models with direct social reinforcement. In accordance with expectation, however, the conditions involving modeling procedures proved to be considerably more powerful than operant conditioning, which produced a slight, although not significant, increase in objective judgments. The corresponding results for the objective children treated subjectively are presented in Figure 26.3.

The over-all findings are essentially the same as those obtained for the subjective children. The experimental treatments were highly influential in changing the children's moral orientations from objective to subjective. Although the differences among the three treatment groups did not reach statistical significance, evidently the conditions utilizing

models were the main contributors to the observed changes.

The two sets of data considered together clearly demonstrate that, at least insofar as moral judgments are concerned, the developmental sequence is in no way prefixed or invariant. Indeed, the developmental stages can be readily altered through the application of appropriate social learning principles, modeling procedures being particularly effective in this respect.

The imitation experiments to which reference has been made have been confined to two-person groups. Currently we are studying imitation in three-person groups simulating different constellations of the nuclear family. Results from these experiments reveal that children are considerably more imitative of adults who control rewarding resources than of rivalrous adults who consume these resources, and that power inversions promote cross-sex imitation (Bandura & Ross, 1963). An experiment comparing imitation of aggressive models who are punished for exhibiting such behavior with that of models who amass considerable rewards through their aggression has also been completed.

The results yielded by this series of experiments strongly suggest that much of a child's behavior repertoire is acquired through imitation by the child of attitudes and patterns of behavior exhibited by adult models. Once acquired, these personality patterns can be effectively strengthened and maintained by direct reinforcement procedures.

REFERENCES

Bandura, A. *Relationship of family patterns to child behavior disorders. Progress Report.* Stanford University Project No.

M-1734. Washington, D.C.: U.S. Public Health Service, 1960.

Bandura, A. Social learning through imitation. In M. R. Jones (Ed.), *Nebraska Symposium on Motivation*. Lincoln: University of Nebraska Press, 1962.

Bandura, A., and Huston, A. C. Identification of film-mediated aggressive models. *Journal of Abnormal and Social Psychology*, 1961, *63*, 311–318.

Bandura, A., & McDonald, F. J. The influence of social reinforcement an the behavior of models in shaping children's moral judgments. *Journal of Abnormal and Social Psychology*, 1963, *67*, 274–282.

Bandura, A., Ross, D., & Ross, S. A. Transmission of aggression through imitation of aggressive models. *Journal of Abnormal and Social Psychology*, 1963, *67*, 575–582.

Bandura, A., Ross, D. & Ross, S. A. Imitation of film-mediated aggressive models. *Journal of Abnormal and Social Psychology*, 1963, *66*, 3–11.

Bandura, A. & Ross, D. A comparative test of the status envy, social power and the secondary reinforcement theories of indificatory learning. *Journal of Abnormal and Social Psychology*, 1963, *67*, 601–607.

Erikson, E. H. *Childhood and society*. New York: W. W. Norton & Co., 1950.

Freud, A. *The ego and the mechanism of defense*. London: Hogarth Press, 1939.

Freud, S. *New introductory lectures in psychoanalysis*. New York: W. W. Norton & Co., 1933.

Gesell, A., and Ilg, F. L. *Infant and child in the culture of today*. New York: Harper & Bros., 1943.

Keller, H. *The story of my life*. New York: Doubleday, 1927.

Mowrer, O. H. Identification: A link between learning theory and psychotherapy. In *Learning theory and personality dynamics*. New York: Ronald Press, 1950.

Nash, M. Machine age Maya; The industrialization of a Guatemalan community. *American Anthropological Association*, 60 (2), 1958.

Parsons, T., & Shils, E. A. *Toward a general theory of action*. Cambridge, Mass.: Harvard University Press, 1951.

Piaget, J. *The moral judgment of the child*. Glencoe, Ill.: Free Press, 1948.

Riechard, G. A. Social life. In F. Boas (Ed.), *General anthropology*. Madison, Wis.: C. D. Heath, 1948.

Schramm, W., Lyle, J., & Parker, E. G. *Television in the lives of our children*. Stanford, Calif.: Stanford University Press, 1961.

Walters, R. H. Lleyellyn-Thomas, E., & Acker, C. W. Enhancement of punitive behavior by audio-visual displays. *Science*, 1962, *136*, 872–873.

CHAPTER 27

Typology Theory

Introduction

One of the most remarkable individuals in psychology is Hans J. Eysenck (1917–   ), who is as productive as Albert Ellis but who ranges over the whole field of psychology like a colossus. He is an independent thinker who operates in an essentially simple way: he wants facts, not theories; he wants results, not explanations; he demands clear thinking, not pious hopes. An iconoclast, he is constantly in the center of controversies. His keen wit and clear thinking, as well as his prodigious accomplishments, have made him one of the world's most important psychologists.

One of Eysenck's many areas of interest and expertise is the mapping out of personality; that is, the determination of the real dimensions of this nebulous concept. What is exciting about his findings is his apparent conclusion that one of the oldest theories of personality dimensions—that developed by the Greek physician Hippocrates some 24 centuries ago—has been validated by his own factor analytic investigations using multivariate research techniques.

H. J. EYSENCK
The structure of personality

Theories about the structure of personality go back at least as far as the ancient Greeks, and the theory of the four humours and the four temperaments corresponding to them is of very respectable antiquity. In its most widely accepted form, it is due to the Greek physician Galen who lived in the second century of our era. The famous German philosopher Immanuel Kant accepted this theory in his widely read textbook of psychology which he entitled *Anthropologie,* and his descriptions of the four temperaments have become widely quoted. He followed custom in conceiving of them as being separate categories into one or other of which every person could be sorted, without any possibility of overlap or change (H. J. Eysenck, 1960). This was clearly not in accord with reality, and towards the end of the nineteenth century various psychologists pointed out that a better description of personality could be achieved by using two orthogonal dimensions, along each of which people could be distributed continuously. Wilhelm Wundt postulated that one of these dimensions would segregate the strong from the weak emotions, i.e., the melancholic and choleric temperaments from the phlegmatic and sanguine; as his other dimension he postulated one which divorced the changeable temperaments, the choleric and sanguine, from the un-

changeable ones, the melancholic and the phlegmatic (Eysenck & Eysenck, 1967). Figure 27.1 shows in diagrammatic form this combination of the theories of Kant and Wundt.

The work summarised in this figure was almost entirely of a subjective character; in other words, what these various philosophers, physicians, and psychologists were doing was to look for uniformities of conduct in the lives of the people whom they were able to observe, and reduce these uniformities to a description of a categorical or a continuous type. They made no attempt to formulate specific theories about the formal structure which was so well described in their word pictures, and they made no attempt to demonstrate by experimental or statistical means the accuracy or otherwise of their hypotheses. Implicitly, however, it is clear that the theories in question were essentially *hierarchical* in nature. The concept of an emotional person depends essentially on the occurrence of a variety of traits in the same person. In other words, we would expect a person who was anxious also to be worried, unhappy, quickly aroused, egocentric, etc.; conversely, we would expect a calm person to be also steadfast, persistent, carefree, hopeful, contented, and so on. Similarly, a changeable person would be active, playful, easygoing, and histrionic; an unchangeable one would be thoughtful, reasonable, serious, and high-principled.

Hypotheses of this kind are, of course, testable. What is implied is, in fact, *correlations between observable traits,* and it

H. J. Eysenck, "The Structure of Personality." From H. J. Eysenck, *The Biological Basis of Personality.* Courtesy of Charles C Thomas, Publisher, Springfield, Illinois 62717, U.S.A.

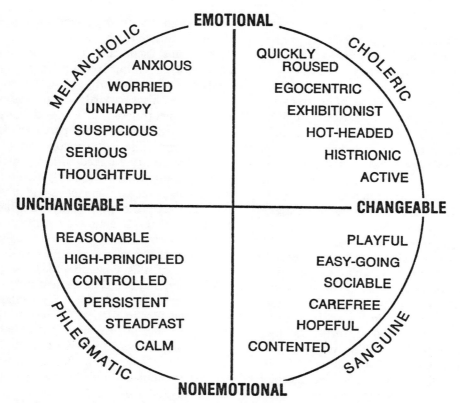

FIGURE 27.1. Traits traditionally describing the "four temperaments" of Galen. The actual descriptions are adapted from I. Kant, and the arrangement about the two major axes is as suggested by W. Wundt.

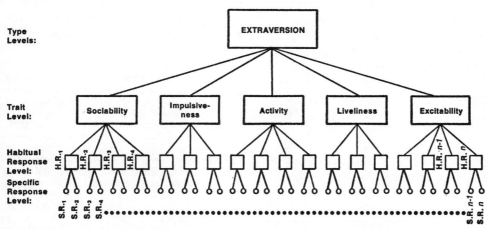

FIGURE 27.2. Hierarchical model of personality. Types are supraordinate concepts built up on the observed intercorrelations between traits. Reprinted with slight changes from H. J. Eysenck (1947).

is a great contribution of the early psycho-
metrists to have seen the possibility of applying correlational methods to this field
and to have carried out a number of
studies along these lines. A very detailed
discussion has been given of these early
efforts elsewhere (H. J. Eysenck, 1960),
and there would be little point in dupli-
cating this discussion here. Let us merely
note that in all essentials, whether carried
out on normal or abnormal subjects, on
adults or on children, on male subjects or
on females, and making use of ratings,
questionnaires, objective tests or other
methods, results have very generally verified a two-dimensional system of the kind
shown in Figure 27.1. The dimension labelled there emotional versus nonemotional has variously been called emotionality, neuroticism, stability, ego-
strength, anxiety, and so forth, but the
identity of the underlying concept has
been very clearly demonstrated. With
respect to the changeable-unchangeable
dimension, the tendency has been to label
this trait one of extraversion as opposed
to introversion. Figure 27.2 shows in
some detail the conception of extraversion
as a personality dimension based upon the
intercorrelations between a number of
different traits, in this case those of sociability, impulsiveness, activity, liveliness,
and excitability. It is clearly an empirical
question whether in actual fact sociability
correlates with impulsiveness, activity
with liveliness, and excitability with all the
others in a random group of 100 or 1,000
subjects, and, as stated before, the
evidence suggests that the correlations are
indeed all positive and reasonably high,
however the traits may be assessed. The
traits themselves are in turn, of course,
based on empirical evidence of a similar
kind; in other words, persons who behave
in a sociable manner in one situation tend

to behave in a sociable manner in other
situations, and so forth.

The terms used, such as neuroticism
and extraversion-introversion, are immediately suggestive of psychiatric abnormality.[1] This is so partly because, as in
the case of neuroticism, they refer directly
to emotional illness, and partly it is
because terms like extraversion and introversion are often linked with psychiatrists like Jung, who is frequently credited
with having invented these terms and having discovered the personality variable
denoted by them. In actual fact neither of
these two statements is true; as we have
noted above, the theory of a personality
dimension of this type goes back very
many years, and Jung's statement of it is
only one among many. Nor is it true that
he was the first to suggest the terms extraversion and introversion; these had
been in use in Europe for several hundred
years before Jung. Jung did, however,
make one important contribution, which
was to suggest that the two ends of the
extraversion-introversion continuum were
related respectively to two varieties of
neurotic disorders which he labelled the
psychastenic and *hysteric* respectively.
Later work has partly borne out this
hypothesis. Psychastenics, or as we would

---

[1] The connection between "emotionality" as a
personality variable of constitutional origin, and
proneness to nervous disorders (neuroticism) is
already adumbrated in Robert Whytt's famous "observations on the nature, causes, and cure of those
disorders which have been commonly called nervous, hypochondriac, or hysteric" (R. Whytt, *An
essay on the vital and other involuntary motions of
animals,* 2nd ed., Edinburgh: Hamilton, Balfour &
Neill, 1763.) On p. 93, for instance, he points out
that "those disorders may, peculiarly, deserve the
name of *nervous,* which, on account of an unusual
delicacy, or unnatural state of the nerves, are produced by causes, which, in people of a sound constitution, would either have no such effects, or at
least in a much less degree."

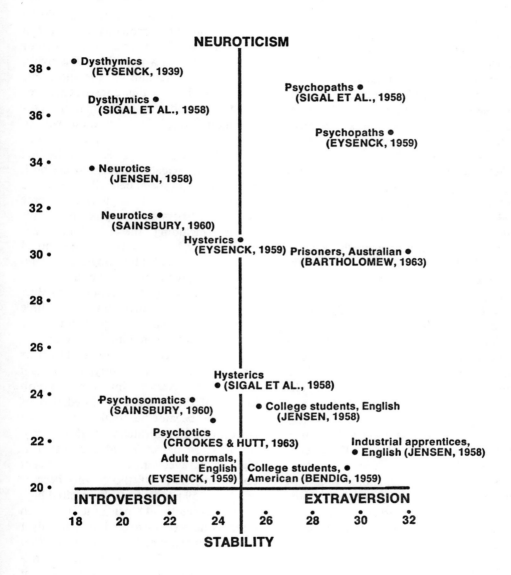

FIGURE 27.3. Scores of various neurotic, criminal, and normal groups on the Maudsley Personality Inventory. Reprinted with some additions from the Manual of the American edition (Eysenck, 1959).

now prefer to call them, *dysthymics* (i.e., neurotic patients suffering from anxiety, reactive depression, phobias, and/or obsessive-compulsive symptoms) do indeed tend to combine high neuroticism with a high degree of introversion; and hysterics, while above normal on neuroticism, tend to be much more extraverted than dysthymics. However, they are not more extraverted than normals on the whole, as shown in Figure 27.3, which quotes some typical studies carried out on a variety of groups by various authors using the Maudsley Personality Inventory (H. J. Eysenck, 1959).[2]

It will also be seen in this figure that the groups having high extraversion scores in addition to high neuroticism scores are convicts and psychopaths of various kinds. Thus we might say that people of the melancholic temperament, those combining a high degree of emotionality with a high degree of introversion, are apparently predisposed to develop dysthymic reactions; on the other hand, people of a choleric temperament, those highly emotional and highly extraverted, develop psychopathic, criminal, and delinquent behaviour patterns. There would be little point adducing all the evidence available on these relationships; a very detailed account is given in Eysenck and Eysenck (1967), bearing out the general picture shown in Figure 27.3. Nor are these relationships confined to European or English speaking countries; similar relationships between personality and behaviour patterns have been observed for instance in Australia, India, Japan, and a variety of other countries and cultures.

[2] The M.P.I. was constructed by the writer to measure N (neuroticism) and E (extraversion-introversion), and has been widely used. It has since been superseded by the E.P.I. (Eysenck & Eysenck, 1964). Also available is the Junior E.P.I. (S. B. G. Eysenck, 1965), which has been constructed for use with children.

Strictly speaking, the observed correlation between high N-high E scores and criminality, and between high N-low E scores and neurosis, does not prove that the personality traits predispose the individual to neurosis or crime; it might be argued that the personality traits are a consequence of neurotic breakdown or punishment following criminal activity, or that both personality traits and crime and neurosis are the consequences of some common cause. Something corresponding to this last hypothesis will, in fact, be argued in a later chapter, in which we shall try to show that certain inherited neurophysiological structures affect both personality and social behaviour. Here we will rest content with arguing that some form of "personality predisposition" theory (including the possibility that "personality" itself is in part determined by biological-neurophysiological factors) is in good agreement with the facts. Consider the following study reported by Burt (1965). Seven hundred and sixty-three children, of whom 15 per cent and 18 per cent later became habitual offenders or neurotics, respectively, were rated by their teachers for emotionality/neuroticism and for extraversion/introversion. Follow-up of the children disclosed that of those who became habitual offenders, 63 per cent had been rated as high on emotionality; 54 per cent had been rated as high on extraversion, but only 3 per cent on introversion. Of those who became neurotics, 59 per cent had been rated high on emotionality; 44 per cent had been rated as high on introversion, but only 1 per cent on extraversion. Thus we see that even the probably rather unreliable ratings made by teachers of their pupils at school can predict with rather surprising accuracy the later adult behaviour of these children. The concordance is surprising because luck and other unforeseeable circumstances of life must play a large part in determining whether a person prone to crime or neurosis does in fact succumb, and other personality traits such as psychoticism and intelligence obviously also play a part in the social adjustment of the person. However that may be, the figures as they stand argue rather convincingly for the predetermination of later conduct, whether criminal or neurotic, by personality.

The picture that emerges from a great variety of different studies then is a fairly clear and concise one. At the highest and most inclusive level of personality description, we are apparently dealing with two main dimensions, the one ranging from high degrees of emotionality to very low emotional reactivity, the other ranging from high degrees of introversion to high degrees of extraversion. Both of these scales are continuous, and the majority of people have been found to give scores intermediate between the extremes; very high scores in either direction are relatively rare. It is, of course, possible to describe personality in other terms; many American authors have preferred to use descriptive scales at the trait level, that is, to measure sociability, impulsiveness, activity, liveliness, excitability, and so forth directly. There are two reasons why this may not turn out to be a very successful choice.

In the first place, these traits are not independent but quite highly correlated, and a system of description purely in terms of correlated traits leaves out what may be the most important variable of all, namely that which underlies these correlations and gives rise to the higher-order type-level concepts of extraversion and emotionality. In the second place, it has been found that while concepts like extraversion and neuroticism are easily replicable from one investigation to another, concepts at the trait level are very elusive and very difficult to reproduce from one study to another. This is true even when the instruments used are identical; when they differ, then the outcome tends to be one of uttermost confusion. Cattell and Guilford, for instance, have both carried out very extensive investigations using their respective instruments; results from their statistical investigations have demonstrated two separate sets of traits which show hardly any overlap at all. Yet when the intercorrelations between these traits are studied, it is found that quite similar type-level concepts of extraversion and neuroticism emerge (Eysenck & Eysenck, 1967). To say this is not to deny that concepts at the trait level may be very useful under certain circumstances, may have wide practical applicability, and may in due course reach the level of reproducibility which at the moment characterises concepts at the type level. All that is being suggested is that for the time being, trait-level concepts are very much more elusive, and that type-level concepts are of so much wider import that it would seem reasonable to devote considerable energy to an investigation of their psychological meaning and their possible biological background. As far as this book [*Biological Bases of Personality*] is concerned, at any case, we shall be dealing in the main with extraversion-introversion and neuroticism-stability rather than with the various traits, the intercorrelations between which give rise to these higher order concepts.

How can we relate these two dimensional concepts with theories current in experimental psychology? Let us begin with emotionality or neuroticism; introversion-extraversion will be dealt with in the next chapter. Jones (1960) has put the point very well: "Neuroticism or vulnerability to neurosis implies low tolerance for stress whether it be physical as in painful situations, or psychological as in conflict or 'frustration' situations. In learning theory terms an individual scoring high on the factor of neuroticism would be characterised by a high level of drive in avoidance situations. High appetitive drives are not necessary to the theory and it may be that the high drive of neurotics is aroused only in situations of threat or ego-involvement." This high level of drive must be considered, as we have pointed out before, in relation to the Yerkes-Dodson law. It will be remembered that this law states that too high level of drive exerts a negative influence on performance. There are several theoretical reasons why this should be so; the best known of these is perhaps that associated with the Iowa group (Farber, 1954; Spence, 1956; Taylor, 1956) in which use is made of the Hullian concept of excitatory potential as a multiplicative function of habit and drive strengths. As Jones (1960) points out, "in a situation in which only a single habit is evoked, an increase of drive is expected to improve performance but, where repeating response tendencies are operative, of which only one is scored correct by the experimenter, the effect of changes in drive strength is considered to depend on the number and comparative strength of the competing tendencies. When the correct response is based on a relatively weak habit strength, increased drive is deleterious in that the stronger incorrect tendencies gain relatively more in excitatory potential and have, therefore, an enhanced probability of evocation. During learning, as the relative strength of the correct tendency increases, increased drive becomes progressively less injurious and ultimately advantageous when the correct response is prepotent. In the complex situation, involving competing tendencies, increased

drive may also lower efficiency by raising new incorrect competing responses above the threshold value of excitatory potential."

An alternative hypothesis has been put forward by Mandler and Sarason (1952) and by Child (1954). According to these authors, a heightened drive state is linked with a number of previously learned response tendencies, frequently emotional in nature and irrelevant to the task in hand; these response tendencies disrupt performance by competing with the correct response. According to Child, such disruption occurs only when the task already involves competing tendencies, but it is difficult to see why such a limitation should be necessary. An example may make clear the nature of this particular hypothesis. Savage and Eysenck (1964) required emotional and nonemotional rats to learn to escape from a conditioned fear situation by jumping a barrier from one compartment into another. The emotional animals had higher latency scores; that is, they performed this learned task less successfully. The reason appeared to be that they responded to the stimuli with "freezing"; i.e., this previously learned response tendency competed with the correct response of jumping.

The Farber/Taylor/Spence theory concerned itself with the energising effects of emotion; the Mandler/Sarason/Child hypothesis took into account the stimulus aspects of drive. Jones (1960) has considered a third alternative theory which is concerned with the stimulus properties of drive as such. The example he gives is taken from the field of discrimination learning. "Discrimination is most difficult to achieve when the positive and negative stimuli are most nearly alike, i.e., when they have most elements in common. The incidental experimental stimuli contribute to what they have in common and one of these is the drive stimulus. The stronger the drive, the more intense the drive stimulus, the greater its share of the stimulus complex, the greater the similarity between the positive and negative stimuli and, therefore, the greater the difficulty of discrimination. This effect will be opposed to any energizing value of increased drive and the interaction of the two effects would determine the optimal level of drive, thus producing a pattern of results similar to those reported by Yerkes and Dodson.'' Jones has also suggested a fourth possibility, to wit, that increasing task difficulty, irrespective of the degree and nature of response competition, increases drive in a manner analogous to the drive increment

postulated as following frustration. These four hypotheses are, of course, not mutually exclusive; and all the postulated effects may conceivably contribute to the interaction between drive and performance.

The results of experimental studies relating to this general theory have been reviewed by Jones (1960), who concludes that "from the review it is abundantly clear that our preceding formulation of theoretical expectations was altogether too flexible for precise validation. Whereas the great majority of the studies reviewed produced results consistent with that formulation, this consistency was only achieved after a post hoc placement of the experimental situation along the stress-difficulty dimension. The relative

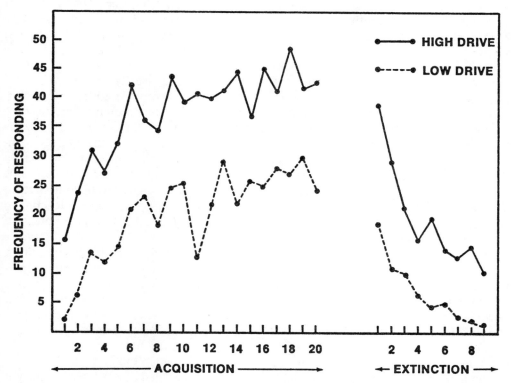

FIGURE 27.4. Acquisition and extinction of eyelid conditioned responses in high- and low-drive groups. Reprinted with permission from R. A. Willett, in H. J. Eysenck (1964).

difficulty of the experimental task is clearly of importance in determining the nature and direction of group differences in learning and may well be the most important single factor. Furthermore it is a factor which can be objectively and quantitatively controlled . . . stress is by contrast a nebulous concept the quantification of which is scarcely possible, but the stress situations derived by many investigators clearly affected the performance and probably the learning efficiency of their subjects, and differentially affected groups selected in terms of personality variables, relevant to abnormal psychology . . . psychological stress, induced by such devices as failure stimulation, generally interacted with personality variables in a manner consistent with our theoretical expectations, but the complexity of the factors contributing to 'psychological stress' was evident in many studies."

Some examples may be useful in making clear the successes as well as the failures of the neuroticism-drive theory combined with the essential features of the Yerkes-Dodson law. To begin with, let us consider eyeblink conditioning as an example of a task where increase in drive might be expected to be related monotonically to improvement in performance. The reasons for this expectation are, of course, (1) that the task is a relatively simple one in that there are no existing habits connected with the conditioned stimulus which might be expected to interfere with the establishment of the new response, and (2) that the strength of the unconditioned stimulus is never such as to trigger off those hypothetical "previously learned response tendencies, frequently emotional in nature and irrelevant to the task in hand" which are posited by Child, Mandler, and Sarason to disrupt per-

formance by competing with the correct response. Willett (1964) has directly manipulated the drive variable and has demonstrated, as shown in Figure 27.4, that frequency of conditioned responses both during acquisition and during extinction is very significantly greater in the high drive group than in the low drive group.

Making use of a similar argument, Spence and Taylor (1951) have argued for a positive association between eyeblink conditioning and anxiety. Some of the work related to this hypothesis has been reviewed by Spence (1964), who confines himself to work using the Taylor Manifest Anxiety Scale as a measure of the personality variable. Other studies using the M.P.I. neuroticism scale have been reviewed in H. J. Eysenck (1965). At first sight the general picture which emerges is rather confused, as about half the studies, notably those carried out in Iowa, have positive results, whereas the remainder find low and usually insignificant relationships between anxiety or neuroticism and eyeblink conditioning. One possible way of resolving this impasse is by reference to the fact that the theory under consideration is a "process" rather than a "status" theory; in other words, while different individuals are hypothesized to have differential potentials for reacting to emotion-evoking stimuli, these potentials can only be translated into observable behaviour under specified conditions, that is, under emotion-provoking conditions. Unless conditions are such that emotion, anxiety, or fear is in fact evoked, no correlation between behaviour and neuroticism or anxiety will be observed. Spence has suggested that the manner in which the eyeblink conditioning test is carried out in his laboratory is sufficiently threatening and nonreassuring to make it likely that some degree of emotion or anxiety was in fact evoked; most other workers have tended to try and reassure subjects about the situation to such an extent that no emotional reactions were evident. If this explanation be true, and of course there is no direct evidence on this point, then most of the results reported fall into line very neatly.[3]

Our second example is taken from the field of paired associate learning. The study chosen was published by Standish and Champion (1960) and constitutes a direct test of Spence's hypothesis regarding the interaction between drive and correct and incorrect responses. Standish and Champion argue that where task difficulty is determined by such features as "association value" of list elements, the necessary conditions for testing Spence's hypothesis about the interaction of drive level and task difficulty level may well be absent. Spence's hypothesis requires that "correct" responses be dominant in performance if a high drive group is to be superior to a low drive group, and that the obverse conditions prevail if a low drive group is to be superior to a high drive group. Standish and Champion contend that in the case of an "easy" list of nonsense syllables regarded as easy simply by virtue of the high association values of its elements, incorrect responses may still be dominant for much of any learning period. Hence a comparison of the performance of groups of different drive levels on such a task could not necessarily

be expected to yield the results predicted on Spence's hypothesis.

Accordingly, Standish and Champion designed an experimental procedure especially relevant to this hypothesis. First they constructed an easy list of stimulus and response words, by using common associates in the Kent/Rosanoff list such as "foot—land; hungry—food; deep—shallow." A difficult list was then formed by employing the same stimulus words, but this time pairing them with words given rarely in free association according to the Kent/Rosanoff list. The difficult list was made up of combinations such as "foot—cheese; stem—heavy; sheep—loud."

Since the aim of the experiment was to contrast performance where correct responses were dominant with performance where incorrect responses were dominant, each subject had to learn the easy list first to a criterion of two correct repetitions plus eight further trials. These ten trials are labelled trials 1 to 10. Having completed the list to this criterion, each subject learned the difficult list, also to a criterion of two correct repetitions plus eight further trials. The first ten trials of the difficult list are also labelled trials 1-10 and the last ten trials A-J. It can be seen that trials 1-10 of the easy list and trials 1-10 of the difficult constitute a crucial comparison. In the former case the correct response is clearly dominant; in the latter case the incorrect response is clearly dominant. In trial A-J of the difficult list, the correct response is dominant again, these ten trials being at the same stage of learning as trials 1-10 of the easy list. Exposure time of both stimulus words and pairs was three seconds throughout with eighteen seconds separating trials. The score taken was the latency in tenths of a second of the subject's response to the stimulus words. The

[3] Ominsky and Kimble (1966) have published a paper supporting this view. Spence and Spence (1966) have recently shown that under "masking" condition, i.e., when the subject is confused about the purpose of the experiment, there is no correlation between anxiety and conditioning; this finding is damaging to the Spence hypothesis.

results of the experiment are shown in Figure 27.5, where subjects are divided in terms of their questionnaire responses into high drive, medium drive, and low drive. It will be seen that on the easy list, as expected, the high drive subjects do best, whereas on the difficult list, again as expected, the low drive subjects do best. On the last ten trials of the difficult list, it is again the high drive subjects who perform best. All these results are in direct conformity with hypothesis.

Willett (1964) repeated the experiment exactly, but substituted groups in whom high and low drive had been induced experimentally for the groups in the Standish and Champion experiment which had been chosen according to questionnaire responses. His results showing mean response latency are shown in Figure 27.6; there is a superficial dissimilarity from

Figure 27.5 because Standish and Champion recorded reciprocal latency, whereas Willett reported direct latency values. However, the crucial feature of the Willett experiment is that under all conditions the high drive group performs better even on the first ten trials of the difficult list. This is completely contrary to the Spence hypothesis and to the Standish and Champion results and is very difficult to explain in their terms. Nor is this the only study of its kind where the relationship between list difficulty level and situation-induced anxiety drive has been studied; Willett and Eysenck (1962) also found no interaction between drive level and difficulty level but rather a simple facilitation by the higher drive condition in an experiment on the serial rote learning of nonsense syllables.

It is, of course, possible to put forward

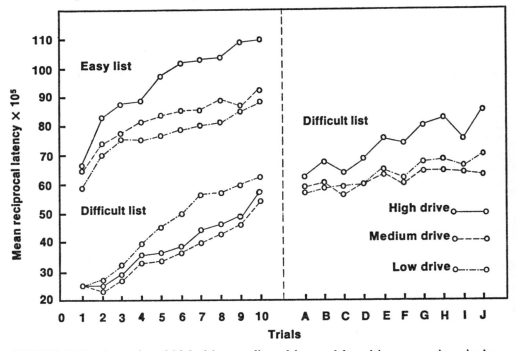

FIGURE 27.5. Latencies of high drive, medium drive, and low drive groups in paired-associate learning tasks under different conditions of difficulty. Reprinted with permission from Standish and Champion (1960).

hypotheses to explain the apparent contradiction in this experiment, which is typical of the rather confused literature on this subject. One might postulate that the task itself produces a stress which is itself due to the interaction between rate of stimulus presentation and the relative intelligence of the subjects. Standish and Champion used university subjects; Willett and Eysenck used industrial apprentices of a rather lower level of intelligence. Or the explanation may lie in the relatively greater extraversion of these apprentices as compared with students; it has been generally found that students on the whole are more introverted, industrial apprentices more extraverted than the aver-

age. These and many other hypotheses can be put up to explain the observed discrepancies; but of course there is no direct evidence to support any of these theories, and until more direct proof is forthcoming we must conclude that the striking confirmation of Spence's results achieved by Standish and Champion cannot be accepted at face value. The same problem arises in connection with most of the evidence that has been put forward in relation to the general hypothesis under consideration. Most of the studies are positive, many of them quite strikingly so; but there are always other studies which give negative results or which are at best inconclusive. To say this is not to deny the

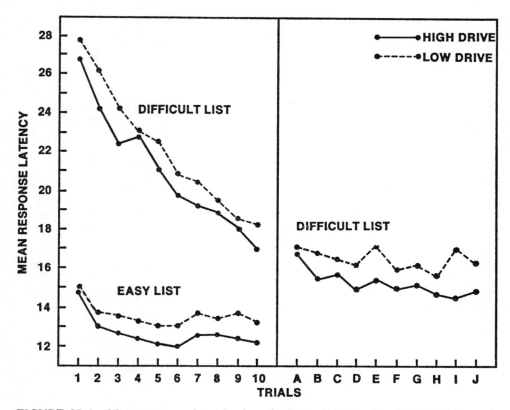

FIGURE 27.6. Mean response latencies in paired-associate learning for high-drive and low-drive groups under different conditions of difficulty. Reprinted with permission from R. A. Willett, in H. J. Eysenck (1964).

importance, relevance, and ingenuity of the theory under consideration; it is merely to draw attention to the very complex ways in which the variables involved are associated and to the difficulty of measuring any of them in isolation.

REFERENCES

Bartholomew, A. A. Extraversion-introversion and neuralicism in first offenders and recidivists. *British Journal of Delinquency,* 1959, *10,* 120–129.

Bendig, A. W. College norms for, and concurrent validity of, the Pittsburgh revision of the Maudsley Personality Inventory. *Journal of Psychological Studies,* 1959, *11,* 12–17.

Burt, C. Factorial studies of personality and their bearing on the world of the teacher. *British Journal of Educational Psychology,* 1965, *35,* 368–378.

Child, I. L. Personality. *Annual Review of Psychology,* 1954, *5,* 149–170.

Crookes, T. G. and Hutt, S. J. Scores of psychotic patients on the Maudsley Personality Inventory. *Journal of Consulting Psychology,* 1963, *27,* 243–247.

Eysenck, H. J. *Dimensions of personality.* New York: Praeger, 1947.

Eysenck, H. J. *The structure of human personality.* London: Methuen, 1960.

Eysenck, H. J. Maudsley Personality Inventory. London: University of London, 1959.

Eysenck, H. J. *Maudsley Personality Inventory.* London: University of London, 1959. (American edition, San Diego: Educational and Industrial Testing Service, 1962.)

Eysenck, H. J. (Ed.). *Experiments in motivation.* New York: Pergamon, 1964.

Eysenck, H. J. Extraversion and the acquisition of eyeblink and GSR conditioned responses. *Psychological Bulletin,* 1965, *63,* 258–270.

Eysenck, H. J., and Eysenck, S. B. G. *Eysenck Personality Inventory.* San Diego: Educational and Industrial Testing Service, 1964.

Eysenck, H. J., & Eysenck, S. B. G. *Personality structure and measurement.* San Diego: R. R. Knapp, 1967a.

Eysenck, S. B. G. *Manual of the Junior Eysenck Personality Inventory.* San Diego:

Educational and Industrial Testing Service, 1965.

Farber, I. E. Anxiety as a drive state. In M. R. Jones (Ed.), *Nebraska Symposium on Motivation.* Lincoln: University of Nebraska, 1954.

Jones, H. C. Learning and abnormal behaviour. In H. J. Eysenck (Ed.), *Handbook of abnormal psychology.* New York: Basic Books, 1960.

Mandler, C., & Sarason, S. B. A study of anxiety and learning. *Journal of Abnormal Psychology,* 1952, *47,* 166–173.

Ominsky, M., & Kimble, G. A. Anxiety and eyelid conditioning. *Journal of Experimental Psychology,* 1966, *71,* 471–472.

Saintsbury, P. Psychosomatic disorders and neuroses in outpatients attending a general hospital. *Journal of Psychosomatic Research,* 1960, *4,* 261–273.

Savage, R. D., & Eysenck, H. J. The definition and measurement of emotionality. In H. J. Eysenck (Ed.), *Experiments in motivation.* New York: Pergamon, 1964.

Sigel, J. J., Star, K. H. & Franks, C. M. Hysterics and dysthymics as criterion groups in the study of introversion-extraversion. *Journal of Abnormal and Social Psychology,* 1958, *57,* 143–148.

Spence, K. W. *Behavior theory and conditioning.* New Haven: Yale University Press, 1956.

Spence, K. W. Anxiety (drive) level and performance in eyelid conditioning. *Psychological Bulletin,* 1964, *61,* 129–139.

Spence, K. W., & Spence, J. T. Sex and anxiety differences in eyelid conditioning. *Psychological Bulletin,* 1966, *65,* 137–142.

Spence, K. W., & Taylor, J. A. Anxiety and strength of UCS as determinants of amount of eyelid conditioning. *Journal of Experimental Psychology,* 1951, *42,* 183–188.

Standish, R. R., & Champion, R. A. Task difficulty and drive in verbal learning. *Journal of Experimental Psychology,* 1960, *59,* 361–365.

Taylor, J. Drive theory and manifest anxiety. *Psychological Bulletin,* 1956, *53,* 303–320.

Willett, R. A. Situation-induced drive and paired associate learning. In H. J. Eysenck (Ed.), *Experiments in motivation.* New York: Pergamon, 1964.

Willett, R. A., & Eysenck, H. J. Experimentally induced drive and difficulty level in serial rote learning. *British Journal of Psychology,* 1962, *53,* 35–39.

CHAPTER 28

Direct Decision Theory

Introduction

This final selection, by Harold Greenwald (1910–   ), is different in many ways from the others in this book, perhaps most different from the first selection, by Sigmund Freud. Greenwald is an example of a third-generation theorist-therapist. The first generation consisted of those who more or less started out from scratch, without much knowledge of what others were doing or thinking; they were the seminal, original thinkers. We would put the big three (Freud, Adler, and Jung) in this category, as well as J. L. Moreno and Fritz Perls. Second-generation theorists such as George A. Kelly, Ludwig Binswanger, and Karen Horney were indoctrinated in a particular theory and then went off on their own. A third-generation theorist, such as Greenwald, Carl Rogers, or Albert Ellis, usually had a wide acquaintanceship with a variety of personality theories and consequently was sophisticated about them. Such theorists either came to original conclusions about the nature of human nature or established their own theories, or else they became eclectics.

Greenwald is important as a personality theorist because he probably represents more people in the field of applied psychology than any other individual considered in this book. So we have a paradoxical situation: the first theorist, Sigmund Freud, is exceedingly well known and probably has the greatest number of expressed followers in psychology, while Greenwald is probably among the least well known of the contributors; but he nevertheless represents by far the greatest proportion of psychiatrists, psychologists, social workers, and counselors.

Greenwald's chapter represents a kind of correction to all the others. In its deceptively casual manner, its evident lack of discipline, and its lighthearted manner, this selection shows a practitioner-theorist at work. It demonstrates how a well-trained person (Greenwald was trained as a psychoanalyst by Theodore Reik) thinks and operates in the accomplishment of his work.

The lesson of this section is that eventually all those concerned with personality theory must fall back on their own common sense and their own interpretations of what they have learned from others—teachers, textbook writers, theorists, patients, or counselees, among others. All must operate in terms of their experience in life to come to a unique, individual, idiosyncratic theory of personality. This should be the most important message of this book.

HAROLD GREENWALD
Treatment of the psychopath

In dealing with the severe character disorder of the psychopath we are dealing with more than individual pathology; we are also dealing with a problem that has broad social implications. The psychopath's aberrant behavior frequently consists of acting destructively toward others around him and toward society in general.

One of the problems in talking about psychopaths is that the term is not a very fashionable one. As a matter of fact many efforts have been made to change it. Psychopathy has also been called constitutional inferiority, moral insanity, perverse personality, and more recently, sociopathy (Chrzanowski, 1965).

Henderson and Gillespie (1952) described three basic types of psychopath; predominantly aggressive, the predominantly passive or inadequate, and the predominantly creative. Because the term psychopath is often used in a judgmental sense and many authorities have stated that psychopaths cannot be treated, a new term that is more respectable had to be invented. For example, "neurotic character disorder" is a term that Abrahamsen (1960) uses. He includes the rapist, the murderer, the pathological liar and swindler, the marriage wrecker, the Don Juan, the imposter, the nymphomaniac, the drug addict, the homosexual, and the alcoholic.

Another reason why psychopathy is an important social problem is stated by Ackerman (1958) when he defines psychopathy as a social disease that is contagious and virulent. My subjective impression is that psychopathy has increased greatly in the last fifteen years. For more than ten years, I have been working on a book describing the kind of world that psychopaths inhabit, and I cannot finish the book because this world appears to be growing larger all the time. For example, "hip" language, which used to be primarily the property of people in this kind of world, is today familiar to many of us, and certainly to the youth generation. The language they speak, as well as many other of the characteristic behaviors which used to be confined mainly to psychopathic groups, such as smoking marijuana and participating in group sex, are now increasingly widespread (Winick, 1965).

The behavioral symptoms, as described by Ackerman, include impulsiveness, antisocial conduct, defective control and judgment, lack of foresight, shallow emotionality, egocentricity, magic omnipotent thinking, power striving, grandiosity, inability to empathize with others, failure to respect the rights of others, lack of genuine guilt, failure to learn from experience, and deviant sexual behavior. In fact, so extreme are these symptoms in many cases that it is my impression that psychopathy is often a defense against a more serious disorder. I know from my clinical experience in dealing with psychopaths that when a psychopath stops acting out he will often either sink into a deep

Harold Greenwald, "Treatment of the Psychopath." Reprinted from *Voices,* 1967, *3,* 50–60, with permission of the Journal of the American Society of Psychotherapists.

depression or begin to show overtly psychotic symptoms. Harry Stack Sullivan (1956) once said, "For the life of me, I can't tell the difference between psychopathic personality and psychosis" (1956).

Usually when we talk about the psychopath we are talking about the *unsuccessful* psychopath. The reason why we generally do not discuss the successful psychopath is because we would then have to discuss many of the rulers of our world. The sociologists Sorokin and Lundeen maintain that when measured by the same yardstick, the moral behavior of any ruling group tends to be more criminal than that of the ruled population in the same society. Many of the symptoms discussed, such as lack of morals and apparent lack of guilt, exist widely among people of power and influence.

It is amazing how little empathy is shown for psychopathy. Many authors writing about schizophrenia have tried to see it from the inside. In discussing neurotics, and even homosexuals, we are willing to admit that there is possibly some neurosis or homosexuality in ourselves. But in practically all the literature discussing the psychopath there is a complete lack of the kind of empathic understanding that psychotherapists are supposed to have. I think that this inability to see the disorder from the "inside" may be one of the factors leading to our attitude of therapeutic nihilism and our belief that psychopaths cannot be treated. Perhaps this is a disorder so virulent and so contagious that most of us do not dare look at it too closely for fear of being contaminated. We must learn how to deal with this problem first in ourselves before our entire world is destroyed. One can readily imagine what might happen if some psychopath, in a position of really effective power (without any restraints), were suddenly to obtain possession of

some of the nuclear weapons now in existence.

In discussing the psychopath, I feel there are two broad categories. There is the sociopath—the individual who is conforming to the norms of the milieu in which he grew up. Personally, I prefer to limit the term sociopath to that type of psychopath—the kind of person, for example, who grows up in certain sections of large urban communities where antisocial behavior, including drug addiction, prostitution, and robbery, is so widespread that in order to be properly adjusted to society, he grows up to be a deviant. This is how he successfully adapts to his social group. This kind of person is different from the second category of psychopath, who grows up in a milieu that does not share such norms. While I think one of the growing problems today is that our entire milieu is becoming one in which psychopathy is the norm, it is still true that when one finds people with similar symptoms and with the same way of behaving who grew up in supposedly more normal surroundings (by which psychotherapists generally mean middle-class surroundings), then we have the problem of the individual psychopath or the character neurotic.

The inability to see a differentiation between the two has caused much confusion in this area.

Now, what does the psychopath really feel like? This is what puzzled me, and only when I reached an understanding of this inner feeling was I able to get some perception of the condition. Can you imagine yourself a Jew suddenly dropped into Nazi Germany and surrounded by SS men during the height of the Hitler terror against the Jews? What feelings of morality would you have? What kind of ability would you have to empathize with the people around you? What immediate gratification would you want to post-pone? What would there be that you would not be willing to do? This is how the psychopath/sociopath views the world around him. He believes himself sur-rounded by deadly enemies. His early life experience has usually been such that this estimate is correct. He has grown up in the kind of milieu, whether broadly social or limited to his family, where he felt sur-rounded by enemies, and therefore had no hopes beyond survival and enjoyment of immediate gratifications because every-one was against him anyway.

Though we describe psychopaths as lacking morality, this is not completely true. What we do often find is that their morality may not be the morality of the majority culture. They frequently have a special morality of their own. For exam-ple, say a psychopath witnessed an ac-quaintance committing a murder. We would think it his duty to report it *to* the police. But the psychopath, because of his particular upbringing, would feel his duty was to protect his friend *from* the police. This would be a moral position, though different from the moral position that most of us have. Sometimes it seems to me that we may be witnessing the birth of a new morality. When I think of my younger patients I realize that their sexual behavior would have appeared highly im-moral thirty years ago. Yet to them, the present day widespread premarital sexual freedom on the part of both males and females does not appear particularly im-moral.

The use of marijuana was at one time confined to a small group. A girl in Mississippi recently wrote asking me what to do about a boy friend who smokes "doped" cigarettes. I could sense the moral horror she experienced. Yet many take a far more tolerant attitude about

marijuana now, and there is even a move-ment afoot for its legalization.

One of the descriptions one reads again and again, which I find dubious, is that psychopaths are usually free of anxiety (Ellis, 1963). To me, their anxiety is ob-vious. My experience is that psychopaths will not admit to anxiety. However, if a workable relationship is established in therapy, then the anxiety becomes quite clear, despite their many ways of acting out in dealing with its avoidance.

One important factor in treatment, however, is the problem of counter-transference—our own feelings about the psychopath. At a conference in Pitts-burgh a year ago a frank psychiatrist con-fided to me: "You know, if I were going to go crazy, and if I could choose the way I would go crazy, I would prefer to be a psychopath." Similarly, some profes-sions—psychologists, psychiatrists, or social workers—whom I have seen for training analyses, have asked if I could help them become psychopaths. One such trainee recently said at a first interview, "What I would like is to be able to do whatever I choose and not feel bad about it. The hell with everybody else; just get mine, that's what I would like to do." I believe that some aspect of psychopathy is in all of us because this kind of behavior sounds quite attractive to most of us. However, the problem is that while at one level it sounds attractive, at another level it is very difficult for any of us to accept the fact that we may have psychopathic traits. To accept our own psychopathy and to admit that we find some of this behavior attractive is so difficult that it becomes almost impossible for us really to establish a therapeutic relationship with psychopaths. Another difficulty arises from their skill in evoking hostile, punitive reactions by their compulsive aggressive rebelliousness and their calm assumption that our zeal is a hypocritical mask for our own selfish goals.

When I first started to treat psychopaths, I found it very difficult to establish a cooperative relationship, a relationship of the kind that is workable, the kind one gets with other types of patients. I can tell you some of the problems I encountered and some of the things I tried to do, and I admit that I had difficulty doing them. We therapists always maintain that we are free of moralizing, but many psychopathic patients have told me of going from therapist to therapist, and sooner or later in the treatment each therapist said, "How could you behave that way? What would this world be like if everybody behaved the way you do?" These patients are very skillful in eliciting this kind of response. It is therefore absolutely essential for the therapist to keep his morality to himself, at least in the beginning. This was one thing that I had to learn to do in dealing with the psychopath. One way to help establish a working relationship is to be ready to use one's own psychopathy.

Psychopaths are frequently involved in manipulations. The ones in therapy are usually inadequate manipulators. Since they are inadequate, and continually manipulating, the therapist's job is to show them how to manipulate properly. For example, a woman came to see me for her first interview dressed in a rather ragged cloth coat. She said she just happened to find my name in the phone book; actually she did not want me to know that she had heard me speak at an expensive resort. It was six months before she wore the first of her three mink coats to a session. She had dressed poorly at first in order to be charged a low fee. It turned out that her husband was a "poor banker" (I had never heard of such a thing but that's the

way she described him) and she was involved in an intense "life and death" struggle to get the things she wanted from him; a 15-carat diamond, a larger and more expensive apartment, additional servants, a larger car, etc. Her husband was determined to give her as little as possible. So I helped her. I showed her how to deal with him to get all the things she wanted. I was perfectly willing to help her. Eventually, we established such a good relationship that I treated her daughter and her son-in-law; the son-in-law's parents came to see me several times; and even the husband came. One major difference between the wife and husband was that he was a much more successful manipulator than she was.

Another case concerns a young woman who came to see me some years ago. She was being kept by a very wealthy man (to the tune of about $30,000 to $40,000 a year). At the same time, she was having a number of other affairs. The man who was keeping her had sent her to an attorney for legal advice. Everything she discussed with the attorney, such as her extracurricular sexual activities, was reported by the attorney back to her boy friend. The boy friend naturally was not pleased when he found out that he was paying so much for what others were receiving free. She had gone through two or three similar experiences before she came to see me. Obviously the first thing I had to do was to establish a trusting relationship. When the boy friend called me and suggested that we have lunch at an expensive restaurant, I accepted and explained to my patient what I was planning to do. I met the boy friend, and when he commented about the terrible situation between them, asking, "Is she still sleeping around?" I responded, "Sleeping around? You mean she never told you?

She has tremendous fear of sex. Why do you think you have given her two hundred and fifty thousand dollars so far, during which time you have only laid her five times? Why do you think it has been so rare? It's because she is so frightened of sex." Of course, she got the message back from her boy friend, who then became very tender and wanted her to go more often for therapy so that she would get over this horrible fear of sex. Now, I was scheming. I was apparently being more manipulative than anyone else involved in the situation, but on this basis I was able to establish a much better relationship and a much better transference with this girl than I had before. (Incidentally, despite her acting-out, she actually *did* have serious sexual fears, and what I had said was the literal truth.)

A major problem with psychopaths in office treatment is that of fees. One of the things that often happens when a doctor does establish a good transference is that the patient stops paying. If he likes you, why should he pay you? This liking is such a rare gift that surely payment isn't necessary. Therefore, the next problem in the treatment of a psychopath is what to do about the fee. He tries to make you feel like the most crass, commercial, exploitative person in the world for even asking for a fee. The patient has had so much trouble, and finally has found you, the one person in the world who can understand him. How can you ask for money under those circumstances? When this point in therapy is reached, it is the key test in many ways. From bitter experience, I know that if you do not collect the fee, you can continue to treat them for the next three or four years without fee, but nothing will happen except that they will stop the therapy because they believe that if they succeed in this ploy, they are really smarter than you are. If they are

smarter, why should they listen to you or do anything that you suggest? The question of the fee becomes crucial in the treatment of the psychopath, and the only thing I have found to be effective is to spend every session discussing the fee. Not setting limits; that does not appear to work. If you tell them, "All right, I will give you two months and if you do not pay we will stop treatment," the psychopath will be convinced that it is your fault he failed again. He will tell you that he could have been cured if only you had had a little more faith in him. But you're just like everybody else. So it does no good to set limits if you are interested in treating these people. What you have to do is to discuss payment of fee continually. Rather than face the anxiety that this provokes, they will sometimes pay. You must work this through or you cannot touch them in therapy.

The next problem in treating psychopaths is that of seduction. I am discussing not only sexual seduction, for psychopathic personalities practice many types of seductive behavior in their attempts to manipulate. A patient of mine who was a theatrical producer once said to me, "I've had several plays offered to me but I'm not going to take any of them because I'm waiting for your next book. I'm sure I can make a helluva play out of your next book." This was an attempt at seduction, because if I had given him the book, we would have gotten involved in details, and of course therapy would be impossible under those circumstances.

Another patient offered to double my fee. He said he could well afford it. I thanked him and explained that I did not think this was a good idea because I could not see that his financial condition had improved sufficiently to warrant an increase. If it should change, I would be willing to take an increase in fee, but until that time I saw no reason to do so. It was only then that he told me one of the reasons he had left his last analyst. That therapist had started with a fee of $50 per session. The patient then said, "I'm raising you to a hundred dollars a session," and the psychiatrist was very happy. After two months, the patient said, "I'm sorry I can't afford the fee of a hundred; I'm reducing it to fifty again." The psychiatrist was unhappy, but what could he do? Two weeks later, the patient left treatment and sought me out. If I had agreed to his raising my fee, he might also have left me, for once he was able to raise and lower the fee at will he felt he had outsmarted the therapist. A third patient who is a successful psychopath, a self-made millionaire and a wielder of great power at a comparatively young age, once started a session by saying, "You know what you do, Harold? Tell you what you do. Have you got your passport in order? I don't know when, but I'll call you one day—we'll hop on a plane—we'll go to Rome, Venice, and Paris."

There have also been attempts at sexual seduction by several female and two male patients. They do it quite cleverly, unlike the ordinary neurotic, who might just say, "I like you, I want you, I need you." One patient recently said to me, with a tear in her voice as she lowered her eyes, "I now know what my problem is. I never had any acceptance. Nobody ever accepted me." When I agreed, she continued, "I'm not even sure that you can accept me." When I asked her why, she replied, "Well, you might accept me verbally, but not really fully and completely." Slowly I drew from her (or so she made it seem) that the only acceptance a person with her kind of problem would really appreciate would be sexual. When I explained that I did not think such acceptance would be helpful, she said, "Won't you feel like a

fool when it is discovered some day that this is the best kind of therapy for a patient like me?" For a while she had me wondering if she might be right.

One woman challenged me: "I know all the books say you're not supposed to sleep with your patient, but how do you know? Has there ever been a controlled experiment done on the effects of sleeping with a patient?" I had to admit that I knew of no such experiment.

Another patient made it very clear that she had been homosexual for a number of years and her last analyst had seduced her. She said, "He was a son of a bitch. It was nasty; he shouldn't have done such a thing and besides he was a lousy lay. But I was heterosexual for eight years after that incident." When I saw her, she was still acting heterosexually. She had a seven-year-old daughter. She was involved with another woman and at this point she indicated that we should have an affair. She implied that if we did, it would prevent her from getting involved in a homosexual relationship. She faced me with a choice that was morally difficult, because by refusing, in a sense I permitted her to drift into another homosexual relationship. However, she had organized it this way—created it—and was willing to go through with a homosexual relationship to pay me off for not having accepted her. I could give still other examples of seductive behavior on the part of psychopathic patients, some of whom revealed a remarkably keen understanding about my own sexual fantasies which they were offering to gratify.

The basic treatment plan that I follow or try to follow with psychopaths is to try to indicate to each patient the fact that he and I are not so different; that there are similarities between us. Advice about manipulation is one way of doing this. Another way is to be frank about my selfish needs. One patient said, "Don't give me any bullshit that the treatment won't be good without the money." I replied, "No, the most important thing is that I like to get paid because I like money. While it also happens that the treatment will not be effective without it, the most important reason for wanting the money is that I like to get paid."

This they can respect much more than moralizing. So one of the first things to do in treatment is to indicate our similarities. I will give an even more dramatic example. A pimp came to see me and started to discuss his way of life. He said, "You know I'm ashamed to show myself and so on, but after all, it's a pretty good way to live and most guys would want to live that way, you know, to live as a pimp. It's not bad—you get girls out hustling for you—why shouldn't you do it? Why shouldn't anybody do it?" I said, "You're a jerk." He asked why. I replied, "Look, I live off the earnings of call girls. I wrote a book about them (Greenwald, 1958); I got respect for it; I got famous from it; they made a movie out of it. I made much more money off call girls than you ever will, and you, you schmuck, you can get arrested any day and be sent to jail for ten years, whereas I get respect, honor, and admiration." This he could understand. He saw that somebody whom he considered similar to him had a superior way of accomplishing the same ends.

Another patient with whom I dealt in this way had previously been extremely inadequate, unable to finish school or hold a job. She said to me once, referring to the fact that she had been enormously promiscuous before, "You know, I know you were as low in the gutter as I am, just like me, but somehow, you son of a bitch, you learned how to get out of it, and I'm going to learn that from you!" This is the beginning of a constructive relationship. They see that the therapist has similar problems, similar drives, similar feelings—that all of us have them, but that some of us have learned how to deal with them in ways that are more successful.

Another thing that helps foster the proper relationship is that when they attack society's hypocrisy, I find no necessity to defend it. I happen to agree with most of them that there is a tremendous amount of hypocrisy in our society, and I think it is because I agree with them that I have been better able to work with them.

What usually happens is that they develop a curiosity about how I did manage, since I am so much like them, to get away with it and be successful. At the point where they develop this curiosity I can begin to show them the self-destructiveness of their behavior. When they realize that the problem with their behavior is not that it is immoral or bad for society, but that it is self-destructive, it is an effective way of reaching them. After that, they will usually ask, "What should I do?" And it is at this point that they are ready to listen to the hard lesson the therapist has to drive home, which is—*to learn control*. I do this in a variety of ways. For example, in sessions with this kind of patient I will insist on certain controls. I will ask them not to smoke; I will ask them to lie down on the couch—something I do not necessarily demand all the time. In group therapy, I will ask them not to touch one another. Until I did that, I had a number of fights in groups. Now I do not permit group members to touch one another in affection, and that prevents them from hitting another group member over the head with a painting, as one did, or throwing a water carafe at me, as another did.

Almost every psychopath (this is practically a diagnostic sign) will, at one time or another, want to borrow one of the books in my library and usually there is a desperate urgency about it. One man, who had not completed elementary school and could hardly read, wanted to borrow a textbook of psychiatry (Henderson & Gillespie, 1952) so he could, as he put it, show his girl friend that we're buddies. And this, too, cannot be allowed (though you might do it with other patients), because they have to learn control. After some of these controls are established I go on to more, because it is in our battle over control that early problems are relived. Their major problem is that they did not learn controls when they were young; one of the characteristics of psychopaths is that many of them were enuretic as children and did not develop proper controls. So among the things I have done to make· this conscious is to prohibit them from using the bathroom before a session, which leads to a big fight. I am willing to fight this out with argument and discussion, and even though they will defy me for a long time, I continue to insist. In group, of course, I prohibit socializing, and I try to prohibit their socializing with other patients, which they will frequently do. Psychopathic patients will very frequently try to get involved in a relationship with other patients they meet in the waiting room.

In addition to making the problem of control the central problem in therapy (by demanding control within the session), I indicate that the reason why they do not control themselves, is that they do not really *believe* that they *can* control themselves. (This type of treatment is useful not only with psychopaths but with many other character disorders.) Underneath the inability to control is lack of confidence in their ability. For example, a promiscuous girl complained that she did not understand her promiscuity. She ex-

plained that often she could have stopped herself from casual relations but did not think she would be able to, so she finally said to herself, "Oh, the hell with it," and gave up. This is why getting them to control themselves within the session becomes so valuable—because you demonstrate that they *are* able to control themselves under those circumstances. They are able not to smoke; they are able to sit in one place; they are able to say hello when they come in, and good-by when they leave, even if they were angry. These are things I request from such people, who have poor impulse control, which establishes the whole pattern of control.

Within this context it is important to indicate that the ability to control oneself leads to greater freedom. This is hard for them to see—that actually, if you know you have control, you are much freer. If every one of us knew we had complete control of our emotions, we would be free to experience the huge rage that might be boiling up in us, or to experience the lust that we might have for somebody who should be outside the pale. The ability to control leads to greater internal and external freedom. As a young woman said to me, "Now, as I am getting greater confidence in my ability to control myself, I can go out with a lot of men that I did not dare to go out with before because I didn't think I could control myself and would have to go to bed with them."

Another thing that happens as these people start to practice control is that they find that it gives them pleasure; it becomes one of the most ego-building experiences they have ever known. One young lady was very concerned about going out with a married man because, while she liked him and was attracted to him, she was very fearful that she would not be able to control herself; that she would have to go to bed with him, and that this would upset her other boy friend, who was aware of the situation. When for once she did control herself and did not go to bed with the married man, she was so excited and so pleased that she called me and said ecstatically, "I did it—I controlled myself and it was great! I said no, and I'm so happy."

Similarly, another patient, who had been involved in a homosexual affair, having decided that she was "going straight," that she did not need women any more and was able to control herself, also described this with great joy and happiness. A male patient who was always being fired because, upon being criticized by his boss, he would have to tell the boss off in no uncertain terms, was able to stop reacting in that way and reported, "I experienced the anger. It made me feel so good that I didn't have to blurt out and lose this job because it's a good job."

With control established, the next step is to facilitate the verbal expression both of their hostility and, even more important, of what is hidden behind the hostility in practically all these patients—their enormous dependency needs.

With the establishment of self-control, most patients find less need to control others. Frequently the need to control and manipulate others is based on the fear of losing control if something unexpected were to happen. Therefore they control and manipulate in an effort to prevent any unforeseen circumstance which might threaten their precarious self-control system.

Because I am interested in this whole problem of how to treat psychopaths, I have tried hypnotherapy on occasion. Robert Lindner in his book *Rebel Without a Cause* (1944) and Lewis Wolberg in a personal conversation, as well as others who have dealt with psychopaths, have pointed out that hypnoanalysis is useful in treatment. *Rebel Without a Cause* is a study of the treatment of the psychopath with hypnoanalysis. Hypnosis of the psychopath is often a short-cut to a workable relationship. One girl, after the first hypnotic session, said "Did you see what happened? Did you see how my shoulders went down? What a pleasure, not to have to keep them up against the whole world, to let yourself go and for once be dependent on somebody else." Their deeply buried dependency is enormous and a great deal of their anger and hostility is often caused by the fact that this dependency has been frustrated for so long.

With a few, though all too few, it has been possible to transform psychopathy to creativity. Of course, not everyone is creative, but in one case, for example, a man who was never able to finish anything in his life was able to write a novel: a novel which described his experiences in therapy in a fictional way. He was able to vent much of his hostility and dependency in his writing. The creative person, one who can transform his psychopathy to creativity and utilize his creative potential, need not abide by all of the norms of ordinary society. Creative people often do not have to work from nine to five, for example, as do those of us who are less fortunately endowed. Also, the grandiosity of the psychopath is useful for the creative person. Every really creative person has a kind of grandiose self-esteem. A creative person gets an idea—those of us who lack that creative grandiosity know that other people have had that idea but they do not care—they feel that they are going to do more with it than anybody ever did before, so that grandiosity is useful to them on the creative side. Another way in which this sometimes works, and the reason why I had some success with it, is that several of them, as they established identification with me, identified with what they considered my creative ability. The fact that I had written books made it possible for the man I mentioned to write books. The fact that I had some of my own paintings hanging on the walls of my office (and obviously I am not a skilled painter) made it possible for some of them to start painting and to think seriously of painting or sculpture or some other of the graphic arts.

One of the biggest problems I used to have in dealing with psychopaths was the psychosis which often lies underneath the defense. On one hand, if they continue to operate as psychopaths, they can get themselves into such serious trouble that they may be jailed for many years, or even executed. On the other hand, if the psychopathic defense is removed, they may break down into a schizophrenic, paranoiac, or manic-depressive psychosis requiring hospitalization. However, by emphasizing the problem of control, you deal with the underlying problems, because, as they learn to control themselves, they can also control the psychoticlike behavior which lies underneath the psychopathy and the self-destructiveness. This technique gives you an opportunity to study the problem, and when you motivate and help establish controls, these help control possible psychotic behavior.

One thing I discovered in working with people who have had psychotic breaks is that most of them described a particular moment when there was a choice of whether to stay in control or let go. A patient who became catatonic described the particular moment when, as she was sitting in an airport, she found out that her lover had a date with somebody else. At that point she knew that she could get up or she could let herself drift into a catatonic stupor. She chose to let herself

drift in, but the choice point was there. You will find, again and again, if you speak to patients who have broken down, and if you search for it, that there is always a point at which they had a choice, and it is at that point that they still have the possibility of controlling themselves. If they have confidence in their ability to control themselves they can exercise it.

Similarly, in every kind of acting out there often seems to be a choice point. The psychopathic problem of acting out has been indicated. Often, the major problem of psychopaths is impulsive behavior, and here again is a choice point at which they can exercise control.

In working with psychopaths, I have found some contributing factors which often show up. Frequently their history shows early lack of control, such as incontinence and enuresis. Frequently also, they have a confusion of lateral dominance which, too, leads to problems of control.

Many of them learned early in life that the way to survive was to play off one parent against the other, or one sibling against the other. In therapy they attempt to repeat this tactic by trying to play off the present therapist against previous therapists or simultaneously to visit other therapists. One such patient went to the length of seeing another therapist and myself for three months before she made her choice, and only then did she inform me of this choice.

Closely tied in with the tendency to divide and conquer is their enormous ability to arouse hostility in others. This they demonstrate most dramatically in group therapy, and if left to their own devices they will attempt to create such dissension in a group as to lead to its dissolution. Here firmness on the part of the therapist in demanding that the psychopathic patient cease his destructive behavior while indicating to the other patients how they are being provoked into anger is required.

One type of psychopath I have encountered chooses a psychopathic way of life out of feelings of profound despair. One such woman explained to me, "I was thinking of committing suicide and then I decided to choose evil instead. Now that I search for evil, I do not feel like committing suicide."

The establishment of the ability to control leads to more than a controlled psychopath. It leads to the development of an individual capable of substituting the verbal expression of hostility or anger when appropriate, rather than a driven creature who compulsively *has to* behave destructively. In turn, this new-found ability and self-confidence leads to the wish for the development of the ability to form meaningful and satisfying relationships, rather than self-destructive or exploitative ones. If the controlled psychopath has difficulties in this area, he is usually motivated to continue therapy as a neurotic and can be treated as such.

The therapist who is interested in treating the psychopath must not only be willing to withhold moralizing but must also be certain enough of his own controls to be nondefensive and free to be in contact with his own antisocial, manipulative, and psychopathic trends.

The ability to deal with psychopathy is an example of the ability really to deal with the dark destructive forces that stand ever ready to destroy the individual and society.

REFERENCES

Abrahamsen, D. *The psychology of crime.* New York: Columbia University Press, 1960.

Ackerman, N. *Psychodynamics of family life.* New York: Basic Books, 1958.

Chrzanowski, G. The psychotherapeutic management of sociopathy. *American Journal of Psychotherapy,* 1965, *19,* 3.

Ellis, Albert. The treatment of a psychopath with rational emotive psychotherapy. In *Reason and emotion in psychotherapy.* New York: Lyle Stuart, 1963.

Greenwald, H. *The call girl: A social and psychoanalytic study.* New York: Ballantine Books, 1958.

Henderson, D., & Gillespie, A. *A textbook of psychiatry.* New York: Oxford University Press, 1952.

Lindner, R. *Rebel without a cause.* New York: Grune & Stratton, 1944.

Sullivan, H. S. *Clinical studies in psychiatry.* New York: Norton, 1956.

Winick, C. Marihuana use by young people. In *Drug addiction in youth.* New York & Oxford: Pergamon Press, 1965.

Name Index

Abercrombie, J., 160
Acker, C. W., 326
Ackerman, N., 346
Acton, Lord John, 97
Adler, Alfred, 31, 32, 33, 36, 50, 52, 266, 288, 289, 345
Adler, Gerhard, 51n
Adorno, T. W., 87
Alexander, F. M., 293
Allport, F. H., 82
Allport, Gordon W., 81, 82, 83, 85, 87, 89, 90, 92, 94
Angel, Ernest, 129n
Angyal, A., 239
Ansbacher, Heinz L., 32n
Aquinas, Thomas, 109
Argyle, M., 87
Aristotle, 240
Aron, B., 256, 264

Bales, R. F., 89
Balint, Michael, 215, 216
Balken, E. R., 255, 264
Bandura, A., 309, 321, 322, 323, 324, 325, 326, 327
Barrett, W., 206
Bateson, G., 243
Beach, F. A., 241
Beardsley, R. K., 213
Beck, Aaron, 301, 309
Beethoven, Ludwig von, 231, 235
Bekhterev, V. M., 198, 199, 200
Bell, Sanford, 22
Bellak, L., 264
Bel'skiy, P. G., 195
Benedict, Ruth, 216, 217, 218, 241, 244
Bennett, Lillian, 82
Benton, A. L., 164
Bergson, H., 239, 240
Bernard, L. L., 241, 242
Berne, Eric, 266, 267, 305

Binswanger, Ludwig, 128, 129, 190, 345
Blau, A., 160
Bleuler, E., 15, 22, 56
Block, J., 82
Breuer, Josef, 1, 2, 3, 4, 5, 6, 7, 8, 9, 12, 21
Buber, Martin, 65
Buehler, Karl, 305
Burt, Cyril, 301, 336

Cannon, W., 239
Carr, H. A., 81
Cattell, R., 239, 337
Caudill, William, 217
Champion, R. A., 341, 342, 343
Charcot, Jean-Martin, 1, 8, 9
Cherry, L., 309
Child, 338, 340
Christenson, J. A., Jr., 255
Chrzanowski, G., 346
Cleveland, S. E., 159, 160, 161
Coan, R. W., 306
Combs, A. W., 264
Converse, P. E., 86
Coomaraswamy, A. K., 209
Corsini, R., 306
Crawford, M. P., 249
Critchley, M., 164
Cronbach, L. J., 91

Darwin, Charles, 246
Daudet, Leon, 56n
Davison, G. C., 309
Deabler, H. L., 264
DiGiuseppe, R., 303
Dobrynin, N. F., 193
Doi, L. Takeo, 212, 213, 214
Dostoevsky, Fyodor, 96
Dreisch, H., 239

Eccker, W. F., 264

Edwards, A. L., 88
Eliot, T. S., 103
Einstein, Albert, 236, 286
Ellenberger, H. F., 129n
Ellis, Albert, 245, 248, 297, 298, 300, 301, 302, 303, 304, 305, 308, 312
Ellis, Havelock, 23
Erikson, Erik, 210, 276, 277, 327
Evans, R. I., 210
Eysenck, Hans J., 331, 332, 333, 334, 335, 336, 337, 338, 339, 340, 342, 343
Eysenck, S. B. G., 332, 336, 337

Farber, I. E., 338
Fenichel, O., 160, 239
Ferenczi, Sandor, 27
Fisher, Seymour, 159, 160, 161
Fleming, E. E., 256, 258
Fordham, Michael, 51n
Fosdick, Harry Emerson, 223n
Frank, J. D., 208
Freed, H., 264
Frenkel-Brunswik, Else, 87
Freud, Sigmund, 1, 2, 16, 31, 36, 38, 50, 59n, 107, 109, 130, 132, 209, 218, 220, 227, 239, 240, 242, 244, 266, 267, 287, 288, 289, 291, 294, 295, 296, 305, 327, 345
Fromm, Erich, 106, 189, 190, 239, 240, 251, 305

Galen, 333
Gannushkin, P. B., 197
Gardner, M., 241
Gart, J. J., 206
Gerstmann, J., 164
Gesell, A., 327
Gibson, J. J., 83
Gillespie, A., 346, 353
Glasser, William, 312, 313, 315, 316, 319
Goethe, J. W., 40n, 296
Goldfarb, W., 247, 248
Goldfried, M. R., 309
Goldstein, Kurt, 166, 167, 172, 173, 174, 176, 239, 240, 241
Greenacre, P., 209

Greenwald, Harold, 345, 346, 352
Grieger, R., 298, 302, 304
Gurwitch, G., 190
Guthrie, G. M., 86

Haas, W. S., 204, 206
Hall, Stanley, 12
Harper, R. A., 300, 302, 304
Harrison, R., 264
Heidegger, Johann, 190
Helson, H., 82
Hertz, R., 160
Henderson, D., 346, 353
Holtzman, W. H., 87
Horney, Karen, 63, 189, 220, 221, 240, 251, 305, 345
Howells, T. H., 242, 248
Hull, R. F. C., 51n
Hunt, J. McV., 82
Huston, A. C., 323
Huxley, Aldous, 73, 104
Huxley, T. H., 103

Ilg, F. L., 326
Isona, Fujiko, 218

James, William, 174
Janet, P., 9, 11
Jones, H. C., 337, 338, 339
Jung, C. G., 14, 15, 22, 27, 31, 50, 51, 56n, 57, 61n, 195, 240, 244, 334, 345

Kanifer, F., 309
Kanitz, J. M., 298
Kant, Immanuel, 84, 332, 333
Kierkegaard, Søren, 67, 73, 190, 225
Kell, B. L., 77n
Keller, H., 322
Kelly, George A., 106, 107, 110, 113, 301, 310, 312, 345
Kimble, G. A., 341n
Kingsbury, F. A., 81
Kipling, Rudyard, 212
Klages, L., 195
Korzybski, Alfred, 301
Kovalev, A. G., 191, 193
Krafft-Ebing, R. von, 32
Krasner, L., 205

Kretschmer, E., 152
Kropotkin, P., 246
Krutch, Joseph Wood, 101, 103
Kuo, Z. Y., 241
Kutner, B., 264

La Piere, R., 82
Lashley, K. S., 241
Lazurskiy, A. F., 195, 196
Leeper, R. W., 167
Lenski, G., 89
Leont'yev, A. N., 193
Levinson, D. J., 87
Levi-Strauss, C., 210
Levy, D. M., 239, 243, 247, 249
Lewin, Kurt, 295
Lincoln, Abraham, 102
Lindner, Robert, 254
Lipgar, Robert M., 74n
Llewellyn-Thomas, E., 326
Luce, R. D., 272

McClelland, D. C., 83
McDonald, F. J., 327
McDougall, William, 83, 91, 117, 240, 244, 245
McFarland, J. H., 161
McGuire, William, 51n
McKendry, Margaret S., 86
McNeil, H., 77n
Mahoney, M., 309
Mainord, Willard H., 315, 316
Makarenko, Anton, 177, 178, 188
Mandler, C., 338, 340
Marcus Aurelius, 97
Marmor, J., 242
Maruyama, Masao, 218
Maslow, Abraham, 212, 226, 238, 239, 240, 241, 244, 245, 249, 250, 251, 304, 316
Maslow, Bertha, 239n
Masserman, J. H., 264
Maultsby, M. C., 304
Mawardi, Betty, 86
May, Rollo, 129n, 240
Mayman, M., 264
Mead, George H., 138, 139
Mead, M., 243
Meehl, P. E., 91
Meichenbaum, D. H., 309

Mencius, 210
Mendel, Gregor, 242
Miller, D. R., 82
Miller, N., 303
Mischel, W., 309
Mooney, Ross L., 74n
Morgan, C. D., 255
Morris, K. T., 298
Moses, Elizabeth, 86
Mowrer, O. H., 122, 315, 323
Munn, N. L., 168, 175
Murphy, G., 239, 248
Murphy, R., 303
Murray, Henry A., 162, 239, 254, 259
Myasishchev, V. M., 188, 189, 191, 193, 200

Naccarati, Sante, 152
Nakamura, Hajime, 217
Namenwirth, J. Z., 89
Nash, M., 322
Newcomb, T. M., 86
Niebuhr, R., 241
Nikol'skiy, V. N., 195

Odbert, H. S., 89
Oedipus, 25
Ogilvie, D. M., 89
Ominsky, M., 341n
Orwell, George, 104

Paige, Jeffrey, 90
Pande, Shashi K., 202, 203, 206
Parker, E. G., 325
Parsons, T., 323
Pasquarelli, B. A., 264
Pastore, N., 244, 245, 301
Pavlov, I. P., 189, 191, 194, 196, 197, 199, 200
Perls, Frederick (Fritz), 285, 286, 312, 345
Perry, Ralph Barton, 100
Petrov, P. M., 195
Petrova, A. Ye., 195
Petrullo, L., 82
Piaget, J., 327
Piatrowski, Z., 256
Planck, Max, 227, 236
Popper, J. M., 161

Radhakrishnan, S., 206
Raiff, H., 272
Rank, Otto, 31, 240
Rapaport, D., 255
Raup, R., 239
Read, Herbert, 51n
Reik, Theodore, 345
Reincourt, A. de, 210
Ribble, M., 239, 247
Riechard, G. A., 322
Rodgers, David A., 74n
Roe, Anne, 74n
Rogers, Carl, 63, 64, 77n, 106, 239, 240, 251, 345
Roosevelt, Franklin Delano, 103
Rorschach, Hermann, 195
Rosenzweig, S., 256, 258, 264
Ross, D., 324, 329
Ross, S. A., 324
Rotter, J. B., 256, 264
Rubinshtein, S. L., 192, 196
Russell, Bertrand, 109

Sanford, Nevitt, 92
Sanford, R. N., 87
Sarason, S. B., 338, 340
Sartre, Jean Paul, 172, 173, 174, 175, 176
Savage, R. D., 338
Scheinfeld, A., 239, 243
Schilder, P., 160
Schoefield, W., 210
Schopenhauer, Arthur, 54, 61
Schooland, J. B., 241, 248
Schramm, W., 325
Sheldon, William H., 151, 152, 310
Sherif, M., 162
Shils, E. A., 323
Skinner, B. F., 73, 81, 94, 95, 106
Smet, Walter, 74n
Smith, R. J., 213n
Spemann, H., 239
Spence, J. T., 341n
Spence, K. W., 75, 338, 340, 341, 342, 343
Spitz, R., 247, 248
Spranger, Eduard, 85
Standish, R. R., 341, 342, 343
Stein, M., 264

Stephenson, William, 68n
Stern, Guenther, 170, 171, 174
Stern, William, 189
Stone, P. J., 89
Stouffer, S. A., 82
Streich, Eugene, 74n
Sukhanov, S. A., 197
Sullivan, Harry Stack, 106, 109, 189, 305, 347
Szasz, T. S., 209

Tagiuri, R., 82
Taylor, Bayard, 40n
Taylor, J., 338, 340
Texler, L., 303
Thompson, C. E., 264
Thorndike, Edward, 245
Thurstone, L. L., 160
Tillich, Paul, 208n
Tomkins, S. S., 264
Trilling, L., 209
Truax, C. B., 204
Turner, H. H., 86

Uznadze, D. N., 192

Vander Veer, A. H., 264
Van-Su, 193
Varon, Zipporah, 239n
Vernon, P. E., 83, 85
Vine, D. C., 242, 248

Walker, E. L., 83
Walters, R. H., 326
Wapner, S., 161
Watson, John B., 94, 241
Watts, A. W., 209
Weider, Arthur, 255n
Weiss, P., 239
Werner, H., 161
Wheelis, Alan, 316
Whytt, Robert, 334n
Willett, R. A., 339, 340, 342, 343
Williams, R. M., Jr., 87, 89
Williamson, E. G., 207
Wilson, W. C., 87
Winick, C., 346
Winkelman, N. W., 272
Wolfle, D., 249
Wolfle, H. M., 249

Woodworth, R. S., 169, 170, 297
Wundt, Wilhelm, 332, 333
Wyatt, F., 256

Young, P. T., 239

Zunin, Leonard, 312, 313

Subject Index

A-B-C theory of personality, 303
Absolutism, 108
Absolutistic thinking, 303
Acculturation, 246; resistance to, 251–252
Act-completed needs, 250
Activity, 274
Adequacy of behavior, 229-230, 231
Adult ego state, 267, 268, 269
Adulthood, 207–208
Affection, 109
Affective theories of personality, 308
Aggression, 33, 197; imitation, 324–327
Allopsychic phobias, 132
Amae, 213, 214, 216, 218
Amaeru, 214, 215, 216, 217, 218
Ambivalence, 35
Analytical psychology, 50–62
Animal, 139, 142; intelligent conduct, 143
Antiinstitutionalism, 277, 283
Anxiety, 167, 168, 171, 172, 197; behavior range, 173, 174, 175; compulsion neurosis, 33; disruption of continuity, 131, 132; dreams, 18; eye blink conditioning, 340; purpose, 173–174
Apersonal theories of personality, 307
Asian personality theories, 202–219
Attitude, concept of, 192, 193
Attitude test, 69
Authoritarian Personality, The, 87
Autism, 302
Autistic transactions, 274
Auto-eroticism, 23, 24

Behavior: biological base, 305; control, 99, 101; democratic philosophy of, 95; emotions, 169, 170, 171, 173, 174; environmental bases, 305; personality traits, 82; reinforcement, 100; scientific study, 95, 96
Behavioral choices, 125
Behavior modification, 94
Bird songs, 141, 143
Blushing mania, 46–47
Brave New World, 73, 104
Bungling, 19

Canalization, 248
Character, 194
Characterology, 135
Child ego state, 267, 268, 269
Childhood recollections, interpretation of, 37
Children: Eastern culture, 207; personality development, 147, 148; Soviet upbringing theories, 178–187; training, 246; Western culture, 207
Choice corollary, 125
Cognition, 109, 308
Cognitive theories of personality, 308
Collective psyche, 55, 56, 57, 58, 59, 60
Collective unconscious, 55, 56, 61
Compulsion neurosis, 32-49; prognosis, 48; safeguard, 36-38; washing, 40
Compulsion of repetition, 294, 295
Conation, 109
Concepts, 124
Concretist thinking, 122
Condensation, 18
Conditioned reflex, 103, 191, 192, 294
Conditioning, 103

Conflicts, 221, 222, 223, 224, 225
Consciousness, 8, 10, 11, 14, 18, 149, 150; psyche, 56, 57; splitting, 9
Conservation of energy, 227, 235, 236
Constitution (inheritance), 292, 293
Constitutional inferiority, 356
Constitutional theory, 160–165
Construct validation, 91
Construed alternatives, 116–117; behavioral choices, 125; neurotic paradox, 122
Contingencies of reinforcement, 100
Continuity, 130, 131; anxiety, 131, 132
Control: behavior, 99, 101; disguised, 100; psychopath, 352–356; punishment, 96, 100, 103–104
Coprophilism, 24
Counter-compulsion, 34, 48
Countertransference, 348
Covariation, 87–89
Creativity, 227, 231, 232, 233, 234, 235, 236, 237; psychopath, 354
Cultural conserves, 233, 235
Cultural consolidation, 280
Cultural designing, 98
Cultural patterns, 97, 98; controlled, 101; scientific design, 103
Cultural relativity, 241
Cyclothymia, 48, 49

Day-dreaming, 290
Death instinct, 295, 296
Delusions of persecution, 133
Delusions of reference, 133
Democracy: philosophy, 98, 99; science of man, 105
Dependency, 216, 217
Desacralization of life, 279, 283
Desert, The, 316
Deterministic theories of personality, 307
Deviant behavior, 315

Diagnosis, 114–115
Dialectical materialism, 190
Directionality of behavior, 119; personal construct, 121
Direct decision theory, 345–356
Discrimination learning, 338
Disorder, 167, 168
Displacement, 18
Dominant, principle of, 195
Double personality, 8
Doubt, 34
Dreadful, The, 131
Dreams, 17; analyzing, 16, 18; collective psyche, 61; emotions, 39
Dream-work, 18
Drive, 38; experiments, 342; eyeblink conditioning, 340; level, 341; need-press theory, 258; neurotics, 338; stimulus, 339
Dynamic theories of personality, 307
Dysthymics, 336

Economic values, 85–86
Ecstasy, 168
Ego, 11, 267; weak, 268
Ego alienation, 209–210
Ego states, 267
Elementaristic theories of personality, 306
Emotion, 39, 40, 166–176, 308; behavior, 169, 170, 171; purpose, 171–172
Emotionality, 334n
Emotionless behavior, 170, 171, 172
Emperor worship, 218, 219
Empiricism, 84, 85
Empty organism, 81–82
Encroachment, 133
Endogenous theories of personality, 207
Energy, 117, 227, 235
Environment, 95; behavior changes, 96, 101
Environmental force, 257, 259, 261
Erogenous zones, 23
Erythrophobia, 199
Esthetic values, 85–86

Ethical issues of science, 73
Exclamatory sounds, 142
Existential theory, 128–137, 189, 190; analysis, 129
Exogenistic theories of personality, 307
Experiential learning, 68–69; psychotherapy, 68–69, 70–79
Experimentation, 108
Extraversion, 336, 337
Extraneous fantasies, 274
Eyeblink conditioning, 340

Factors, 83–84
Farber/Taylor/Spence theory, 338
Faust, 52
Fear, 168, 171, 172, 174
Femininity, 161, 162
Freedom, 94, 95; behavior control, 100; democratic philosophy, 99
Freudianism, 108, 128
Function pleasure, 305
Future influence theory of personality, 308
Futuristic thinking, 288–292, 293

Game, 144, 147, 148
Game analysis, 272
Games People Play, 272
Generalized other, 144, 145, 146, 148, 149
Gestalt theory, 285
Gesture, 139, 140, 143; as symbols, 139, 140
Godlikeness, 34, 35, 38, 44, 47, 48, 52, 53, 60
Grandiosity, 302
Group therapy, 210
Guilt feelings, 35, 36, 48

Habits, 149, 294
Hedonism, 278, 283
Heredity, 242, 243
Heuristic realism, 84, 85–90; restraint on trait research, 91
Historical mistakes, 291, 292
Holistic theories of personality, 306
Homosexuality, 24, 45
Humanist orientation, 280, 281
Hygiene, 200

Hypnosis, 8, 9, 12, 27
Hysteria, 3, 6, 7, 9, 10
Hysterical conversion, 7
Hysterical dissociation, 9
Hypnoanalysis, 354
Hypnoidal states, 8, 9
Hypnosis, 200; psychopath, 354
Hysterical neuroses, 334, 336

Id, 267
Identification, 323
Identity, 313, 317, 318; image, 316; success vs failure, 316, 317
Imitation, 62, 141, 142, 323; nurturance, 323, 324
Impatience, 286, 287
Indecision, 34
Indeterministic theories of personality, 307
Individual autonomy, 319
Individuality, 60, 62, 73
Individual psychology, 31–49
Infantile sexuality, 21, 22, 23, 24, 26; theories, 25
Inferiority complex, 33, 34, 35, 42, 47, 48, 53
Instinct, 36–37, 38; animal, 243, 245, 246; collective psyche, 61; theory, 239
Instinctoid tendencies, 304
Instrumental needs, 250
Interpretation of Dreams, 16
Intersubjective verification, 76
Intimacy, 274
Iowa studies of intelligence, 77
Irrationality, 109, 113; personal construct theory, 126

Japanese personality theory, 213–219
Joy, 175–176

Kent/Rosanoff list of paired associates, 341

Language, 139, 142, 143, 144; hands, 142; vocal gestures, 148
Law of the excluded middle, 109–110, 111–112
Laziness, 115–116

Leadership hunger, 274
Learning, 320
Letters from Jenny, 89, 90
Libido, 23, 26, 132, 227
Life style, 39, 46, 48, 49
Love, 247, 248, 250; need, 318

Macrosplanchic classification, 152
Magic, 58, 59
Magical thinking, 112
Mandler/Sarason/Child hypothesis, 338
Manipulation, 72
Marxist-Leninist teachings, 190
Masculinity, 161, 162
Masochism, 23
Masturbation, 199
Maudsley Personality Inventory, 335, 336
Meaningful covariance, 85
Meaningful dimensionalism, 85
Meaningful morphogenesis, 85
Measurement of social traits, 151, 152; intelligence criteria, 157–158; morphological measurements, 155; reliability, 155
Measure of Man, 101
Melancholia, 48
Mental illness: deviant behavior, 315; reality theory, 314
Microsplanchic classification, 152
Miserliness, 135, 136
Misplaced concreteness, fallacy of, 81
Models, 322; aggression, 325–327; moral judgement, influence on, 327–329
Moral insanity, 356
Morality, 60
Moral judgements, 327–329
Morphologic types, 152; measurements, 155
Motivation, 108, 109, 113; choice corollary, 125; conceptualization, 115–116; construct alternatives, 116–117; diagnosis, 114; directionality, 119, 121; energy, 118; push and pull theories, 118–119; rewards, 122
Mourning, 291

Musturbatory thinking, 302, 303

Narcissism, 216
Needs, 240; basic, 242, 245n, 250; gratification, 250; identity, 313; instinctoid, 244, 246–252; neurotic, 250; Thematic Apperception Test, 258
Needs-press theory, 254–264; thema, 260
Neo-Freudianism, 189–190
Nervism, 200
Neuropsychic hygiene, 200, 201
Neuroses, 24; basic needs, 251; etiology of, 196; formation of symptoms, 198; Japanese psychiatry, 213; obsessive, 199; pathenogenesis, 26–27, 196, 197; personality, 189–201; retired business man, 290
Neurosis of the system, 198
Neurotic conflicts, 221, 223, 224, 225
Neurotic Constitution, The, 36
Neuroticism as a personality trait, 336, 337, 338
Neurotic paradox, 121–122
1984, 104
Nirvana, 295, 296, 305
Novelty of behavior, 229, 230, 231
Nuclear physics, 236
Nurturance, 323, 324

Objective theories of personality, 306
Objective thinking, 122
Object love, 215, 216
Oedipus myth, 25
Operant reinforcement, 94–105
Operationalism, 122
Order, 167
Organism, The, 167, 169

Paired associate learning, 341
Parental dependency, 216, 217
Parental ego state, 267, 268, 269
Parent-child relationship, Soviet theory, 178–187
Passive object love, 215, 216
Past, 289, 290, 291, 292

Past influence theories of personality, 308
Pastime, 274
Patience, 286
Perfectibility, 95, 96
Permissiveness, 246
Personal dispositions, 83
Personal constructs, 106, 107, 108, 110, 113–114; directionality of behavior, 121; nature of, 123–124; neurotic paradox, 122; psychotherapy, 121
Personalism, 80–92, 189
Personality: analysis, 85; direction, 193; experimental studies, 195; heredity, 304; hierarchical model, 333; irrelevance in study of, 90; maintainers, 305; measurement of traits, 150–158; origins, 305, 306–308; physiological nature of, 191; social nature of, 189–190, 193; Soviet theory, 177–201; structural diagram, 269; traits, 81, 82
Personality organization, 147, 148; social community, 149
Personal psyche, 55, 56, 59, 61
Personal theories of personality, 307
Personal unconscious, 57
Person-centered therapy, 63–79
Person perception, 82
Perverse personality, 356
Perversions, 24
Phobia, 132; preceding paranoia, 133, 134
Physical image, 317
Physical measurements, 151
Play, 104, 144
Pleasure, 176
Political values, 85–86
Positive reinforcement, 104
Positivism, 83
Post hypnotic suggestion, 8
Predisposition, 130
Press, 257, 259; environmental forces, 261
Prestige, 58
Primary love, 215, 216
Principles, 295

Projective tests, 195
Property, 149
Psychadelic therapy, 210
Psychastenics, 334, 336
Psyche, 55, 56
Psychiatry, 129
Psychic inflation, 53, 54, 55, 56
Psychoanalysis, 1, 30, 52; existential, 129; Freud's theories, 107; resistance, 28; Western society, 206, 210
Psychodrama, 226, 234, 235
Psychopath, treatment of, 346–356; anxiety, 348; behavioral symptoms, 346; creativity, 354; empathy, 347; morality, 348; seductive behavior toward therapist, 351; self-control, 352
Psychosocial theory, 221–225
Psychotherapy, 64, 200, 203–210; basic needs, 251; decision-making process, 204–206; ethical issues, 73; experience, 64–67; experiential learning, 66–67, 68–69, 70–71; group, 210; insight, 120; integration, 206–208; learning, 66–67, 68–69; love, 203–204; motivational research, 119–121; resistance, 120–121; science, 67–69, 70–79; subjectivity, 64, 65, 67; therapist-client relationship, 65–69, 70
Punishment, 96, 99; behavior control, 100, 103–104

Q sort, 69
Qualitative theories of personality, 307
Quantitative theories of personality, 307

Rational-Emotive theory, 297, 298–310
Rationality, 109, 113; instinctive, 243; personal construct theory, 126
Rational processes, 39, 40
Reality therapy, 312, 313–320
Recognition hunger, 273
Reflexes, 170

Regression, 24, 292

Reinforcement, 100, 104; moral judgements, 327

Relativity theory, 236

Relevance, 111–112

Religion: covariance with prejudice, 87–89; extrinsic and intrinsic orientation, 87; values, 85–86

Repression, 10, 11, 12, 13, 17, 18, 20; formal, 26; psychic development, 58; temporal, 26

Resistance, 10, 14, 17, 20

Responsibility, 99

RET, *see* Rational Emotive Theory

Retirement, 290

Retrospective person, 291

Rewards, 122, 247, 248

Right and left body sides, 160–165; sex role characteristics, 160–165

Rituals, 274

Rorschach test, 129, 133, 195

Sadism, 23, 35

Safeguarding, 36–38

Schizophrenia, 318

Science: absolutism, 108; behavior study, 97, 98, 101, 102–103; communication of findings, 76–77; conflict with experientialism, 70–73, 78–79; methodology, 75–76; psychotherapy, 67–69, 70–79; subjectivity, 74–75, 78; use, 77–79

Science of man, 95, 99, 101, 102, 105

Script analysis, 272

Sechenov and Botkin theory, 200

Self: development, 144, 146, 149, 150; unconscious, 149

Self-acceptance, 69

Self-actualization, 238–252

Self consciousness, 149

Self-control, 354

Self-discovery, 67

Self-rating, 302

Sense data, 170

Set, 192

Sex-role characteristics, 160–165

Sexuality, 20, 21; development, 21–22, 23, 24, 25; infantile, 21–22, 23, 24, 25

Significance, 192, 193

Situationism, 82, 83

Skepticism, 277

Skinner box, 94

Social act, 139, 140

Social group, 144, 145, 146, 147, 148, 150

Social learning theory, 321–329

Social nature of personality, 189–190

Social organization, 60, 61

Social relations, 33, 35, 37, 48, 49

Social science, 72, 73

Social traits, measurement of, *see* Measurement of social traits

Sociometric theory, 226–237

Sociopathy, 356

Soviet personality theory, 177–201

Splitting of consciousness, 9

Spontaneity, 227, 229, 230, 232, 233, 234, 235, 236, 237; theater of, 229

Static theories of personality, 307

Stimulus hunger, 273

Structural analysis, 267–269

Structure hunger, 273

Studies on Hysteria, 2, 6, 21

Study of Values, The, 85

Subjective theories of personality, 306

Subjectivity, 64, 67; scientific, 74–75, 78, 79

Subject-predicate language structure, 108; fallacy, 110–111, 122

Sublimation, 13, 29

Superego, 267

Superiority complex, 34, 35, 43, 44, 47, 48, 49

Symbol, 18, 139, 140, 142, 144; gesture, 139, 140; thought, 143; word, 143

Taboos, 59

Talent-capacity-expression needs, 250

Taylor Manifest Anxiety Scale, 340

Technological orientation, 280, 281

Tendencies, 83, 84

Thema, 259–260

Thematic Apperception Test, 254–264; depth interpretation, 263; formal analysis, 263; reliability, 264; uses, 264
Theoretical values, 86–87
Therapist-client relationship, 65–69
Thinking, 140, 145
Third Force psychology, 316
Thought, 143
Time, 286–289
Time structuring, 273–275
Traitology, 82
Traits, 81, 82, 83, 84, 91; analysis of, 85, 86; common sense, 89; factorial, 89; idiomorphic study, 89–90; modifiable, 243; names, 89; typology, 332, 333, 337; validation, 89, 90, 91
Transactional analysis, 266–274; complementary transactions, 269, 270; crossed transactions, 270, 271; ulterior transactions, 270–272: angular, 271; duplex, 272
Transference, 19, 27, 28, 214
Transvaluation, 18
Typology theory, 331–343

Unconditional reflex, 199

Unconscious, 8, 10, 11, 14, 18, 28, 58; analysis, 52, 59–60; assimilation, 51; evidence of existence, 319; psyche, 57; suppression, 12
Unconscious self, 149
Uniformity, 102

Values, 85, 86
Vocal gesture, 139, 141, 142; thought, 143
Voss, Lola, case of, 133

Walden Two, 73, 94, 103
Washing compulsion, 40, 41
Ways of Thinking of Eastern Peoples, 217
Well adjusted man, 251–252
West, Ellen, case of, 129, 135
Wit, 15
Withdrawal, 274
Word Association Test, 129, 133
Words, 143
Work, 104
World-design, 129, 135; anxiety, 132; continuity, 130, 131; mental illness, 137

Yerkes-Dodson law, 338, 340
Youth, 277

Zen Buddhism, 305

BOOK MANUFACTURE
Composition: Fox Valley Typesetting Service
Menasha, Wisconsin
Printing and binding: R.R. Donnelley & Sons Company
Crawfordsville, Indiana
Internal design: F.E. Peacock Publishers
art department
Cover design: Martin Alt
Type: Times Roman